(9)

Sandhya

Bal Krishna Shivram

ISLAMIC SHURA
Religion, State and Democracy

ISLAMIC SHURA

Religion, State and Democracy

Dr. Obaidullah Fahad
Department of Islamic Studies,
Aligarh Muslim University, Aligarh

SERIALS PUBLICATIONS
NEW DELHI (INDIA)

First Published - 2007

ISBN: 81-8387-062-7

Published by

SERIALS PUBLICATIONS
4830/24, Ansari Road, Darya Ganj
New Delhi-110002 (India)
Phone : 91-11-23245225
Fax : 91-11-23272135
E-mail : serials@satyam.net.in,
serialspublications@vsnl.net
Web : www.seriealspub.com

To

Maulana Rahmatullah al-Athari

Acknowledgements

Apart from the dignitaries mentioned in the 'Introduction' of the work, I would like to thank the scholars whose discussions with me has enriched the study. In particular the late Professor Ziaul Hasan Faruqi, the late Professor Mushirul Haq, the then Vice-Chancellor of the Kashmir University who were the examiners of my Ph.D. and M.Phil. thesis respectively; Dr. Abdul Haq Ansari whose suggestions and useful comments corrected my misperceptions, must be duly acknowledged.

In March 1988, I visited Pakistan and thoroughly discussed with a number of academicians who shared their provocative thoughts. Prof. Zafar Ishaq Ansari, Dr. Mahmud Ahmad Ghazi and Dr. Anis Ahmad all then in International Islamic University Islamabad; the late Khurram Murad, Secretary General, Jammat-e-Islami Pakistan; Dr. Asrar Ahmad, Amir Tanzim Islami Lahore; Javed Ahmad al-Ghamidi the director of al-Mawrid and editor of Mîthaq monthly Lahore and Hafiz Salahuddin Yusuf the Ahl Hadith writer are to be necessarily noted. I am indebted to them all.

I am especially in the debt of Hafiz Abdullah and Ayyub Munir both then amongst the leaders of Islami Jamiat Talba Pakistan; the late Khalid Masud and Muhammad Ahsan Tahami, both then in the Qaid-e-Azam Library Lahore; Abdul Jabbar, then a post graduate student in the International Islamic University Islamabad; Maulana Amin Usmani, the general secretary of Islamic Fiqh Academy New Delhi; Dr. Muhammad Raziul Islam Nadvi in Idarah Tahqiq wa Tasneef Islami Aligarh, all of them along guiding me to the valuable sources.

I am grateful to Prof. Muhammad Salim Khan ex-Dean Faculty of Social Sciences, AMU, Prof. Abdul Ali and Dr. Abdul Majid Khan, both my colleagues in the Department of Islamic Studies and Dr. Towqueer Alam Falahi in the Department of Sunni Theology AMU who provided me useful suggestions to make the title of the book more appealing and attractive. Mr. Muhammad Naim Khan has, as before, done a superb job of composing the book and making it more readable. I should heartly acknowledge his services. Of course, none of those mentioned here in any way are responsible for the views expressed in the following pages.

CONTENTS

INTRODUCTION
Shura: Origin and Background

The *Qur'ān* describes the life of Muhammad (SAW) as the *Uswah Hasanah* (the beautiful pattern of conduct).[1] This position of the Prophet (SAW) in Islam has been a commonly and uniformly held view of all Muslims throughout history. In the *Ummah* there is no dispute on this central position of the Prophet (SAW) in Islam. And since his principal achievement was to lay the foundations of a state based on Islamic teachings the Muslims are bound to follow his example in this respect as well.[2] Every step of the Prophet (SAW) and of the Muslim community in Makkah was a step towards the establishment of the Islamic state. In a late Makki verse the *Qur'ān* emphasizes the importance of political power on the side of Islam. The Prophet (SAW) was told to pray that Allah (SWT) may grant him the assistance, support and protection of political power (*Sultanan Naseerah*).[3] Allah (SWT) grants political power for a specific purpose which he states in the most general term: that 'His *Ummah* must enjoin the good and forbid the eveil'.[4] The *Qur'ān* lays down numerous other collective duties[5] that cannot be discharged unless Muslims have first established a state with mobilized power[6] and centralised leadership that itself derives authority from obedience to Allah (SWT) and the Prophet (SAW).[7] That all good deeds outside this framework are rendered useless is pointed out in an early Madni Surah.[8]

All that one needs to note is that the colonial period of Muslim countries was the inevitable outcome of Kingship (*Mulukiyah*). Once Kingship, disguised as *Khilafah*, became the established and accepted form of political leadership and organization, the eventual decline, defeat and dismemberment of the *Ummah* also became inevitable. Muslims were themselves responsible for giving a direction to their history that could lead only to defeat and humiliation. As a consequences, more than 1200 years later, the European powers met little more than nominal resistance to their rule. It was if the erosion of moral conviction had also shaped the Muslims once indomitable zeal for political power and domination. The great zeal and energy for world power and exploitation displayed by the European colonizers was too great for the depleted political, material, spiritual and intellectual resources of the Muslims in the eighteenth and nineteenth centuries. The extent of political unawareness persuaded Arab leaders to accept 'freedom' from the Uthmaniyah state as a fair reward for subservience to the West.

Colonizing the Polity

For this treachery to Islam the Arabs have paid a terrible price. The same framework of nation-station that are secular, in European terms as well as in Islamic terms has also been imposed by the colonial powers on the rest of the *Ummah*.[9]

The most serious development of the colonial period was that for the first time in their history, Muslims were persuaded to think of political issues outside the framework of Islam. This period not only introduced new issues in politics it also changed the language of politics. The more the Muslim intellectuals looked at Europe, the more they became convinced that they would have to create European-style institutions to fill the political vacuum caused by the defeat and disintegration of political authority in Muslim areas of the world. They, under the patronage of the colonial powers, had to learn and absorb not only new political facts but also new political concepts. A new bag to conceptual tools, complete with its own language, history and worldview was signed, sealed and delivered to the new Muslim colonial elite. For example some Indian thinkers believed that despite the advent of British rule India could still be treated as *Dar al-Islam*. They preferred to line under the illusion that the Europeans were Christian and *Ahl al-Kitab* and they were their long lost half-brothers in faith. The democracy that was developed to give European's preference for secularism a moral face, was regarded to Muslim elites, as the very core of the Islamic political ideal of *Shura*. The sad fact was that the Muslim political thought in this period was concerned with one objective alone – to appease the Europeans and to cultivate the favour of their new masters. During this period Muslim political thought was not concerned with the political goals of Islam; its one and only concern was the protection and promotion of the status and economic interests of the Muslim colonial elites within the colonial system. These elites made use of Islam only to the extent necessary to gain respectability and to retain their place within the fold of Islam. For all political purposes they abandoned such political goals of Islam as *amr bil maruf wa nahy anil munkar* (ordering good and forbidding evil) and sovereignty for Allah (SWT).

While all this logically followed the victory of European colonial power over the Muslim world, there was something else that was also equally logical: the emergence of an Islamic movement to challenge the power of the west and to defeat and dispossess the subservient elites, their governments and the nation state system. The colonial powers paid scant attention to the fact that the Islamic state is an integral part of Islam. Islam is incomplete without the

Islamic state. If the *Qur'ān* and the *Sunnah* are the spirit of Islam, the Islamic state is the body in which the spirit finds its fulfilment. The Islamic state is the natural habitat of the Muslim. Every Muslim longs to live in an Islamic state.

Now the time has come to make an all out effort to expose the true nature of the political ideas, institutions and processes introduced into Muslim societies under the influence of colonialism and to re-organize their political, social and economic life in a way that fully incorporates the injunctions of Islam and to ensure that a socially healthy, politically coherent and economically efficient and vigorous *Ummah* will emerge.[10]

Shura and *Khilāfah*

The sovereignty (*Hakimiyah*) of Allah (SWT) and the vicergerency (*Khilafāh*) of man are two pillars of the political structure of Islam. Every human being is created with the purpose and necessary ability of becoming, by the conscious exercise of one's discretion, a (*Khalifah*) vicegerent of Allah. This is a heavy responsibility, which demands full determination and complete effect. When a man has its full realisation of and determines on its discharge, he becomes what is called 'Muslim'. The exercise of the authority of vicegerency is thus legalised.

Before becoming 'Muslim' one is a potential vicegerent, but henceforth he is an actual authorised vicegerent.

The authority of vicegerency is exercised at every step, and in every aspect of life. All private and public, individual and social matters are equally the field of its application. Every individual is required to exercise this authority wholly according to his discretion, in his private life, unless there is a Commandment of Allah (SWT) or the injunction of the Prophet (SAW) contrary to it. But in public matters and social problems man is obliged to adopt a certain path, a particular method- the method of '*Shura*' (mutual consultation).

The word '*Shura*' signified that the social/political body is set up for consultation on any problem. The members of *Majlis al-Shura* sit together, discuss, deliberate and arrive at decisions. What comes out of this common consultation is equally binding on every member irrespective of his personal view point. Thus the Arabic word '*Shura*' is an act, an idea, a social technique and a political institution.

The concept of '*Shura*' has its origin in the idea of human vicegerency. Everyman is the vicegerent of Allah (SWT), and thus is legally on equal footing with any other man. His authority is not inferior to that of any other. Now when a group of men are faced with a common problem they have an occasion for the exercise of their authorities. The natural procedure for this is mutual consultation and decision. This decision is not the decision of any particular member or members but it is the common decision of the whole group. Obviously till the problem retains its common character the decision is binding on every member unless he leaves the group. Thus *Shura* is nothing but the manifestation of the individual authority in problems of social/political nature. It is not a passive acceptance of any decision by the members of the group. It is on the contrary, an active participation of the individuals in the performance of their responsibility as regards the problems of common interest. Thus the concept of '*Shura*' is of fundamental importance to the Islamic political theory.

Origin of *Shura*

This concept is based upon the verse of the Holy Qur'ān '*amruhum shura bainahum*' (their problems are decided by their mutual consultation). It is necessary to fully understand the verse in order to press our inquiry deeper into the concept of *Shura*.

The word which is very significant in this verse is '*Amr*' meaning problems. This word is general in its connotation. It covers every aspect of social life. The dynamic march of history creates new problems at every step. A living community as to face a constant flux of problems relating to the different aspects of life, social or economic, political or legal, legislative or judicial, civil or military. Every problem that challenges the genius of the Muslim community demands that they should bring their heads together, ponder over it and hammer out the proper solution by common consultation. This is the way in which they can share in the responsibility of their vicegerency.

A second thing, revealed by little reflection, is that this verse gives more a social spirit than a legal code. The verse belongs to a *Makki Surah*. And as every one knows, *Makki Surahs* convey the spirit and not the laws. Their focus of attention is the interior of man, not the exterior. They train mind, purify heart and build character. They do not subject human relations to legal codes. Moreover, the context of the verse is not of a legal nature. It is enumerating the qualities of Muslims, they are intent on *Salah* and *Infaq*; they keep aloof from vice and vulgarity. And included in this list, is the attribute that they decide their common problems through consultation. It is evident therefore that the verse presents the mental attitude of Muslims. It gives the spirit of Islamic social life. In fact mutual consultation and cooperative approach to problems is to the Islamic body social what blood is to the physical body. If blood is not in sufficient quantity the body will tend to weaken, and will be an easy prey to disease, but if it is in sufficient quantity the body will develop and attain sound health.

Theorization of *Shura*

But to say that *Shura* is the spirit of the Islamic social/political life does not denote that the verse has no legal utility. To divest the verse from any legal bearing is as wrong as to deny its spiritual aspect. If the legal structure of society is the manifestation of its spirit, the guardian of its values, and one of the potent instruments for attaining its purpose and goal, then there is no reason why the Islamic legal structure should not perform all these functions. And it is here that the verse assumes that great legal significance which is rightly attributed to it.

This discussion has made two points very clear. Firstly, the concept of *Shura* is the direct outcome of the theory of human vicegerency which Islam advocates. Secondly, the *Shura* is the basic spirit of Islamic society, which runs through its veins, its organs, institutions and associations in general.

The political system of Islam, being an integral part of the Islamic society, must be pervaded with the spirit which runs through the society as a whole. As every Muslim is the vicegerent of Allah (SWT), so in the eyes of law he has equal political power. This essentially democratic concept determines the character of Islamic political system for ever. As every one has equal political power the opportunity to influence political decisions can be claimed by every one as his fundamental right. *Shura* is the means through which this aim can be achieved in society. Thus all questions relating to the technique of Islamic political system, for example elections, their conduct and procedure, determination of constituencies, setting up of representative bodies, formation of governmental bodies, and finally electing the whole democratic structure of Islam would be convincingly resolved through the concept of *Shura*.

Concept of *Tawkil*

Now the first difficulty is that common consultation is not possible in large states. It may be practicable in very small states like the city-states of Greece. But even in such city-states, as history shows, all decisions were not taken through common consultation.

The second difficulty is that every one is not competent enough to pass judgement on every problem. Moreover competence varies greatly from men to men in relation to the same problem. Generally the majority of the people stand on one pole, that of least competence, and a very small number stands on the opposite pole. Therefore the incompetency of the general masses is a great obstacle in the way of common consultation.

Thirdly, certain problems are by their very nature are such that they can not be put to public discussion and consultation either because it is dangerous to reveal them or because they demand prompt decision and efficient execution.

Finally it is just possible that problems of general interest and state-wide importance may not be put for common consultation due to certain factors, internal or external. A disturbed atmosphere in a bear situation may render common consultation sometimes impossible. But like every other democratic system, Islam solves all these difficulties by its system of representation. In Islam representation implies the delegation of political power or the authority or vicegerency of the masses to their representatives who are competent. In the Islamic legal term this can be called a sort of '*Tawkil*'. We find different kinds of '*Tawkil*' in different spheres of Islamic society. There is a kind of '*Tawkil*' in business transactions, in property matters, in custody of orphans, in the matters of marriage etc. The general trend of Muslim jurists is that '*Tawkil*' is justified in every sphere of life except where it is prohibited by *Ijma* like *al-ibadat al-badaniyah* (physical prayers). Such is the wide range of '*Tawkil*'. The system of representation is nothing but a function of '*Tawkil*' in political matters. Therefore the concept of representation.is nothing new or alien to Islam. It is on the contrary, a very vital aspect of the social/political life of Islam.

A thorough study of political system of the Prophet (SAW) and of the Four Caliphs will reveal that the system was democratic in spirit, its political technique was common consultation and election of representatives and that in form it was representative government. These constitute the essential and integral features of an Islamic government. Other details of the system do not directly follow from the texts of the *Qur'ān* and the *Sunnah*.

This mode conforms to the nature of all Islamic legislation which is characterised by complete flexibility making it possible to continually build it up through the interpretation and application of its rules. In this respect there is no difference between Islamic legislation in the political field or in any other field of human activity. For if we assume that the Prophet (SAW) had established some specific system of government or had designated a person as the caliph to succeed him, or determined one single way of choosing him then that course of action would undoubtedly have suited the Islamic *Ummah* after his death and would, most probably have remained so far many generations after him. But it is doubtful whether one system could continue to be applied to generations of Muslims in different countries where Islam had spread and where their diverse social, economic and other circumstances would have affected changes in the political system.

For this reason, the Prophet (SAW) left the matter of choosing the ruler and the determination of the system of government to Muslims to decide according to their interests and the requirements of the time, place and changing circumstances; and nothing decreed was binding on them except the general rules of Islamic law in regard to consultation, justice, freedom and equality, and the ordinances and high moral values which the Prophet (SAW) had promulgated during the Madni period, that is, from the inception of the first Islamic state until he passed away.

Methodology

The present work is a humble attempt to show the main features of Islamic *Shura* and compare it with the modern executives. The discussion on the origin and development of the institution in the Islamic history was quite essential. Therefore the first two chapters analysed the problem in the historical perspective. Other problems relating to *Shura* – whether or not the Amir is bound by the decisions of the *Shura*; how the members of *Shura* would be elected; what would be prerequisites for its membership; women would be allowed to participate in its functions or not; what would be status and rights of non-Muslim citizens regarding *Shura* functioning etc. – have been discussed in detail in succeeding chapters. And finally a comparison between Islamic *Shura* and modern democracies is made thoroughly.

I owe my initial interest in this work to the motivations and brotherly encouragements of Dr. Muhammad Ahmadullah Siddiqui (Professor, Western Illinois University, Macomb, U.S.A.) to study and undertake the research on the topic. A further incentive came from the learned discussions of Prof. Nijatullah Siddiqui (then in King Abdul Aziz University, Jeddah) in which he pointed out the basic importance and emergent necessity of a clear picture of *Shura* system in Islam.

I must acknowledge that all this could still not have materialized but for the kind co-operation of Institute of Objective Studies, New Delhi. It was the Institute that provided me a chance to work on a project entitled "An Anthology of Political Terms in Islam". In course of completion of this project I collected all the relevant material on Islamic political system. It was the Institute that facilitated to complete the work on such an original and highly complicated topic.

In this regard, I must give expression to my heartly-felt thankfulness to Mr. Amanullah Khan, the then Assistant Secretary General of IIFSO (International Islamic Federation of Students Organizations, Kuwait) who provided me a chance to visit the libraries of Pakistan and Malaysia in March 1988 and October 1989 respectively. And during a visit to Hong Kong, Singapore and China, I benefited from a number of scholars whose names could not be mentioned. Their hearty encouragements, help and cooperation, discussion and deliberation must be acknowledged.

I heartly express my gratitude to my beloved teacher Dr. Ishtiaq Ahmad, former professor, Department of Political Science, A.M.U., Aligarh for his kind cooperation and ready assistance throughout this period. He, infact, helped me greatly in planning and successfully completing my work.

It will be share injustice – even ingrateful to me – not to mention, the learned scholars as Professor M.Y.M. Siddiqui, Dr. F.R. Faridi (Aligarh), Dr. Mumtaz Ali, Dr. Zeenath Kausar (Malaysia) and even those who go here un-named, whose hearty help, co-operation and good wishes through word or deed brought me inspiring moments of satisfaction and relief.

The Incharges of various libraries in the country and abroad, are beyond any thankfulness because without their help and keen interest, the work might not be completed. In this regard the name of Mr. Kabir Ahmad Khan, Asstt., Librarian, Library, Institute of Islamic Studies, A.M.U., Aligarh can not be neglected. He has been supported and encouraged me since the day I came to Aligarh.

Last but not the least is my wife, Tahera Fahad, who provided me, to her complete disadvantage, with the mental peace and homely relief without which no external aid could have done any good.

Qasr-e-Fahad
University Fort Enclave
Baraouli Road,
Aligarh-202002

Obaidullah Fahad

NOTES AND REFERENCES

1. The *Qur'ān*, 33: 21.
2. Hamid Enayat, *Modern Islamic Political Thought*, London, Macmillan Press, 1982, p. 2.
3. The *Qur'ān*, 17: 80.
4. The *Qur'ān*, 3: 104, 110.
5. The *Qur'ān*, 24: 2; 5: 38.
6. The *Qur'ān*, 8: 60.
7. The *Qur'ān*, 4: 59.
8. The *Qur'ān*, 47: 33.
9. See for detail, Kalim Siddiqui, *Nation States as Obstacles in the total transformation of the Ummah*, The Muslim Institute, London, 1985; also his paper, Beyond the Muslim Nation States, The Open Press, London, 1982.
10. Muhammad, Mahathir, Islamization of knowledge and Future of the Ummah, in *Toward Islamization of Disciplines*, International Institute of Islamic Thought, U.S.A. 1989, p. 19.

*****

1

SHURA IN THEORY AND PRACTICE UNDER THE PROPHET (SAW)

Qur'ānic Notions

Islamic concept of *Shura* (mutual consultation) is not only premier in nature but also pays a cordial role in Islamic polity and system of governance. It could be said without hesitation that it is not inevitable in the political life of the Islamic *Ummah* but also invariable in all walks of the social and communal life. For example, when the Qur'ān narrates the issues and problems of suckling out of the divorce, it gives due importance to the mutual consent:

وَالْوَالِدَاتُ يُرْضِعْنَ أَوْلَادَهُنَّ حَوْلَيْنِ كَامِلَيْنِ لِمَنْ أَرَادَ أَنْ يُتِمَّ
الرَّضَاعَةَ وَعَلَى الْمَوْلُودِ لَهُ رِزْقُهُنَّ وَكِسْوَتُهُنَّ بِالْمَعْرُوفِ لَا
تُكَلَّفُ نَفْسٌ إِلَّا وُسْعَهَا لَا تُضَارَّ وَالِدَةٌ بِوَلَدِهَا وَلَا مَوْلُودٌ لَهُ
بِوَلَدِهِ وَعَلَى الْوَارِثِ مِثْلُ ذَٰلِكَ فَإِنْ أَرَادَا فِصَالًا عَنْ تَرَاضٍ مِنْهُمَا
وَتَشَاوُرٍ فَلَا جُنَاحَ عَلَيْهِمَا

The mothers shall give suck to their offspring for two whole years, if the father desires to complete the term. But he shall bear the cost of their food and

> clothing on equitable terms. No soul shall have a burden laid on it greater than it can bear. No mother shall be treated unfairly on account of her child, or father an account of his child. And heir shall be chargeable in the same way. If they both decide on weaning by mutual consent, and after due consultation, there is no blame on them."[1]

As this verse comes in the midst of the regulations on divorce, it applies primarily to cases of divorce where some definite rule is necessary as the father and mother would not, on account of the divorce, probably be on good terms, and the interests of the children must be safeguarded. However, the wording is perfectly general. It has been held that the principle applies equally to the father and mother in wedlock: each must fulfil his/her part in the fostering of the child. On the other hand, it is provided that the child shall not be used as an excuse of hard bargain by either side. By mutual consent they can agree to some course that is reasonable and equitable.[2]

In individual life, the *Qur'ān* instructs the Muslims to go ahead only through the process of mobilisation, agreement and mutual consent in the shorter field of educating and nursing the children, and does not permit anyone of the parents to despotism, state being individual writ large, logically Islam does not permit any body to behave with the whole *Ummah* in political and social affairs in an autocratic manner.[3] Therefore, the *Qur'ān* guides the Prophet (SAW) to consult with his companions:

فَاعْفُ عَنْهُمْ وَاسْتَغْفِرْ لَهُمْ وَشَاوِرْهُمْ فِى الْأَمْرِ فَإِذَا عَزَمْتَ
فَتَوَكَّلْ عَلَى اللهِ

> So pardon them and ask forgiveness for them and consult with them on the matter and when you decide, put your trust in Allah (SWT).[4]

This verse was revealed after the Battle of Uhud which was fought on the advice of his companions though he was of the opinion to stay in Madinah and defend it from inside. The events during this battle showed that the Prophet's (SAW) view was more correct and sound. Despite this, after these events, Allah (SWT) ordered His Prophet (SAW) "to ask forgiveness" for the companions and to consult with them on every matter in which consultation was needed. The *Qur'ānic* text, quoted above, revealed that consultation with the companions was essential and definite even if the majority's advice may be seemingly wrong as had happened in case of Uhud. This leaves no room for any doubt that *Shura* was one of the basic principles of the Islamic political system and one of its highest values which the Muslim *Ummah* should always and under all circumstances adhere to.[5]

Some scholars assert that the word *al-Amr* in the above mentioned verse, makes "consultation" necessary regarding the system, the power and the government. *Al-Amr* conveys the meaning that every aspect of the system: the problems of municipality, national and provincial affairs, political and social ordinances, legislative rules and regulations, appointment and dismissal of the governors, delegation and deprivation of the authorities and alike are to be consulted.[6]

In an other verse, Allah (SWT) has praised to those Muslims who conduct their affairs through consultation:

وَالَّذِيْنَ اسْتَجَابُوْا لِرَبِّهِمْ وَاَقَامُوا الصَّلٰوةَ وَاَمْرُهُمْ شُوْرٰى بَيْنَهُمْ
وَمِمَّا رَزَقْنٰهُمْ يُنْفِقُوْنَ

And those who hearken to their Lord, and establish regular prayer and who conduct their affairs by mutual consultation and who spend out of what We bestow on them for sustenance.[7]

In this verse the description of the believers as those "who conduct their affairs by mutual consultation" denotes that *Shura* is one of the traits of Islam which should adorn Muslims whether they are only a "group" without state (which was the situation of the Muslims in Makkah) or are in a "state" as was the case of the Muslims in Madinah.[8]

The general literary style of the *Qur'ān* is to describe the *Salah* (prayer) alongwith the *Zakah* or *Infaq* (to spend in the way of Allah). But here, contrary to this, *Shura* is mentioned in between prayer and *Infaq*. The reason is very simple. The spirit of collective system of Islam and the original form of its structure is preserved in *Salah* (prayer). The *Salah* system of Islam indicates how to stand unitedly and collectively for the service to Allah's religion, how to select the most aware of Islamic *Shariah* and God-fearing persons from amongst for leadership, how to obey the leader unhesitatingly under the *Hudud* (limitations) of Allah (SWT), how the leader is obligated not to order against the will of Allah (SWT); and how even lower section of the society is free to criticize and check if the leader is committing any wrong, even in the midst of the prayer in performing the *arkan* (essential parts) of the *Salah* and the Imam is bound to correct himself. The *Salah* is a mirror to political and social system of Islam. We have to be united for the establishment of religion like in *Salah* to select the most aware of religion and God-fearing person of us, to obey him undoubtedly and to control him from any wrong without fear. This explains the relation between *Salah* and political system of Islam, and because of that co-relationship the *Shura* system was emphasised upon in due course of *Salah* and *Infaq*.[9]

In addition to these two verses, there is an even stronger evidence stressing the mandate of Shura.[10] It is in the *Qur'ānic* verse in *Surah Āl-Imran* which states:

وَلْتَكُن مِّنكُمْ أُمَّةٌ يَدْعُونَ إِلَى الْخَيْرِ وَيَأْمُرُونَ بِالْمَعْرُوفِ
وَيَنْهَوْنَ عَنِ الْمُنكَرِ وَأُولَٰئِكَ هُمُ الْمُفْلِحُونَ

> And there must arise from you a group which invites to goodness and enjoins right and forbids wrong. And such are the successful.[11]

The verse already referred with, does not indicate as to whether the decision reached after consultation is binding upon the ruler and there is no guarantee of compliance. This verse also does not suggest that what could be done to prevent the ruler if he deviates from the decision reached after consultation. This verse, however, establishes a mandate that there must exist among the people a strong and united group who call for goodness and for observing the right and forbidding the wrong. It is a general mandate to be observed by the rulers and the ruled both. Hence, there is no right greater than justice and no wrong worse than tyranny.[12]

The Qur'ān has described the story of the Prophet Sulaiman and the queen of Saba. It is in the holy verses that when the letter of the Prophet (Sulaiman) demanding her submission to Allah (SWT) came to the queen, she did not decide independently ad autocratically instead, she consulted with her chiefs and ministers:

قَالَتْ يَا أَيُّهَا الْمَلَأُ أَفْتُونِي فِي أَمْرِي مَا كُنتُ قَاطِعَةً أَمْرًا حَتَّىٰ
تَشْهَدُونِ

> The queen said, "O chiefs, counsel me in this matter; I do not take a decision in any matter without consulting you."[13]

The scholars assert that this pagan queen always consulted in matters of importance. Naturally the Muslims upon whom "consultation" has been made obligatory manage their social and collective affairs by mutual understanding and common sharing.[14]

Traditions of the Prophet

Prophetic traditions have emphasised "consultation" so much that one may derive it as a general rule that the ruler shall consult the *Ummh*.

عن علي رضى الله عنه قال قلتُ يا رسولَ الله الأمرُ ينزل بنا بعدك لم ينزل فيه قرآن ولم يُسمع منك فيه شيءٌ قال: إجمعوا له العابدَ من أمتى واجعلوه بينكم شورى ولا تقضوه برأى واحدٍ

Ali (RA) reports that he asked: O the messenger of Allah (when) we face a situation after you in which there is no guidance in the Qur'ān, nor we had heard from you any thing regarding the matter (what we will do)? The Prophet (SAW) replied: "collect the God-fearers among my *Ummah*, consult with them and do not decide individually.[15]

عن ابن عباس رضى الله عنه قال: لمّا نزلت وَشَاوِرْهُمْ فِى الأمرِ قال رسول الله صلّى الله عليه وسلّم: أما إن الله ورسولَه لغنيّان عنها، ولكن جعلها الله رحمة لأمتى، فمن استشار منهم لم يعدم رشدًا ومن تركها لم يعدم غيًا.

Ibn Abbas (RA) reports that when the verse "And consult with them in the matter" was revealed, the Prophet (SAW) explained "Beware Allah and His messenger do not need it, but Allah (SWT) has bestowed His mercy upon my *Ummah*. One who consults the people never loses the right guidance, and one who ignores it is prone to misguidance.[16]

عن ابن عمر رضى الله عنهما عن النبى صلى الله عليه وسلّم

قال: من أراد أمرا فشاور فيه وقضى هدى لأرشد الأمور.

Ibn Umar (RA) has quoted the Prophet (SAW) "One who likes to do something, consults with the people and decides, would be guided to the right way."[17]

عن أبى هريرة رضى الله عنه قال قال رسول الله صلّى الله

عليه وسلّم: إذا كان أمراؤكم خيارُكم وأغنياءكم سمحاءكم،

وأموركم شورى بينكم فظهر الأرض خير لكم من بطنها، وإذا

كان أمراؤكم شرارُكم وأغنياءُكم بخلاءُكم، وأموركم إلى نساء

كم فبطن الأرض خير لكم من ظهرها.

Abu Hurairah (RA) says that the Prophet (SAW) has narrated that "when your leaders are from the best, your wealthy people generous, and your affairs are decided upon after consultation, then the surface is better for you than underground, and when your leaders are corrupt, your rich avaricious and your affairs entrusted to your women, then the underground is better for you than its surface.[18]

عن أنس رضى الله عنه قال قال رسول الله صلّى الله عليه

وسلّم: ماخاب من استخار ولاندم من استشار.

Anas (RA) has quoted from the Prophet (SAW) that: not failed who made an *Istikhara* (sought to obtain the Devine favour) and never become ashamed who consulted.[19]

عن جابر رضى الله عنه قال قال رسول الله صلّى الله عليه

وسلّم: إذا استشارَ أحدكم أخاه فليُشر عليه.

Jaber (RA) narrates on behalf of the Prophet (SAW) that, "when any one from you seeks counsel from his brother, he should give his advices".[20]

عـن أبى هريرة رضـى اللّـه عـنه قال: مارأيت احدًا أكثر مشاورةٍ لأصحابِه من رسول الله صلّى الله عليه وسلّم.

Abu Hurairah (RA) has said, "I have never seen any one else who sought counsel of his companions more than the Prophet (SAW)".[21]

Pre-Islamic Arabia

Before the advent of Islam, the uncultured Bedouin Quraish, though unorganised, had some basic qualities which could support, to a large extent, the establishment of a strong state. They had distinctive features of centralized and collective system. The state of Qusay and its influence upon the entire Arabs is a clear example. During this period one can see an initial stage of parliamentary system of government in which the delegates of Quraish used to meet and decide their important affairs with mutual consent.[22] Undoubtedly, this society was democratic in spirit. Tribes were natural social units which were governed by representatives. No doubt in certain regions like Yaman, there were monarchies, but the majority of the tribes were essentially small democracies. Monarchical spirit was not only alien to but even antagonistic to the free Arab society. The prominent feature of the tribal government was the representative system, a fact which is beyond doubt. Difference of opinion may arise about certain of its characteristics, its scope and degree of development. The general technique of representation was neither direct nor indirect in the precise sense of these words. The head of the tribe and his counsellors, that is, the heads of different clans constituting the tribe, were not chosen either through general election or by representatives. They emerged from within the clans and the tribes as a whole in the course of a gradual and long natural process. Every one aspiring for leadership had to go through a series of social ordeals. Various occasions were provided now and then in which their ability exhibited. Thus whoever won the admiration of the tribe and captivated the hearts of the majority was adopted the head of the tribe or the clan. It was never hereditary. If the son was not competent, and did not bear certain qualities, he was not recognised as a successor. His place passed on to free contesters. On the other hand if he proved his worth the Arabs did not be grudge his exalted position. He could continue in the office of his father after him. Neither this nor that lineage was the sovereign. What was sovereign was a set of democratic qualities.

If this representation is right then upon this view the Arab representative system was not a matter of few days in which through elections representatives were installed for a period of three or five years. It was rather a continuous natural process, self developing in the light of a definite criterion and culminating in the emergence of a tribal head or the representatives of different clans.

Dar al-Nadwah

The government of the tribe had the tribal representative at its head and the representatives of the clans as his '*Shura*'. Here a remarkable point should be noted. The members of the *Shura* were not nominees. They were either the general body of the clan representatives or a certain chosen from among these. Such was the character of the representatives government in the pre-Islamic society, a clear picture of which can be observed in the Government of Quraish in Makkah. Historical evidence is sufficient to trace a representative government in Makkah. It consisted of the representatives of different clans, each in-charge of a particular portfolio, like *Siqaya, Liva, Imarah* etc. Though it can not be claimed that this government was purely democratic, yet this much is beyond doubt that decisions in important problems were taken by the representatives of the clans in a very free and cooperative atmosphere. All the decisions were equally binding on each clan no matter whether it had first approved it or not. We know that the historical decision to murder the Prophet (SAW) was taken after a good deal of discussion by the different clan representatives of Quraish who had assembled in a house named *Dar al-Nadwah*. It was like the parliament house of the modern world. According to Ibn Hisham after the migration of the Prophet (SAW) to Madinah frightened Quraish met in *Dar al-Nadwah* (the parliament house), the house of Qusay b. Kilab. Quraish never decided any important matter without consultation. To decide matters of importance, they used to meet together in this house and decide.[23] This discussion has been referred to in the *Qur'ān* as follows:

وَإِذْ يَمْكُرُ بِكَ الَّذِينَ كَفَرُوا لِيُثْبِتُوكَ أَوْ يَقْتُلُوكَ أَوْ يُخْرِجُوكَ وَيَمْكُرُونَ وَيَمْكُرُ اللَّهُ وَاللَّهُ خَيْرُ الْمَاكِرِينَ

> Remember how the unbelievers plotted against you to keep you in bonds, or slay you, or get you out (of your home). They plot and plan, and Allah too plans, but the best of planners is Allah.

The Prophetic Consultations

It indicates that the Quraish were familiar with a system of government that was based on mutual understanding and consent. The Prophet (SAW) turned this initial quality into a mature one. He established the Islamic state on the base of the *Shura*. This is the reason why Tabatabai has claimed that the Prophet (SAW) had usually consulted with his companions,[24] and that why Ibn Khaldun has declared that "he always consulted with his companions in special and general affairs and specially with Abu Bakr.[25]

Military Campaigns

In all the military expeditions, the Prophet (SAW) of Islam consulted with his companions specially with those living in the centre *e.g.* Madinah. The weak and numerically small Muslim community of Madinah was infact living after the migration in an island surrounded by formidable forces of opposition and hostility. The greatest danger to which the Muslims were exposed was genuinely feared from the Makkans whose clutches the Prophet (SAW) and his followers had narrowly escaped from. In this situation, in the second year of migration, the Muslims came up against the infidels in the decisive battle of Badr which was to prove the turning point in the destiny of Islam. When the Prophet (SAW) sent a group to intercept the commercial caravan, news came to him that a strong Makkan army was on its way to engage him in a battle. The Prophet (SAW) thereupon summoned his followers and asked for their advice. He really wanted to know the reaction of the *Ansar*, for, their original compact with him implies their defending him in Madinah and did not put them under any obligation to take part in a military expedition outside their territory. The migrants responded first and assured him of their help and loyalty. The Prophet (SAW), however, repeated his question and the migrants gave the same reply but the Prophet (SAW) put the same question again for the third time. Now the *Ansar* realised that the question was meant for them. Sad bin Muād immediately got up and replied, "O Prophet of Allah, it seems as if you mean us and you want to have our answer. Perhaps you think, O Prophet of Allah, that the *Ansar* have undertaken to help you on their own territory alone. I want to tell you on behalf of the *Ansar* that you may lead us where you like; align with whom you may desire or break relations with whom you may think fit; you may take whatever you desire from our property and give us as much as you want; for, whatever you would take from our property would be dearer to us than what you would leave for us. We would follow whatever you would command us. By Allah (SWT), if you go ahead until you reach Bark Ghimdan (a place of Yaman) we will accompany you, and by Allah (SWT) if you plunge into the sea, we will also plunge with you.

Then Miqdad got up and said, O Prophet of Allah, we will not say as the children of Israel said to Moses: Go thau and thy Lord and fight, we will sit here; we will fight with you on your left and on your right, in your front and in your rear.

The Prophet (SAW) was delighted to hear the replies given by his companions. He said, "Go ahead and have glad tidings.[26]

In the same battle, there is another example of consultation and democratic procedure in another form. Here the experienced and intelligent persons gave their advice on their own without being called to *Shura*. When the Quraishi army halted on reaching a river valley near Badr and Muslims pitched their tents on the further side of the enemy, Hubab b. Mundhir called upon the Prophet (SAW) to enquire: "O Prophet of Allah, is this a place which Allah (SWT) has ordered you to occupy, so that we can not leave the place, or is it a matter of opinion and military tactics? "No", replied the Prophet (SAW), "it is a matter of opinion and military tactics and everything can be done to ambush the enemy". Hubab then said, "O Prophet of Allah, it is not the place we should occupy". He suggested another place nearest to the water more suitable to fight enemy. The Prophet (SAW) agreed and ordered his men to move on there.[27]

The Prophet (SAW) again, when the prisoners of Badr were presented before him, consulted his companions. He said to them that Allah (SWT) has empowered you over them. Umar stood and said, "O Prophet of Allah, they had declared you liar and they had taken you out, so slay them". The Prophet (SAW) avoided him. Abu Bakr was of the opinion that "they are your relatives so pardon them and accept the ransom in exchange". Abdullah b. Rawaha said, "O, Prophet of Allah, you are in a valley of firehood, inflame it and throw them into it". The Prophet of Islam (SAW) was silent and did not respond to any one. He stood and entered his room. The people guessing that he will follow Umar. Some told that the opinion of Abu Bakr would be implemented. The others were in favour of Abdullah b. Rawaha.

Muhammad (SAW) came out and said, "Allah softens the hearts of some people so far that these become softer than kilk; and He makes the hearts of others so hard and stiff that these are more hard than stones. Your example, O Abu Bakr, is like Ibrahim who said, those who will follow me would be among us and those who deny me, O Allah you are Merciful and Forgiving for them; and your example, O Abu Bakr, is like Isa who said, "O Allah, if you punish them they are your own servants, and if you forgive them, you are All-Powerful and All-Wise". And your example, O Umar is like Nooh who said, "My Lord, leave not on the earth any dweller from among the disbelievers". You are family members, none of them would be freed except after the payment of ransom or would be killed.

The Prophet (SAW) implemented the opinion of Abu Bakr. Later on the *Qur'ānic* Verses were revealed and Umar's view was favoured:

مَاكَانَ لِنَبِيٍّ أَنْ يَكُونَ لَهُ أَسْرَى حَتَّى يُثْخِنَ فِي الْأَرْضِ
تُرِيدُونَ عَرَضَ الدُّنْيَا وَاللَّهُ يُرِيدُ الْآخِرَةَ

> It does not behave a Prophet to keep captives until he has crushed down the enemies in the land. You desire the gains of this world, but Allah desires the Hereafter.[28]

In the same battle, when the Makkans sent to ransom their prisoners, Zaynab sent the money for Abul As, she sent with it a necklace which Khadijah had given her on her marriage to Abul As. When the Prophet (SAW) saw it his feelings overcome him and said, "If you would like to let her have her captive husband back and return her money to her, do so. "The people at once agreed and they let him go and sent her money back".[29]

Battle of Uhud

And in the battle of Uhud Prophet's plan was to remain in the city, leaving the invaders there alone and fight only when they decided to enter the city. He suggested that Muslims should hold fast to Madinah; reinforce themselves therein, and keep out the Quraish. Should the enemy decide to attack, the Muslims would fight from within and knowing their own ground, should be better able to repulse the enemy. Abdullah b. Ubayy agreed with the Prophet (SAW) and explained: O, Prophet of Allah, in the past we always fought our enemies in Madinah by placing our women and children safely in the upper stories of the houses ad building walls connecting one house with another on the peremeter of the city, thus making the town a single fortress. When the enemy advanced on us, the women and children would hit them with stones with which they had been amply provided while we would meet them with our swords in the streets. Our city, O, Prophet of Allah has never been violated by any enemy outside our city without loss to ourselves. Please listen to me in this matter and follow this wise plan which inherited from the greatest leaders and wise men of Madinah who have gone before.

The Prophet (SAW) as well as the prominents among his companions, whether *Muhajirs* or *Ansar*, agreed with this view. However, the young Muslims who had not participated in Badr, as well as others who had witnessed Badr but became thereafter convinced that Muslim power was invincifle, desired to go out of Madinah and meet the enemy in the open. They were disturbed by the idea that unless they spoke to this effect, they might be suspected of cowardice. One of them said: "I hate to see the Quraish return to Makkah saying that they have locked up Muhammad in the houses and buildings of Yathrib and have prevented him and his companions from going out. Such propaganda would undoubtedly incite the Quraish to commit further acts of aggression. Then they would enter our very orchards and plantations. This show by Quraish of their numbers and strength would incite the Arab tribes and Abyssinian clients to follow them. We should not allow them to blockade us again and to cut off our roads to the outside world". A number of other speakers spoke in favour of going out to meet the enemy.

Muhammad (SAW) led the prayer of *Jumu'ah* and informed the congregation that their victory depended on their patience and careful preparation for war. After the *Asr* prayer, he returned home with Abu Bakr (RA) and Umar (RA), who helped him put on his armour and handed to him his sword. In the meantime the people were waiting outside and arguing with one another. Usayd b. Hudayr and Sad b. Muadh who had argued in favour of remaining in Madinah, addressed the people in these words, "You must have noticed that the Prophet (SAW) was of the opinion that we should remain in Madinah and meet our enemy here, but you dissuaded him from this position against his will. It is better to delegate the matter to him entirely follow his verdict and obey him". As the Prophet (SAW) came out of his house, they came to him pleading that they did not mean to disagree with him. They declared that they were prepared to abide by "his" and Allah's (SWT) judgement whatever that may be. Muhammad (SAW) answered "The Prophet is not one to put away his armour and sword once he puts them on until Allah's (SWT) judgement is rendered between him and his enemies".[30]

Thus the Prophet (SAW) showed a way that once the community had made up its mind after deliberation, it should not alter it in a haste.

Battle of Ahzab

In the battle of *Ahzab* when the Prophet (SAW) had news of enemies' design to wipe the Muslims out of existence he conferred with his companions how to meet the threat. It was decided after a thorough discussion to fight a defensive war resisting the attack of the enemy on the city instead of facing the coalition in a pitched battle outside Madinah. It was the Persian companion called Salman al-Farasi who advised to dig a trench on the side Madinah lay open to cavalry attack. Salman is reported to have said, "O Prophet of Allah, when we feared a charge by the cavalry we used to dig trenches to keep the invaders at bay". The Prophet (SAW) agreed to his suggestion and decided to have a trench dug in the open ground lying to the north of Madinah.[31]

In the same battle when Muslims were placed in a desperate position, the air of security and fear enveloped the city and the conditions pressed hard upon them the

Prophet (SAW) sent to the leaders of *Ghatfan* (enemy) and offered them a third of the dates of Madinah on the condition that they would go back with their followers and leave him (the Prophet) and his men. Peace was concluded to an unsigned agreement between them. When the Prophet (SAW) wanted to act he consulted his companions. He called for Sad b. Muadh and Sad b. Ubadah and told them of it and sought their advice. They said, "Is it a thing you want us to do, or something Allah has ordered you to do which we must carry out? The Prophet said: I deem my opinion better for your sake. By Allah, I would not do it were not that I have seen the Arabs have shot at you from one bow, and gathered against you from every side". Infact the Prophet (SAW) wanted to break their offensive against Madinities. Sad b. Muadh said, "we and these people were polytheists and idolators, not serving Allah nor knowing Him, and they (*Ghatfan*) never hoped to eat a single date of ours except as guests or by purchase. Now, after Allah has honoured and guided us to Islam and made us famous by you, are we to give them our property? We certainly will not, We will give them nothing but the sword until Allah decides between us. The Prophet (SAW) said, "you shall have it so". Sad took the paper and erased what was written, saying, 'Let them do what they could do against us'.[32]

In this case, the Prophet (SAW) had a opinion and implemented it to some extent. But after the consultation with his followers, he gave up the idea and did not make any compromising treaty.

Khaybar Battle

During the campaign of *Khaybar*, when the Prophet (SAW) halted near to the enemy's fort, Hubab b. al-Mundhir asked him, "Is this a place which Allah has ordered you to stay, or is it a matter of opinion". Then Hubab suggested to encamp in the higher place far from the fort so that their arrows may not hit the Muslims. The Prophet (SAW) accepted his advice and ordered Muhammad b. Maslamah to search in a place far from their fort and protected from the plague".[33]

During the same battle, on the advice of Hubab b. Mundhir, the Prophet (SAW) ordered to cut down certain types of date-trees, but later Abu Bakr's stand was accepted. Abu Bakr said, 'O Prophet, Allah has promised you for *Khaybar* and He will carry out His promise. Do not cut out the date-trees'. Then the previous order was cancelled.[34] The *Qur'ān* incidentally, testified to the validity and usefulness of both the opinions:

مَا قَطَعْتُم مِّن لِّينَةٍ أَوْ تَرَكْتُمُوهَا قَائِمَةً عَلَىٰ أُصُولِهَا فَبِإِذْنِ
اللَّهِ

> "Whatever palm-trees you cut down, or whatever you left standing upon their roots, it was only by Allah's leave."[35]

Similarly, Sad b. Ubadah's advice against giving a half of the produce of Khaybar to Ghitfan in the expedition as a price of their withdrawal from Jewish territory was also accepted by the Prophet (SAW).[36]

In *Shawwal* 7 A.M./Feb 629 A.D. the Prophet (SAW) decided to send an expedition towards *al-Jinab*, but he could not make up his mind as to who should be asked to command it. He, therefore, consulted Abu Bakr and Umar who jointly recommended the name of Bashir b. Sad al-Khazraji and their advice was readily accepted.[37]

Hunayn Battle

During the *Hunayn* expedition, the release of the prisoners of *Hawazin* was affected only after much deliberations and pursuations. On his way back from Taif the Prophet (SAW) stayed over at *Jirana* having a large number of Hawazin captives. A deputation from Hawazin came to him after embracing Islam and said that the disaster which had befallen upon them had ruined them. They requested for mercy for Allah's sake. One of the Hawazin Banu Sad b. Bakr, Zuhayr Abu Surad said, 'O Prophet of Allah, in the captives are your paternal and maternal aunts and the women who suckled you and used to look after you. Had we acted as foster parents for Al-Harith b. Abu Shimr or Al-Numan b. al-Mundhir and then got into the position in which you hold us we could hope for his kindness and favour, and you arc thc best of trustworthy men'.

The Prophet (SAW) asked, "which are dearest to you? Your sons and your wives or your cattle?" They replied, 'Do you give us the choice between our cattle and our honour? Nay, give us back our wives and our sons, for that is what we most desire'. He said, "so far as I and the B. Abdul Muttalib have they are yours. When I have prayed the noon prayer with the men then get up and request" we ask the Prophet's intercession with the Muslims, and the Muslims' intercession with the Prophet (SAW) for their sons and wives". I will then give them to you and would make an application on their behalf. After the noon prayer, they did as the Prophet (SAW) had ordered them. The Prophet (SAW) said what he had promised to say. In reply, the *Muhajirs* and *Ansar* said that what was their's was the Prophet's. But al-Aqra b. Habis on his behalf and on behalf of banu Tamim said, "No" banu Uyayna b. Hisn said "No" on his behalf an on behalf of banu Fazarah and so did Abbas b. Midras for himself and banu Sulaym, but banu Sulaym said, "Not so, what is our's is the Prophet's". Abbas said to B. Sulaym, 'you have ashamed me. Then the Prophet (SAW) said, "He who holds his right to these captives shall have six camels for every man from the first booty I take". The women and children were returned to their men thereafter.[38]

In the battle of Taif the Prophet (SAW) used for the first time the *Minjanique* (catapult) against the besieged. He consulted with his followers. Salman Farasi suggested, 'O Prophet of Allah, In my opinion you should fix the catapult against their fort. We in the country of Iran had used the catapults against the forts and these were planted against us too. We were injured and the vise versa. If the catapult is not used, the siege may be prolonged'. Then the Prophet (Saw) executed the advice and fixed it himself.[39]

In the same battle, when the siege was prolonged to fifteen days, the Prophet (SAW) called Nawfal b. Muawiyah al-Duili for consultation. He advised: "O Prophet of Allah, the fox is in the burrow. If you will stay at it, you will catch it; and if you leave it, it will not harm you". The Prophet (SAW) understood the point and ordered to withdraw.[40]

In the battle of Tabuk, with the withdrawal of the Byzantine and the binding of the frontier provinces with treaties and covenants of peace, the Prophet (SAW) had no reason to march any further. Thereupon, he called his followers to take advices. Umar b. al-Khattab said, 'If you were ordered to march, march surely. The Prophet (SAW) replied, 'Had I was ordered to march, I would have never called you to consult in this matter' Then he said, 'O Prophet of Allah, the Byzantine has a big army and none of them is Muslim. You have come nearer to them as you like. They have become frightened now. In my opinion you should return back this year until Allah has created any other situation'.[41]

Hudaibiyah Treaty

In the event of peace-treaty of Hudaibiyah, there are many examples of consulting the companions. Bukhari has reported that the Prophet (SAW) set out in the company of more than one thousand of his companions in the year of Al-Hudaibiyah, he garlanded his animal to be sacrified, assumed the state of *Ihram* for *Umrah* from that place and sent a spy from Khuzaah tribe. The Prophet (Saw) proceeded on till he reached a village called Ghadir al-Ashtat. There his spy came and said, "The Quraish have collected in a great number against you, and they have collected against you the Ethiopians, and they will fight with you, and will stop you from entering the Kabah and prevent you". The Prophet (SAW) said, "O people, give me your opinion. Do you recommend that I should destroy the families and off-springs of those who want to stop us from the Kabah? If they should come to us for peace then Allah will destroy a spy from the pagans, or otherwise we will leave them in a miserable state". On that Abu Bakr said, "O Allah's messenger, you have come with the intention of visiting this house and you do not want to kill or fight anybody. So proceed and whoever should stop us from it, we will fight him". After hearing them, the Prophet (SAW) said, "Proceed on, in the name of Allah".[42]

On another occasion, in Hudaibiyah the Prophet (SAW) asked to go to Makkah for diplomatic negotiations. Umar told him that he feared that his life will be in danger there, as there were none of Banu Adiy b. Kab in Makkah to protect him and Quraish knew of his enmity and he had always been hard whenever he was to deal with the infidels. He recommended that a man more suitable than him should be sent, namely Uthman. The Prophet (SAW) summoned Uthman and sent him to Abu Sufyan and the chiefs of Quraish to tell them that he had not come for war but merely to visit the Makkah, the house and to venerate its sanctity. At this juncture, one of the followers of the Prophet (SAW), disagreed with his opinion and it was not discouraged by the Prophet himself.[43]

Family Issues

Consultations on other matters of communal interest, religious, social and political, were also frequently held during the Prophet's period. In the scandal about Aisha, returning from the expedition of al-Mustaliq, when the hypocrites and some of the sincere Muslims too spread a rumour, he gathered the followers and put his difficulties before them. In the mosque he addressed his men. After praising Allah he said: "what do certain men mean by worrying me about my family and say false things about them? By Allah, I know only good of them, and they say these things of a man of whom I know not but good, who never enters a house of mine but in my company". Then Usayd b. Hudayr stood up and said, "If they are of Aus let us rid you of them, and if they are of the Khazraj give us your orders, for they ought to have their heads cut off." Sad b. Ubadah got up and said, "By Allah, you lie. They shall not be beheaded. You would not have said this had you not known that they were of Khazraj. Had they been your own people you would not have said it, "Usayd replies, "liar yourself you are a disaffected person arguing on behalf of the disaffected". Feeling ran so high that there was almost fighting between these two clans the Prophet (SAW) left and entered his house. He called Ali and Usamah b. Zayd and sought their advice. Usamah said, "They are your family and we and you know only good of them, and this is a lie". As Ali said, "women are plentiful, you can easily change one for another. Ask the salve girl, for she will tell you the truth". So the Prophet (SAW) called Burayrah to ask her, and Ali got up and gave her a violent beating, saying, "Tell the Prophet the truth", to which she replied, "I know only good of her. The only fault I have found with Aisha is that when I am kneading dough and tell her to watch it she neglects it and falls asleep and the sheep comes and eats it".[44]

And in the end, Aisha had not to wait for long when the verses attesting her innocence were revealed by Allah:

إِنَّ الَّذِينَ جَاءُوا بِالْإِفْكِ عُصْبَةٌ مِّنكُمْ لَا تَحْسَبُوهُ شَرًّا لَّكُم
بَلْ هُوَ خَيْرٌ لَّكُمْ لِكُلِّ امْرِئٍ مِّنْهُم مَّا اكْتَسَبَ مِنَ الْإِثْمِ وَالَّذِي
تَوَلَّى كِبْرَهُ مِنْهُمْ لَهُ عَذَابٌ عَظِيمٌ لَّوْلَا إِذْ سَمِعْتُمُوهُ ظَنَّ
الْمُؤْمِنُونَ وَالْمُؤْمِنَاتُ بِأَنفُسِهِمْ خَيْرًا وَقَالُوا هَٰذَا إِفْكٌ مُّبِينٌ

> "Those who have invented the slander, are some of your own people. You should not, however, regard this matter as evil for it has good in it for you. Whoever took any part in this, earned his sheer of the sin accordingly, and the one, who had the greatest share of responsibility in it, shall have a terrible punishment. When you have heard of it, why did not the Believing men and Believing women have a good opinion of themselves, and why did they not say, "This is a manifest slander".[45]

Religious Affairs

In this case one can see that the Prophet (SAW) consulted his companions even in his family matters. In religious matters too, he took the advice of the Muslims. How to call and gather the faithful for prayers in the mosques was a problem in the early days after the *Hijrah*. The Prophet (SAW) disliked the customs of the Jews and Christians like kindling fire or the use of bell and horn to send for the people. At first the Muslims used to come by themselves for prayer at the appointed time without any announcement or call. While different propositions were being considered, Allah guided the Muslims to the method of giving the call to prayer. Abdullah . Zayd heard a voice in a dream, and came to the Prophet (SAW) saying, 'A phantom visited me in the night. There passed by me a man wearing two green garments carrying a clapper in his hand, and I asked him to sell it to me. When he asked me what I wanted it for. I told him that it was to summon people to prayer, whereupon he offered to show me a better way'. Then he suggested the institution of *Azān*. When the Prophet (SAW) was told of this, he said that it was a true vision if Allah so willed it, and that he should go with Bilal and communicate it to him so that he might call to prayer as he had a more penetrating voice. Bilal performed *Azān*. Umar heard him in his house and came to the Prophet (Saw) dragging his cloak on the ground and saying that he had seen precisely the same vision. The Prophet (SAW) said, 'Allah be praised for that'.[46]

Similarly, one finds that the selection of the site for the Prophet's mosque at Madinah[47] and the establishment of the institution of the *Muakhat*[48] were also made after consultations. The distribution of the landed property obtained as booty from the Jewish clans of Madinah among the poor immigrants (and a few poor Ansar also) was affected only after consultation with, and concurrence of, the leading men of the Ansar.[49] In the same way, after Bahrayn was annexed to the Islamic state and the Prophet (SAW) wanted to give some landed property to the Ansar there, the latter are reported to have declined the offer, unless the immigrants were also given an equal share.[50]

The Prophet (SAW) consulted his companions so much that Abu Hurairah has said, "I have never seen any one else who seeks consultation of his companions more than the Prophet".[51]

NOTES AND REFERENCES

1. The *Qur'ān*, 2: 233.
2. Yusuf Ali, A., *The Glorious Qur'ān – Translation and Commentary*, American Trust Publications, U.S., 1977, p. 93 f. No. 266.
3. Rida Rashid, *Tafsir al-Manar*, al-Manar ed. 1376 A.H., Vol. II, p. 414.
4. The *Qur'ān*, 3: 159.
5. El-Awa, M.S., *On the Political System of the Islamic State*, American Trust Publications, Indiana, 1980, p. 87. Regarding this concept and the circumstances in which this verse was revealed, see: Sayid Qutb, *Fi Dhilal al-Qur'ān*, Dar al-Marifa, Beirut, 1971, Vol. 4, pp. 118-120.
6. Al-Ghamidi, J.A., *Islam Ka Siyasi Nizam*, Dar al-Ishraq, Lahore, 1986, pp. 13-18.
7. The *Qur'ān*, 42: 38.
8. Syed Qutb, *op. cit.,* Vol. V, p. 299.
9. See for detail: Islahi, Ameen Ahsan, *Tadabbur-e-Qur'ān*, Faran Foundation, Lahore, 1978, Vol. VI, pp. 178-180.
10. The *Qur'ān*, Āl-Imran: 159, Al-Shura: 38.
11. The *Qur'ān*, 3: 104.
12. Rida Rashid, *Tafsir al-Manar*, *op. cit.* Vol. IV, p. 45.
13. The *Qur'ān*, 27: 32.
14. Abu Faris, M.A., *Al-Nizam al-Siyasi Fi al-Islam*, Beirut 1984, pp. 80-81.
15. Al-Suyuti, Jalaluddin Abdurrahman bin Abu Bakr, *al-Durr al-Manthur Fi al-Tafsir bi al-Mathur*, Beirut, Vol. 10, p. 6; Alusi, Syed, Mahmud, *Rooh al-Maani*, Beirut, Vol. 25, p. 46.
16. *Ibid.*, Vol. II, p. 90.
17. *Ibid.*, Vol. VI, p. 10; Alusi, *Rooh al-Maani*, *op. cit.*, p. 46.
18. al-Khatib, Waliuddin Muhammad b. Abdullah, *Mishkat al-Masabih,* edited by Naseeruddin Albani, Damascus, Vol. II, p. 695.
19. Al-Suyuti, *al-Durr al-Manthur*, *op.cit.,* vol. II, p. 90.

20. Ibn Maja, *al-Sunan*, edited by Muhammad Fuad Abdul Baqi, Cairo, Part II, p. 1233, hadith No. 3747.
21. Al-Suyuti, *al-Durr al-Manthur*, *op. cit.*, Vol. II, p. 90.
22. Ibn Hisham, Abu Muhammad Abdul Malik, *Al-Seerah al-Nabawiyah*, Dar al-Fikr, Cairo, Vol. I, pp. 141-142.
23. Ibn Hisham, *op. cit.*, Vol. II, p. 502.
24. Tabatabai Syed, Muhammad Hussain, Al-Mizan fi *Tafsir al-Qur'ān*, Tehran, 1376 A.H., Vol. IV, p. 58.
25. Ibn Khaldun, Abdur Rahman, *Al-Muqaddimah*, Cairo, p. 237.
26. Ibn Qayyim, *Zad al-Maād*, Vol. I, pp. 342-343, Ibn Hisham, *op. cit.*, Vol. I, p. 614. Bukhari and Muslim have also related the conversation with a little variation.
27. Ibn Hisham, *op. cit.*, Vol. I, p. 620.
28. The *Qur'ān*, 8: 67. This tradition is quoted from Ibn Hanbal, Ahmad b. Muhamad, *al-Musnad*, ed. Ahmad Muhammad Shakir, Egypt, 1948, Vol. V, pp. 227-230.
29. Ibn Hisham, *op. cit.*, Vol. II, p. 297.
30. *Ibid.,* Vol. III, pp. 7-8.
31. Waqidi, *Kitab al-Maghazi*, Oxford University Press, 1966, Vol. II, pp. 444-445.
32. *Ibid.*, Vol. III, pp. 239-240.
33. *Ibid.*, Vol. II, pp. 643-644.
34. *Ibid.*, Vol. II, p. 644.
35. The *Qur'ān*, 59: 5.
36. Waqidi, *op. cit.*, Vol. II, p. 651.
37. *Ibid.*, Vol. II, p. 728.
38. Ibn Hisham, *op. cit.,* Vol. IV, pp. 135-136. Waqidi, *op. cit.*, Vol. III, p. 950-952.
39. Waqidi, *op. cit.*, Vol. III, p. 927.
40. *Ibid.*, Vol. III, p. 936-937.
41. *Ibid.*, Vol. III, p. 1018-1019.
42. Bukhari, Mohammad b. Ismail, *Al-Jame al-Sahih.* Kitab al-Maghazi, Vol. III, pp. 31-32.
43. Ibn Hisham, *op. cit.*, Vol. III, p. 363.
44. *Ibid.*, pp. 344-346.
45. The *Qur'ān*, 24: 11-12.
46. Ibn Hisham, *op. cit.,* Vol. II, pp. 128-129.

47. Bukhari, bab al-Masajid, bab al-hijrah, kitab al-Buyu.
48. Ibn Hisham, *op. cit.*, Vol. I, pp. 234.
49. Al-Zurqani, *Sharh al-Mawahib al-Ladunniyah*, Ist ed., Cairo, 1325 A.H./1907-08 A.D., II, p. 87.
50. Bukhari, Fazail al-Ansar.
51. Al-Suyuti, *Al-Durr al-Manthur*, *op. cit.*, Vol. II, p. 90.

*****

2

EVOLUTION OF SHURA UNDER THE FOUR CALIPHS

Caliphs' Method

Next to the precepts and practice (*Sunnah*) of Mohammad (SAW) the Four Guided Caliphs are deemed to be the models of rectitude and worthy to be followed by the faithful. It is because the interpretation of the *Qur'ān* and the *Hadith* by the companions of the Prophet (SAW) and the importance attached to these by the first Four Caliphs are considered to be trustworthy and authentic by Muslims. Any course of action adopted by these Caliphs is unfailingly looked upon by the devout as rightful, while measures rejected by them are considered to be wrong.

The extent to which the Four Caliphs followed the Islamic system of *Shura*, if studied in the light of authentic texts, would lead one to the conclusion that not only did these Caliphs follow the *Sunnah*, but they also gave it a concrete shape.

Maimun bin Mehran says that "when any issue was brought before Abu Bakr, he first sought its solution in the *Qur'ān*. If he got it in the Holy Book he decided the case according to it. In case he did not get any guidance in the *Qur'ān* and he himself knew any *Hadith* throwing light on the matter, he gave his judgement in accordance with it. Failing this, he enquired from the *Sahabah* (Companions of the Prophet) whether in their knowledge the Prophet (SAW) had pronounced any judgement relevant to the case. Frequently some *Sahabi* cited a *Hadith*, at which Abu Bakr expressed his happiness thanking Allah that there still lived some who could recall the Prophet's traditions. However, in case this method failed, the first Caliph convened an assembly of the representatives of the people (*Shura*) and gave his decision according to the consensus evolved at it. Caliph Umar, too, followed a similar practice. When he failed to get any guidance from the *Qur'ān* or the tradition of the Prophet in any matter he tried to find if there was any pronouncement of Abu Bakr pertaining to the issue in hand, if he came to know of any such decision of his predecessor, he gave his judgement according to it. Failing this, he called a meeting of scholars, and if they came to an agreed conclusion, he gave his decision according to it".[1] Leaders and representatives of the *Ummah* who were consulted by the Guided Caliphs, and constituted the *Shura* and formed a definite group known to the people. A Caliph could not arbitrarily decide whom to call and consult in order to decide an issue. Rashid Rida has written that the Guided Caliphs knew who are the leaders of the *Ummah*. They were persons with a deep understanding of religious matters and were the *Ulul amr* (people at the helm of affairs) who were called whenever necessity arose.[2] Names of some of these leaders of the people and religious scholars are still known and hence it is possible to determine the political status of those constituting the *Shura*. Allama Qasim says that when Abu Bakr had to deal with an important issue which required consultations with those well-versed in *Fiqh* and those who were endowed with deep insight, he invited selected people from among the *Muhajirs* and the *Ansar*. He consulted people like Umar, Uthman, Ali, Abdur Rahman bin Auf, Muaz bin Jabal, Ubai bin Kaab and Zaid bin Thabit. Such were the people who, according to Qasim, were deemed by Abu Bakr to be worthy of being consulted to resolve different problems during his caliphate. Umar, too followed the same method.[3]

According to Ibn Khaldun the position that was held by Abu Bakr during the life-time of the Prophet (SAW) was later enjoyed by Umar under the caliphate of Abu Bakr, and, during the term of Umar, Ali and Uthman held the same position.[4]

Ibn Sad has cited Saeed bin al Mosayyib to the effect that Umar hesitated to decide the complicated issues without consulting Ali and Uthman.[5]

Abbas, the uncle of the Prophet Mohammad (SAW) enjoyed a very high prestige during his life and after his death. This is clear from the fact that Umar always gave his final verdict only after consulting Abbas.[6] whenever the second calipah was confronted with a complicated problem he would say to Abbas, "only you have the right to resolve such problems".[7]

Ibn Hajar says that Umar consulted the eminent Qur'ānic Scholar Ubai bin Ka'ab on different issues and decided matter according to his advice.[8]

Malik bin Aus Hadthan Basri says that he himself was '*areef* i.e. the leader of his community, during the caliphate of Umar.[9]

Ibn Taimiyah writes that on issues regarding which no clear guidance could be obtained from the *Qur'ān* or the *Sunnah*, Umar held extensive consultation.[10]

Mohammad Hussain Haikal, a modern Egyptian historian says that Umar based his state politics on the *Shura*.[11]

Imam Shobi writes: "Anyone wishing to arrive at authoritative judgement to resolve problems ought to adopt the procedure adopted by Umar, who gave his judgement in consultation with the *Sahabah*.[12]

Commenting on the period of the Guided Caliphs, Syed Amir Ali writes that they put the affairs of the state before the assembly of state officials, prominent *Sahabah* and tribal chiefs which was held in the Masjid Nabawi and did not take any decision without consulting such an assembly. Thus, according to him the Islamic system of government during the first thirty years was nearer to the democratic system of the present times.[13]

After the age of the Guided Caliphs the Muslim state became despotic in nature. However, after half a century Umar Ibn Abdul Aziz restored the pristine Islamic system of government. Mughirah says that the Caliph had a number of councelors before whom he used to put the issues raised by the people in search of solution.[14]

Appointing the head of state

Like other democratic systems, in the Islamic system of government, procedure of election of the head of state is of primary importance since this gives a clue to the true nature of the state. This helps one to decide whether the system is despotic or whether the will of the people is the decisive factor in it. If in a system the head of the state is elected by the common people or their representatives, it is a democratic system in which the people enjoy freedom and liberty and the real power is vested in the people who elect as their ruler a person whom they regard as their well-wisher and who, in their opinion, can fulfill their expectations and aspirations. They can divest their head of state of his powers the day they are sure that he has proved himself unworthy of the faith they had reposed in him. But if a state makes a person head of state without taking into consideration the will of the people and if the will of an individual in it has the force of law, it can truly be said that democracy has been banished from it.

Ibn Khaldun gives the following description of the system of election of the head of state, according to the Sunnis:

Election of a caliph depended on consensus among the *Sahabah.* The right of election to the office vests in the *Ahl al-hall wa al-aqd.* Once a person is elected by the *Ahl al-hall wa al-aqd* the body of the *Ummah* is bound to obey him.[15]

Qazi Abu Yala al-Farra had described as follows how a caliph ought to be elected and what kind of person should be elected to the post:

"When *Ahl al-hall wa al-aqd* assemble to elect an *Amir*, they would consider the cases of those who fulfil the requirements of an *Imam.* And they would bring that person forward for offering oath of allegiance who is most excellent among them and possesses the qualifications of *Imamah* to the highest degree and to whom people would not hesitate to offer their oath of allegiance. And when after their diligent enquiries, they choose one amongst them, they offer the position of *Imamah* to him and if he accepts it, all of them offer their oath of allegiance to him and thus their allegiance to him would be confirmed and the entire *Ummah* would be bound to obey him".[16]

In the light of the above description, it is worth looking into the details of the election of the Guided Caliphs which are given below:

According to a number of traditions cited by *Sahih* of al-Bukhari, Prophet Mohammad (SAW)[17] said that he was not nominating anyone as his successor nor should nearness to him or family relationship with him be any consideration in their selection.

Oath of Allegiance to Abu Bakr

After the demise of the Prophet (SAW), the *Ansar* of Madinah on the strength of their services and sacrifices for the faith, thought that the caliph should be elected from among themselves. So they decided to offer their oath of allegiance to their leader Saad bin Ubadah. When representatives of the Muhajirs heard this, among whom Abu Bakr, Umar and Abu Obaidah occupied eminent positions, they immediately went to *Saqifah Bani Saaedah* where the Ansar had gathered for offering oath of allegiance to Saad bin Ubadah and explained to them the political situation in the country.

In his speech Abu Bakr Said:

> "You certainly deserve whatever you have said about your qualities and merits but the people of Arabia are not aware of any leadership other than that of the Quraish. Hence they would not be satisfied with the leadership of any other tribe."[18]

After saying this, he suggested the names of Umar and Abu Ubaidah to the assembled people.

This speech of Abu Bakr opened the eyes of the wise among the *Ansar* and they started expressing themselves in favour of his proposition. Zaid bin Thabit, an eminent *Ansari* said:

"Don't you know that the Prophet (SAW) was a *Muhajir*. Hence, the Arabs can be satisfied with the leadership of the *Muhajirs*. So only a muhajir ought to be caliph. We should continue be the hands and arms of the successor of the Prophet as we have been the hands and arms of the Prophet."[19]

Then Umar spoke of the excellence of Abu Bakr and his religious fervour and nobility, adding:

"This is the person who was given by Mohammad (SAW) the honour of leading an important thing like *Salah*. Is there anyone among you who claims to be superior to one whom the Prophet (SAW) treated as superior?"[20]

Ansar with one voice said that they dare not to consider themselves superior to Abu Bakr. Then all the representatives of the *Ansar* and the *Muhajirs* present there, came forward to offer their oath of allegiance to Abu Bakr. The next day, Abu Bakr went to the Masjid Nabavi and Umar spoke to the congregation about the great services rendered by Abu Bakr in the cause of Islam. Thereafter, all the rest of the *Muhajirs* and the *Ansar* offered the oath of allegiance to him and the process of offering the oath of allegiance by the common people was completed.[21]

Ali, it is said; did not offer his oath of allegiance to Abu Bakr for several months as he was not consulted in the matter of the election of the Caliph. But there are evidences against the denial of Ali to offer oath of allegiance to Abu Bakr. For example, Hakim, Ibn Saad and Baihaqi have said that after receiving allegiance from all those present when Abu Bakr was addressing the congregation, he noticed the absence of Zubair and Ali. He summoned both the senior personalities and said to them:

"You are relatives of the Prophet of Allah. Do you want there to be dissention and disintegration among the *Ummah*? If such is not the case why have not you offered your oath of allegiance to me?" On hearing this, both of them came forward and offered their oath of allegiance to him.[22]

According to several accounts, Abu Sufyan and others had tried to dissuade Ali from offering allegiance but he rebuked Abu Sufyan that such things could lead to the creation of dissention and disintegration among the *Ummah.*[23]

In this context Ibn Sad has cited a most clear statement of Ali who is reported to have said that at the demise of the Prophet (SAW) when he considered his own position he recalled that Mohammad (SAW) had asked Abu Bakr to lead the prayers and hence he (Ali) had accepted the leadership of such a personage in worldly affairs too.[24]

Amar bin Hareeth asked Saeed bin Zaid if any one had desisted from offering oath of allegiance to Abu Bakr. Saeed replied that none of them had done so except those who had become apostates or were about to become apostates. Amar bin Hareeth further asked if any one among the *Muhajirs* had refused to offer oath of allegiance. Saeed bin Zaid replied that, on the contrary, the *Muhajirs* went on offering allegiance continually even without being invited to do so.[25]

Sad bin Ubadah was the only person who, according to some accounts, did not offer oath of allegiance to any Caliph till his death. He even stopped prayers in mosques alongwith other Muslims. It was considered imprudent to force him to follow the discipline of the *Ummah* and hence he was allowed to do what he liked.[26]

According to some accounts Sad bin Ubadah was later convinced by the arguments of Abu Bakr and accepted the claim of the *Muhajirs* for Caliphate. He said:

> "You are right. We are the ministers while you are the rulers."[27]

Ibn Taimiyah says:

"None of the companions said that anyone other than Abu Bakr among the *Muhajirs* deserves caliphate. Some *Ansar* opposed this on the ground that there should be an *Amir* from amongst themselves and another from amongst the *Muhajirs*. Then, all the *Ansar* took the oath of allegiance except for Saad bin Ubadah. Since Saad was himself a candidate for caliphate, he did not take the oath of allegiance (to Abu Bakr). None of the companions said that anyone among the Quraish deserved Caliphate more than Abu Bakr (neither the bani Hashim nor the non-bani Hashim). These are the things that are well-known to all the scholars conversant with the Sunnah."[28]

Oath of Allegiance to Umar

It is generally believed that the election of Umar as caliph took place in an undemocratic manner. It is said that Abu Bakr himself selected him as his successor, since, in his opinion, he was the most suitable person to be a caliph. But this is absolutely wrong and is not borne out by fact.

The truth is that Abu Bakr was the *Amir* and ruler of the *Ummah* and it was his duty to think of the welfare of the community. Hence he deemed it proper to nominate his successor during his life time so that there were no differences and dissentions among the *Ummah* on the issue. But he could not do so simply because he himself thought it was advisable. Since consensus among the *Ummah* was indispensable for the purpose, he asked Abdur Rahman bin Auf for his opinion regarding the suitability of Umar for the post. Abdur Rahman bin Auf replied that the qualities of Umar far exceeded the words of praise uttered by Abu Bakr. However, he said that Umar was somewhat harsh by nature. Abu Bakr disagreed saying, Umar had to be harsh when he saw that he (Abu Bakr) was being unduly lenient in order to maintain a balance between surgery on the one hand and applying ointment and bandaging on the other, adding that when he himself was unduly strict, Umar became soft like wax and recommended the adoption of a soft policy. After this Abu Bakr consulted Uthman who wholeheartedly supported the selection of Umar.[29] Abu Bakr discussed the matter with Saeed bin Zaid, Usaid bin Hudair and other *Muhajirs* and *Ansar*.[30]

Some people objected to Abu Bakr's preference for Umar saying that he would be answerable to Allah for nominating an unduly harsh person as his successor. To this Abu Bakr replied that he would say to Allah that he had nominated the most excellent person among the *Ummah* as a caliph.

Ibn Qayyim writes that the assessment of Abu Bakr regarding the suitability of Umar was based on the fact that his own selection was due to his being among the *Ahl al-hall wa al-aqd* which happened to be true of Umar too and hence the *Ummah* would not object to his selection as caliph.[31]

However, in spite of all these extensive consultation Abu Bakr did not utilize his position to impose his will on the people, but finalized the selection of Umar after he had obtained the consensus of the people in the matter. When he fell fatally ill, he addressed a gathering of the *Sahabah* as follows:

"O my people, as you see, Allah had decided to end my days in this world. After my death you will need a person who can be your guardian and guide in your affairs, can lead you in your prayers; face your enemies and rule over you. If you wish, you can elect any one as caliph after discussing the matter among yourselves. And if you wish, I may help you in nominating someone as caliph. I swear by

Allah that I would not leave any stone unturned in my attempt to do so."

After Abu Bakr had said this, his eyes were filled with tears due to the fear of the Day of Judgement and the entire audience started shedding tears and everyone said with one voice:

> "You are better and more knowledgeable than us. So, please nominate a caliph by exercising your judgement."

On hearing this, Abu Bakr said that he would think about the matter and would select the most excellent person from amongst them as caliph.[32]

In the light of the above fact it would not be correct to assert that the selection of Umar took place without ascertaining the consent of the people. The only objection to the selection of Umar as caliph could be his harsh attitude. But this was contradicted by Abu Bakr. Umar, too, shared this opinion about himself. He once said that the harshness that was noticed by people in his attitude during the prophethood of Mohammad (SAW) was due to the soft and lenient attitude of the Prophet.[33]

This was the reason why nobody opposed Umar's appointment as caliph. Once Abdullah bin Abbas said to him that not even two persons had opposed his nomination for caliphate.[34]

Oath of Allegiance to Uthman

The manner of the election of Uthman was the clearest evidence of the democratic process. As has been said above only the *Muhajirs* of Quraish could shoulder the burden of caliphate during the early period of Islam. Achieving consensus among the *Ummah* over the election of anyone else was difficult. Umar had once said that caliphate would be confined to those who had participated in the Battle of Badr, till even one among them was alive, after which those who fought in the Battle of Uhud would deserve it, and only then others would be considered suitable for the caliphate according to their status, while those who embraced Islam after the Conquest of Makkah would not be entitled to become caliphs.[35] In other words, according to Umar, the *Ummah* would take into account the sacrifices of the people in the cause of Islam and their long association with the faith in the matter of the selection of a caliph and that nobody was to be considered suitable for this position of eminence unless he deserved it.

During the last moments of his life, Umar was asked by the *Sahabah* to nominate his successor.[36] He, himself, thought that Ali deserved this position because of his manifold qualities and that Ali's appointment to the caliphate would be in the best interest of the *Ummah*,[37] because of his being among the first to embrace Islam, his participation in the Battle of Badr, his scholarship and his most Allah-fearing nature. Umar's son Abdullah too, concurred with this opinion of his.[38] However, in spite of these considerations, he refused to nominate anyone. He once asked Abdullah bin Abbas to remember that he had not nominated anyone as his successor.[39] Instead, he constituted a panel consisting of Ali, Uthman, Talha, Zaubair, Sad bin Abi Waqqas and Abdur Rahman bin Auf and asked its members to select one from among themselves for caliphate after necessary consultations.[40] These six members of the panel were the most outstanding people belonging to the *Ummah* whose lofty character and nobility were known to everyone and whose peity and Allah-fearing nature was such that the Prophet (SAW) himself had given them glad tiding of their going to paradise.[41] These six people enjoyed the confidence of the people to such an extent that Umar once said to them that he had assessed the opinion of the people about them and found no difference of opinion regarding them except that there were disagreement amongst themselves, and hence if there were any dissentions, these would be caused by them.[42]

Umar asked the panel of six to take the help of other eminent people of the *Ummah* like Abdullah bin Umar, Abdullah bin Abbas and Hasan, with the stipulation that these additional personages would only act as consultants and only a person among the six members of the panel should be given the responsibility of shouldering the burden of caliphate.[43] If none of those six were appointed to the position, it could lead to the disintegration of the *Ummah*, he worried.

After constituting this panel of six consisting of *Muhajirs* he asked the eminent *Sahabi* Abu Talha to form a committee of fifty from among the *Ansar* whose job should be to force the members of the panel to select one amongst themselves as *Amir* within three days of his death.[44]

After the demise of Umar, the panel of six appointed by him held a number of sessions for three days, discussing the issue of selecting his successor to the caliphate, without arriving at any agreement. Seeing this, Abdur Rahman bin Auf asked his panel colleagues if anyone of them was willing to withdraw from contest in favour of other. In response to his, Zubair said that he would cast his vote for Ali, while Talha and Saad offered to withdraw in favour of Uthman and Abdur Rahman bin Auf respectively.[45] Abdur Rahman assured the fellow panelists that he did not wish to be a caliph and ask them if they would abide by his decision. Every one immediately said that he was willing to do so.[46] Other members of the panel followed suit.[47]

After this, Abdur Rahman bin Auf tried to elicit the opinion of the *Ummah* regarding Uthman and Ali. Madinah was already a centre of the *Muhajirs* and the

Ansar. On hearing of the martyrdom of Umar and being keen to learn about the selection of a new caliph, governors of different provinces, tribal leaders and eminent people from a large number of towns had also gathered at Madinah. Adbur Rahman bin Auf tried to elicit the opinion of all these people. He consulted *Ahl al-Rae* (those whose opinion carried weight) and asked the common people who they thought would be the person most suited for being a caliph. He came to the conclusion that the majority of the people wanted Uthman to be the next caliph. On the next day he addressing all the *Muhajirs* and the *Ansar* in the Mosque told them that he had tried his best to elicit public opinion, after which he had come to conclusion that the majority was in Uthman's favour and was prepared to acknowledge him as its *Amir* and hence he (Abdur Rahman bin Auf) was going to put the band of caliphate round Uthman's neck.

After this speech of Abdur Rahman bin Auf, Ali was the first person who came forward to take his oath of allegiance to Uthman. All the others present at the gathering followed him and offered their oath of allegiance to Uthman.[48]

In the words of Ibn Atheer, all the members of the *Shura* arrived at a consensus acknowledging Uthman as their caliph.[49] Imam Ahmad bin Hanbal, a great scholar of the traditions of the Prophet (SAW) writes that the number of people who offered allegiance to Uthman far exceeded that offered to any of the other Guided Caliph.[50]

Oath of Allegiance to Ali

During the closing years of the caliphate of Uthman definite signs of infirmity and disintegration become discernable in the Islamic state and a most vicious element was bent upon creating disturbances and mischievous elements started raising their head. All this resulted in the assassination of Uthman which shook the foundation of the state spreading chaos and disorder throughout its length and breadth. To disperse this storm and to restore normalcy became a herculean task. It was under such circumstances that the election of Ali to the caliphate took place. Of the six personages whom Umar had deemed to be the representatives of the *Ummah* only Ali, Talha and Zubair were alive, Ali said to the other two that he was prepared to offer his oath of allegiance to either of them, if they so wished. Alternatively, he asked them to offer their oath of allegiance to him.[51] Both of them said that they considered Ali to be most suitable for caliphate. There are authentic accounts to the effect that in spite of his initial unwillingness the *Muhajirs* and the *Ansar* ultimately prevailed upon him to agree to accept the burden of caliphate.[52] According to Ibn Sad, all the people of Madinah, including the *Sahabah* and other prominent people offered their oath of allegiance to Ali.[53] There were a handful of *Muhajirs* who did not accept Ali as their caliph and, in the words of Ibn Atheer, all the *Ansar* took oath of allegiance for Ali except a very small group.[54] Among those who did not offer their oath of allegiance to him, or most hesitated to do, there were some who first wished to ascertain the will of the *Ummah*. They were prepared to offer their allegiance to him if people in all Islamic countries showed their willingness to do so.

Shura Under Abu Bakr

There were two important decisions of Abu Bakr regarding which it is generally believed that they were taken contrary to the advice rendered by the *Shura*, preferring his own judgement to that of *Ahl al-hall wa al-aqd* (those at the helm of affairs). The first of these is that of waging war against those who refused to pay *Zakah*.

Riddah Wars

The monster of apostasy raised it head through out Arabia after the demise of the Prophet (SAW). Among the apostate tribes there were some who discarded the yoke of Islam altogether, while others either flatly refused to consider the payment of *Zakah* as their religious obligation or abstained from this payment without denying that it was so.

Abu Bakr wanted to wage war against all these three elements. There was no difference of opinion among the *Sahabah* against suppressing the first of these three tribes – those who had gone back on their acceptance of Islam as their faith. However, the *Sahabah* were hesitant to fight against the other two elements. Abu Hurairah was foremost among the *Sahabah* who held this opinion. He said that a person became a Muslim after reciting the *Kalimah al-Tauheed* (affirmation of faith in the unity of Allah) and said that he wondered if it would be proper to use force against those who had not renounced their faith in the oneness of Allah, on the ground that they were refusing to pay Zakah. He said to Abu Bakr:

"How can you start a *jihad* (holy war) against these people since the Prophet of Allah has said that he had been asked (by Allah) to fight against people till they affirmed their faith in His unity. Once they have done so, the security of their life and property is guaranteed, unless it becomes necessary to do so in the cause of Islam, and they are accountable only to Allah."

Abu Bakr replied that for the protection of one's life and property affirmation of faith in the unity of Allah was not enough as it entailed meeting two important prerequisites – *Salah* (Prayer) which everyone owed to Him for giving him the breath of life and *Zakah* which had to be paid by everyone in return for the material benefits that have been bestowed on him. He added that both these obligations were equally important and could not be separated from each other, and that is why the Holy *Qur'ān* always mentioned them together. Hence, he said that Jihad had to be waged against those refusing to pay Zakah just as it had to be waged against those who refused to perform *Salah*. According to Ibn Qutaiba, Abu Bakr cited the tradition of the Prophet (SAW) too in this context which clearly mentioned that guarantee of life and property was contingent upon the performance of *Salah* and the payment of *Zakah* only. According to Muslim, Abu Bakr added saying that "by Allah if they would refuse to pay a rope being already paid to the Prophet, I will wage fighting on the refusal of that. Zakah is a due right in the wealth. By Allah I will fight against those who would distinguish prayer from *zakah*." On hearing the above mentioned arguments Umar responded spontaneously saying that he was convinced that Abu Bakr was right and started kissing his hands in sheer ecstacy.[55]

This incident is described in detail alongwith the arguments by most of the traditionists. Bukhari has quoted in brief; Muslim has followed almost the same line and Ahmad bin Hanbal has narrated it six times. The text is as follows:

وقد روى الجماعة فى كتبهم سوى ابن ماجة، عن أبى هريرة قال لأبى بكر: علام تقاتل الناس وقد قال رسول اللّٰه صلّى اللّٰه عليه وسلّم: أمرتُ أن أقاتل حتى يَشهدوا أن لا الٰه الّا اللّٰه وأنّ محمّدًا رسول اللّٰه فإذا قالوها عصموا منّى دماءهم وأموالهم إلّا بحقِّها. فقال أبوبكر: واللّٰه لو منعونى عناقًا – وفى رواية عقالا – كانوا يؤدّونه إلٰى رسول اللّٰه صلّى اللّٰه عليه وسلّم لأقَاتلَنّهم علٰى منعها، إنّ الزكٰوة حق المال واللّٰه لأقاتلنّ من فرق بين الصّلٰوة والزّكٰوة" فقال عمر: فما هو إلّا أن رأيتُ اللّٰه قد شرحَ صدرَ أبى بكر للقتال فعرفتُ أنّه الحقّ.

From the above, it is clear that in the matter of waging *Jihad* against those who were refusing to pay *Zakah* Abu Bakr had acted after obtaining the consensus of the *Ummah* by convincing it with the strength of his arguments.

Dispatching Army under Usama

The other case in which Abu Bakr is said to have rejected the advice of *Ahl al-hall wa al-aqd* (those at the helm of affairs) relates to the appointment of Usama as the leader of the army and acted according to his personal judgement. This misunderstanding has arisen due to a lack of knowledge of the facts of the case.

It was not Abu Bakr but the Prophet (SAW) who had given the command of an army to Usama. However, the Prophet (SAW) died before this army could be dispatched for the campaign for which it was meant.

Due to the conditions that prevailed in the country following the Prophet's death, the *Sahabah* advised Abu

Bakr not to send this army to the battle front but to use it to quell the disturbances that had broken out within the country. However, Abu Bakr said that it was not possible for him to abstain from doing what had been urged by the Prophet (SAW) again and again, even on his death bed. When Umar asked him not to undertake this campaign Abu Bakr replied that he would not desist from sending the army even if the entire people of Arabia were against this measure and even though as a result of this, birds would claw him and eat him up. This speech of Abu Bakr opened the eyes of all and they were satisfied with his decision in the matter. Then Umar informed Abu Bakr of the demand of same people that someone with a high stature and wide experience be appointed commander of the army in place of Usama bin Zaid on the ground that it would be most humiliating for honourable members of the army to be led by one who was so young and was begotten by a slave.

Abu Bakr declined to concede this demand, saying that it was the Prophet (SAW) himself who had chosen Usama to lead the army. According to Ibn Jareer Tabari the *munafiqs* (hypocrites) had taunted and reproved him for this selection of his.[56] Even then the Prophet (SAW) has appointed Usama as commander in spite of this and had said to his critics that he was not surprised that they were taunting him on Usama's appointment since they had earlier criticized the selection of his father as a commander, even though he eminently deserved to be a leader and was his great favourite and his son was also his favourite.[57]

Setting high or low ancestry as a measure of ability or lack of it only befitted the hypocrites (*munafiqs*) since abolition of privileges based on this standard was one of the main objectives of Islam. Abu Bakr could also not go against a decision already taken by the Prophet (SAW). So, when some of the *Sahabah* thought that the army might not accept the leadership of Usama they approached Umar to convey their feelings to Abu Bakr. When Umar did so, Abu Bakr was greatly enraged. He asked Umar how he dared to advise him to dismiss one who had been appointed by the Prophet (SAW).[58]

War Against Rome

The above incident shows that when Abu Bakr was faced with the demands of the people which went against the principles of Islam and the directives of the Prophet (SAW), he preferred the latter to the former.

When Abu Bakr put the facts of the case of Usama before the *Sahabah* they were not merely satisfied with his decision but supported him wholeheartedly in the matter.

The importance attached by the first caliph to the opinion of the *Shura* is clear from the proceedings of the consultative meeting attended by eminent *Sahabah* to discuss the issue of war against Rome. Prominent among those present at the meeting were Ali, Uthman, Abdur Rahman bin Auf, Saad bin Abi Waqqas, Saeed bin Zaid and Abu Ubaidah bin Jarrah and the *Sahabah* who had participated in the Battle of Badr from amongst the *Ansar* and the *Muhajirs*. Abu Bakr informed the assembled gathering that the Prophet (SAW) had turned his attention towards Syria (which was part of the Roman Empire) but had died before he could take any steps in the matter. Abu Bakr told them that he now wished to send an army in Syria and wanted to elicit the opinion of the assembly. Umar said that he agreed with the proposal, adding that it was Allah who had guided Abu Bakr to take the correct decision in the matter. He asked the Caliph to send as many horses and men as possible for the campaign. He was sure that Allah would make the followers of His true faith victorious and would make the Muslims strong.

Abdur Rahman bin Auf reminded Abu Bakr that the Romans were very cunning and constituted a strong military power. He, therefore, was against attacking them without adequate preparations. He advised the Caliph to send the cavalry and surround the territory of the Romans and repeat this a number of times every day. He said that this would greatly harm the Romans and their belongings would be taken as booty, and this would also result in a blockade of the enemy. He added that this should be followed by mustering the tribes of Yaman, Rabiya and Mudar. He said to the Caliph that after these preparations he should either lead the war against the Romans personally or direct it from a distance.

Uthman was of the view that Abu Bakr was a well-wisher of the Ummah and ought to go ahead unhesitatingly and take whatever steps he considered best in its interest. Talha, Zubair, Saad, Saeed bin Zaid and others present supported Uthman asking to Abu Bakr to take whatever steps he deemed necessary. Ali was initially silent on this occasion. But when the Caliph requesting him to express his opinion, he said that whether or not he (Abu Bakr) lead the army personally he would be victorious over the enemies. When Abu Bakr asked Ali on what basis he was giving such glad tidings, he replied that he had heard the Prophet (SAW) say that the Islamic faith would overcome all its opponents and enemies until it was completely established and that its followers overcome all others.

Then Abu Bakr addressed the people, saying that Allah had blessed them with the boon of Islam and with the divine inspiration of participating in *Jihad* (holy war) and had made them superior to the followers of other faiths and hence they should proceed to the Syrian front to fight against the Romans. The Caliph added that he was nominating their leaders and was awarding them pennons. He enjoined on the people to obey Allah and not to go against the commands of their leaders.[59]

Awarding the Jagirs

Such was the attitude of Abu Bakr relating to military affairs. He consulted prominent *Sahabah* even on issues concerning the administration of the state and in the interpretation and elucidation of the Islamic *Shariah*. In such affairs Umar was his especial adviser. When Abu Bakr started implementing the *Sunnah* of the Prophet (SAW) by awarding fallow lands to people as *Jagirs* (rent-free estates) so as to strengthen the economy of the country and to increase national income, Oyainah bin Hisn and Aqra bin Hā bis approached the Caliph requesting him to allot to them as *Jagirs* some barren pieces of land in their area which were lying unutilized as they were unfit for cultivation and promised to start farming these lands after making them fertile. Abu Bakr acceded to their request and gave a document transferring these lands to them and asked them to get the document attested by Umar. When these persons went to Umar for the purpose, he was furious. He snatched away the paper from them, spat on it with contempt and tore it into pieces. The two become very angry and used harsh words against him. Umar said that the Prophet (SAW) had showered them with benevolence when Islam was weak and since Allah had now made the religion strong they ought to earn their livelihood through hard work. Both of them went to Abu Bakr and said to him angrily that they were not sure he or Umar was the Caliph. Abu Bakr replied that Umar deserved to be Caliph but had declined his offer to assume the caliphate. In the meantime Umar too reached there and expressed his displeasure at the action of the Caliph. He asked Abu Bakr whether the lands that he had allotted to these two belonged to him personally or to the entire *Ummah*. The Caliph replied that the lands belonged to all the Muslims. Umar asked him that if such was the case why he had given these lands only to these two persons, ignoring the claims of all other Muslims. Abu Bakr replied that he had consulted the *Sahabah* who were present on the occasion in the matter. Umar, then suggested to the Caliph that whenever he consulted people sitting around him or convened the assembly of the entire people to hold consultation he should keep some scope for his own views also. To this Abu Bakr remarked that this was why he was of the opinion that it was he (Umar) who deserved to be caliph but he had, instead, installed him (Abu Bakr) in the seat of caliphate.[60]

One feature of the system of *Shura* during the period of the Guided Caliphs was that whenever a *Sahabi* thought what was right and his opinion was confirmed in the light of the Qur'ān and the *Sunnah*, he was most vehement in putting forward his point of view and employed all the arguments and his full rhetorical force to convince the *Sahabah*. This was why, according to some accounts, in the case of the army of Usama when Umar put before the first Caliph objections of some *Sahabah* and suggested a change in the command of the army, Abu Bakr caught him by the beard in sheer rage. In the same way, when Abu Bakr accepted the advice of some prominent *Sahabah* regarding the allotment of barren lands, Umar became furious and spat on the deed of the allotment of these lands and tore it into pieces.

Compilation of the Qur'ān

Another example of the important role of the *Shura* during the caliphate of Abu Bakr relates to the compilation of the verses of the *Qur'ān*. This issue assumes great importance when in the Battle of Yamama one thousand and two hundred Muslims were killed, including 39 prominent *Sahabah* and *Huffaz al-Qur'ān* (those who had learnt the *Qur'ān* by heart), this being just one of the several battles in which large number of the Prophet's companions were killed.

Abu Bakr realized the need to take measures to preserve the authenticity of the *Qur'ān*. But he was reluctant to undertake anything which had not been done during the life of the Prophet (SAW). However, Umar took up courage and impressed upon the first caliph the need to do something in the matter. He said that if steps were not taken to compile the *Qur'ān* there was the danger that its large portions would be lost. Abu Bakr asked Umar how he could do something not done by the Prophet (SAW). To this Umar replied that the compilation of the Holy Book was a virtuous undertaking.

On being urged by Umar to undertake this task again and again, the first caliph was convinced of the need to do so. He called Zaid bin Tahbit the *Katib* (scribe) of the *Wahi* (divine Revelation to the Prophet) to collect the verses of the *Qur'ān* and compile them. Zaid bin Thabit said that if had been asked by the caliph to remove a mountain from its place, this task would not been as difficult as that of the compilation of the *Qur'ān*. Then he raised the same objection to the measure as that initially raised by Abu Bakr himself. The first Caliph gave the same reply as was given to him by Umar. Ultimately, after some hesitation Zaid bin Thabit too, was convinced of the need to do so. He collected different parts of the *Qur'ān* most carefully inscribed on pieces of cloth, bark of trees and palm leaves or those that had been learnt by heart by others or by himself. For example, he got two verses of *Surah al-Taubah* which had been preserved by Khuzaimah Ansari and the verse of *Surah al-Ahzab* which he had himself heard from the lips of the Prophet (SAW) and had also been preserved by Khuzaimah Ansari. He included this verse in the compilation after it was attested by two other *Sahabah.* All those pages on which the *Qur'ān* was compiled by Zaid bin Thabit were kept in the safe custody of Abu Bakr. They were then looked after by Umar and after his death they were handed over to Hafsa the mother of faithful.[61]

The Punishment of Sodomy

Abu Bakr held consultations on the issues of *Fiqh* (Islamic Jurisprudence) too. A person was arrested and brought before Khalid. He was charged with the crime of sodomy. Khalid referred the matter to Caliph Abu Bakr since there was no mention of the punishment for such a crime in the *Qur'ān* or the *Sunnah.* The Caliph conferred with his advisers on the issue, giving his personal opinion that death should be the punishment for a sodomite. His advisers were about to concur with his opinion when Ali said that such an unnatural and loathsome act should not be punishable merely with death but with the harshest and most exemplary punishment so that no one would dare to commit such a crime in the future. He further said that the Arabs considered the cutting off of the nose and ears as the most humiliating punishment and a blot on the face of humanity. In his opinion Ali continued the punishment meted out for such a disgusting crime should be harsher than that of the cutting off of the nose and ears and suggested that the criminal should be burnt alive. Abu Bakr accepted this suggestion of Ali and asked Khalid to pronounce judgement accordingly.[62]

The above examples show that the first Caliph established the Islamic system of *Shura* and consulted the scholars and *Ahl al-Raae* (those whose opinion carried weight) in the disposal of all national and political issues, thus keeping alive the *Sunnah* of the Prophet (SAW).

Shura under Umar

Umar the second Caliph of Islam, like Abu Bakr, maintained the *Shura* system of Islamic state. During his caliphate the most vital and fundamental thing was the establishment of the Consultative Assembly. Whenever an important question come up for decision, the Consultative Assembly was called and no question was decided without free debate and without the consent of the majority. The whole body politic of Islam was divided at that time into two groups, namely, the *Muhajirs* and the *Ansar*. They were the leaders of the people, and the whole of Arabia looked upon them as their representatives.

Members of both groups always necessarily took part in the deliberations of the Assembly. The *Ansar* consisted of two tribal groups, the Aus and the Khazraj and it was considered essential that members of both the groups should be present in the Assembly meetings. The history tells us that Uthman, Ali, Abdur Rahman b. Auf, Kab and Zaid b. Thabit were included in the members of Assembly.[63] The assembly was called in the following manners: A public crier went out in the capital calling the people to prayers. When the people had collected, Umar would enter the Prophet's Mosque and pray two *Rakats* of *Salah* with them. He would then ascend the pulpit and address the congregation on the matter in hand.[64] In ordinary matters of daily occurrence, decisions of this congregation were considered sufficient. But for deciding matters of great importance a general assembly of the *Muhajirs* and *Ansar* was convened. The pay of the soldiers, organization of secretariat, appointments of civil officers, freedom of trade of foreigners and assessment of import duties and other questions of State were decided by free discussion in the Consultative Assembly. These assemblies were held not merely out of piety, but because as explained by Umar, caliphate was not lawful without consultation.[65]

Two-Chamber *Shura*

The Consultative Assembly was called only on special occasions when vital issues had to be decided. There was another council in which current administrative and other questions of lesser importance were discussed. This council met always in the Prophet's Mosque and only the *Muhajirs* took part in it. Daily reports from districts and provinces that arrived in the Caliph's court were presented to this council by Umar who consulted with them on any details that called for discussion. Baladhuri speaks of this council as follows: "The *Muhajirs* used together in the Mosque and Umar used to sit with them and talk with them about world affairs".[66]

Distribution of the Captured Lands

When Umar had some leisure from military expeditions, that is, after Arabian Iraq had been completely conquered in 16 A.H. and the victory of Yarmuk had shattered the power of the Romans, he turned his attention to the organization of land revenue administration. The first obstacle that confronted him in this connection was the insistence of the army commanders that the entire conquered territory should be handed over to the army in estates and the inhabitants made their serfs and slaves. Immediately on the conquest of Iraq, Umar had ordered Sad b. Waqqas to take census of the people. Sad took the census very carefully and submitted his report. On comparing the number of the army with that of the inhabitants it was found that three men would fall to the lot of each soldier. Umar had made up his mind at that very time that land should be left in the possession of the inhabitants who should be left free.[67] But some of the eminent companions like Abdur Rahman b. Auf and others supported the army. Bilal was so persistent in this matter that Umar exclaimed in annoyance, "May Allah save me from Bilal." Umar argued, if the conquered lands were divided up among the army, wherefrom they would get the necessary finance for the raising and equipment of armies in future for defence against aggression and for the maintenance of peace and order in the country. Abdur Rahman B. Auf contended that the lands belonged to those who had conquered them, and future generations had no right to them. Then a general assembly comprising all *Muhajirs* and five representatives from each of the two tribes of *Ansar* namely, Aus and Khazraj, was called.[68] Ali, Utman and Talha supported Umar, but no decision was arrived at, and the assembly continued in session for several days. Then Umar suddenly recollected verses 8-10 of *Surah al-Hashr* which speak of "the poor who had fed, those who were expelled from their homes and properties" and of "those who come after". These verses proved decisive and Umar inferred form them that coming generations had a share in the conquests; and if the lands were divided up among the conquerors, nothing would be left for the coming generations. The Caliph advanced his contention in a powerful speech, so that the whole audience acclaimed it unanimously. On the basis of Umar's inference the principle was established that countries conquered would be the property of the state and not of the conquering forces and former occupants of lands would not be dispossessed.

Military Organization

The consultation was sought about military organization too. It is said that Abu Hurairah who had been appointed governor of Bahrain brought five lakh dirhams of the land revenue of the province to Madinah. A sum of five lakhs was wonder at the time. Umar would not believe Abu Hurairah's report and wondered whether the governor was quite in his senses. The latter repeated that he had brought five lakhs with him. Umar was still doubtful and asked whether the governor could count up five lakhs. Abu Hurairah assured him that he knew the figures and repeated lakh five times. When Umar was at last really convinced he called the Consultative Assembly and sought their opinions as to what was to be done with such a large amount of money. Ali, Uthman and other companions offered various suggestions. Walid b. Hisham said, he had seen the rulers of Syria maintaining a war department and a register of the army. The idea appealed to Umar who then decided to keep a register of the army and organize a war department.[69]

There were, at the time at Madinah three expert genealogists who were also well-versed in accountancy namely, Mahzamah b. Naufal, Jubair b. Mutam and Aqil b. Abi Talib. The keeping of genealogies was a hereditary science among the Arabs, but these three gentlemen were distinguished as genealogists throughout the country. Umar commissioned them to prepare a register of the whole of Quraish and the *Ansar*, giving the name and parentage of each person. They presented a sketch, in which were entered first the Hashimitis, then the family of Abu Bakr, and after him that of Umar. The scheme was prepared in view of the actual succession of the Caliphate. If it had been adopted, there was fear of the Caliphate becoming an object of family ambitions. Umar, therefore, rejected it and said that they should begin with the near relatives of the Holy Prophet (SAW) and then enter the names in the order in which they receded farther and farther away from the Holy Prophet (SAW) in relationship, until they came to Umar's family when his name should be written.[70]

Construction of Canals

Umar consulted with the governor of Egypt and its leading personalities in the matter of Amir ul Muminin's Canal, which joined the Nile to the Red Sea. There was a general famine in Arabia in 18 A.H. Umar commanded all his district and provincial officers to purchase large quantities of food stuffs and send them to Arabia. The order was complied with, but the land routes from Syria and Egypt were so long that the import of food stuffs from these countries proved very tardy. Umar invited Amar b. al-As, governor of Egypt to come to Madinah with him a party of responsible persons to solve the problem. When they arrived at the capital, the Caliph told them that if the Nile were connected with the Red Sea, Arabia would never have any fear of scarcity, for the carriage of food stuffs by the land route was tedious and slow. Umar told them to seek consultation among themselves and to inform him the result. Next day, when the delegation came to the court, Umar noticed their hesitation and unwillingness. He further, discussed the matter and convinced them fully. Amar, then went back, took the work in hand and built a canal from Fustat to the Red Sea.[71]

Appointment of Governors

In the appointment of governors and other officials, Umar consulted with his companions and appointed the honest and capable men for the posts. On important posts, selection was made openly in the Consultative Assembly. Uthman b. Haneef's appointment was made in this wise. At times, the inhabitants of districts or provinces were asked to select honest and capable men, and the persons so selected were appointed officers over them.[72]

The man appointed to an office of state was given an instrument of instructions, in which his appointments, powers and obligations were stated,[73] and which was witnessed by a number of *Muhajirs* and *Ansar*.

New Islamic Calendar

Umar sought for companions' opinion about introducing the new calendar. In 16 A.H. he was one day presented with a draft on which was written one word *Shaban*. Umar asked how he should know whether *Shaban* of the previous was meant or of the current one. Thereupon he called the Consultative Assembly, at which all prominent companions were present and the question of fixing an era was discussed. Most of those present suggested that the Persian method should be adopted. Harmuzan, King of Khazistan who had embraced Islam and settled down at Madinah, said that the method current in his country called *Mahruz* was convenient as it indicated both the day and the month. The question arose next as to the date from which the era was to commence. Ali suggested it should begin from *Hijrah* and all agreed to it. The Holy Prophet (SAW) had migrated in the month of *Rabiul Awwal* when the year had already run two months and eight days. The era should have started thus from Rabiul Awwal. But as the year begin in Arabia with the month of Muharram, the date was pushed back two months and eight days, and the era was made to commence from the beginning of the year.[74]

Custom Duties

Ushur were an innovation of Umar and these began with the consultation of companions this wise. Muslims who went to foreign lands for trade had to pay an import duty at ten percent on their merchandise according to the laws of those lands. Abu Musa Ashari reported the fact to Umar who ordered that import duty should be charged at the same rate form merchants of those countries coming to the Muslim countries for trade. The Christians of *Manbij* who had not yet come under the rule of Islam applied to Umar for permission to trade in Arabia on payment of *Ushur* (or custom duties at ten percent). The caliph holds the Consultative Assembly and sought the public opinion. The companions gave the permission and the same rule was extended to Muslims and *Dhimmis* though the rates were different. The foreigners paid ten percent, *Dhimmis* five percent and Muslims two and a half percent.[75]

Distribution of Booty

After the conquest of Qadisiyah (14 A.H./635 A.D.) Saad the commander-in-chief, ordered that the treasures of the royal places should be brought and accumulated in one place. There were vast riches comprising thousands of rare and priceless heirlooms transmitted and preserved from the Kayani dynasty down to the time of Anusharwan such as the coats-of-mail and swords of the monarchs of the celestial Empire of China, the Raja Dahar, the Emperor of Rome Numan b. Mundhir, Siyawash and Bahram Chobin, the poniards of Kisra, Hurmuz and Qaiqubad and the gembedizened crown and kingly robes of Anusharwan. The most wonderful and exquisitely magnificent of all was a carpet which the Persians called the 'Spring'. After the season of 'ethereal mildness' was over, the carpet was used for the feast of wine. Hence the carpet was provided with all the paraphernalia of spring which art and wealth would assay to imitate. In the centre was a parterre of verdure bordered on all sides with ornamental avenues around which trees and plants of various descriptions grew laden with buds and flowers and fruits. Strongest of all, every thing was worked in gold, silver and precious stones. The ground work was of gold and silver, the leaves of silk and the fruits of gems.

The carpet and other ancient relics were sent to the caliph's court in their entirety so that the Arabs might view the spectacle of the grandeur and magnificence of Persia as well as of th might and glory of Islam. Umar called the companions and sought advice with regard to the celebrated carpet. The public opinion was that it should not be distributed but be preserved, Umar himself was inclined towards this view. Ali was alone to disagree with it. He insisted to distribute it among the Muslims. He persistently told that if the caliph had preserved it how could be prohibit those wishing to possess unlawfully in future. At his insistence the carpet also had to be distributed and cut into pieces.[76]

Juristic Issues

Though the second caliph himself was a great jurist and his opinion alone sufficed to establish the dicta of law, even then brought most of questions in the Consultative Assembly, where matters were discussed with the greatest freedom and acumen. The historians write that Umar never adjudicated upon any question which had not been decided already.[77] Shah Waliullah analyses the situation and says, "It was Umar's practice to consult the companions and hold discussions with them until veils were lifted and conviction was attained. For this reason Umar's dicta were accepted throughout the East and the West".[78]

The cases decided by Umar in consultation with the companions were not small in number, and full details of them are to be found in the history. For instance, Baihaqi reports case of the bath of *Janabah* or sexual purification (particulars of which are given by Baihaqi). Umar commanded that the *Muhajirs* and the *Ansar* should assemble, and the question was put in the Assembly. All the companions except Ali and Muadh who differed, agreed on one opinion. Umar said, "If you gentlemen who fought the Battle of Badr differ so, what would happen to the coming generations?" The matter was referred to the noble wives of the Holy Prophet (SAW) and their opinion was made law by Umar.[79]

Similarly, there was a difference of opinion among the companions with regard to the number of *Takbirs* or repetition of the magnificatory formula in the funeral prayers. Umar invited the companions to a general assembly at which it was decided to make an inquiry as to what the Holy Prophet (SAW) had done in this respect the last time. It was found that in the last funeral prayers, the Holy Prophet (SAW) had said *Takbir* four times and the question was decided upon by consultation and discussion.[80]

War Affairs

In war affairs too, Umar used to take advice with the companions. In the Battle of Qadisiyah he ordered that the troops should mustered and equipped in the best order and intimated his intention to command the whole force in person. He, accordingly, entrusted the divisional command of the vanguard to Talha and that of the right wing to Zubair, while Abdur Rahman b. Auf was appointed to the command of the left wing of the army. When the army was drawn up, he made over the charge of the caliphate to Ali and leaving Madinah advanced toward Iraq. The activity thus displayed by Umar created wide spread enthusiasm and every one girded up his lions to meet death in the face. At Sarar, a spring three miles from Madinah, the first hault was ordered. As, for certain reasons, it was not expedient that the Caliph should go personally to the battle field, Umar convened a general council of war at Sarar and invited the opinion of every one present. All unanimously exclaimed that the expedition could not terminate successfully unless it was headed by the caliph himself. The elite fo the companions, however, who would weigh the pros and cons of the affair, gave a contrary opinion. Abdur Rahman b. Auf said, "War has two sides. Supposing we are defeated and some harm befalls you then Islam will be no more." Umar got up and made a stirring speech and wound it up by addressing the people thus, "I had a mind to follow your counsel but the elite of the companions do not acquiesce in this view." In short, it was unanimously resolved that Umar should not lead the expedition in person.[81]

Likewise, in regard to the Battle of Nihawand, Umar called the companions to the Prophet's Mosque with the letter sent by Ammar b. Yasir the governor of Kufa. He addressed the people regarding it out, "O people of Arabia, this time the Persians, one and all, have girded up their lions to sweep off the Muslims from the face of the earth, tell me what do you propose to do now?" Talha b. Ubaidullah rose and said, "O commander of the Faithful, experience has made you wise. We know no more than this that we obey whatever you order us to do." Uthman spoke next and observed, "In my opinion orders should be issued to the governors of Syria, Yaman and Basra to march with their respective forces toward Iraq while you should personally start from Madinah at the head of the Madinites. At Kufa all the troops should assemble under your standard and then we may proceed in the direction of Nihawand." All approved of this view but Ali was silent. Umar glanced at Ali who spoke thus, "If the entire forces stationed in Syria and Basra were mobilized, the frontier enemies would obtain possession of those territories and if you were to leave Madinah the whole of Arabia would become involved in internecine agitation rendering our control even our own country a matter of difficulty. I am of opinion that you should not personally leave Madinah but issue orders to the governors of Syria, Yaman, Basra and other provinces instructing them to dispatch one third of the forces under their command." Umar approved of this counsel and said that he already held the same view but that he did not like to pronounce his decision without consulting others.[82]

Case of plague

During the year 18 A.H. virulent plague broke out in Syria, Egypt and Iraq and many a towering personality of Islam succumbed to it. The epidemic appeared toward the close of the year 17 A.H. and raged with the greatest rigour for many months. When Umar first heard of it he personally went to the infected area to concert measures for its suppression. On arriving at Surgh he learned from Abu Ubaidah and others, who had hastened to the spot to receive him, that the virulence of the plague was increasing by leaps and bounds. Umar sent for the First *Muhajirs* and the *Ansar* and invited expression of their opinion. Different counsels were offered by the various people but the *Muhajirs* of the period of victory unanimously exclaimed that it was against the dictates of prudence that the Caliph should halt there. Umar acquiesced in the soundness of the advice and abade announce that all were to march tomorrow. Abu Ubaidah was an extreme fatalist. He in a tone of passion cried out, "Fliest thou, O Umar away from God's will?" Umar bore this acrid remark with an unsuffled mien and calmly replied" "Yes I fly from Allah's Will, but toward Allah's Will."[83]

These examples are sufficient to prove that Umar though none of the states around him was democratic, established a powerful democratic state in which all the matters were discussed freely and decided entirely with consultations.

Shura Under Uthman

It has been discussed already that Uthman was appointed as caliph through the mutual consultation among the *Ansar* and the *Muhajirs*. All the members of Consultative Assembly, as Ibn Athir[84] has stated, agreed upon the selection of Uthman. Ahmad b. Hanbal, who has a vast and deep vision in the Holy Traditions, has elaborated the point that the general consensus was so much in this regard that no other highteous Caliph could got so support.[85]

In the outgoing period, when there was an anarchy and disturbance throughout the country, Uthman could not hammer the spirit of consultation. To make a critical analysis he called for the *Ansar* and the *Muhajirs* to whom he said, "You are my partners and a representatives of the Muslims, give your advice what to do to cool the abnormal situations." On the advice of the companions, he sent few experienced persons in different parts of the country so that they might find out the real causes and their remedies.[86]

These few examples from the history of the Four Guided Caliphs prove the importance, validity and lawfulness of consultation with the *Ummah* or their representatives in the affairs of Islamic state. The Caliphs were really deserved to be titled '*Khalifah*' (successor of the Prophet) because they followed the Islamic political principles laid by the Prophet (SAW) *i.e.* the consultation, justice, freedom and equality in the true sense of the terms.

After going through the cases cited above in detail, one may conclude that the *Shura* system during the period of Four Caliphs was implemented with due importance. During the period of Umar al Farooq, it was developed in its highest degree. The issues were put to the Consultative Assembly and after due deliberations the problems were resolved. In the matters of greater importance the general assembly was called and the general body of Madinah or its representatives participated the discussion.

Secondly, both the religious and worldly affairs, were presented to the *Shura* for its decision. Administrative as well as legal aspects were discussed and after reaching to a consensus the final verdicts were given. In case the consensus was not possible, the opinion of majority was followed.

Thirdly, the head of state was either nominated as was done in the case of second Caliph, or proposed by *Majlis al Shura* as was practiced in the selection of Uthman, or selected by eminent *Sahabah* and was presented, later, to the general public for approval as was followed in the election of Abu Bakr or was elected by the people directly as was in the case of Ali.

The final authority lied with the people. He could not be imposed upon the people in a despotic way. The approval of the Muslims, directly or indirectly, was considered essential.

NOTES AND REFERENCES

1. Al-Darmi, Abu Mohammad Abdullah, *Al-Sunan*, al-Matba al-Nizami, Kanpur, 1293 A.H., pp. 32-33; al-Baihaqi Abu Bakr Ahmad b. Hussain b. Ali, *al-Sunan al-Kubra*, Vol. X, p. 115, Ibn al-Qayyim al-Jauziyah, Shams al-Din Muhammad, *I'elam al-Muaqqieen an Rabb al-Alameen*, Vol. I, pp. 51-52.
2. Rida, Rashid, *Tafseer al-Qur'ān al-Hakeem*. (Tafsir al-Manar) Al-Manar Press, Egypt, 1328 A.H., Vol. V, p. 214.
3. Alauddin Ali al-Muttaqi, *Kanzul Ummal fi Sunan al-Aqwal wa al-Afaal*, Hyderabad, 1951, Vol. III, p. 451.
4. Abn Khaldun, Abdur Rahman, *Al-Muqaddimah*, Cairo, p. 210.
5. Ibn Hajar al-Asqalani, *Fath al-Bari, Sharh al-Bukhari*, Egypt, 1301 A.H., Vol. XII, p. 263.
6. Abn Kathir, Abul Fida Ismail b. Umar, *Al-Bidayah wa al-Nihayah*, Matbaah al-Saadah, Egypt, 1939, Vol. III, p. 107.
7. Ibn al-Qayyim al-Jauziyah, *I'elam al-Muaqqein, op. cit.*, Vol. I, p. 14.
8. al-Asqalani, Ibn Hajar, *Al-Isabah fi Tamyiz al-Sahabah*, Maktaba al-Tijariyah al-Kubra, Egypt, 1939, Vol. I, p. 32.
9. al-Muttaqi, Alauddin Ali, *Kanzul Ummal, op. cit.*, Vol. III, p. 172.
10. Ibn Taimiyah, Taqiuddin Abul Abbas Ahmad, *Minhaj al-Sunnah al-Nabaviyyah fi Naqdh e Kalam al-Shiah al-Qadriyyah*, Vol. III, pp. 162-163.
11. Haykal, Mohammad Husain, al-Farooq Umar, Vol. II, Cairo, 1364 A.H., p. 208.
12. Baihaqi, *Al-Sunan al-Kubra, op. cit.*, Vol. X, p. 109.

13. Ameer Ali, *A Short History of the Saracens*, N. Delhi, 1977, p. 56. Hasan Ibrahim Hasan, *Tareekh al-Islam al-Siyasi*, Cairo, 1935, Vol. I, p. 570.

14. Al-Baihaqi, *Al-Sunan al-Kubra*, *op. cit.*, Vol. X, p. 110.

15. Ibn Khaldun, *Al-Muqaddimah*, *op. cit.*, p. 191.

16. Al-Farra, Abu Yala Muhammad, *Al-Ahkam al-Sultaniyah*, (ed.) Mohammad Hamid Al-Fiqqi, Matba Mustafa al-Babi al-Halbi, Egypt, 1938, p. 8.

17. Al-Bukhari, Abu Abdullah mohammad b. Ismail, *Al-Jame al-Sahih*, Vol. VI, Matba Mustafa al –Babi al-Halbi, Egypt, 1345 A.H., p. 15.

18. *Ibid.*, Vol. VIII, pp. 210-211.

19. Hakim, Abu Abdullah Mohammad b. Abdullah, *Al-Mustadrak ala al-Sahihain fi al-Hadith*, Dairah al-Maarif, Hyderabad, 1340 A.H., Vol. III, p. 776; al-Suyuti, Jalaluddin, *Tarikh al-Khulafa*, Matba Mujtaba, Delhi, pp. 46-47.

20. Al-Suyuti, *Tarikh al-Khulafa*, *op. cit.*, p. 47; Ibn Hanbal, Ahmad b. Mohammad, *Al-Musnad*, (ed.) Ahmad Mohammad shaker, Dar al-Maaref, Egypt, 1949, Vol. I, pp. 133-134.

21. Al-Bukhari, *Al-Jame al-Sahih*, *op. cit.*, Vol. IX, pp. 100-101.

22. Al-Suyuti, *Tarikh al-Khulafa*, *op. cit.*, p. 47.

23. Ibn Taimiyah, *Minjah al-Sunnah*, *op. cit.*, Vol. I, p. 13.

24. Ibn Saad, Mohammad, *Al-Tabaqat al-Kubra*, Dar Sader, Beirut, 1957, Vol. III, p. 130.

25. Tabari, Abu Jafar Mohammad b. Jareer, *Tarikh al-Rusul wa al-Muluk*, Leiden, 1893, Vol. III, p. 36.

26. Ibn Qutaibah, Abu Mohammad, Abdullah b. Muslim, (ed.) Mohammad Taufeeq al Kutbi, *Al-Imamah wa al-Siyasah*, Cairo, 1909, Vol. I, p. 12.

27. Tabari, Abu Jafar Mohammad b. Jareer, Tarikh al-Rusul wa al-Muluk, *op. cit.*, Vol. III, p. 199.

28. Ibn Taimiyah, *Minjah al-Sunnah. Op. cit.*, Vol. I, p. 139.

29. Ibn al-Athir, Izzuddin Abul Hasan, *Al-Kamel fi al-Tarikh*, Dar Sader, Beruit, 1965, Vol. II, p. 425.

30. Ibn Saad, *Al-Tabaqat al-Kubra*, *op. cit.*, Vol. III, p. 141.

31. Ibn Qayyim al-Jauziyah, *I'elam al-Muaqqein*, *op. cit.*, Vol. I, p. 187.

32. Ibn Qutaibah, *Al-Imamah wa al-Siyasah*, *op. cit.*, Vol. I, pp. 22-23.

33. Hakim, *Mustadrak*, *op. cit.*, Vol. I, p. 136.

34. Qazi Abu Yusuf, Yaqub b. Ibrahim, *Kitab al-Kharaj*, Matbaah Salafiyah, Cairo, 1346 A.H., pp. 7-8.

35. Ibn Saad, *Tabaqat*, *op. cit.*, Vol. III, p. 248.

36. Bukhari, *Al-Jame al-Sahih*, Part IX, *op. cit.*, p. 100.

37. Ibn Athir, *Al-Kamel fi al-Tarikh*, *op. cit.*, Vol. III, p. 66.

38. Ibn Abdul Barr, Yusuf b. Abdullah b. Muhammad, *Al-Isteeaab fi Marefah al-Ashāb*, (ed.) Ali Mohammad al-Bajavi, Maktabah Nahdhah, Egypt, Vol. III, p. 1154.

39. Ibn Saad, *Tabaqat*, *op. cit.*, Vol. III, p. 256.

40. Al-Tabrezi, Waliuddin Mohammad b. Abdullah al-Khateeb al-Umari, *Mishkat al Masabeeh*, (ed.) Mohammad Naseruddin al-Albani, Al-Maktab al-Islami, Damascus, Vol. III, p. 248.

41. *Ibid.*, p. 240.

42. Ibn Saad, *Tabaqat*, *op. cit.*, Vol. III, p. 249.

43. Ibn Qutaibah, *Al-Imamah wa al-Siyasah*, *op. cit.*, Vol. I, p. 26.

44. Ibn Saad, *Tabaqat*, *op. cit.*, Vol. III, p. 42.

45. Ibn Qutaibah, *Al-Imamah wa al-Siyasah, op. cit.*, Vol. I, p. 29.

46. Hākim, Mustadrak, *op. cit.*, Vol. III, p. 310.

47. Ibn Qutaibah, *Al-Imamah wa al-Siyasah, op. cit.*, Vol. I, p. 30.

48. Ibn Saad, *Tabaqat, op. cit.*, Vol. III, p. 43. Ibn Kathir, *Al-Bidayah wa al-Nihayah, op. cit.*, Vol. VII, p. 147.

49. Ibn Athir, *Al-Kamel fi al-Tarikh*, Vol. III, pp. 71-72.

50. Ibn Taimiyah, *Minjah al-Sunnah, op. cit.*, Vol. III, p. 162.

51. Ibn Athir, *Al-Kamel fi al-Tarikh, op. cit.*, Vol. III, pp. 190-191. Tabari, *Al-Tarikh, op. cit.*, Vol. IV, p. 427.

52. *Ibid.*

53. Ibn Saad, *Tabaqat, op. cit.*, Vol. III, p. 31.

54. Ibn Athir, *Al-Kamel fi al-Tarikh, op. cit.*, Vol. III, p. 191.

55. Ibn Qutaibah, *Al-Imamah wa al-Siyasah, op. cit.*, Vol. I, p. 20. See for details, Abu Izzah, *al-Shura am al-Istibdād*? *al-Mujtama*, No. 38, where all the sources of *hadith* are quoted: *Sahih Bukhari bi Sharh al-Kirmani*, Vol. 8, p. 73; *Sahih Muslim bi Sharh al-Nawawi*, Cairo 1929, Vol. I, p. 200; *Musnad* Ahmad, ed. Ahmad Muhammad Shakir, Hadith No. 67, 117, 238, 239, 334, 335; Ibn al-Atheer, *al-Kāmil*, Vol. 2, p. 143; ----, *al-Bidayah wa al-Nihayah*, Vol. 6, p. 213; Hafiz Dhahabi, *Tarikh al-Islam*, Vol. 1, p. 349.

56. Tabari, *Al-Tarikh, op. cit.*, Vol. III, p. 184.

57. Bukhari, *Al-Jame al-Sahih, op. cit.*, Vol. VI, p. 19.

58. Tabari, *Al-Tarikh, op. cit.*, Vol. III, p. 226.

59. Waqidi, *Futuh al-Sham*, (ed.) Abdul Hamid Ahmad Hanafi, Egypt, p. 2.

60. Abu Ubaid Qasim b. Sallam, *Kitab al-Amwal*, Cairo, 1353 A.H., p. 276.

61. Bukhari, *Al-Jame al-Sahih, op. cit.*, Vol. VI, pp. 225, 226.

62. Ibn Hazm, Abu Mohammad Ali b. Ahmad b. Saeed, Al-Muhalla, Etypt, 1352 A.H., Vol. XI, pp. 380-381.

63. Ibn Saad, *Tabaqat, op. cit.*, Vol. III, pp. 282-283.

64. Tabari, *Tarikh, op. cit.*, Vol. IV, pp. 98-99.

65. Ibn Abi Sheebah, Abu Bakr Abdullah b. Mohammad b. Ibrahim b. Uthman, *Al-Kitab al-Musannaf fi al-Ahadith wa al-Aathār*, (ed.) Abdul Khaliq al-Afghani, Hyderabad, 1867, Vol. III, p. 139.

66. Quoted by Shibli Nomani, *Al-Farooque*, Azamgarh, 1956, Vol. II, p. 16.

67. Tabari, *Tarikh, op. cit.*, Vol. IV, pp. 30-31.

68. Qadi Abu Yusuf Yaqub b. Ibrahim, *Kitab al-Kharaj, op. cit.*, p. 14.

69. Al-Baladhuri, Ahmad b. Yahya, *Futuh al-Buldan*, Dar al-Nashr le al-Jamein, 1957, pp. 635-636.

70. Tabari, *Tarikh, op. cit.*, Vol. III, p. 614.

71. Tabari, *Tarikh, op. cit.*, Vol. IV, p. 100.

72. Qadi Abu Yusuf, *Kitab al-Kharaj, op. cit.*, pp. 64-65.

73. Tabari, *Tarikh, op. cit.*, Vol. IV, pp. 34, 35.

74. *Ibid.*, pp. 38, 39.

75. Qadi Abu Yusuf, *Kitab al-Kharaj, op. cit.*, pp. 161-162.

76. Tabari, *Tarikh, op. cit.*, Vol. IV, pp. 21-22.

77. Qadi Abu Yusuf, *Kitab al-Kharaj, op. cit.*, p. 106. Shibli Nomani (Al-Farooque, *op. cit.*, Vol. III, p. 123) has cited some examples in this regard. He has the opinion that Umar, while issuing the Fiqhi ordinances considered the consensus of companions. The matters in which difference of opinion arose were discussed and decided in the assembly of companions.

78. Shah Waliullah, *Izalah al-Khifa an Khilafah al-Khulafa*, Vol. II, p. 140.
79. *Ibid.*, Vol. II, p. 88.
80. See for details, Shibli Nomani, *Al-Farooque*, Vol. II, *op. cit.*, pp. 216-217.
81. Tabari, *Tarikh, op. cit.*, Vol. III, pp. 480-481.
82. Shibli Nomani, *Al-Farooque, op. cit.*, Vol. I, pp. 166-167.
83. Tabari, *Tarikh, op. cit.*, Vol. IV, pp. 57-58.
84. Ibn Athir, *Al-Kamel fi al-Tarikh, op. cit.*, Vol. III, p. 79.
85. Ibn Taimiyah, *Minjah al-Sunnah, op. cit.*, Vol. III, p. 162.
86. Urjoon Sadeq Ibrahim, *Uthman b. Affan*, Cairo, 1947, p. 99.

*****

3

LEGAL STATUS OF *SHURA*

The most important element of Islamic political system is the *Shura*. Almost all the theologians and Muslim intellectuals consider it an essential organ of an Islamic state. However, they differ on the issue as to whether the *Khalifah* is bound to accept the decisions of this body or whether he can ignore it. There are broadly three schools of thought among the Muslim thinkers who hold widely divergent views on this issue.

According to the exponents of the first of these schools, Islam enjoins on the *Khalifah* to consult the *Shura*, but he is not bound to abide by its judgement. Rather, after holding consultation with its members he can accept the advice of either the majority or the minority of the body, as he deems fit, keeping the interests of the *Ummah* and the rules of Islamic law in mind. This opinion is held by most of the *Ulama* of the early period of Islam as well as the contemporary scholars.

The second viewpoint is that the *Khalifah* is absolutely bound to follow the decisions of the *Shura* and that he has no right to enforce any law which has been disapproved by this body, especially in matters of policy and those directly concerned with social welfare. Those holding this point of view also think that if any *Khalifah* violates the decisions of the *Shura*, it has the right to dismiss him. However, they are of the opinion that an issue relating to everyday life as well as those of a subsidiary nature, details and administrative matters, the *Khalifah* is bound to consult the *Shura* but is not bound to follow its advice. This viewpoint is shared by a majority of contemporary scholars.

According to the proponent of the third school of thought, the role of the *Shura* in decision making depends upon the demands of the time and considerations of the welfare of the community. They say that if the *Ummah* thinks that the *Khalifah* should follow the decisions taken by the *Shura* in certain circumstances and on certain issues he should do so, but if it is of the opinion that the *Khalifah* is at liberty to tackle certain issues according to his own judgement this is also proper and lawful, since, in the opinion of these scholars, this is a subsidiary issue and not one related to the *Shariah* directly. This is the viewpoint of a number of contemporary scholars.

Shura is Optional

The scholars who do not think that the *Khalifah* is bound to follow the advice of the *Shura* and are of the opinion that he is at liberty to act as he deems fit on basic as well as subsidiary issues, cite the verse 159 of *Surah Al-Imran* and advance two arguments based on it in support of their stand.

This verse focuses on the issue of forgiveness for the companions of the Prophet (SAW) who had advised him to attack the Makkan pagans after coming out of Madinah, while he was of the opinion that it would be advisable for the believers to defend themselves while remaining inside the town. Scholars of this school of thought say that the Prophet (SAW) was not bound to follow his companions because they had been proved to be wrong and were in need of forgiveness and also because his status was superior to that of his companions.[1]

The above argument does not have much validity since the fact that Allah (SWT) had asked His Prophet (SAW) to forgive his companions, does not mean that they ought not to be consulted or that their decisions ought not to be accepted when the Prophet (SAW) says that in matters in regard to which there is no guidance from the *Qur'ān*, he himself could make mistakes since to err is human.

Quranic Cocept of *Azm*

Another argument based on the above-mentioned *Qur'ānic* verse is that its words *Fa iza Azamta fa Tawakkal ala Allah* (and when you have taken a decision, put your faith in Allah) indicate that in administrative and political matters this directive to consult people is intended to strengthen the hands of the Prophet (SAW) and to afford his satisfaction. This means that consultation is in any case necessary and after it one should go ahead and take whatever action is necessary to his heart's satisfaction, putting one's trust in Allah (SWT). Once the Prophet (SAW) is satisfied it does not matter whether the opinion that he has accepted is that of the majority or the minority.[2]

Elucidating this verse Qatadah says that Allah (SWT) instructed Prophet (SAW) to go ahead and set according to his firm decision and be stoodfast in matters relating to Him. In his exegesis of this verse Qurtubi adds the words, "and do not bother about the advice of the peopoe".[3]

Rabi bin Anas says that Allah (SWT) asks the Prophet (SAW) once he taken a decision he should stick to it and put his trust in Allah (SWT). Qurtubi has cited similar sayings and exegesis.

Ibn al-Jauzi has clarified this verse to the effect that once the Prophet (SAW) has taken a firm decision he ought to put his trust in Allah (SWT) and not on consultations.[4]

In his exegesis of this verse Imam Razi says tht it is not necessary to put one's trust in a conclusion that emerges from consultation. Since trust should only be put on help and guidance received from Allah (SWT). According to him the purport of this verse is that in all matters servants of Allah (SWT) ought to put their trust in no one except Allah (SWT).[5]

In his exegesis entitled *Al-Siraj al-Muneer* Imam Sharbini says that once a firm determination is taken after consultation, trust should be reposed in Allah (SWT) and not on the consultations, adding that trust in Allah (SWT) does not mean completely ignoring all policies, but that keeping the contingent factors and resources in mind the matter in hand should be handed over to Allah (SWT).[6]

Imam Shaukani writes that once a firm decision is taken in any matter after consultations and one's heart is satisfied, it should be implemented, putting trust in Allah (SWT). He says that there is another interpretation of this verse also, which is to effect that one should do what he has decided to do and trust should be reposed in Allah (SWT) rather than on consultation.[7]

Imam Qushayri says that Allah (SWT) is asking to Prophet (SAW) not to trust the opinion of any human being and for all his actions he would be responsible to him and he would not be absolved for his responsibility in any matter.[8]

Baghawi writes that Allah is telling his Prophet (SAW) in this verse to repose his faith in Him and not in the advice of the people. In other words, he is asking the Prophet (SAW) to stand up on the command of Allah (SWT), put his faith only on Him and seeking help and guidance only from Him.[9]

Imam Nasafi interprets the verse to the effect that once the Prophet (SAW) forms a definite opinion after consultations, he should put his trust in Allah (SWT) rather than on consultation for implementing the correct decision.[10]

Zamakhshari has given the exegesis of this verse in the following words:

'When you have taken a definite decision after holding consultations, put your trust in Allah (SWT) for implementing the appropriate and correct opinion since only Allah (SWT) knows what is good and expedient for you, which can be understood neither by you nor by your advisers.'[11]

Mahmood Bablali has elaborated the meaning of the verse further by saying that Allah (SWT) has asked his Prophet (SAW) to take steps according to the opinion he forms after holding consultations, irrespective of whether it is contrary to the opinion of the majority or even of the entire assembly of the *Shura*, since what is good is not confined to the majority.[12]

Ahmad Naar opines that what Islam enjoins is seeking advice and holding consultations. He says that Imam is not bound to follow the advice of the majority of the *Shura*, nor can it be imposed on him, since consultations merely meant for seeking guidance. However, he also holds that the *Amir* can also not be allowed to act as an autocrat so that he gives up holding consultations with the *Shura*, the correct course being that he should adopt what he considers to be the better and the correct opinion.[13]

The above mentioned interpretations of the verse from *Āl-Imran* raise a number of questions, such as what the term 'azm', on which the whole structure of this argument stands, means. Arabic literature and dictionaries of the language show that there are a number of different connotations of the word satisfaction with the action that one has decided to take,[14] intention to implement some decision,[15] doing anything without hesitation and a firm determination to implement some design.[16]

In the light of the above mentioned connotations of the term *azm*, the verse from the *Āl-Imran* referred to above means putting one's trust in Allah (SWT) and implementing some decision regarding which one's heart is satisfied, the soundness and propriety of which is confirmed by one's conscience and a firm decision to implement what is decided, whether such a decision is in accord with the opinion of the *Shura* or contrary to it. The use of the term '*azm*' in the verse neither proves that the decision of the *Shura* is binding on the *Khalifah* nor that he has the right to deviate from it. Against this background *Tawakkul* (putting trust in Allah) means that once the *Shura* has been consulted in some state affair and any action has been decided upon, it should be implemented using all available resources, not allowing any hesitation or fear of criticism to interfere with its implementation and trust should only be reposed in Allah (SWT). Hinting at such a meaning of the term *azm*, a contemporary scholar has interpreted the verse of *Āl-Imran* to the effect that Allah (SWT) has not specified whether the word *azm* used in it refers to the decision of the Prophet or that of the *Shura*. Rather, it is meant to have a general application, asking for the implementation of a decision which is to one's satisfaction, whether it is the Prophet's decision, or that of the *Shura*. This scholar is of the opnion that those who say that in this verse the word *azm* refers to the firm determination of the Prophet (SAW) to implement his decision, are merely trying to extract a meaning from this verse which is absolutely unwarranted.[17]

Another scholar avers that use of the term *azm* does not amount to a denial of the role of the *Shura*, adding that the verse of *Āl-Imran* is not intended to mean that the decision of the *Ummah* is not binding on the head of the state, but that once the Muslim community expresses its agreement on a certain specific policy, there ought to be no hesitation in implementing it.[18]

This is why Imam Razi says that the term *Tawakkul* in the verse from *Āl-Imran* should not be interpreted to mean that deliberations should be given up altogether, which, he says, is the viewpoint of the ignorants who aver that consultations would go against the injunction of *Tawakkul*. According to him, *Tawakkul* really means that people should take resources at their disposal into consideration, but instead of being proud of them, they should be steadfast in the path of justice and truth.[19]

In his *Tafsir al-Khazin*, Baghdadi interprets the verse to the effect that after being satisfied with the outcome of consultation, once a firm determination to implement it has been taken trust should be put in Allah (SWT), by praying for divine help and guidance. In other words, according to him, though trust should be reposed in Allah (SWT), consultations do not amount to a negation of *Tawakkul*.[20]

From the above elucidation of the verse from *Āl-Imran* is it clear that the word *azm* does not stand in the way of the acceptance of the decisions of the *Shura*.

Another point that arises from such an interpretation of the above mentioned verse is that the texts (*Nusus*) that have been cited by Tabari, Qurtubi, Baghavi and Zamakhshari have no bearing on the issue of the *Shura* since all these citations are concerned with an issue regarding which Allah has expressed His will through revelations and it is an axiom with all the faithfuls that a matter relating to which there is some divine revelation goes out of the pale of the *Shura* since this body can only take up matter regarding which there is no clear guidance from the *Qur'ān* and the *Sunnah*.

The second categories of texts (*Nusus*) are those that are related to reposing trust in divine help and guidance (*Tawakkul*), which, as has been said above, does not negate consultation and worldly considerations.

Arguments from Hadith

Scholars who think that the *Khalifah* is not bound to abide by the decisions of the *Shura*, cite a *Hadith*, too, in support of their stand, according to which the Prophet (SAW) told Abu Bakr and Umar that he would not oppose a decision on which both of these companions were in agreement.[21]

The above mentioned *Hadith* is interpreted by these scholars to mean that the Prophet (SAW) has expressed his preference to the opinions of these prominent companions of his by saying that these should be accepted, whatever be the opinion of the majority of his companions. The purport of the *Hadith* appears to be that the Prophet (SAW) emphasizes the weight of the opinions of Abu Bakr and Umar even if they go against that of the majority of his companions. This tradition is also confirmed by another one that is attributed to Ibn Abbas that the verse '*wa shawirhum fil amr*' has been revealed in the context of consultation with these two prominent companions of the Prophet (SAW).[22]

However, the above mentioned *Hadith* raises four questions which negate the stand of those who base their arguments on it.

The first of these objections is that this *Hadith* is a *dhaeef* one, since its narrators are Shahr b. Haushab, Abdur Rahman b. Ghanam and Abdul Hamid b. Bahram, the first of whom is deemed to be unreliable by a majority of *muhaddithoon*[23], the status of the companions of the Prophet (SAW) of the second one is controversial[24] while the last one has been considered unreliable.[25]

The second objections that may be made is that even if this *Hadith* is given credibility it cannot be established on its basis that the Prophet (SAW) accepted the opinion of the two prominent companions even if the opinion of the majority of his companions was against it. The Prophet (SAW) only said that when these prominent companions of his were in agreement on an issue, he would accept their judgement and would not oppose it. It was possible that the agreement on any issue between the two eminent companions would be the result of agreement between all or at least the majority of the companions and hence the question of any disagreement between the opinions of the two companions and that of the majority of one would not arise. It was also possible that the opinion of the majority of the companions is against that of the two senior companions, in which case the Prophet (SAW) would not accept the opinion of the latter since the *Hadith* does not mention any comparison between the two eminent companions on the one hand and the majority of the *Sahabah* on the other.

The third question that arises in this context is that, even if for the sake of argument this *Hadith* is accepted as authentic along with the interpretation that has been sought to put on it, how can it be interpreted to mean that the Prophet (SAW) would implement the decision of the two companions even in opposition to that of the majority of the *Sahabah*? The *Hadith* concerned merely says that the Prophet (SAW) would not oppose the two eminent companions. He did not say that he would act according to their opinion.[26] This *Hadith* only says that the Prophet (SAW) would accept the opinion of the two companions. The issue of its implementation is not clearly stated in it.

The import of the above-mentioned *Hadith* may be discussed from another angle also. Even if it is accepted that the Prophet (SAW) implemented the decisions of the two eminent companions it is not necessary that the opinions of the companions would have been opposed by the *Sahabah*; the fact is that the opinions of these two senior companions reflected the will of the entire *Ummah*. They represented the majority of the companions. While Abu Bakr was famous for lenity, tolerance and forgiveness, Umar was known for his uncompromising and rigid attitude. If the two were in agreement on a particular issue, it was thought that a middle way had been found with which the majority of the companions were satisfied. Hence by saying that he would implement the opinion over which there was agreement between the two companions the Prophet (SAW) in effect meant that he would follow the judgement of the majority of the companions since it would not only have the sanction of the majority but would also be a moderate one.

The commentary of "*Wa shawirhum fil amr*" by Ibn Abbas has been received through two different channels. While al-Hakim narrates it and considers it authentic,[27] Baihaqi cites it in his *Sunan*.[28] According to a second channel, it is not an authentic tradition[29] since al-Kalbi has attributed it to Abu Swaleh who, in his turn, has ascribed it to Ibn Abbas and the authenticity of these two narrators has been questioned by the *muhaddithoon.*[30] Even if it is accepted that both the channels of the *Hadith* are authentic and that *Hadith* refers to Abu Bakr and Umar, this can, at best, considered the opinion of Ibn Abbas and it does not lead one to the conclusion that the Prophet (SAW) did not find it necessary to consult other companions. Aalusi writes that even if these words refer to the two senior companions, it only means that they deserved to be consulted more than others but it does not at all show that consultations were to be confined only to these two.[31] Imam Razi says that the persons who were asked to be consulted were the companions who had been accorded the privilege of pardoning and forgiving people. While it may be conceded that Umar was included in this category, Abu Bakr was certainly not one of them since he did not have to deal with defeated persons, and hence he cannot be covered by the verse.[32]

The Prophetic Events

Those who think that the caliph is not bound to follow the decisions of the *Shura*, base their arguments on certain incidents in the life of the Prophet (SAW), too, prominent among which were those related to the Peace Treaty of Hudaibiyah and the prisoners captured during the Battle of Badr. The incident regarding the peace Treaty of Hudaibiyah has been dealth with in detail in chapter I of the present work. Referring to this significant historical event, these scholars aver that on several occasions the Prophet (SAW) implemented his own judgement which was contrary not merely to the opinion of the majority of the companions but that of all of them. They cite the following instances in this connection:

1. When the treaty was being drafted, the Muslims said that they would not write anything except *bismillah al-Rahman al-Rahim* (In the name of Allah, Most Gracious, Most Merciful) but the firm pronouncement of the Prophet (SAW) was that the expression *bismika Allahumma* (In your name, O Allah') should be written and this decision of his was implemented.

2. When Abu Jandal came there, the Muslims objected to his being handed over to the Makkan pagans on the grounds that he had embraced Islam and that the agreement had not finalized till then, but the Prophet (SAW) acceded to the claim of the pagans in the matter.

3. When the Peace Treaty had been signed the Prophet (SAW) asked the Muslims to offer sacrifice of animal (*nahr*). When they refused to do so, he himself performed sacrifice and after this others, too, came forward to offer sacrifice.

According to these scholars, the above incidents show that the leader of the *Ummah* can act according to what he thinks proper even if all the Muslims are opposed to his decision. They aver that these incidents are conclusive arguments in favour of the right of *Khalifah* to overrule the *Shura*, since according to Islam, the practice of the Prophet (SAW) is one of the bases of law-making in an Islamic state.

These scholars say that incidents related to the Peace Treaty of Hudaibiyah cannot be ascribed to divine revelations since the *Surah al-Fath* was revealed on the Prophet's return from Hudaibiyah. They add that had the steps taken by the Prophet (SAW) been in accordance with divine revelations, no Muslim would have dared to oppose them, since anyone who knowingly opposes a revelation is deemed to be a *kafir* (non-believer). Hence, they ask how one can expect the companions of the Prophet to oppose these revelations since the *Qur'ān* itself praises their listening to and obeying it.[33] If any person says that in taking these steps the Prophet (SAW) was guided by unrecited revelations (*wahy ghair matlu*)[34] the answer to this would be that this makes the position still more clear, since this shows that going against the majority of the *Shura* has the sanction of divine revelation.[35]

Peace Treaty Examined

A number of points arise in connection with the Peace Treaty of Hudaibiyah. The first of them is that there are several clear indications relating to this event which show that all steps were taken in the light of divine revelations and it is agreed upon among all the faithfuls that steps determined by divine revelations are beyond the jurisdiction of the *Shura*.

Imam Bukhari[36] gives a detailed account of this Peace Treaty. According to him, before the Prophet (SAW) could reach Makkah, his she-camel sat down at a place. At this the Prophet (SAW) said that she had been stopped by the Being that had prevented elephants from reaching Makkah.

The point is made still clearer from the incident that when Umar objected to certain provisions of the Peace Treaty the Prophet (SAW) said that he was a bond slave and messenger of Allah (SWT) and hence he could not act against His command lest He should destroy him. No clearer evidence is needed to prove that the Peace Treaty of Hudaibiyah was concluded in the light of divine revelations. Had this not been the case, the Prophet (SAW) would have said to Umar that he (Umar) was prefering his own opinion but if he was a true believer he should bow down before his (the Prophet's) opinion, while according to Bukhari were to the effect that he was the messenger of

Allah (SWT) and could not disobey Him and that He would help him.[37] And a matter regarding which there is a divine revelation cannot be taken up for discussion by the *Shura*.[38]

Elucidating the above tradition, Imam Qastalani writes that Umar was admonished by the Prophet (SAW) over his disagreement with some clauses of the Peace Treaty and it became clear that the Prophet (SAW) had taken these steps according to the command of the Being who had made his she-camel stop.[39]

There can be a number of conjectures about the objections that were raised by Umar and other companions of the Prophet (SAW) over the Peace Treaty of Hudaibiyah. While leaving Madinah the Prophet (SAW) had held consultations with his companions at Ghadeer al-Ashtat over the impending battle and they had advised him to prefer a peace treaty and to avoid confrontation unless they were practically prevented from entering the Kabah shrine. But after this the conditions changed radically and the she-camel on which the Prophet (SAW) had riding refused to move forward with his caravan. His companions said that Qaswa (his she-camel) had become obdurate. The Prophet (SAW) said that this was not so since it was not her habit to behave in this way, but that it had been stopped by the Being that had stopped the elephants in their track. He said that he was swearing by the Being who controlled the breath of his life that if the enemies put forward conditions which were in keeping with reverence for Allah (SWT) he would certainly accept them. After this, the Prophet (SAW) ordered the she-camel to move and she sprang into action. From this point the circumstances changed and the matter went beyond the purview of public opinion and the people of the *Shura* and the Prophet (SAW) started acting according to divine commands, even when they came into conflict with his initial intentions and the advice of his companions, since the command of Allah (SWT) had to be given precedence over their advice. It is possible that some of the Prophet's companions did not realize this change in the state of affairs and this is why they objected to some of the terms of Peace Treaty of Hudaibiyah.[40]

Another conjecture that can be made in this regard is that the companions of the Prophet (SAW) knew that there was a divine revelation in the matter but they had not have the slightest doubt about the victorious outcome of their campaign due to the fact tat they did not doubt the veracity of the dream f the Prophet (SAW) and had no inkling of the incident that had taken place on their way to Madinah which deprived them of a decisive victory. When they were on the verge of achieving it and this had given a rude psychological shock to them and they were depressed and disappointed for a long time so that they initially ignored the injunction of the Prophet (SAW) to perform sacrifices of animals (*nahr*) and they complied with the command of the Prophet (SAW) when they were aroused from this state of depression and psychological tension. Such psychological tensions can prevail upon any person, since no human being is innocent except for the Prophets of Allah and no one goes out of the pale of true faith on this ground, since such natural tensions are beyond the control of ordinary human beings.[41]

Prisoners of Badr

According to these scholars another significant event in this connection is the one that relates to the prisoners taken after the Battle of Badr, in whose case the Prophet (SAW) overruled the opinion of his companions and acted according to his own judgement, with only Abu Bakr supporting his stand.[42]

This argument is controverted from a number of angles. The first thing is that the Prophet (SAW) had not gone against the opinion of the majority but had in fact implemented it. Quite a few *Sahabah* were of the opinion that the prisoners be set free after receiving ransom. *Sahih* of Muslim[43] has recorded the entire incident thus:

In the beginning when the Prophet (SAW) held consultation with his companions, Abu Bakr and Umar gave their respective opinions. However, on the next day there was a divine guidance, hearing which the Prophet (SAW), and Abu Bakr started crying due to fear of being reprimanded by Allah. On being asked by Umar why they were crying, the Prophet (SAW) said that he had released the prisoners on receiving ransom on the advice of his companions while Allah (SWT) had revealed a following verse:

مَاكَانَ لِنَبِيٍّ اَنْ يَّكُوْنَ لَهٗٓ اَسْرٰى حَتّٰى يُثْخِنَ فِى الْاَرْضِ
تُرِيْدُوْنَ عَرَضَ الدُّنْيَا وَاللّٰهُ يُرِيْدُ الْاٰخِرَةَ

> It is not fitting for an Apostle that he should have prisoners of war until he hath thoroughly subdued the land. Ye look for the temporal goods of this world but Allah Looketh to the Hereafter.[44]

This shows that other *Sahabah* had also supported the opinion expressed by Abu Bakr and that the stand that had been taken by the Prophet (SAW) was influenced by the advice of the *Sahabah* too.[45]

Syed Rashid Rida has written clearly that the decision of the Prophet (SAW) to release the prisoners of war against the payment of ransom was in accordance with the opinion of the majority of the *Sahabah* and not that of Abu Bakr alone, basing his assertion on authentic *Ahadith*.[46] In the same way the *Tafsir* of Tabari contains such traditions and authentic references also testifying to the fact that the majority of the *Sahabah* were in favour of releasing the prisoners on receiving ransom.[17]

One may ask why Allah (SWT) had admonished the Prophet (SAW) when he had acted according to the opinion of the majority of his companions, since it is not possible to arrive at a correct decision in a matter which comes under the jurisdiction of *Ijtihad* because the opinion of the minority may be correct as well as that of majority and the Prophet (SAW) had not made any mistake in following the advice of the majority and for this he did not deserve any admonishment.

The answer to this objection is that Allah had admonished the Prophet (SAW) not because he had accepted the advice of the majority and released the prisoners since sanction for release of prisoners of war against ransom and seizure of booty remained part of Islamic law till the end. Admonishment by Allah (SWT) was actually meant for condemning those who gave precedence to material gains over the Day of Judgement.[48] The Prophet (SAW) and Abu Bakr cried because of their fear of Allah and piety as well due to the fear that the *Sahabah* might fall for the temptations of the world, forgetting the Day of Judgement. Otherwise also a true believer bursts into tears on listening to the *Qur'ān*ic verses which remind him of the blessings showered by Allah (SWT).[49] And even if it is conceded that the Prophet (SAW) was reprimanded by Allah (SWT) since he had not accepted the opinion of the majority of his companions, this all the more establishes the correctness and expediency of following the opinion of the majority which makes it incumbent on an *amir* to abide by the decisions of the *Shura*.[50] Hence in either case the evidence of the prisoners of the Battle of Badr cannot be cited in support of the stand that it is not binding on the *amir* to follow the advice of the *Shura*. On the contrary, it only shows that he is bound to do so.

Caliphs' Examples

These scholars say that the Guided Caliphs, too, had often ignored the opinion of the majority. For example, Abu Bakr appointed Usama bin Zaid as the commander of the army against the advice of the *Sahabah*. Dr. Hasan Huwaidi says that this incident of the history of Islam clearly proves that the *amir* is not bound by the decisions of the *Shura*, adding that he can adhere to the opinion and stand that he deems to be correct till the end and has the authority to implement it.[51]

Mahmood Bablali writes that if anybody says that Abu Bakr had taken this step to implement a decision taken by the Prophet (SAW) whch had been held up due to latter's death, the answer to this is that this may be true but when Abu Bakr emphasised the need for acting according to the will of the Prophet (SAW) and insisted on sending the army under the command of Usama his decision in this respect was contrary to the opinion of the majority, adding that senior *Sahabah* were against this and they opposed this step initially and expressed their displeasure at it. According to Bablali this action of Abu Bakr shows that the *amir* has the right to act according to his own opinion.[52]

However, the incident relating to Usama army is not a suitable one for arguing for or against the authority of the *Shura*. Since in this case Abu Bakr had only carried out the will of the Prophet (SAW). As stated above, the Prophet (SAW) had prepared this army and due to his serious illness this force had camped itself outside Madinah. The only step that was taken by Abu Bakr was to send this army to the front after the death of the Prophet (SAW).[53] This is why it is wrong to say that Abu Bakr had stuck to his stand and had acted against the decision of the *Sahabah*. It is true that he resisted the opposition of the *Sahabah* to this move forcefully. However, he did call them for consultation and insisted that the will of the Prophet (SAW) should be respected,[54] saying that it was improper to oppose it and the *Sahabah* were ultimately convinced, and it was only then that the army was sent to the front. Some scholars appear to be of the view that any difference of opinion negates the role of *Shura*, though a correct opinion can only be evolved through discussion.[55] There may be difference of opinion among members of the *Shura* on any issue. This can also result in parities insisting on their respective stands and defending them vigorously until a decision is finally arrived at.

These scholars cite another instance from the history of the Guided Caliphs to establish that an *amir* need not abide by the decisions of the *Shura*. It is related to Abu Bakr's insistence of waging war against the apostates who were refusing to pay *Zakah* while the *Sahabah* wanted him to adopt a moderate policy in the matter.[56] When he was asked who were the people with whose help he would wage this war Abu Bakr replied that he was prepared to fight alone till he is beheaded.[57]

A number of arguments can be raised against this contention. The tradition according to which Abu Bakr had said that he was prepared to fight aloe is not contained in *Sahihain* of Bukhari and Muslim nor has the *Musnad* of Ibn Hanbal narrated it. Only Ibn al-Arabi narrates it, but does not cite any authority in his support. Then it is difficult to believe that all the *Sahabah* should have been opposed to waging war against the apostates so that Abu Bakr should have been ready to come out to wage this war alone.[58]

Another point in this connection is that it was not an issue that was fit for *Ijtihad* but one of enforcing the will of the Prophet (SAW). In support of his stand Abu Bakr cited a *Hadith* to the effect that the Prophet (SAW) had said that Allah (SWT) had commanded him to go on fighting the people till they confessed to the faith that there was no God but Allah (SWT) and that Mohammad (SAW) was His Prophet, adding that their life and property were safe so long as they fulfilled their obligations in respect of these commands. Abu Bakr argued that the payment of *Zakah* was obligatory on the basis of people's possessions, so how those who refused to pay *Zakah* coluld enjoy the security of life and property.[59] Abu Bakr wanted to implement a clearly stated command of the Prophet (SAW) which was beyond the jurisdiction of the *Shura*. Issues related to the common welfare and *Ijtihad* could be placed before the *Shura* but a matter like *Zakah* was beyond its pale since its payment was obligatory in Islamic *Shariah*.[60]

If some one raised an objection to the above-mentioned argumentation saying that the decision of Abu Bakr was based on his own opinion since there was no authoritative injunction in the matter and even if the above-mentioned *Hadith* is accepted as a definite pronouncement, it was being cited by Umar and other *Sahabah* too in support of their stand. And since this *Hadith* could be interpreted in two different ways, it was definitely a matter which was fit for *Ijtihad* and decision could only be taken by the *Shura*. However, this did not happen and Abu Bakr considered his own opinion rightful and so he implemented it.[61] Two things can be said in reply to the above contention:

It is not true to say that there was no definite authority behind Abu Bakr's stand. According to some traditions the first Caliph had also cited the Prophet (SAW) to that effect that the faithful had been enjoined to wage war no three issues; that they should confess to their faith in these being no God but Allah (SWT), that they offer *Salah* and that they pay *Zakah*. This is confirmed by an authentic *Hadith* cited by Bukhari and Muslim according to which the Prophet (SAW) had said that he had been commanded by Allah (SWT) to wage war on three issues: that they bear testimony that there is no God except Allah (SWT) and Mohammad (SAW) is His Prophet, that they offer *Salah* and that they pay *Zakah*, adding that if they did all this, they would be accountable to Allah (SWT) if they do not fulfil their obligations in these respects.[62] Any ambiguity in the *Hadith* cited earlier has been removed by this one. This is also confirmed by the statement of Abu Bakr before the *Sahabah* that there is no difference between *Salah* and *Zakah*, the two being twin sisters and that the *Qur'ān* mentions these two together. The *Sahabah* had to submit to the judgement of Abu Bakr after listening to these arguments of his.

Difference between the *Sahabah* on the one hand and Abu Bakr on the other on this issue arose since according to the former there was no definite authoritative pronouncement in the matter or because they were not aware of it. It is possible that they had forgotten it and were reminded of it by Abu Bakr. It is also possible that they had paid attention to the earlier part of the *Hadith* and had ignored its concluding parts so that while they stressed the importance of true faith and *Salah* they might have forgotten the stress laid on *Zakah*, which is part of the *Hadith*. They might have thought that those who were showing reluctance to pay *Zakah* at the time might agree to do it later. However, when Abu Bakr made it clear that there was no difference in importance between *Salah* and *Zakah* and that it was obligatory to wage war on the issue of non-payment of *Zakah* and cited authentic *Ahadith* in support of his contention, the *Sahabah* were convinced about the correctness of his stand. Such a situation was also there on the news of the demise of the Prophet (SAW) but the First Caliph had confirmed the news of his death after citing relevant verses of the *Qur'ān*.[63] Initially there was a difference of opinion among the *Sahabah* on the issue due to their lack of awareness of authentic texts on this behalf. However, once they were confronted with such texts they were convinced of the stand of Abu Bakr. This is confirmed by the words of Umar that he uttered on this occasion, "Allah (SWT) has opened the heart of Abu Bakr to receive the truth. I realise that what he has said is true". According to a tradition, Abu Rajaa Atardi says that people had gathered and Umar was kissing the head of Abu Bakr saying again and again that had he (Abu Bakr) not been alive all of them would have been destroyed.[64]

If it is conceded that there was no authentic text relating to the issue and the text on which the *Sahabah* based their arguments ultimately convinced of the opinion of Abu Bakr, the question arises as to why the *Sahabah* gave up their opinions and agreed with that of his. Did they bow down before his opinion without being satisfied with his arguments? They were wrong if they gave up their opinion simply out of sense of a obedience to the *amir*, since they looked upon the apostates as Muslims and still they obeyed the Caliph. In this way they were guilty of obeying him in implementing what amounted to a sinful decision – that of waging war against the faithfuls.[65]

However, the facts were quite different. In reality the *Sahabah* had bowed down before the opinion of Abu Bakr after being completely satisfied with its soundness. So this case caste no reflection on the obligation of the *amir* to abide by the decisions of the *Shura*.[66]

The third instance that is cited to support the contention that the Caliph is not bound to abide by the decision of the

Shura relates to the issue of the distribution of conquered lands of Iraq. It is said that Caliph Umar had converted these lands into state property, ignoring the opinion of the *Sahabah*.[68] This matter has been thoroughly dealt with earlier which shows that Ali and Muadh were in agreement with the second Caliph on this issue and that a majority of the numbers of the *Shura* were also convinced of his stand in the matter after prolonged deliberations.[68] On the contrary, according to some accounts though Umar had taken the decision to distribute these lands, he reversed his decision when the *Sahabah* advised him not to do so.[69]

According to a third source, Caliph Umar had issued orders for the distribution of the lands among the ordinary Muslims as advised by the *Sahabah*, but later he asked them to give these lands in return for other monetary benefits, and when they agreed to do so, he imposed a tax on these lands and converted them into state property.[70]

Hence, none of the above-mentioned accounts show that Caliph Umar had acted against the decision of the majority.

Withdrawal of the Property

Scholars who are of the opinion that a Caliph is not bound to abide by the decision of the *Shura* cite another instance to support their contention. They refer to the fact that Caliph Umar withdrew half of the property of eminent *Sahabah* (who were also provincial governors) like Abu Hurairah, Amr bin Aas, Ibn Abbas and Saad bin Abi Waqqas without holding any consultations, making the property part of the *Baitul Maal*. They argue that had consultations with the *Shura* been obligatory, the second Caliph would not have taken such a step without consulting this body.[71]

This argument is also fallacious. Though it is the right of the *Ummah* to be consulted in matters of general interest there are also matters regarding which the head of state can act according to his own judgement, keeping in mind the common interests and welfare of the community. Obligation to *Shura* does not mean that every issue, big or small, should be placed before it for its opinion. A caliph is expected to have the capability and the sagacity to take necessary steps in time and to take prompt decisions.

Another thing worth mentioning in this connection is that Caliph Umar kept an account of the property of every governor at the time of his appointment to the post and watched the rate at which the wealth of the incumbent was increasing, so as to guard against oppression, wasteful expenditure and corruption on his past. He had issued direction to the governors to enter Madinah in broad daylight and not in the darkness of the night so that they are unable to hide their belongings. While appointing a governor, Umar prepared a document and got it witnessed by the *Ansar* and the *Muhajirs* asking the would be incumbent not to oppress anyone physically or materially and not to make use of his position for his personal benefit or that of his relatives. He was also forbidden to ride excellent horses, to put on nice clothes, to consume bread made from fine wheat flour and not to deprive people of their necessaries of life. Caliph Umar also sent his informers to the provinces who reported to him on the doings of every governor.[72] Every appointee to the governor's post had to accept all the above-mentioned conditions and to be prepared to render every kind of account. In such a state of affairs there was no need to consult the *Shura*.

Method of Succession

Scholars who hold the view that a caliph is not bound to consult and follow the advice of the *Shura* base their contention on the manner of succession of the caliph also. According to them, had taking the opinion of the *Shura* been obligatory and had the *amir* been bound to abide by the decisions of this body, Umar would not have been appointed caliph nor could he, in his turn, confine the selection of his successor to six persons of his choice. On the other hand, these scholars aver that when Caliph Umar was on his death-bed he was asked by the *Muhajirs* to nominate some one as his successor, and the dying caliph replied that if he were to nominate anyone he would be doing what had been done by one (Abu Bakr) who was superior to him and if he did not do so, then too he would be following a better person (the Prophet SAW) who had not nominated any successor. They say that the *Muhajirs* did not question the caliph's right of nominating anyone as his successor on the ground that this was under the jurisdiction of the *Shura*, thus providing evidence that the decisions of the *Shura* cannot be imposed on the head of state.[73]

The above-mentioned argument, too, is not very sound, Muslim *Ulama* are unanimous in holding the view that caliphate can only be conferred upon a person with the will of the people expressed through his election. There is no scope for forced allegiance in Islam. The nomination of Umar by the first caliph after consultations with the men of affairs would not have been valid until it was confirmed by the consent of the common people. Muslims had every rights to refuse to elect as their caliph the person who had been nominated by Abu Bakr. It is a different matter that they did not do so.[74] In fact they confirmed his choice by offering allegiance to the person nominated by him. Except for the Shia, followers of all other Muslim sects are unanimously of the view that there are two ways of appointing a caliph – through election or through consensus.[75] This is why Mawardi has written that nomination for caliphate in Islamic history amounted to nothing more than candidature. It did not at all mean that Muslims were compelled to accept a person who had been nominated, otherwise there would have no necessity of obtaining allegiance from the common people.[76] The method of *Istikhlaf* (nomination of some one for caliphate) did not mean the negation of the *Shura*. Caliph Umar has himself said that if anyone takes oath of allegiance without consulting the *Ummah,* his oath would have no force, nor would it be proper for the person to whom the oath is offered to accept it, lest if might lead to both the parties being killed.[77]

Nomination was merely a stage in the election of a caliph. It was thus that Abu Bakr had nominated Umar as his successor on his death-bed while Umar, in his turn, had nominated a panel of six persons, suggesting that one of them be elected caliph.[78]

Rational Arguments

Those who are of the opinion that the caliph is not bound to follow the decisions of the *Shura* also advance the following arguments, based on reasoning and logic, to support their contention:

1. The *Qur'ān* commands the faithfuls to obey Allah (SWT), His Prophet (SAW) and their *Ulul amr*;[79] but making the *amir* bound by the decisions of the *Shura* implies that people have the right to disobey him, since in this way the opinion of the *amir* is deemed to carry the same weight as that of the common people and no power can deprive the *amir* of the right that Allah (SWT) has conferred on him.[80]

2. The caliph or *amir* too, has the right to do *Ijtihad.* He can derive conclusion from the study of the authentic texts and pronouncements to tackle problems. As a *mujtahid* he

has the right to ignore the opinions of others and to act according to his own judgement, since *taqlid* (following others and not having one's own opinion) is forbidden to a *mujtahid*.[81]

3. A caliph is totally accountable for all his actions and hence he cannot be compelled to implement the decisions of others which he does not deem to be sound.[82] It is neither just nor reasonable to compel him to implement a decision to which he is opposed and then to be held solely responsible for the consequences of its implementation.[83]

4. The principle of following the opinion of the majority is an un-Islamic one since had it been Islamic the Prophet (SAW) would have laid down specific rules and procedures concerning it so that there was no controversy over it. But the Prophet (SAW) did not establish any such system, nor did he follow this principle as a general rule.[84] The *faqihs*, too, have not devised any rules concerning the matter and this issue had not been dealt with in any of their writings.[85] Had there been an established practice of following the majority opinion, they would certainly have taken it up as a topic of discussion and would have laid down its rules and procedures. The concept of following the majority opinion is merely that of the western thinkers and has no connection with Islam.[86]

5. The opinion of the majority is not necessarily right and just,[87] since the soundness and authority of an opinion depends not on its being held by a majority but on its intrinsic worth. Islam does not deem majority opinion as a yardstick for determining the rights and wrongs of a matter, since it is possible that the opinion of a single individual is more sound than that of the majority.[88] These scholars base their contention on certain verses of the *Qur'ān* in which Allah (SWT) has said that very often the common people are bereft of true knowledge[89]. These scholars are of the

view that Islam prefers the judgement of a small number of selected persons who are gifted with wisdom and insight rather than that of the crowd of common people.[90]

An analysis of the above-mentioned arguments would lead one to the following conclusions:

There is no contradiction between obedience to the *amir* and his obligation to abide by the decisions of the *Shura*. Obedience to the *amir* is itself incumbent on his not issuing a sinful command and not transgressing the sphere of Allah (SWT) and His Prophet (SAW). Abiding by the decisions of the *Shura* also depends upon their being based on directions found in the *Qur'ān* and the *Sunnah*. Hence, the limitations that have put on the powers and the authority of the *amir* also include his following the advice of the *Shura* and people would be bound to obey him only if he acts according to its decisions and would not transgress them.

Muslims in general do not deny that a caliph has the capacity and the right to do *Ijtihad*, since it is absolutely necessary for him to do so when he is dealing with settling desputes and pronouncing judgements in legal cases. When an *imam* is occupying the seat of justice, he would have to give full expression to his capacity to do *ijtihad*. He is confronted with many issues which demand that he draw inferences based on authentic sources and hence no limits can be imposed on the *imam* in the matter of doing *ijtihad*. The *ijtihadi* pronouncements of the Prophet (SAW) and the First and Second Caliph are found in the accounts of the Islamic history and *siyar*. Special mention in this connection may be made of the *ijtihad* done by Caliph Umar on the issues of gathering people for *Salah* of *Tarawih*, implementing hudud on the consumption of alcoholic drinks, prevention of *mut'ah* deeming triple divorce as permissible, enacting the laws of inheritance, punishment for killing a person to avenge the killing of numbers of a group and no enforcement of criminal laws for crimes committed in extenuating circumstances or in a drunken state. In matters of details like these it is not proper to voice opposition or to raise controversies. It is more advisable to obey the *amir* in such things and it is obligatory on the part of the common people to accept the decisions of the *amir* based on *Ijtihad* to ensure that the *Ummah* is safe from mischief, disputes and disintegration.[91]

From the above it is clear that the obedience to the rulers relating to secondary issues based on *ijtihad* is binding on the people. In this context, Ibn Taimiyah has said that the *amir* ought to consult the *Shura* and if he obtains some direction from the *Qur'ān* or the *Sunnah* or a consensus among the faithful (*ijm'a*) he is bound to follow it, adding that if there is an issue over which there is a difference of opinion among the Muslims, he should listen to the opinions and arguments of everyone and then he should act according to what he deems to be nearest to the instructions he finds in the Holy Book and the *Sunnah*.[92]

Hence, while the *amir* has the right to do *ijtihad* and act according to his own opinion when dealing with details, with implementation of decisions and deriving conclusions from authentic texts, it is essential for him to consult the *Shura* and act according to their advice in tackling of social and political issues, and those relating to the general welfare of the society like peace treaties, war covenants, general policy on education and civic amenities etc.[93] This is so since in such matter there are greater possibilities of the majority opinion being more sound.[94]

Such a distinction between issues needing *ijtihad* and those that did not, was commonly accepted by *Sahabah*. Muslim historians write that when there was some issue which required deriving conclusions from the *Qur'ān* or the

Sunnah, Caliph Umar consulted a few selected persons but when a new policy was to be adopted or some step relating to the welfare of the common people was to be taken up, he convened a general assembly of the *Ansar* and the *Muhajirs*, as was done in the issue of distribution of conquered lands of Iraq.[95]

As far as the third argument given above is concerned, it is true that only the Caliph cannot be held responsible for the consequences of any step taken by him if he has done so after consulting the *Shura*, which according to the *Qur'ān* is an institution, that is based on the concept of collective discussion and a collective sharing of responsibilities. Whether the consequences of a step taken after consulting the *Shura* turn out to be useful or harmful, their responsibility is that of the *Shura* and ultimately of the entire *Ummah*.[96] However, since the Caliph has the necessary authority and the machinery to implement such collective decisions, the responsibility of their implementation rests with him.[97]

As regards the contention that the principle of the acceptance of the majority opinion being un-Islamic, the following arguments can be advanced to counter it.

There is no evidence in Islamic history to show that the Prophet (SAW) ever rejected majority opinion. On the contrary, there is every evidence to establish that he always bowed down before the decision taken by a majority. An outstanding example of this is that on the occasion of the Battle of Uhud, respecting the opinion of the majority of the *Sahabah*, he decided to come out of Madinah to fight the enemies, while his personal opinion was that it would be better for his forces to defend themselves while remaining stationed in Madinah. This is why Shaikh Makhloof writes that in the *Sunnah* there is not a single instance of the Prophet (SAW) ignoring the opinion of the *Sahabah* after consulting them.[98]

The Prophet (SAW) did not lay down any rules and procedures to determine the majority opinion, nor did he establish any system for the working of the *Shura*, since Islam was for all ages and all places and would guide its followers till the Day of Judgement and provide basic directions on all political and social matters. Had a system of *Shura* been established taking into account the conditions prevailing in Arabia during his prophethood it could have been found impracticable in changed circumstances later. There was an additional difficulty also. The *Sahabah* would have deemed such a system as part of the religion though it is not directly connected with it. While pointing this out, the *Sahabah* had supported the election of Abu Bakr by saying that there was no reason why they should not elect him to manage their worldly affairs since the Prophet (SAW) had selected him to manage their religious affairs.[99]

Faqihs had neither worked out any rules and procedures for determining majority opinion nor had they dealt with in detail with voting since these matters are related to the evolution of political consciousness and the cultural and social progress of nations. With progress in science and arts the level of political consciousness among the people has also gone up, so that their mental attitude and intellectual standards have become quite high and they have started giving thought on such issues. The *faqihs* of earlier times are not to blame since problems of those times were quite different from what they are now. However, there are some who go so far as to accuse them of not giving any lead on political issues and institutions to avoid facing the wrath of the rulers and hence they share the responsibility for the damage that had been done to the social order and the anarchic conditions that had prevailed as a result.[100] This criticism of the *faqihs* is unfair, since the conditions prevailing at that time have to be taken into consideration in comprehending their matter of bringing about reforms.

During the period of the Guided Caliphs, the *Shura* system existed in practices and hence there was no need to discuss to procedure that it entailed. However, later, when real caliphate was replaced by personal rule and monarchy, creating a wide gulf between the rulers and the common people, the *ulama* and the *faqihs* withdrew from the polluted atmosphere of politics and started concentrating on cultural and moral values, character building and protection of Islamic beliefs and practices. At that time the social organization of the *Ummah* was in the hands of individuals and institutions while the sphere of the state was confined to levying of texes and tributes, military conquests, annexations and defence. Under such circumstances the *faqihs* concentrated their attention on a correct enunciation of articles of faith, preservation of pristine purity of religious observances and propagation of Islam. They used the method of gradual evolution on the one hand and conducted discussions on the issues of *imamah* and *khilafah* and wrote books on the duties and qualities of a caliph and on the characteristics and powers of a government that runs alone the lines of the Islamic *Shariah* on the other. Thus they indirectly criticised the existing rulers who they lacked the merits required by Islam and were ignoring the duties enjoined by them by the Islamic *Shariah*.[101]

It is wrong to say that Muslim jurists (*faqihs*) had no idea at all of the principles of taking decisions according to the majority opinion. In fact, they employed these in setting various issues of *fiqh* and are interspersed here and there in their writings. Accordeing to Dr. Mohammad Ziauddin al-Rayyis,[102] the principle of following the majority opinion has existed in Islamic political thought for centuries. In this context, he cites Imam Ghazali who holds that if oath of allegiance is offered to two *imams*, the allegiance of that *imam* would be valid who has a larger number of followers, since, according to Imam Ghazali, majority is the best source of determining preference.[103] After citing this opinion of Ghazali, Dr. al-Rayyis asks whether there could be a clearer enunciation of the principle of the validity of majority opinion. He also cites Ibn Taimiyah to the effect that Abu Bakr became *imam* through the offer of oath of allegiance to him by the general body of the *Sahabah.*[104] He bases his argument on the words of Mawardi who has said that if there is a difference of opinion in the appointment of the *imam* of a mosque, the decision should be according to the opinion of the majority.[105] He adds that some *ulama* of principles of jurisprudence have enunciated the principles that majority opinion ought to prevail.[106] Shaikh Abu Hamid al-Sāih,[107] too, cites the sayings of several *faqihs* and has come to the conclusion that the principle of abiding by the majority opinion prevailed during the early period of Islam, adding that this principle was followed even while taking important decisions and political steps. An instance of this is that a panel of six persons was nominated before his death by Caliph Umar for the selection of his successor, with the provision that if four persons were on one side and two on the other, the decision of the majority should be acceptable and if the opinions are divided into two groups equally, the opinion of the group that included Abdullah bin Umar (a member of that panel) should be considered final because Abdullah could not be the candidate for the post as he had been debarred by Umar himself. Commenting on this incident, Abdur Rahman Abdul Khaliq says that had the principle of following the decision of the majority been un-Islamic the *Sahabah* would not have agreed with this opinion of Caliph Umar and would have rejected it as a heresy. This shows that the principle of abiding by the decision of the majority is part of the Islamic *Shariah* and not a novel or unfamiliar practice in Islamic history.[108]

Dr. Mohammad Abdullah al-Arabi makes a most cogent remark to rebut the argument that majority opinion is no guarantee of rightfulness (in support of which the *Qur'ān*ic verses have been cited), by saying that the correct interpretation of the verse is that they are related to religion, faith and the Day of judgement and not to everyday affairs for which the head of state or *amir* is elected, who consults the people in managing these affairs.[109] Mohammad al-Ghazali writes that these *Qur'ān*ic verses, talking about the ignorance and misguidance of the majority, were revealed to refer to pagans ad non-believers and ought not be applied to Muslims, adding that the Prophet (SAW) had said that there can be no overwhelming majority among the faithfuls on anything that is mean.[110]

While it is possible to argue that the majority may also be wrong in its judgement and the minority may have justice on its side, the probability of the minority holding a perverse view is much greater than the majority. However wise, pious and well-intentioned an individual may be, he cannot avoid being led by his personal attitudes and tendencies. On the contrary, there is lesser possibility of such personal attitudes and tendencies affecting collective decisions.[111] In fact, there can be no guarantee that an individual would not take a wrong stand. Because of its limitations, the intellect of a person suffers from many defects and weaknesses from which it cannot be entirely freed. The utmost that can be done is to protect it from errors and weaknesses as far as possible and the best way to do this is to accept the judgement of the majority, since mankind has not yet discovered a better way of doing so.[112]

Shura is Binding

The second group of scholars holds the view that the *amir* or caliph is absolutely bound to abide by the opinions of the *Shura*. According to them, while the *amir* has every right to put forward his point of view and to try convince others of its correctness, he is duly bound to implement the decision of the majority.

Implications of *Qur'ānic Azm*

The two *Qur'ān*ic verses that are cited in this context are interpreted by these scholars in such a way as to support their contention.[113] According to them the word '*azm*' means accepting and implementing the decision of the majority. This interpretation is based on the reported practice of the Prophet (SAW) of withdrawing his own opinion and giving precedence to that of the *Sahabah*. For example, on the occasion of the Battle of Uhud, while his personal opinion was that the Muslims should defend themselves from inside Madinah, he bowed down before the advice of the *Sahabah* and came out to fight the enemies, which resulted in the defeat of the Muslims. It was after this incident that the above-mentioned Surah of *Āl-Imran*[114] was revealed, instructing the Prophet (SAW) to keep holding consultations with the *Sahabah* and not to ignore the institution of the *Shura* simply because its wrong advice had resulted in the defeat of the Muslims. Allah (SWT) asked the Prophet (SAW) not to hesitate to accept the decision of the majority in future too.

In his exegesis of this verse, Dr. al-Jamal writes as follows:

> "When an opinion finally emerges, accept the decision of the majority, be steadfast in it and repose trust in Allah in implementing it."[115]

Syed Rashid Rida,[116] Jalal Mohammad al-Munajji[117] and Shaykh Muhammad al-Ghazali[118] have given similar interpretations to the verse.

In answer to the objection that the word '*azm*' does not mean abiding by the opinion of the majority but taking a firm decision it may be said that while it is true that the literal meaning of the term is 'taking a firm decision', it can also be given a connotation in *Shariah* in common parlance.

The verse about the *Shura* says that the affairs of the Muslims are managed by mutual consultations in which the principle of consensus or abiding by majority decision has to be observed, since if an individual or a group is given the right to act arbitrarily after listening to the opinions of others, consultations become absolutely meaningless. Allah (SWT) does not say that the Muslims are to be consulted in the management of their affairs but that affairs are conducted with mutual consultation. This command is not fulfilled merely by holding consultation but it involves that the decisions that are taken by a majority ought to be followed.[119]

If someone objects to the above-mentioned interpretation of this verse by saying that while the obligation and indispensability of holding consultations is understandable, this does not necessarily imply the opinion of the *Shura* being binding, it may be contented that if consultations are held and the viewpoint of the majority is known and even after all this the majority decision is not implemented, the very purpose of consultations is defeated and hence the obligation to hold consultation in itself implies that the decisions that emerge from them are implemented.

These scholars cite *Ahadith*, too, in support of their contention that the decisions of the *Shura* are binding on the *amir*.

This is a *Hadith* attributed to Ali that when the Prophet (SAW) was asked as to what '*azm*' meant he replied, "to consult the people whose opinion carries weight and then to act according to their advice".[120]

Prophetic Explanations of *Azm* and *Hazm*

The terms *azm* and *hazm* are near synonyms. Another *Hadith* which is attributed to Khalid bin M'adan and Abdur Rahman bin Hussain clarifies the connotation of the word *azm* still further. According to it, when some one asked the Prophet (SAW) what *hazm* meant, he replied,

مشاورةُ أهل الرّأى ثم اتّباعهُم

"consult some one whose opinion carries weight and them accept his advicc".[121]

As already stated above, the Prophet (SAW) once said to Abu Bakr and Umar that if both of them were in agreement on an issue, he would not oppose them.[122]

لَو اجْتمعتمَا فى مشورةٍ ما خَالفتكمَا

The explanation of the terms *azm* and *hazm* by the Prophet (SAW) makes it absolutely clear that, according to the verse from *Al-Imran*, the decision of the majority that emerges after consultations with the *Shura* is binding on the *amir*.

However, the experts of Ilm al-*Hadith* do not consider the tradition attributed to Ali *Sahih*. Nasiruddin Albani says that it has not been possible for the scholars to trace its chain of transmission to examine its authenticity.[123] Imam Ibn Hazm[124] and Shaikh Ahmad Shakir,[125] too, look upon this tradition as unauthentic. And though the chain of transmission of the second *Hadith* cited above is *Sahih*, it is a *mursal* one,[126] and a *mursal hadith* is regarded as *dhaeef*. As has been described above, the third *hadith* is also deemed to be *dhaeef*.[127]

Majority was never Overruled

These scholars base their contention that it is binding on the caliph to abide by majority opinion in the *Shura* on the practice of the Prophet (SAW) too. According to them, the Prophet (SAW) consulted people on various military and state matters and implemented the decisions of the majority. They aver that there is nothing in the history of Islam to establish that the Prophet (SAW) ever rejected the advice of the majority after holding consultation with the *Shura*.[128] In this connection they refer especially to the incidents of the Battle of Uhud, the details of which are as follows:

In the year 3 A.H. the Quraish decided to avenge their defeat at the Battle of Badr and, gathering a large army, hitched their camps near the Uhud hill. The Prophet (SAW) received detailed reports regarding this enemy force in time. He convened a meeting of the military high command early in the morning to hold consultations on the adoption of a proper strategy and tactics to deal with the situation. At first he recounted a dream that he had the previous night in which he saw that some cows were being slaughtered and that his own sword was somewhat broken. He also dreamt that he had a strong protective armour on and was riding a sheep, when people asked him to interpret his dream, he said that some among his people would be slaughtered like cows and that a strong protective armour refers to the city of Madinah and the sheep refers to the army.[129] Then he consulted his companions, expressing his own opinion that they should defend themselves from inside Madinah and if the enemies tried to enter the lanes of the town they should be killed by menfolk as well as by women, the latter of whom should shoot them down with arrows showered from roof-tops. He was of the opinion that if the Muslims came out of Madinah to fight, they would be at a disadvantages. However, the zealous and young *Sahabah* who had been deprived of taking part in the Battle of Badr deemed the proposal of the Prophet (SAW) as shameless and cowardy. They were not prepared to consider themselves weak and helpless before their enemies. With one voice they demanded that they should come out of Madinah to fight the enemy forces. After the Friday prayer the Prophet (SAW) came out putting on his armour and gave a call for marching out of Madinah. On this the senior *Sahabah* started talking to one another in undertones that the Prophet's opinion was that the Muslims should defend themselves while remaining within Madinah. They were afraid he had become angry since this opinion of his was overruled. So they went to the Prophet (SAW) and said to him that they were prepared to remain in Madinah if this was what he thought more advisable. To this, he replied that it did not behove a Prophet to withdraw from the battle after putting on his armour till the fighting was over. He added that he had expressed his opinion but they had insisted on coming out of Madinah, so that in a situation of confrontation with the enemy it was advisable for them to be pious, patient and firm in their stand. After he came out of Madinah with his companions and participated in the Battle of Uhud, in which violation of his command by the archers led to the defeat of the Muslims. Sixty verses of the *Surah Al-Imran* were revealed on this occasion, which included, those relating to holding consultations with the *Shura*.[130]

This battle was fought near the Uhud hill after coming out of Madinah to implement the decision of *Shura* which was contrary to his own opinion and in this battle Muslims had to face defeat. In spite of all this, the verses that were revealed on this occasion include an injunction to consult the *Ummah* in all matters. Commenting on this incident, Dr. Abdul Aziz Kamil says:

"The Prophet had made a complete plan, but the *Sahabah* erred twice – once by insisting on coming out of Madinah and then by violation of his command on the part of archers who left their appointed place. But this did not deprive them of their right of expressing their opinion, nor was the principle of the *Shura* discarded by the society. It is from experience and by making mistakes that we learn our lessons. It is our duty to discuss and debate matters with an open mind and keep the principle of consultation before our eyes."[131]

Dr. Abdul Munim al-Namir says that the incident of the Battle of Uhud alone is enough to establish that it is obligatory for the *amir* to abide by the decision of the *Shura*, adding that it is not proper for him to ignore the advice of the *Shura* and to impose his own will on it.[132]

Shaikh Mohammad Ghazali says that when it became clear that the opinion of the majority in favour of fighting outside Madinah was a mistake and that the defeat in the Battle of Uhud was the result of the weaknesses of the Muslims, the command of Allah (SWT) that was revealed to the Prophet (SAW) on that occasion was that the *Shura* ought not to be ignored while taking decisions on important matters even though in this case the opinion of the majority had turned out to be wrong.[133] Dr. Ahmad Shawqi al-Fanjari asks whether the Islamic concept of the *Shura* was changed after the Muslims had to face defeat in the Battle of Uhud as a result of their collective decision and whether

Allah (SWT) asked the Prophet (SAW) not to heed their advice henceforth. Answering these questions in the negative, Dr. Fanjari says that the *Qur'ān* was revealed neither for the Prophet (SAW) alone nor exclusively for his age, adding that it was intended to guide the people for thousands and lakhs of years. He says that this was the reason why the command to abide by the advice of the *Shura* remained in force even after the Battle of Uhud, and Allah (SWT) asked this Prophet (SAW) to adopt a policy of pardon and forgiveness towards his companions, to treat them well and to involve them in consultations.[134]

In this context Amin Ahsan Islahi has cited the following comments of Abu Bakr Jassas:

"And it is not justified to say that the command for consulting the *Sahabah* was given merely to reassure them and to enhance their prestige and honour or only in order to teach the *Ummah* to follow the method adopted by the Prophet (SAW) in dealing with such affairs. Otherwise, if the *Sahabah* felt that when they applied their minds on an issue under discussion and formed some opinion about it, it would not be acted upon nor would it receive any regard from any angle, it would have had an effect on them opposite to reassurance and gain in prestige and they would have been afraid their opinions were being solicited neither for acceptance nor for being translated into action but merely for the sake of being tendered.[135]

Commenting on the above remarks of Jassas, Islahi says that this elaboration of his makes it clear that according to him the injunction to go on consulting the *Sahabah* was not just a formality and for show but in order to implement the decisions arrived at after holding consultations with them.[136]

Three Lessons

Three points emerge from the incident of the Battle of Uhud:

The first of these is that the Prophet (SAW) had accepted the decision of the majority on the occasion as he was satisfied with its advisability, since it is possible that an *imam* withdraws his own opinion and accepts that of the *Shura*. However, being convinced of – the advisability and propriety of a decision in a specific matter does not imply that the *imam* is bound to abide by all its decisions. To be inclined towards what deems to be fair and just is not the same thing as necessarily acceding to the opinions of others without being satisfied with it. It should be assumed that whether it be the *imam* or a member of the *Shura*, he would accept what is true and just what emerges out of a discussion. If this does not happen, it would militate against the spirit of the *Shura* and holding consultations would be pointless.[137] It is true that it should be presumed that the head of state would accept a just advice, and if he does not do so, it merely means that he is not satisfied with it and that he has not rejected it only for the sake of opposing it and because of any feeling of hostility towards the *Shura*.[138]

If the facts of the incident of the Battle of Uhud are taken into consideration, one would reach the conclusion that the Prophet (SAW) had not withdrawn his opinion with any degree of satisfaction and that he had expressed his opinion after recounting and interpretation of the dream but had later withdrawn his opinion in view of the majority which was quite different from his own.

Some scholars wonder how one would find out who is right and who is wrong if there is a difference of opinion between the head of state and members of the *Shura* on an issue regarding which there is no clear guidance in the *Qur'ān* or the *Sunnah* and what would be the touchstone for the right conclusion if the opinion of the majority of the members of the *Shura* is ignored, even though they are deemed to be the most sagacious members of the *Ummah* whose opinions carry weight and who are well-versed in the *Qur'ān* and the *Sunnah*. And they ask if it is presupposed that the head of state would form a correct judgement, why cannot the same be presumed about the *Shura*, a body which has the selected men of wisdom and intellect, adding that affairs of nations, countries and states cannot be run on the basis of the good opinion of the people since certain limitations and rules and regulations are needed for the purpose.[139]

Another point that is raised in connection with the incident of the Battle of Uhud is that the Prophet (SAW) had decided to come out of Madinah to fight not because he had bowed down to the opinion of the majority but since he had put on armour.[140] This contention is a far-fetched one since the Prophet (SAW) had donned his armour only in compliance with the opinion of the majority. Again, when the *Sahabah* later agreed to remain in Madinah, they were withdrawing the opinion that they had expressed earlier, in deference to the opinion of the Prophet (SAW) and not because they were satisfied with it. Their words to the Prophet (SAW) were, "we shall stay on in Madinah if this is your will". The fact is that the Prophet (SAW) rejected this offer of the *Sahabah* in order to end all tension and dissention over the issue and to fortify the decision of the majority as this was an occasion in which there was little scope for anxiety or hesitation since the *Sahabah* had made preparations for leaving the city and were only waiting for the call to march forward. When the crier proclaimed marching orders, all anxiety was removed. It was this firm determination to which the *Qur'ān* refers when it asks the faithfuls not to be victims of anxiety and to put their trust in Allah (SWT), once they have taken a firm decision.[141]

A third point that is raised in relation to the Battle of Uhud is that the *Sahabah* had realised that they were in the wrong, that they regretted it and wanted the opinion of the Prophet (SAW) to be acted upon. Later, when they had to face defeat this realisation on their part was greatly increased and they learnt from the terrible consequences of opposing the opinion of their leader that henceforth they should not oppose the opinion of the *imam* if he insisted on it and ought not to insist on the majority decision being followed.[142]

The above contention is not a valid one since the Prophet (SAW) had neither issued any command for not going out of Madinah to fight nor did he insist on upholding his opinion. He had merely expressed his personal opinion before holding consultations. Had the Prophet (SAW) issued any command, the *Sahabah* would have been compelled to follow it. He gave them sufficient hints to indicate that he was not issuing any command and that the matter was open to discussion and debate. Hence there was no question of any opposition to his command.

This general statement should not mean that no decision of the *imam* or caliph should be opposed and that consequences of such opposition would be disastrous. Even though the Prophet (SAW) was innocent, he gave an opportunity to the *Sahabah* to express their views, withdrew his own proposal in favour of the one put forward by others, so as to establish the validity of the principle of abiding by the decisions of the *Shura* till the Day of Judgement. He accepted the wrong opinion of the majority of the *Sahabah* and yet the *Qur'ān* did not blame him. On the contrary, the Prophet (SAW) was enjoined to keep consulting them and to implement the decision of the majority. Hence, there is no question of the representatives of the people being prevented from expressing their opinion in opposition to that of the head of state and other officials who are by no means innocent.[143]

Those who hold that the head of state is bound by the decisions of the *Shura* base their arguments on the practice of the Guided Caliphs, too, during whose tenure all important decisions and steps were taken according to the opinion of the majority. Instances of these have been described above and need not be repeated here. Amin Ahsan Islahi says that during the period of the Guided Caliphs there is not a single instance to show that after consultation with the people who mattered any step was taken against their unanimous opinion or that of the majority.[144]

According to Shaikh Mohammad Abu Zahrah, the procedure of *ijtihad* adopted by the Guided Caliphs was as follows:

During this period the caliph did not do *ijtihad* personally but convened meeting of the *Sahabah* and put an issue requiring *ijtihad* before them and took his decision in accordance with that of the *Sahabah*. The aim behind the convening of such a *Shura* was to find out if there was some *Sunnah* relating to the issue. In case there was such a *Sunnah*, he decided according to it. If no guidance could he had from the *Sunnah*, the caliph himself did *ijtihad* and expressed his opinion pertaining to the issue in hand to the *Sahabah*. If they agreed with his opinion he implemented it, failing which he enforced the decision of the *Shura* in the matter. If he felt that there was greater weight in his opinion than in that of the *Sahabah* he tried to convince them about his stand so that the issue was resolved without any difference of opinion and the judgement of the caliph was enforced only if the *Sahabah* endorsed it. Very often recourse had to taken to *ijma* (consensus).

Abu Zahrah adds that the Guided Caliphs were themselves elected by a majority. According to Maimoon bin Mahran, who has been cited by Abu Zahrah, Caliphs Abu Bakr and Umar convened assembly of the faithfuls to deliberate the issues and implemented its decisions when there was a consensus among them. As has been mentioned above, during the caliphate of Umar matters were decided by a majority of votes of the members of the *Shura*.[145]

Rationale for Mandatory *Shura*

Those holding the opinion that the *amir* is bound to follow the decision of the *Shura* advance certain other arguments also in support of their stand. For instance they wonder what the value of the *Shura* would be if the decisions arrived at by the majority of its members are not followed.[146] They say that the *Shura* loses its rationale and usefulness if the caliph is given the right to listen to everyone and to adopt the opinion that he himself deems to be proper.[147] Shaikh Mohammad Ghazali says in clear terms that consulting people and then ignoring their opinions and implementing whatever opinion the *amir* likes is no child-play.[148] He adds that an advice which the enforcing authority is not bound to accept carries no weight, and would have no greater significance than that of meaningless sport and entertainment, and an ineffective *Shura* is useless.[149] Shaikh Mohammad Abduh wonders what the significance of the *Shura* is and why Allah (SWT) asks for its establishment if the ruler does not recognise its authority and is not bound by its decisions.[150]

The above arguments may be countered by saying that the importance of the *Shura* cannot be confined to the acceptance of the opinion of its members since the task of the *Shura* is to throw light on the issues in hand[151] and to decide upon the right course of action[152] which accords respect and satisfaction to the people whose opinion matter as well as to the learned scholars.[153]

This argument may be met by saying that all the advantages of the *Shura* would only accrue if decisions arrived at after consultations are binding on the *amir*. These advantages cannot be achieved if the advice of the *Shura* is not accepted. Jassas is right when he says that if the *Sahabah* knew that the efforts that they were making in resolving problems in hand would go waste since their decisions would not be implemented, it would not have resulted in bringing either satisfaction or respect to them, adding that it would, on the contrary, fill their minds with the apprehension that their advice would neither be accepted nor utilised.[154] He says that in such a situation consultations could have led to dissension, disintegration and mischief,[155] which would hardly have resulted in their mental satisfaction or enhancement of their prestige.[156]

The second argument that is put forward by scholars who are of the opinion that the *amir* is bound to follow the decisions of the *Shura* is that the head of state is elected from amongst the eminent members of the *Ummah* as well as those whose opinions carry weight, and his appointment to the high office does not bring about any major change in his mental and intellectual capacities, which are in no way superior to those of other prominent personalities, so that sometimes it is difficult to distinguish between the abilities of the two. So, these scholars wonder how his mental capacities can become superior to those of other thinkers and learned people of the *Ummah* simply because he has been elevated to the post of *amir* from among their ranks. Hence, they assert, a collective opinion is in any case preferable to that of an individual.[157]

The third argument that is given in favour of the view that the decisions of the *Shura* are binding on the *amir* is based on the Islamic principle of equality, according to which the *amir* and an ordinary Muslim have equal status, between whom there can be no valid distinction if they are equal in respect of learning, morality, piety and sincerity. Those who hold this view say that the opinion of the *amir* can prevail over that of the common people only till the latter do not have the courage to say positively that their opinion is better than that of his in the eyes of Allah (SWT).[158]

Majority is Binding

The fourth argument in this respect is based on certain *Ahadith*, according to which the *amir* has been enjoined to act according to the consensus or opinion of the majority in the house. These traditions are interpreted to the effect that the community is nearer to the truth as compared with an individual. Some of these *Ahadith* are as follows:

عن جابر بن سمرة رضى الله عنه قال: خطبنا عمرُ بن
الخَطّابِ فقال: قام فينا رسولُ الله صلّى الله عليه وسلّم
كَقِيامِى فيكُم فقال: من أحب منكم بحبوحةَ الجنّة يلتزم
الجماعةَ فإنّ الشيطانَ مع الوَاحدِ وهو من الإثنَينِ أبعدُ.

A tradition attributed to Jabir bin Samurah is that in an address before a congregation Umar bin Khattab said that the Prophet (SAW) once stood in their midst as he was himself standing amongst them and said that those who wished to enjoy the pleasures of paradise should stand close to the community since Satan kept the company of solitary people and avoided that of two persons at a time.[159]

روى أحمد فى مسنده عن أبى ذرّ مرفوعًا أنّه قال: إثنان خيرٌ من واحدٍ وثلاثةٌ خيرٌ من إثنينِ وأربعةٌ خيرٌ من ثلاثة فعليكم بالجماعة فإنّ الله عز وجلّ لن – أولم – يجمع أمّتى إلا على هدًى.

Imam Ahmad Ibn Hanbal attributes a Hadith to Abu Zarr, according to which the Prophet (SAW) once said that two persons were better than one, three were better than two and four were better than three, asking his followers to stick to the community since Allah (SWT) would not let His *Ummah* stray from the path of righteousness.[160]

عن ابن عمر عن النبى صلّى الله عليه وسلّم قال: لاتجتمع أمّة محمد على ضلالة ابدًا، وعليكم بالسواد الأعظم فإنّه من شذّ شُذّ إلَى النّارِ.

According to Ibn Umar, the Prophet (SAW) once said that his *Ummah* would never agree to stray from the right path and asked his followers to go along with the consensus among the faithfuls since one who isolated himself from the *Ummah* would be consigned to hell.[161]

عن ابن عمر عن النبى صلّى الله عليه وسلّم قال: إنّ الله لا يجمع أمّتى – أو قال أمّة محمّد – على ضلالةٍ، ويدُ الله على الجماعةِ ومن شذّ شُذّ فى النّار.

Hadith attributed to Ibn Umar is that the Prophet (SAW) has said that My *Ummah* would never agree to stray from the right path and that the Hand of Allah is on the community and, a person who isolate himself from the community would go to hell.[162]

عـن ابن عبّاسٍ قال قال رسول اللّه صلّى اللّه عليه وسلّم:

يد اللّه مع الجماعة.

According to Ibn Abbas, the Prophet (SAW) once said that the *Ummah* was blessed by the hand of Al!ah (SWT).[163]

Principle of *Ijma*

The fifth argument of the scholars holding the view that the *amir* is obliged to abide by the decisions of the *Shura* is based on the Islamic principle of *ijma*, according to which all the Muslim *mujtahid*s can arrive at a consensus among themselves on any injunction of *Shariah*.[164] According to Imam Shafi'i, the term *ijma* stands for a consensus among Muslim scholars on any issue provided that the verdict of *ijma* does not run counter to any of the authentic pronouncement. Ibn Jarir Tabari and Fakhruddin Razi hold that the views of the majority are also *ijma*. When Imam Ahmad Ibn Hanbal says that according to his knowledge if there is no opinion against a particular pronouncement, his words have been interpreted to mean that on such an issue there is *ijma*. All the *Ulama* agree that *ijma* is *hujjah* (authoritative source). That is to say, when a consensus is arrived at among the *Ummah* on the interpretation of a text, on the *qiyas*, on any *ijtihad* or on expedient law, it becomes essential for the faithful to abide by it.[165] Ibn Taimiyah says that *ijma* means agreement among all the Muslim *Ulama* and adds that when the *ijma* of the entire *Ummah* is established regarding some injunction no one has the right to go against it, since, according to him, the entire *Ummah* can never agree on something that is degrading. However, he says, there are many issues regarding which there is a misconception in the minds of some people that there is *ijma* but in fact this is not so and there is another pronouncement that is preferable to it. After summing up the whole discussion.[166] Maulana Maududi concludes that even at the present time if there is *Ijma* or verdict of the majority of *ahl al-hall wa al-aqd* on the interpretation of some texts, a *qiyas*, a deduction or a matter of policy or expediency, it would be *hujjah* and would have the force of law.[167]

Ulama commonly believe that *ijma* is possible even in the present age since there are instances of *ijma* taking place on a number of issues, like those of giving one-sixth portion to one's grandmother, the entitlement of one-sixth portion to one's granddaughter even though he has a daughter, depriving one's grandson of inheritance due to the death of his son, prohibiting the consumption of lard, prohibition to marry a lady as well as her maternal aunt etc. In regard to none of these issues was there any clear guidance from the *Qur'ān* or the *Sunnah*. However, there was consensus on these matters and its conclusions became part of Islamic code.

Some Mutazelite *Ulama* and staunch Shiites deny the validity of an *ijma* over which there is consensus among the Sunni *Ulama*, since, they claim that it is not easy for anyone to attain to the status of a *mujtahid*, and there is no commonly agreed yardstick for judging whether or not a person has achieved this status or to differentiate between a *mujtahid* and a common man. Another problem, according to them, is that the *mujtahid*s are spread all over the world. Then, they say, *ijtihad* is needed when there is no definite guidance on an issue and it is difficult for all the *mujtahid*s to agree with the arguments based on assumptions since there are great differences between the points of view of different people and because there are different gradations in their intellectual capabilities. However, the majority of *Ulama* have rejected this contention of the Mutazelite and Shiite *Ulama* on the ground that during the times of Caliphs

Abu Bakr and Umar there were several well-known *mujtahid*s and many arguments based on assumptions were so clear that there was simply no scope for disagreement among them.[168]

Hence, in general, the *Ulama* agree on the authenticity of *ijma* though some Khawarij and Ithna Ashari Shiites do not agree with them on this point. While difference of opinion on the authenticity of the *Qur'ān*ic verses is out of the question, no definite conclusion can be derived from the *Ahadith* cited above, since they are based on *Khabr Wahed* which can only be interpreted to mean that the *Ummah* would be saved from errors.

Some contemporary *Ulama* say that according to most of the *fuqaha*, for an *ijma* it is necessary for *mujtahid*s of all the Muslim countries to be in agreement over an issue, which cannot be translated into practice in present-day conditions. Maulana Maududi says that during the period of the Guided Caliphs there was a regular and well-established political system which was running on the basis of the *Shura*. Hence the decisions of the *ijma* as well as those adopted by majority opinion are well-known and are confirmed by authentic accounts. However, he says, that later when this political system disintegrated and the *Shura* system came to an end, there was no method of finding out on which issues there really was *ijma* and on which there was no *ijma*. He adds that while it is not possible to deny the existence of *ijma* during the period of the Guided Caliphs, if some one makes a claim that was an *ijma* on such and such issue, his claim would be rejected by scholars. Maulana Maududi concludes by saying that for conducting *ijma* and resolving issues through it, the establishment of Islamic system is a pre-requisite.[170]

According to some *Ulama*, even during the period of the *Sahabah* no *ijma* could be held along the lines prescribed by most *fuqaha*. They say that anyone who examines the circumstances and incidents related to the issue of pronouncements by the *Sahabah* and the way in which these *fatawa* of their were given the status of *ijma*, would find that it was not the *ijma* of the kind that is visualised by most. An *ijma* was held according to the collective opinion rather than that of individuals. However this does not mean that all *mujtahid*s had to be consulted. There is no evidence to prove that Caliph Abu Bakr had convened an assembly of all *mujtahid*s or that he had suspended decision on a matter till all the people who were entitled to give their opinion on it were present. Some *mujtahid*s were generally away from Madinah for carrying on trade, propagation of the faith, participating in a Jihad or due to the fact that they were working as government officials. Then the fact is that no unanimity could ever be achieved among the *mujtahid*s over arguments based on *zann*.

This is why Imam Shafi'i is of the view that except for the principles and fundamentals of Islam and matters definitely related to the faith, no *ijma* was possible on any issue. He, for that matter, says that no scholar can claim that there is *ijma* on such and such issue except for definite matters like obligation to offer four *rakats* in *Zuhr* prayer, deeming the consumption of wine to be *haram* and other issues of this nature.[171]

Imam Ahmad bin Hanbal says that anyone who claims that there is *ijma* on any issue is a liar, and anyone who claims that there is a universal *ijma* is a greater liar. He adds that it is possible that some people may express their disagreement on an issue and the remaining people are not aware of this. They should rather say that they do not know whether or not some people had disagreed on the issue.[172]

Qur'ānic verses and Ahadith that have been cited by most of the *fuqaha* do not definitely indicate that *ijma* is an authortative source. This is why Aamidi says that it is possible to have a tentative discussion in the light of these citations but no definite conclusion can be drawn on this basis.[173] It is also for this reason why, after recounting the conditions for *ijma*, Shaikh Mahmood Shaltoot concludes that there is no doubt that even if it is conceded for the sake of argument that it is possible to fulfil the first three conditions of *ijma*, fulfilment of the fourth condition – unanimity among all the *mujtahid*s over a single opinion is impossible. He adds that any issue under discussion can be discussed from a number of angles and hence difference of opinion is natural due to great differences among the *mujtahid*s in their power of understanding and sagacity, availability of resources for discussion and debate and prevailing exigencies and circumstances. Hence, according to Shaikh Shaltoot, the concept of *ijma* on any issue in any age with agreement of all the *fuqaha* is an idealistic one which is almost impossible to realise and it is difficult to enact legislations on its basis. On the other hand, he says, it is possible to adopt a concept of *ijma* which attaches importance to the opinion of the majority or one which has scope for learning about any opposite point of view, both of which, can, in his opinion, form the basis of legislation, since he says, this is the height of human efforts and Allah (SWT) does not impose any burden beyond the capacity of the people. This is, according to Shaikh Shaltoot, what is called collective *ijtihad*.[174] According to Ibn Jareer Tabari, Abul Husain Khayyat Mutazeli, Fakhruddin Razi, and according to one account, Imam Ahmad bin Ḥanbal too, are of the opinion that the majority view should be considered *ijma* if the number of those who opposed to it is very small. Some *fuqaha* hold that majority opinion can be given the status of *ijma* provided that there has not a considerable number of *Ulama* who have been opposed to it throughout the history of Islam, while others says that majority opinion is *hujjah* (authoritative sources) but it cannot be deemed to be *ijma* and still others opine that the opinion of the majority is merely acceptable.[175]

Majority forms *Hujjah*

Those who claim that majority opinion is *hujjah* offer the following arguments in support of their stand:

1. It is mentioned in a number of Ahadith that Allah (SWT) would never allow the *Ummah* of Muhammad (SAW) to take a decision that is degrading and hence, recourse should be taken according to the opinion of the majority. According to one Hadith, the Prophet (SAW) asked his followers to hold on the mantle of the *Ummah*. According to another Hadith, the *Ummah* has the Hand of Allah (SWT) over it. These Ahadith indicate that the opinion of the majority ought to be considered *hujjah*.

2. Members of *Ummah* were unanimous in accepting Abu Bakr as caliph, even though only a majority of the people had taken oath of allegiance to him. Prominent people like Ali and Saad bin Ubadah were initially opposed to his caliphate but even then his *bayah* was confirmed.

3. Accounts given by a large number of narrators make a particular tradition authentic. In the same way, inclination of a majority of *mujtahid*s in favour of a particular opinion is a proof of its soundness.

4. If opposition by a minority invalidates *ijma*, any rule of *Shariah* can be invalidated since no *ijma* can save itself from opposition by one or two persons.

5. The *Sahabah* rejected the opposition of Ibn Abbas to the decision of the majority on the issue of *mut'ah* (usufruct marriage contracted for a specified time and exclusively for

the purpose of sexual pleasure). In this connection there was no debate and discussion between Ibn Abbas and other *Sahabah* on this question. The opposition of Ibn Abbas to the majority opinion on the issue was simply ignored.

6. Authentic pronouncements relating to the innocence of the *Ummah* would be attributed only to the opinion of the majority and this is the sense in which this expression is commonly used in Arabic language and literature.

7. All the decisions taken through consensus pertaining to the period of the *Sahabah* were based on majority opinion. This is why Shaikh Abdul Wahab Khallaf says that these were really the products of the collective deliberations in the *Shura* and were not the personal decisions of any individual and assembly of selected *Sahabah* which was convened by Abu Bakr did not consist of the leaders and representatives of all the Muslims since a large number of these people were away in Makkah, Syria and Yeman and in the battle fields.[176]

8. No pronouncement of the Prophet (SAW) should be deemed to be authentic if it has been received through a single channel and only those of his statements are authentic which have been received through a number of channels. This is one of the cardinal principles of *fiqh*, which also applies to *ijtihad* and *ijma*.[177]

Dr. Mohammad Salam Madkur says that during the period of the *Sahabah* or even that of the Guided Caliphs no *ijma* was ever held in the sense that there was total agreement among the *mujtahid*s on an issue, since cases in which the *Sahabah* pronounced their decisions which have been mentioned by later *fuqaha* in their lists of *ijma* were not *ijma* in the real sense but were in the nature of collective *ijtihad*, as only those who were learned and whose opinions carried weight were required to express their opinions on the issues placed before them and their decision was that of the *Shura* as a whole.[178]

The same thing has been said by Fathi Rizwan who writes that the *ijma*, as has been defined by Muslim scholars, can never take place as it has to be the outcome of total agreement among all the *mujtahid*s of the *Ummah*, meaning thereby that it requires an international *ijma* which is not possible at all. He further says that what these *fuqaha* mean by the term *ijma* is not what the Prophet (SAW) meant when he said to Ali, "Convene an assembly of learned Muslims and hold consultations with them and do not take a decision according to the decision of a single individual." This, according to Fathi Rizwan, means that the Prophet (SAW) merely expressed his preference for collective opinion as compared with that of an individual.[179]

Dr. Abdul Hameed Mutawalli cites Shaikh Mustafa al-Maraghi who has said that in the opinion of Muslim *Ulama* *ijma* is impossible, adding that it was within three centuries of the first phase of Islam tat this issue had become a victim of the confused thinking of the *Ulama*, so that it became impossible to encompass their varying viewpoints. Dr. Mutawalli concludes by saying that a majority of contemporary *Ulama* appear to agree with Shaikh Maraghi, while some of them are of the opinion that conducting *ijma* was impossible even during the early years of Islam.[180]

Zakaria al-Bari holds that *ijma* can only be deemed to be valid when it fulfils certain specific conditions – convening an assembly of *mujtahid*s which should include persons having expertise and experience in different fields and in case of any difference of opinion, the decision of the majority, should be adopted and the ruler should issue orders forthwith for its' implementation. According to him, this is what different *Qur'ānic* verses[181] mean by talking of consultation, obedience to *ulul amr*, and resort to learned people and those who are experts in the principles of *ijtihad* and deduction. He says that *ijma* was held during the age of the *Sahabah* in this way and this was the manner in which Abu Bakr and Umar consulted senior *Sahabah*.[182]

Making a distinction between *ijma* and collective *ijtihad*. Dr. Mohammad Salam Madkur says that this has provided Muslims an easy and convenient way out since decisions of a collective *ijtihad* can be revised and altered by another such *ijtihad* provided that the ruler has not confirmed it by announcing his own decision in the matter. Again, he adds, unlike the decisions of an *ijma*, those of a collective *ijtihad* would not be binding on all Muslims for all the times to come.[183]

From the above-mentioned discussion it may be concluded that *ijma* is really another term for majority opinion and that though there will always be scope for difference of opinion among the *mujtahid*s, it will be the decision of the majority that will be implemented. This makes it quite clear that it is obligatory on the part of the ruler to abide by the decisions of the *Shura* which are arrived at by majority vote.

Theory of Innocence

The sixth argument that is preferred by those who are in favour of the implementation of the decision of the majority of the *Shura* is based on the principle of *ismah* (innocence), according to which the right of the *Ummah* is infringed if decision of the majority, that is, the collective power of the *Shura* is smashed into bits, while, in principle, the *Ummah* as a body is deemed to be innocent and incapable of erring, while the *Amir* is not considered to be so. In such a situation the non-innocent cannot claim preference over the innocent.[184]

In this connection Ameen Ahsan Islahi says that there is no doubt that if an *amir* is convinced that what he thinks is right and that adopting any other measure is fraught with great dangers, he can go on asserting his opinion. However, he adds that the *amir* ought to realise that he is not an innocent being, and so he has no right to insist on the acceptance of his personal opinion to the extent of rejecting that of majority in matters of *ijtihad* or expediency. He says that if the *amir* looks upon his personal viewpoint as something beyond doubt, in effect, he looks upon himself as an innocent personality.[185]

Public Interest

The seventh argument that is advanced by those who are of the view that the *amir* is bound to follow the opinion of the *Shura* is based on considerations of the welfare of the people and expediency. It is contended that if the opinion of the majority does not violate the *Shariah* it should be accepted in the interest of public welfare since this acts as a check on the arbitrariness and dictatorship of the ruler and creates the atmosphere of complete freedom of expression, criticism and accountability.[186] Muhammad Asad says that rulers make terrible mistakes and perpetrate worst tyrannies if they are allowed to act without any check. He adds that this is a sad lesson that one learns from history and a nation that does not learn this lesson becomes a victim of worst kinds of oppressions and tragedies.[187]

There is also a group of *Ulama* and scholars who says that it is for the *Ummah* to specify the legal status of the *Shura*. According to them the question whether or not the *amir* should abide by the opinion of the *Shura* ought to be decided by the *Ummah* itself, keeping in view the demands and exigencies of the age. It has the right to decide whether the opinion of the majority should be enforced or whether, owing to his abilities, the *amir* should be given the power to take decisions himself, keeping the prevailing conditions in mind. This, in effect, means that this matter is related with the understanding and awareness of the common people and their needs and conditions and not with *Shariah.* According to these thinkers this issue is among secondary matters and those of details which depend on the evolution of the collective understanding, democracy and freedom among the people of a particular country. This is why, they say, *Shariah* does not interfere with such issues which lack in stability, and change with changes in prevailing conditions.[188]

Another argument put forward by this group is that this is one of the controversial matters of the *Shariah* with diametrically opposed views held by the *fuqaha* since, according to some authentic texts, decisions of the *Shura* are absolutely final and binding while other texts bestow absolute authority to the *amir*. Hence, these scholars aver, this matte should be left in the hands of the *Ummah* itself to decide.

The above-mentioned arguments are not sound since the principle of abiding by majority decisions may be a secondary issue in the modern parliamentary system but it has a central and fundamental place in Islamic political thought which cannot be altered even by the *Ummah*,[189] though other details of the *Shura* system are amenable to changes. The contention that the issue is controversial in *Shariah* is also not valid, since even though there are arguments in favour of both the opinion, the right to choose one in preference to the other, too, remains with the *Ummah* and any of these can be adopted and others rejected in the light of authentic sources.

When arguments of the three above-mentioned schools of thought are compared, those of the second of these appear to be more sound in the light of the *Qur'ān*, the

Sunnah and the history of Islam. According to it the *amir* is bound to abide by the opinion of the representatives of the community in all basic and crucial matters and he has no right to take decisions regarding such issues without consulting the *Shura*. He has no right at all to take steps in matters which concern the collective interests of the state without obtaining the sanction of the representatives of the people. However, in routine everyday affairs, while the *Amir* ought to consult wise and sagacious people, he is not bound to follow their advice. He has the right to select any of the various opinions expressed by them. It is also not necessary that his consultants should consist only of the representatives of the people. It is enough that those consulted are gifted with sagacity and insight.[190]

NOTES AND REFERENCES

1. Huwaidi, Hasan, *Al-Shura fi al-Islam*, Maktaba al-Manar al-Islamiyah, Kuwait, 1975, p. 8.

2. Islahi, Ameen Ahsan, *Tadabbur Qur'ān*, *op.cit.*, Vol. I, p. 182; Mutawalli, Abdul Hameed, *Mabda al-Shura fi al-Islam*, Alam al-Kutub, Egypt, 1972, p. 14; Tabari, Abu Jafar Mohammad bin Jareer, *Jame al-Bayan an Tafsir Aay al-Qur'ān*, Dar al-Maarif, Egypt, Vol. VII, p. 346.

3. Qurtbi, Abu Abdullah Mohammad bin Ahmad al-*Ansari*, *Al-Jame le Ahkam al-Qur'ān*, Dar al-Kutub al-Arabi, Cairo, 1967, Vol. IV, p. 252.

4. Ibn al-Jauzi, Abul Farj Abdur Rahman, *Zad al-Masir ala Ilm al-Tafsir*, al-Maktab al-Islami, Cairo, 1964, Vol. I, p. 489.

5. Al Razi, Fakhruddin, *Mafateeh al-Ghayb (al-Tafsir al-Kabir)*, Dar al-Kutub al-Ilmiyah, Tehran, Vol. IX, pp. 67-68.

6. Al-Sharbini, *Tafsir al-Qur'ān (al-Siraj al-Munir)*, Dar al-Marifah, Beriut, Vol. I, p 260.

7. Shaukani, Mohammad bin Ali, *Fath al-Qadeer*, Mustafa al-Babi al-Halbi, Egypt, 1349 A.H., Vol. I, p. 630.

8. Qushayri, Abdul Karim bin Hawazin bin Abdul Malik, *Tafsir Soofi Kamil li al-Qur'ān*, ed. Bisyooni, Ibrahim, Dr., Dar al-Katib al-Arabi, Cairo, Vol. I, p. 303.

9. Baghawi, Abu Mohammad Husain bin Maswood, *Maalim al-Tanzeel fi al-Tafsir*, on the margin of Tafsir al-Khazin, Maktaba al-Tijariyah, Egypt, Vol. I, p. 368.

10. Al-Nasafi, Hafizuddin Abdullah bin Ahmad, *Madaarik al-Tanzeel wa Haqaaiq al-Taawil*, on the margin of Tafsir al-Khazin, Mohd. Ameen Damj, Beirut, Vol. I, p. 296.

11. Zamakhshari, Mahmood bin Umar, *al-Kashshaaf an Haqaiq Ghawamiz al-Tanzeel wa Uyoon al-Aqaaveel fi Wajh al-Taweel*, Dar al-Katib al-Arabi, Beirut, Vol. X, p. 432.

12. Bablali, Mahmood, *Al-Shura fi al-Islam*, Dar al-Irshad, Beirut, 1968, pp. 57-60.

13. Naar, Ahmad, *Al-Qital fi al-Islam*, p. 129.

14. Tabrisi, Abu Ali bin Hasan, *Majma al-Bayan fi Tafsir al-Qur'ān*, Dar al-Kitab al-Labnani, Beirut, 1955, Vol. IV, p. 244.

15. Shaukani, *Fath al-Qadeer*, *op. cit.*, Vol. I, p. 360.

16. Ibn Manzoor, *Lisan al-Arab*, 1300 A.H., Vol. XII, p. 399; Zamakhshari, *al-Kashshaaf*, *op. cit.*, Vol. I, p. 432; al-Sharbini, *al-Siraj al-Munir*, *op. cit.*, Vol. I, p. 260; Nasafi, *Madaarik al-Tanzeel*, *op. cit.*, Vol. I, p. 296; Qurtubi, *Al-Jame li Ahkam al-Qur'ān*, *op. cit.*, Vol. IV, p. 252; Abu Izzah, Abdullah, *Al-Shura am al-Istibdad*, *Al-Mujtama*, Kuwait, No. 38, Dec. 1970, p. 23.

17. Abdur Rahman, Abdul Khaliq, *Al-Shura fi Zill Nizam al-Hukm al-Islami*, al-Dar al-Salafiyah, Kuwait, 1975, p. 100; El-Awa, Mohammad Saleem, *On the Political System of Islamic State*, *op. cit.*, p. 113.

18. Abu Zayd, Al-Shura: *Aa Hiya Asasun li Tanzeem al-Mujtama al-Islami am Hilyah yumkin al-Istighna Anha*, *Al-Shahab*, Beirut, September, 1968, p. 5.

19. Al-Razi, *Mafaatih al-Ghayb*, *op. cit.*, Vol. IX, pp. 67-68.

20. Al-Baghdadi, *Tafsir al-Khazin*, *op. cit.*, Vol. I, p. 296; Bhopali, Siddique Hasan, *Fath al-Bayan fi Maqāsid al-Rahmān*, Egypt, 1301, A.H. Vol. 2, p. 130.

21. Mutawalli, Abdul Hameed, *Mabda al-Shura fi al-Islam*, *op. cit.*, p. 15. The author has quoted Tafsir Ibn Kathir, Vol. I, p. 420.

22. Al-Suyuti, Jalaluddin Abdur Rahman bin Abu Bakr, *Al-Durr al-Manthur fi al-Tafsir bi al-Mathur*, Dar al-Thaqafah, Beirut, Vol. II, p. 90. *Tafsir Ibn Abbas* is cited on the margin of the above work.

23. Ibn Hajar, Al-Asqalani, Shahabuddin Abul Fazl, *Tahzeeb al-Tahzeeb*, Dar Saader, Beirut, Vol. IV, p. 369; Al-Albani, Mohd. Nasiruddin, *Silsilah al-Ahadith al-Zaeefah wa al-Mauzuah wa Athruha al-Sayye fi al-Ummah*, Manshooraat al-Maktab al-Islami, Damascus, Vol. III, p. 51.

24. Ibn Hajar, *Tahzeeb al-Tahzeeb*, *op. cit.*, Vol. VI, p. 250.

25. Ibn Hazm, Abu Mohammad bin Ahmad bin Sayeed, *Al-Ihkam fi Usool al-Ahkam,* Maktabah al-Jumhuriyah al-Arabiyah, Egypt, 1970, p. 772.

26. Al-Aalusi, Abul Fazl Shahabuddin Mahmood, *Rooh al-Maani fi Tafsir al-Qur'ān al-Azeem wa al-Sabe al-Mathani*, Dar Ihya al-Turath al-Arabi, Beirut, Vol. IV, p. 107. The author has pointed out that the Prophet (SAW) had said to encourage the two companions and to elaborate the status and dignity they had among the Muslims.

27. Al-Hakim, *Al-Mustadrak alongwith the Al-Talkhees of al-Zahabi*, Maktaba al-Matbooat al-Islamiyah, Halab, Damascus, Vol. III, p. 70.

28. Al-Baihaqi, Ahmad bin Husain bin Ali, *Al-Sunan al-Kubra*, Dairah al-Maarif al-Usmaniyah, Hyderabad, 1354, A.H., Vol. X, p. 109. (Chapter, Aadab al-Qazi).

29. Al-Suyuti, *Al-Durr al-Manthur*, *op. cit.*, Vol. II, p. 90.

30. Al-Albani, *Silsilah al-Ahadith al-Zaeefah*, *op. cit.*, Vol. II, p. 12.

31. Al-Aalusi, *Rooh al-Maani*, *op. cit.*, Vol. IV, p. 107.

32. Al-Razi, *Mafatih al-Ghayb*, *op. cit.*, Vol. IX, p. 67.

33. *The Qur'ān*, 24: 51.

34. Because the *Qur'ān* itself declares that the Prophet (SAW) does not say any thing from his own, his sayings are divided between *Wahy Matlu* (the recited revelation) and *Wahy Ghayr Matlu* (unrecited revelation). See the *Qur'ān*, 53: 3-4.

35. Huwaidi, Hasan, *Al-Shura fi al-Islam*, *op. cit.*, pp. 10-12.

36. Al-Qastalani, Shahabuddin Ahmad bin Mohammad, *Irshad al-Sari li Sharh Sahih al-Bukhari*, Vol. IV, (Bāb al-Shurut).

37. Ibn Kathir, Abul Fida Ismail, *Al-Bidayah wa al-Nihayah*, Maktaba al-Maarif, Beirut, 1966, Vol. IV, p. 164; Ibn Hisham, Abu Mohammad Abdul Malik, *Al-Seerah al-Nabaviyah ma Sharhiha li al-Suhayli*, Mustafa al-Babi al-Halabi, Egypt, 1936, Vol. II, p. 230.

38. Abdur Rahman, Abdul Khaliq, *Al-Shura fi Zill Nizam al-Hukm al-Islami*, *op. cit.*, p. 122; El-Awa, Mohammad Salim, *On the Political System of Islamic State*, *op. cit.*, p. 114, Abu Izzah, Abdullah, *Al-Shura am al-Istibdād*, *op. cit.*, p. 23.

39. Al-Qastalani, *Irshad al-Sari li sharh Sahih al-Bukhari*, *op. cit.*, Vol. IV, (Bāb al-Shurut).

40. Al-Ghazali, Mohammad, *Al-Islam wa al-Istibdād al-Siyasi*, Dar al-Kutub al-Hadithah, Egypt, 1961, pp. 52-53.

41. Mazhar, Jalal, *Mohammad Rasul Allah – Seeratuh wa Athruh fi al-Hadharah*, Maktaba al-Khanji, Egypt, 1970, p. 285.

42. Mutawalli, Abdul Hameed, *Mabda al-Shura fi al-Islam*, *op. cit.*, pp. 15-16.

43. Muslim, *al-Jame al-Sahih bi sharh al-Nawawi*, Dar al-Fikr, Beirut, 1972, Vol. VI, p. 76; Abu Daud, *al-Sunan*, Vol. VII, p. 354; Mubarak Puri, Abdur Rahman, *Tuhfah al-Ahvazi bi Sharh Jame al-Tirmizi*, Vol. V, pp. 373-375.

44. *The Qur'ān*, 8: 67.

45. Abu Izzah, Abdullah, *Al-Shura am al-Istibdād*, *op. cit.*, p. 13.

46. Rida, Rashid, *Tafsir al-Qur'ān al-Karim (Tafsir al-Manar)*, Maktaba al-Qahirah, Egypt, 1960, Vol. X, p. 99.

47. See for detail, Tabari, *Tafsir*, *op. cit.*, Vol. VII, p. 375, Ahadith No. 8189, 8190 and 8191.

48. Ibn Hajar Asqalani, Shahabuddin Abul Fazl, *Fath al-Bari*, *op. cit.*, Vol. VII, p. 326.

49. Al-*Ansari*, Abdul Hameed Ismail, *Al-Shura wa Athruha fi al-Dimiqratiyah: Dirasah Muqaranah*, Al-Maktaba al-Fikriyah, Beirut, 1980, p. 141.

50. Shaltoot, Mahmood, *Al-Islam: Aqeedah wa Shariah*, Dar al-Shuruq, Beirut, 1968, p. 460.

51. Huwaidi, Hasan, *Al-Shura fi al-Islam*, *op. cit.*, p. 18.

52. Bablali, Mahmood, *Al-Shura fi al-Islam*, *op. cit.*, p. 18.

53. El-Awa, Mohammad Saleem, *On the Political System of Islamic State*, *op. cit.*, pp. 97-100.

54. Ibn Asākir, *Tarikh Dimasque*, Vol. I, pp. 433-434.

55. Abu Izzah, Abdullah, *Al-Shura am al-Istibdād*, *op. cit.*, p. 24.

56. Huwaidi, Hasan, *Al-Shura fi al-Islam*, *op. cit.*, pp. 13-14.

57. Ibn al-Arabi, Abu Bakr Mohammad bin Abdullah, *Al-Awāsim min al-Qawasim*, ed. Al-Khateeb, Muhibbuddin, al-Matabaah al-Salafiyah, Egypt, 1387 A.H., p. 47.

58. Al-*Ansari*, Abdul Hameed Ismail, *Al-Shura wa Athruha fi al-Dmiqratiyah*, *op. cit.*, p. 149.

59. Ibn al-Arabi, *Al-Awasim min al-Qawasim*, *op. cit.*, p. 46 with reference to Ibn Hanbal, *Musuad*, Vol. 1, Ahadith No. 67, 117, 239; Ibn Kathir, *Al-Bidayah wa al-Nihayah*, *op. cit.*, Vol. VI, p. 312.

60. Al-*Ansari*, Abdul Hameed Ismail, *Al-Shura wa Athruha fi al-Dimiqratiyah, op. cit.*, p. 149.

61. Huwaidi, Hasan, *Al-Shura fi al-Islam, op. cit.*, pp. 16-17.

62. See for detail, Abu Izzah, Abdullah, *Al-Shura am al-Istibdād, op. cit.*, the author has quoted the following sources: *Sahih al-Bukhari bi Sharh al-Kirmani*, Vol. VII, p. 173; *Sahih Muslim bi Sharh al-Navavi*, Cairo, 1929, Vol. I, p. 200; Ibn Hanbal, *Musnad*, ed. Ahmad Mohammad Shakir, Ahadith No. 67, 117, 239, 334, 335; Ibn Athir, *al-Kamil*, Vol. II, p. 143.

63. *The Qur'ān*, 3:144.

64. Islahi, Ameen Ahsan, *Islami Reyasat, op. cit.*, pp. 35-36. The whole discussion is derived from *al-Imamah wa al-Siyasah* of Ibn Qutaibah.

65. Abdur Rahman, Abdul Khaliq, *Al-Shura fi Zill Nizam al-Hukm al-Islami, op. cit.*, p. 102.

66. See for detail, Al-Ghazali, Mohammad, *Al-Islam wa al-Istibdād al-Siyasi, op. cit.*, p. 75; Al-Ahsari, Abdul Hameed Ismail, *Al-Shura wa Athruha fi al-Dimiqratiyah, op. cit.*, p. 153.

67. Bablali, Mahmood, *Al-Shura fi al-Islam, op. cit.*, pp. 101-105.

68. See for detail, Abu Yusuf, Yaqub bin Ibrahim, *Kitab al-Kharaj*, Egypt, 1392 A.H., p. 26; Al-Tamawi, Sulaiman Mohammad, *Umar bin al-Khattab wa Usool al-Siyasah wa al-Idarah al-Hadithah*, Dar al-Fikr al-Arabi, Beirut, 1969, p. 111. El-Awa, Mohammad Saleem, *On the Political System of Islamic State, op. cit.*, p. 116.

69. Abu Izzah Abdullah, *Al-Shura fi al-Islam, op. cit.*, p. 25, The author has quoted Khateeb Baghdadi, *Tarikh Baghdad*, Vol. I, p. 8 in his support and claimed that Umar wanted initially to distribute the land but he changed his opinion when the companions advised him not to do so.

70. Al-Mawardi, Abul Hasan Ali, *Al-Ahkam al-Sultaniyah wa al-Wilāyāt al-Diniyah*, Matbaah Mustafa al-Babi al-Halabi, Egypt, 1966, p. 174.

71. Huwaidi Hasan, *Al-Shura fi al-Islam*, *op. cit.*, p. 18.

72. Al-Tamawi, Sulaiman Mohammad, *Umar bin al-Khattab*, *op. cit.*, pp. 88, 276.

73. Huwaidi Hasan, *Al-Shura fi al-Islam*, *op. cit.*, p. 20.

74. Moosa, Mohd. Yusuf, *Nizam al-Hukm fi al-Islam*, Dar al-Katib al-Arabi, Egypt, 1963, p. 119.

75. Al-Rayyis, Mohammad Ziauddin, *Al-Nazriyat al-Siyasiyah al-Islamiyah*, Dar al-Turath, Egypt, 1976, p. 212.

76. Hilmi, Mahmood, *Nizam al-Hukm al-Islami Muqaranan bi al-Nuzum al-Muasirah*, Dar al-Fikr al-Arabi, Cairo, 1970, p. 80.

77. Al-Qastalani, *Irshad al-Sari*, *op. cit.*, Vol. X, p. 19.

78. Al-Eili, Abdul Hakim Hasan, *Al-Hurriyāt al-Aammah fi al-Fikr wa al-Nizam al-Siyasi fi al-Islam; Dirasah Muqaranah*, Dar al-Fikr al-Arabi, Cairo, 1974, p. 322.

79. *The Qur'ān*, 4:59.

80. Huwaidi Hasan, *Al-Shura fi al-Islam*, *op. cit.*, p 19.

81. Wafi, Ali Abdul Wāhid, *Al-Hurriyah fi al-Islam*, Dar al-Maarif, Egypt, 1968, p. 109.

82. Zaydān, Abdul Karim, *Al-Shura: Al-Khilaf bain Rayees al-Dawlah wa Ahl al-Shura*, Majallah *Al-Mujtama*, Kuwait, No. 47, Feb. 1971, p. 12.

83. Wafi, Ali Abdul Wāhid, *Al-Hurriyah fi al-Islam*, *op. cit.*, p. 109.

84. Bablali, Mahmood, *Al-Shura fi al-Islam*, *op. cit.*, p. 88.

85. Abu Izzah, Abdullah, *Al-Shura am al-Istibdād*, *op. cit.*, p. 14.

86. Bablali, Mahmood, *Al-Shura fi al-Islam*, *op. cit.*, p. 88.

87. Al-Aqqad, Abbas, Mahmood, *Al-Dimiqratiyah fi al-Islam*, Dar al-Maarif, Egypt, 1971, p. 78.

88. Zaydan, Abdul Karim, *Al-Shura: Al-Khilaf bain Rayees al-Dawlah wa Ahl al-Shura*, *op. cit.*, p. 12.

89. For example see the following verses of the *Qur'ān*: 12: 38, 21, 40; 40: 59; 10: 36; 6: 111, 116; 5: 106; 38: 24.

90. Mahmood Mustafa, *Al-Marxiyah wa al-Islam*, Dar al-Maarif, Egypt, 1975, p. 22; Al-Aqqad, Abbas Mahmood, *al-Dimiqratiyyah fi al-Islam*, *op. cit.*, p. 82; Shalbi, Ahmad, *Al-Islam wa al-Waye al-Siyasi*, A lecture in Umm Darman University, Sudan, Dar al-Maarif, Egypt, 1974, p. 35; Jamal, Ahmad Mahmood, *Ala Maidah al-Qur'ān: Din wa Dawlah*, Dar al-Kitab al-Labnani, Beirut, 1393 A.H., p. 319; Jareeshah, Ali Mohammad, *Al-Mashruyiah al-Islamiyah al-Ulyah*, Maktaba Wahbah, Egypt, 1975, p. 256.

91. Abu Zayd, *Al-Shura: Aa Hiya Asas li Tanzeem al-Mujtama al-Islami am Hilyah Yumkin al-Istighna anha*, *op. cit.*, p. 5.

92. Ibn Taimiyah, Abul Abbas Taqiuddin Ahmad, *Al-Siyasah al-Sharyiah fi Islah al Raee wa al-Rayiyah*, Dar al-Sha'b, Egypt, 1971, p. 182.

93. Al-*Ansar*i, Abdul Hameed Ismail, *Al-Shura wa Athruha fi al-Dimiqratiyah*, *op. cit.*, pp. 166-167; Maududi, Abul Ala, *Islami Riyasat*, Lahore, 1987, pp. 456-457.

94. Islahi, Ameen Ahsan, *Islami Riyasat, Anjuman Khuddam al-Qur'ān*, Lahore, 1977, p. 33.

95. Abu Zahrah, Mohammad, *Al-Mujtama al-Insani fi Zill al-Islam*, Dar al-Fikr, Beirut, 1970, p. 162.

96. Abu Izzah, Abdullah, *Al-Shura am al-Istibdād*, *op. cit.*, p. 14.

97. Al-Fanjari, Ahmad Shauqi, *Al-Hurriyah al-Siyasiyah fi al-Islam*, Dar al-Qalam, Kuwait, 1973, p. 209.

98. Ibrahim, Mohammad, *Al-Shura fi al-Islam: Tatbeeq li Hurriyah al-Rae wa Ilzam al-Hakim wa al-Mahkum*, *Al-Ahram*, Cairo, dated 3.6.1977.

99. Rida, Rashid, *Tafsir al-Qur'ān al-Karim (Tafsir al-Manar) op. cit.*, Vol. IV, p. 201.

100. Abu Izzah, Abdullah, *Al-Shura am al-Istibdād*, *op. cit.*, *Al-Mujtama*, December, 1970.

101. For a detailed study of public involvement in all the social and communal affairs during the rule of Umayyads and Abbasids, See: Munis, Husain, Dr., *Alam al-Islam*, Dar al-Maarif, Egypt, 1973, pp. 104, 209, 516.

102. Al-Rayyis, Mohammad Ziauddin, *Al-Nazriyat al-Siyasiyah al-Islamiyah*, *op. cit.*, p. 250.

103. Ghazali, Abu Mohammad, Hamid, *Al-Radd ala al-Batiniyyah*, Leiden, 1916, p. 63.

104. Ibn Taimiyah, *Minhaj al-Sunnah*, Vol. I, p. 141.

105. Al-Mawardi, *Al-Ahkam al-Sultaniyah*, *op. cit.*, p. 98.

106. Al-Rayyis, M.Z., *Al-Nazriyat al-Siyasiyah al-Islamiyah*, *op. cit.*, p. 368.

107. Al-Sāih, Abdul Hamid, *Hal li al-Akhz bi Rae al-Aktahriyah Asas fi al-Islam*, *Majallah al-Waye al-Islami*, Kuwait, No. 25, April, 1967, p. 60.

108. Abdul Rahman, Abdul Khalique, *Al-Shura fi Zill Nizam al-Hukm al-Islami*, *op. cit.*, p. 104.

109. Al-Arabi, Mohammad Abdullah, *Al-Tanzim al-Hadith li al-Dawlah al-Islamiyah bain al-Shariyah wa al-Qanun*, Dar al-Maarif, Egypt, 1974, p. 4.

110. Abdul Rahman Abdul Khaliq (*Al-Shura fi Zill Nizam al-Hukm al-Islami*, p. 106) has said to the effect that undesired majority referred to in the texts of Hadith are related to pagans and unbelievers because the Muslim *Ummah* as a whole has been declared innocent.

111. Asad, Muhammad, *The Principles of State and Government in Islam*, Dar al-Andalus, Gibraltar, 1961, pp. 49-50.

112. *Ibid.*, p. 50.

113. *The Qur'ān*, 3: 159; 42: 38.

114. "And consult them in affairs, then when you has taken a decision put your trust in Allah."

115. Al-Jamal, Mohammad, Abdul Munim, *Al-Tafsir al-Farid li al-Qur'ān al-Majeed*, Dar al-Kutub al-Jadeed, Egypt, Vol. I, p. 450; Hijazi, Mohammad Mahmood, *Al-Tafsir al-Wāzih*, 1972, Vol. 4, p. 43.

116. Rida, Rashid, *Tafsir al-Manar*, *op. cit.*, Vol. 4, p. 205.

117. Al-Munajji, Jalal Mohammad, *Al-Islam wa al-Shura*, Al-Majlis al-Aala li Shuwoon al-Islamiyah, Egypt, 1970, p. 48.

118. Shaykh al-Ghazali, from his commentary on Mutawalli.

119. Maududi, Abul Aala, *Tafhim al-Qur'ān*, Delhi, 1973, Vol. 4, p. 510.

120. Ibn Kathir, *Tafsir al-Qur'ān al-Azeem*, *op. cit.*, Vol. I, p. 420; Suyuti, *Al-Durr al-Manthur*, *op. cit.*, Vol. 2, p. 90.

121. Al-Baihaqi, *Al-Sunan al-Kubra*, *op. cit.*, Vol. 10, p. 112.

122. Ibn Kathir, *Tafsir al-Qur'ān al-Azeem*, *op. cit.*, Vol. 1, p. 42; Ibn Hajar Al-Asqalani, *Fath al-Bari*, *op. cit.*, Vol. 17, p. 103.

123. Al-Albani, *Silsilah al-Ahadith al-Zaeefah*, Hadith No. 4855.

124. Ibn Hazm, *Al-Ihkam fi Usool al-Ahkam*, *op. cit.*, p. 771.

125. The author while editing Tafsir Ibn Kathir (*Umdah al-Tafsir*, Dar al-Maarif, Egypt, 1957, Vol. III, p. 64) had delited this hadith from the text and did not make any indication in the foot-notes too. It means that the hadith under discussion is not authentic to him.

126. Al-Baihaqi, *al-Sunan al-Kubra, op. cit.*, Vol. X, p. 114.

127. In its narrators there is Shahr bin Haushab who is deemed to be *dhaeef.*

128. Abdul Rahman Abdul Khaliq, *Al-Shura fi Zill Nizam al-Hukm al-Islami, op. cit.*, p. 106.

129. This dream is narrated by Imam Ahmad and is authentic. See: Ibn Hajar Asqalani, *Fath al-Bari, op. cit.*, Vol. 8, p. 348; Ibn Kathir, *al-Bidayah wa al-Nihayah*, Maktabah al-Maarif, Beirut, 1966, Vol. 3, p. 12; Al-Saghani, Abu Bakr Abdul Razzaq b. Humam, *Al-Musannaf*, ed. Habibul Rahman Azmi, Al-Maktab al-Islami, Beirut, 1972, Vol. 5, p. 364.

130. See for detail, Ibn Hajar Asqalani, *Fath al-Bari, op. cit.*, Vol. 8, p. 238; Ibn Kathir, *al-Bidayah wa al-Nihayah, op. cit.*, Vol. 3, pp. 11-13; Al-Saghani, *Al-Musannaf, op. cit.*, Vol. 5, p. 364; Ibn Kathir, *Tafsir al-Qur'ān al-Azeem, op. cit.*, Vol. 1, p. 399.

131. Kamil, Abdul Aziz, *Al-Islam wa al-Asr*, Dar al-Maarif, Beirut, 1972, p. 97.

132. Ibrahim Mohammad (ed.), *Al-Shura fi al-Islam: Tatbiq li Hurriyah al-Rae wa Ilzam al-Hakim wa al-Mahkum, op. cit.*, *Al-Ahram*, 3 June 1977.

133. See his commentary on Mutawalli.

134. Al-Fanjari, Ahmad Shauqi, *Al-Hurriyah al-Siyasiyah fi al-Islam, op. cit.*, p. 213.

135. Al-Jassas, Abu Bakr, *Ahkam al-Qur'ān*, Egypt, 1378 A.H., Vol. 11, p. 49.

136. Islahi, Ameen Ahsan *Islami Riyasat, op. cit.*, pp. 23-24.

137. Huwaidi, Hasan, *Al-Shura fi al-Islam, op. cit.*, pp. 7-13.

138. Zaydan, Abdul Karim, *Al-Shura: Al-Khilaf bain Rayis al-Dawlah wa Ahl-Shura, op. cit.*, p. 13.

139. Abu Izzah, Abdullah, *Al-Shura am al-Istibdād*, *op. cit.*, p. 13.

140. Bablali, Mahmood, *Al-Shura fi al-Islam*, *op. cit.*, p. 64; Huwaidi, Hasan, *Al-Shura fi al-Islam*, *op. cit.*, p. 13.

141. Rida, Rashid, *Tafsir al-Manar*, *op. cit.*, Vol. IV, p. 209.

142. Huwaidi Hasan, *Al-Shura fi al-Islam*, *op. cit.*, p. 13.

143. Al-*Ansari*, Abdul Hameed, *Al-Shura wa Athruha fi al-Dimiqratiyah*, *op. cit.*, p. 204.

144. Islahi, Ameen Ahsan *Islami Riyasat*, *op. cit.*, p. 33.

145. Ibrahim, Mohammad, *Al-Ahram*, 3, June 1977.

146. Audah, Abdul Qadir, *Al-Islam wa Awdauna al-Siyasiyah*, Beirut, 1967, p. 162.

147. Maududi, Abul Aala, *Islami Riyasat*, Lahore, 1987, p. 646.

148. Commentary of al-Ghazali on Mutawalli's book *Mabda al-Shura fi al-Islam*.

149. Al-Ghazali, Mohammad, *Al-Rahmah wa al-Shura, Majallah Liwa al-Islam*, Egypt, Vol. 28, No. 7, April, 1974, p. 47.

150. Quoted from Al-Fanjari, Ahmad Shauqi, *Al-Hurriyah al-Siyasiyah fi al-Islam*, *op. cit.*, p. 213.

151. Bablali, Mahmood, *Al-Shura fi al-Islam*, *op. cit.*, p. 58.

152. Mutawalli, Abdul Hameed, *Mabda al-Shura fi al-Islam*, *op. cit.*, p. 52.

153. Zaydan, Abdul Karim, *Al-Shura: Al-Khilaf bain Rayees al-Dawlah wa Ahl al-Shura*, *op. cit.*, p. 13.

154. Al-Jassas, Abu Bakr, *Ahkam al-Qur'ān*, *op. cit.*, Vol. 2, p. 41.

155. Makhloof, Hasnayn, ed. Ibrahim, Mohammad, *Al-Ahram*, 3, June, 1977.

156. Islahi, Ameen Ahsan, *Islami Riyasat*, *op. cit.*, p. 33.

157. Abu Izzah, Abdullah, *Al-Shura am al-Istibdād*, *op. cit.*, p. 14; Islahi, Ameen Ahsan, *Islami Riyasat*, *op. cit.*, p. 33.

158. Abu Izzah, Abdullah, *Al-Shura am al-Istibdād*, *op. cit.*, p. 15.

159. Ibn Hazm, *Al-Ihkam fi Usool al-Ahkam*, *op. cit.*, pp. 545-546.

160. Al-Suyuti, *Al-Durr al-Manthur*, *op. cit.*, Vol. 2, p. 62; Al-Mubarakpuri, Mohammad Abdur Rahman, *Tuhfah al-Ahwazi bi Sharh Jame al-Tirmizi*, ed. Abdur Rahman Mohd. Uthman, Al-Maktabah al-Salafiyah, Madinah Munawwarah, 1964, Vol. VI, p. 283.

161. Ibn Hazm, *Al-Ihkam fi Usool al-Ahkam*, *op. cit.*, p. 545. The author has declared it as *dhaeef*.

162. Mubarakpuri, Mohd. Abdur Rahman, *Tuhfah al-Ahwazi*, *op. cit.*, Vol. VI, p. 386.

163. *Ibid*, p. 387.

164. Al-Bari, Zakariya, *Usool al-Fiqh al-Islami*, 1971, Vol. 1, p. 70.

165. Maududi, Abul Aala, *Islami Riyasat*, *op. cit.*, p. 459.

166. Ibn Taimiyah, *Al-Fataawa*, Vol. 1, p. 406.

167. Maududi, Abul Aala, *Islami Riyasat*, *op. cit.*, pp. 460-461.

168. Al-Bari, Zakariya, *Usool al-Fiqh al-Islami*, 1971, Vol. 1, p. 70.

169. *Ibid*, p. 75.

170. Maududi, Abul Aala, *Islami Riyasat*, *op. cit.*, p. 459.

171. Imam Shafii, *Al-RiSalah*, ed. Shakir, Ahmad Mohammad, p. 534. Quoted from Al-Bari, *Usool al-Fiqh al-Islami*, *op. cit.*, Vol. 1, p. 80.

172. *Ibid*, p. 81. It does not mean that Imam Ahmad bin Hanbal had rejected the possibility of *Ijma*. He infact, refused to accept the claim of one who asserts without any evidence

that whatever he holds constitutes *Ijma*. See: Maududi, Abul Aala, *Islami Riyasat*, *op. cit.*, p. 460.

173. Al-Bari, Zakariya, *Usool al-Fiqh al-Islami*, *op. cit.*, p. 77.

174. Shaltoot, Mahmood, *Al-Islam: Aqidah wa Shariah*, Dar al-Sharuq, Egypt, 1968, p. 566.

175. Siddiq, syed Mohammad, *Husul al-Mamul min Ilm al-Usool*, Quoted from al-Bari, Zakaria, *Usool al-Fiqh al-Islami*, *op. cit.*, p. 63.

176. Khallaf, Abdul Wahab, *Ilm Usool al-Fiqh*, Cairo, 1956, pp. 54-55.

177. Al-*Ansar*i, Abdul Hameed Ismail, *Al-Shura wa Athruha fi al-Dimiqratiyah*, *op. cit.*, pp. 214-215.

178. Madkur, Mohammad Salam, *Al-Ijma fi al-Tashr'ee al-Islami*, *Majallah Al-Waye al-Islami*, Kuwait, No. 127, July, 1975, p. 19.

179. Rizwan, Fathi, *Al-Islam wa Mushkilat al-Fikr*, Dar al-Maarif, Egypt, p. 176.

180. Quoted from *Al-Ijtihad fi al-Islam*, p. 26; See: Mutawalli, Abdul Hamid, *Azimmah al-Fikr al-Siyasi al-Islami fi al-Asr al-Hadith*, Al-Maktab al-Misri al-Hadith, Alxandria, 1970, p. 130. The author has quoted shalbi, *Al-Madkhal fi al-Tareef bi al-Fiqh al-Islami*, 1959, p. 168, to prove that the scholars claim the *Ijma* which infact constitutes the majority.

181. See for example: *The Qur'ān*, 42: 38; 3: 159; 4: 59; 33: 36.

182. Al-Bari, Zakariya, *Usool al-Fiqh al-Islami*, *op. cit.*, p. 83.

183. Madkur, Mohammad Salam, *Al-Ijma fi al-Tashree al-Islami*, *op. cit.*, p. 19.

184. Abdul Rahman, Abdul Khaliq, *Al-Shura fi Zill Nizam al-Hukm al-Islami*, *op. cit.*, p. 107.

185. Islahi, Ameen Ahsan, Islami Riyasat, *op. cit.*, pp. 32-33.

186. Abdul Rahman, Abdul Khaliq, *Al-Shura fi Zill Nizam al-Hukm al-Islami*, *op. cit.*, p. 107.

187. See for detail, Asad, Muhammad, *The Principles of State and Government in Islam*, *op. cit.*, pp. 30-50.

188. Mutawalli, Abdul Hameed, *Mabda al-Shura fi al-Islam*, *op. cit.*, p. 17; Mutawalli, Abdul Hameed, *Mabadi Nizam al-Hukm fi al-Islam ma al-Maqaranah bi al-Mabadi al-Dasturiyah al-Hadithah*, Manshaah al-Maarif, Alaxandria, 1966, p. 670.

189. It will not be appropriate to mean that the ruler cannot be delegated special powers even in abnormal situation and times of war and political disestablishment. Al-Ansari, Abdul Hameed Ismail, *Al-Shura wa Athruha fi al-Dimiqratiyah*, *op. cit.*, p. 221.

190. Umri, Syed Jalaluddin Ansar, *Islam ka Shurai Nizam*, Lahore, 1983, pp. 22-23, 140-143.

*****

4

SHURA: ELECTION AND ORGANIZATION

How does *Shura* Emerge?

The *Qur'ān*[1] states clearly that in all political and religious matters regarding which no guidance can be obtained from the revelations of Allah (SWT) or *Sunnah* of the Prophet (SAW) should be settled by the *amir* after holding consultations with *Ahl al hall wa al-aqd* (people at the helm of affairs). However, the question arises as to who are the people to be consulted according to the *Qur'ān* – all the *Sahabah* or a specific group of people or a few experienced persons? To answer this question a detailed study of the system of the *Shura* during the prophethood of Muhammad (SAW) and in the period of the Four Guided Caliphs has to be undertaken, since none of the authentic traditions provides any guidance in this respect.[2]

As far as the Prophet (SAW) himself is concerned, he consulted all the *Sahabah* concerning matters of general interest. On the issue of the sharing of booty obtained from Havazin, he tried to elicit the opinion not merely of the eminent *Sahabah* but of all the participants in the battle. On the occasion of the Battle of Uhud, he sought the advice of all the *Sahabah.* He talked to the *Ansar* and the *Muhajirs* both about the Battle of Badr, who, together comprised the *Ummah.* It is true that he consulted only Saad bin Ubadah and Saad bin Muaz on the peace pact with the Ghatfan tribe.

A similar practice was followed by the Guided Caliphs. Caliph Abu Bakr discussed the issues of war against Rome and Persia with all the Muslims, while his successor deemed it necessary to consult all the *Sahabah* on the selection of governors, distribution of lands of conquered territories and delegation of the powers of the caliphate. After the death of Umar, Abdur Rahman bin Auf sought the opinion of all the Muslims, including women, before deciding whether to nominate Uthman or Ali as caliph.

During the caliphate of Umar, there was a *Shura* of the eminent *Sahabah* apart from that of the general body of Muslims in which every Muslim could participate and give his opinion without any let or hindrance. Muslims of conquered territories were consulted in the matter of running their administration.

Details of the system of the *Shura* that prevailed during the prophethood of Muhammad (SAW) and the period of the Four Guided Caliphs show that during these periods the *Shura* comprised the eminent *Sahabah* who represented the entire body of Muslims and enjoyed their full confidence. In the beginning the *Shura* comprised the early adherents of Islam while after Hijrah, the *Ansar* were included in it.

During the period of the Guided Caliphs, two important elements were added to the *Shura.* The first of these consisted of those who had performed glorious services in the propagation of Islam and in the field of administration while the second new element included those who were recognized by the people as well-versed in *fiqh* (Muslim

Jurisprudence) and as scholarly persons endowed with insight. These people were consulted in the day-to-day affairs of the state while the opinion of all the Muslims was elicited on matter concerning the entire *Ummah*.

Three Categories

Hence there were three categories of *Shura* during the period of the Guided Caliphs:

1. The *Shura* of experienced people and experts in various fields who were consulted on purely administrative and technical issues.
2. The *Shura* of the representatives of Muslims and eminent *Sahabah* whose advice was sought in general matters related to *Shariah*. These were the people who constituted what was known as the real *Shura*.
3. The *Shura* of the common people of the *Ummah* eliciting of whose opinion was deemed necessary in administrative matters of common interest like the appointment of officers and governors, declaration of war etc.[3]

The question arises as to what the manner of the selection of the members of the *Shura* during the prophethood of Muhammad (SAW) and the period of the Guided Caliphs was; whether they were elected by the people or were nominated by the Prophet (SAW) or the Caliph himself. The truth is that during this period members of the *Shura* were neither elected according to modern terminology nor were they nominated. Such persons emerged naturally from amongst the *Ummah*. Syed Abul Ala Maududi rightly says:[4]

Natural Representation

Islam rose in Makkah as a movement. It is the common characteristic of a movement that those who are the first to come forward to respond to its call become the mainstay and advisers of its leader. Hence those who were the first adherents of the Muslim faith were naturally deemed to be the comrades and advisers of the Prophet (SAW) whom he consulted in every matter in which he had not received any command from Allah (SWT) directly. Thus, as new people started being added to this movement and its conflict with forces opposed to its was intensified, there emerged those who achieved prominence among the *Ummah* due to their services, sacrifices, insight and wisdom. They were selected not through voting but as a result of their experience and ordeals, which is a more correct and natural process of selection. After this came the incident of *Hijrah*. This followed the fact that about one and a half year earlier some influential people of Madinah had embraced Islam and due to their influence the religion had reached every single home in the tribes of Aus and Khazraj. It was on their invitation that the Prophet (SAW) and other *Muhajirs* left their homes and shifted to Madinah where the Islamic movement assumed the form of a political system and that of a state. So it was only natural that those under whose influence Islam had spread and went on to spreading assumed the leadership of the local population in the new social and political system and it is because of this status of theirs that in the *Shura* of Prophet Muhammad (SAW) a third element (that of the *Ansar*) was included, alongside the early adherents of the faith and tested and tried *Muhajirs*. These people were also selected through the natural process of selection and were such trustworthy persons of the Muslim tribes that had elections been held according to the modern methods, even then it is these people who would have been elected. Thus in the society of Madinah two kinds of people started becoming prominent. First, there were those who had rendered meritorious services for eight to ten years in political, military and proselytizing campaigns so that people started looking up to them on every important issue. In the second category there were people who achieved eminence due to their understanding of and insight into the *fiqhi* (religio-legal) aspects of the *Qur'ān* so that as regards their knowledge in religious matters they were considered next only to the Prophet (SAW). And even the Prophet (SAW) had awarded the certificate of reliability to them by asking people to learn about the *Qur'ān* from such and such person and to resort to such and such person to resolve such and such problem. These two elements also went on being included in the *Shura* through the method of natural selection and no voting was required for their inclusion in the *Shura*. Even if voting had taken place there was none except for these persons who would have been favoured with election by the Muslims. In such a situation there was no need for a formal election.

According to Mohammad Asad, the Arab society had not been able to emancipate itself from tribal ways of life, though Islam had eradicated distinctions between tribes and clans to a great extent and had unified the people with the ties of faith in Islamic universalism. However, he adds, in spite of this, the society was not entirely bereft of the remnants of tribalism, and heads of tribes and clans had full authority to represent their people. He avers that even if general elections would have been held, the same people would have been elected, in which situation, he says there was no need for such elections.[5]

Amin Ahsan Islahi considered members of the *Shura* during the period of the Prophet (SAW) and of the Guided Caliphs as persons who were reliable and worthy of being resorted to. According to him, even though these men of affairs were not elected as representatives of the community in the modern political sense since the present day method of election and not been known at that time, they were the trusted representatives of their respective groups. He adds that one proof of their enjoying the trust of people of their respective groups was that they were resorted to in dealing with the problem faced by the groups. He says that some members of the *Shura* occupied an eminent position among the Muslims owing their insight into religion, like Abu Bakr and Umar who were recognized leaders of the *Muhajirs* and were unexampled in their religious insight and political sagacity while Saad bin Muaz and Saad bin Ubadah were leaders of the Aus and Khazraj tribes. Uthman; Abdur Rahman bin Auf, and Ali were leaders of Banu Umayyah, Banu Zuhra and Banu Hashim respectively and Maaz bin Jabal, Ubai bin Kaab and Zaid bin Thabit were experts in the learning of the *Qur'ān* ad the *fiqh*.[6]

The first objection that has been made regarding the above mentioned thinking is that the *Qur'ān* does not make it clear as to who ought to be members of *Shura*. The edict regarding consultations is couched in such general terms that it embraces the entire *Ummah*. The *Qur'ān* does not deal in detail with constitutional and legal matters or general public affairs. This shows that Muslims have been left free to evolve their own system of *Shura* according to changing conditions and demands of the time and to lay down the qualities and merits they deem necessary for the membership of the *Shura*.[7]

Bases of the Composition

It is true that the *Qur'ān* has not laid down the principles or the framework of the *Shura*, but *Sunnah*, has supplemented and elucidated the Holy *Qur'ān* in this respect and has given it a concrete practical shape. The Prophet (SAW) has not only specified the qualities and merits needed for the membership of the *Shura* but has also put before his followers an example of the manner of their selection, which can be implemented in site of changes in the social and cultural ethos. According to the *Sunnah* members of the *Shura* ought to be true representatives of the people, they should enjoy full confidence of the *Ummah* and liked by it. Confidence reposed by the *Ummah* in them may be due to their skill in dealing with religious and political affairs or because of services rendered by them in *jihads* or by virtue of their moral qualities, intellectual achievements or because of earning fame for insight into *fiqh*. In short, only those persons could be members of the *Shura* who had won the trust and confidence of the people.

It is often said that while the Prophet (SAW) asked all the Muslims to advice him, the people whom he actually consulted were the selected *Sahabah* who were considered by him capable of giving sound advice. These *Sahabah* have been referred to in historical records as *Ahl al hall wa al-aqd.*[8]

Every person was not worthy of being consulted and hence all Muslims were not included in the *Shura*. This state of affairs is confirmed by the historical fact that in the matter of the selection of the caliph, Abu Bakr consulted with the prominent Companions of Madinah. This makes clear that Muslims who were not present in Madinah played no role in the selection of Umar as Caliph, nor were they consulted in the matter. So it would he wrong to say that *Ahl al hall wa al-aqd* comprised the entire body of Muslims.

In view of the above, it is clear that there were the following four bases of the composition of the *Shura*.

1. The *Shura* did not include all the Muslims. However, its members were the natural representatives of the *Ummah*. They enjoyed the trust and confidence of the common people and were popular among them. These selected people who represented the common Muslims in

the *Shura* were consulted as it was not possible or practicable to consult all the Muslims on every issue. Hence, their leaders and elders were called for consultations whenever necessary. And since these members of the *Shura* expressed the feelings of their respective communities, tribes and clans and represented them in every way it may be said that the advice rendered by them truly reflected the will of the *Ummah*.[9]

2. History records that in matters of general and those of all-embracing nature, consultation was undertaken not merely with the representatives and leaders of various groups but every Muslim was given the right to express his opinion and to take part in the discussion. A glaring example of this is the issue of the prisoners of Hawazin in which, after renouncing his own claim, the Prophet (SAW) did not rest satisfied with seeking the advice of the eminent people of the *Ummah* but placed the matter before all the Muslims so as to remove all possible apprehensions. In the same way, every Muslim had the right to express his preference in the matter of the selection of a caliph through the institution of (*bayah*) the oath of allegiance. Abdur Rahman bin Auf even asked travelers coming to Madinah from outside whom they wanted to be the caliph.[10]

3. Muslims living outside Madinah conveyed their choice of the caliph through their representatives since it was not possible to elicit the views of every Muslim in view of great distances and inadequate means of transport and communication. Hence, consultations in the matter had to be confined to people living in the capital. Madinah was the capital of the caliphate and opinions expressed and decisions taken there were taken as those of the whole body of *Ummah*.

In this context Abul Ala Maududi says that the Islamic state was not a national one, since it had come into existence after the propagation of an ideology there had revolutionized the thinking and ethics of the people, as in result of which a new society was created which was based on new social and ethical principles, which, in its turn, resulted in the establishment of a new kind of state which was based on these principles. He adds that in such a state the person who had initiated the revolution naturally became the most trusted one, and after him people reposed their faith in those who were the mainstay of the initiator of the revolution and their leadership was a natural one since none else could be the repository of the trust of the people. In the opinion of Maududi, it was because of this that, in spite of there being complete freedom of criticism from no corner of Arabia did any voice arise asking why only the people of Madinah had monopolished the management of the affairs of the state. He adds that in the conditions prevailing in that period it was simply impossible to hold general elections in the whole of the Islamic state which stretched from Afghanistan to North Africa and it was also not possible for members of the *Shura* to assemble from distant lands for participating in its usual and extraordinary sessions.[11] However, Shaikh Mohammad Abu Zahra writes that people of conquered countries were consulted in running the administration of their respective territories,[12] while Dr. Ibrahim Ahmad al-Adavi says that during the rule of the guided Caliphs, all tribal leaders who came to Madinah participated in the meetings of the *Shura*.[13]

4. In view of the above it may be averred that when the Prophet (SAW) said, "O my people come and advise me" his words were not addressed to some particular *Sahabah* but to all Muslims. And, the issues mentioned above were not of a technical nature, requiring particular expertise and experience, not were the people called upon to give arguments for or against a proposition, but there was a kind of referendum on these issues which was conducted to elicit the opinion and the will of the general body of

Muslims. It is also true that in certain matters the Prophet (SAW) consulted some particular *Sahabah* though, as mentioned above, he is reported to have said, "O my people, come and advise me." Shaikh Mohammad Abu Zahra has written that during the reign of Caliph Umar every Muslim, without any exception, could participate in the meetings of the *Shura*.[14] Almustashar Ali Ali Mansoor has reached the conclusion that during the period of the Prophet (SAW) and the Guided Caliphs the category of people consulted depended upon the issues in hand. If these were of a general nature all the Muslims were consulted and decisions were taken in accordance with the views of the majority, and in case this was not possible it was deemed necessary to elicit the opinion of *Ahl al-hall wa al-aqd* who would have been the representatives of the people or members of parliament in a modern democracy.[15]

Another point that has been raised in this connection is that during the period of the Prophet (SAW) and that of the Guided Caliphs there was no legislative body in the modern sense of the term, having a specified number of members who fulfilled specific conditions, with special qualities and experience expertise. According to those who hold this opinion, those who comprised the *Shura* during the early period of Islam did not constitute a specific assembly but were merely the *Sahabah* or members of some families or their friends and that there were some prominent *Sahabah* and those whose opinions carried weight whose judgements were preferred to those of others.[16]

The fact, however, is that during this period there was a specific group of eminent *Sahabah* who were commonly known as members of the *Shura*. The existence of the *Shura* during the period of the Prophet (SAW) and the Guided Caliphs does not mean that there was a legislative assembly in the modern sense of the term with members having specific qualities and experience.[17] It does not matter whether or not such a selected group of people was called an assembly since its members were popular representatives of the community, enjoying a high social standing whose opinion was elicited on important issues. So it would be wrong to assert that they comprised members or friends of the family of the Caliph, since they owed their position due to not their family relationship or friendship but to their merits, capacities and distinguished services to the *Ummah*.

Ahl al-Hall wa al-Aqd

Nominations to the *Shura* were not left to the likes or dislikes of the caliph. In the period of the Guided Caliphs the *Shura* was an institution through which *Ahl al-hall wa al-aqd* of the state played a decision making role. Nothing was stated in black and white regarding the composition of the *Shura* but both the rulers and the ruled knew what it was. In this connection Abul Ala Maududi says that *Ahl al-hall wa al-aqd* of the state in the period were a number of specific persons who had been occupying such a position from earlier times and were people who had the right to take decisions in matters concerning the *Ummah*, and so according to him, there is no ground for thinking that the caliph could call any one at any time for advice and that no one knew who *ahl al-hall wa al-aqd* (the people managing the affairs of the state) or members of the *Shura* were who enjoyed the right to take decisions on issues concerning the community.[18] After studying the composition and manner of the selection of the *Shura* in the period of the Prophet (SAW) and of the Four Rightly Guided Caliphs it is worthwhile turning to the vast and rich literature of *fiqh* in order to examine the opinions of different *faqihs* (experts in Islamic Jurisprudence) on this important subject.

Defining the Other Titles

The *Qur'ān* mentions the expression Ulul amr in several places[19] while in the *fiqh* literature there exist expressions like Ahl al-*Shura*, *Ahl al-hall wa al-aqd*, *Ahl al-ijtihad* and *Ahl al-ikhtiar*. The question arises whether these five expressions cannote the same thing or whether there is any difference in their meanings. The expression *Ahl al-Shura* was well-known and commonly used during the period of the prophethood of Mohammad (SAW) and that of the Guided Caliphs. The expression became even better known during the caliphate of Umar since he gave a definite shape to the *Shura*. After the period of the Guided Caliphs the term was replaced by *Ahl al-hall wa al-aqd*, *Ahl al-ijtihad* and *Ahl al-ikhtiar*. It can not be said with any definiteness when and by whom this expression *Ahl al-hall wa al-aqd* was first used.[20] In this context the first work is Abul Hasan al Mawardi's *al-Ahkam al-Sultaniyah*. From the utterances of this author, researchers have come to the conclusion that *Ahl al-ikhtiar* who performed the function of the selection and appointment of the caliph were also the *Ahl al-hall wa al-aqd*.[21] In this respect, Mawardi follows his contemporary Qazi Abu Yala and adds that *Ahl al-ikhtiar* were also called *Ahl al-ijtihad*.[22]

Later, in the seventh century A.H., Imam Nawawi, the Shafi'ite *faqih* said that the *Ahl al-hall wa al-aqd* who elected the caliph comprised the *Ulama*, the tribal heads and representatives of the common people who had the requisite qualifications of a witness in a court of law, namely, that they should be Muslims, free, who bear the *Shariah* obligations, and articulate etc.[23]

In his book entitled Usool al-Din Imam Baghdadi equates *Ahl al-ikhtiar* with *Ahl al-ijtihad*,[24] while the Hanafite *faqihs* say that once the nobles have taken their oath of allegiance for a person, his caliphate is confirmed.[25]

From the above paragraphs it can be concluded that there is no difference in the meaning of terms like *Ahl al-hall wa al-aqd*, *Ahl al-ijtihad* and *Ahl al-ikhtiar* and that these terms may be used interchangeably. However, the question that remains unanswered is what these terms denote as regards the composition of the *Shura*. For example, Dr. Abdul Munim al Bahi asks what Imam Nawawi means by the term *Rusa*, whether it refers to a particular group or to all the leaders of the representatives of people, and what the expression 'representatives of the people' means, whether it refers to the wealthy and influential people or prominent individuals who represented the common people.[26]

Shaikh Ahmad al Fazili asks what Imam Nawawi means by the word *Ulama* and to which *Ilm* (field of learning) it refers to; the *Ilm* that helps one to identify a person who deserves to be an *imam* or caliph or one which produces in a person the capacity for *ijtihad* or a person who has the knowledge of the rules of *Shariah* without being capable of doing ijtihad.[27] So, he asks, why Imam Baghdadi says that the *Ahl al-hall wa al-aqd* are the *Ahl al-ijtihad*. He further asks if Baghdadi refers to the *imams* who have attainted the status of *mujtahids* or to those who had special expertise for selecting a suitable caliph from among a number of candidates for the position.

Answering the questions raised by himself, Dr. Al-Bahi says that if by the term *Ahl al-hall wa al-aqd* Imam Nawawi refers to a specific group of nobles, it means that the *Shura* comprised this particular group and people dealing with political and social affairs were not eligible to be it's members. Such an interpretation of the words of Al-Qalansi, the teacher of Shaikh Baghdadi, has not been given by any other authority nor has any other *faqih* supported it. And if Baghdadi has equated *Ahl al-hall wa al-aqd* with *Ahl al-Ijtihad*, the matter had become more complicated, instead of being made clear.[28] Similarly, *Faqihs* of the Hanafite school have not clarified what they mean by *Ashraaf*.[29] However, Imam Mawardi and Qazi Abu Yala al-Farra have said that members of the *Shura* should fulfil the following three conditions[30]:

1. Adalah, abstinence from cardinal sins and avoidance of minor ones.

2. *Ilm*, learning, which should enable him to identify those deserving the caliphate and to be aware of the qualities and qualifications needed by a caliph. This means that, according to these *faqih*, members of the *Shura* need not possess requisite scholarship to be able to do *ijtihad*.

3. Sagacity and insight to select the best person for caliphate.

Though the above-mentioned stipulations are rather general, they can, to a certain degree, help in selecting those who are eligible to be members of the *Shura*, whether they are found among the *Ulama* or those concerned with political affairs or among the common Muslims.

The following conclusions may be drawn from the above discussion:

1. Political thinkers mean the same thing by the terms *Ahl al-Shura*, *Ahl al-hall wa al-aqd*, *Ahl al-ikhtiar* and *Ahl al-ijtihad*.

2. According to scholars of the *Shariah*, the term *Ahl al-hall wa al-aqd* refers to leaders of the people and respectable persons who were experienced and were well-known for their grasp of political affairs and had earned the confidence and goodwill of the people.

3. Experts in the principles of Islamic jurisprudence and political thinkers given two different interpretations of the

term *Ahl al-hall wa al-aqd.* While the latter consider knowledge of social and political conditions all that was necessary to entitle a person to the membership of the *Shura*, since, according to them, this was enough to enable him to make the correct choice of a caliph, in the opinion of the former *Ulama*, it was essential for a member of the *Shura* to be capable of doing *Ijtihad*, since any person who is unable to do so, did not deserve to join the ranks of the *Ahl al-hall wa al-aqd.*[31]

Connotations of *Ulul Amr*

The next question that arises is what was meant by expression Ulul amr. This term occurs in two verses of the *Qur'ān*:

يَآ أَيُّهَا الَّذِيْنَ اٰمَنُوْٓا أَطِيْعُوا اللّٰهَ وَأَطِيْعُوا الرَّسُوْلَ
وَأُولِي الْأَمْرِ مِنْكُمْ فَإِنْ تَنَازَعْتُمْ فِيْ شَيْءٍ فَرُدُّوْهُ
إِلَى اللّٰهِ وَالرَّسُوْلِ إِنْ كُنْتُمْ تُؤْمِنُوْنَ بِاللّٰهِ وَالْيَوْمِ
الْاٰخِرِ ذٰلِكَ خَيْرٌ وَّأَحْسَنُ تَأْوِيْلًا

> "O ye who believe! Obey Allah and obey the Prophet and those charged with authority among you. If ye differ in any thing among yourselves, refer it to Allah and His Apostle, if ye do believe in Allah and the Last Day: that is best and most suitable for final determination."[32]

وَإِذَا جَآءَهُمْ أَمْرٌ مِّنَ الْأَمْنِ أَوِ الْخَوْفِ أَذَاعُوْا
بِهٖ وَلَوْ رَدُّوْهُ إِلَى الرَّسُوْلِ وَإِلٰٓى أُولِي الْأَمْرِ
مِنْهُمْ لَعَلِمَهُ الَّذِيْنَ يَسْتَنْبِطُوْنَهٗ مِنْهُمْ

> "When there comes to them some matter touching (public) safety or fear, they divulge it. If they had only referred it to the Apostle, or to those charged with authority among them, the proper investigators would have tested it from them (direct)."[33]

Zamakhshari says that the term *Ulul amr* refers to righteous people. According to another authority the expression means army commanders, while still another authority suggests that it refers to the *Ulama*.[34] Commenting on second of the two verses cited above, he says that the expression *Ulul amr* refers to eminent companions of the Prophet (SAW), experienced persons or army commanders.[35]

Ibn Kathir has cited traditions of the Prophet (SAW) in his commentary on the first of the two verses from which it appears that the term *Ulul amr* means *amirs* of righteousness and justice.[36] He has also cited the words of Ibn Abbas and a group of the followers of the *Sahabah* to the effect that in these verses *Ulul amr* refers to the *Ulama*.[37] Ibn Kathir had indicated his preference for the opinion that the verses refer in general terms to both the *Umara* and the *Ulama*. Tabrisi has cited a number of exegeses of the first of the two above-mentioned verses. According to one of these the term *Ulul amr* means the *Umara* while a second one says that it refers to the *Ulama* since this was the category of people who were resorted to instead of officials and governors in resolving controversial issues. According to a third exegesis the expression cannotes the *imams* who were the descendants of the Prophet (SAW). The author interprets the second of the verses cited above by saying that the term *Ulul amr* used in it refers to the innocent *imams*,[39] and he has cited another authority according to which the expression means army commanders and governors, while, he says, still another exegesist says that the term connotes the scholars and the *faqihs* who were the companions of the Prophet (SAW).

Razi[40] says that the term *Ulul amr* means *Ahl al-hall wa al-aqd* but he has not made it clear as to whether *Ahl al-hall wa al-aqd* comprised the *Ulama* of *Shariah* or those of *Usool* (principles of jurisprudence). One is not sure whether *imam* Razi is here referring to the *Ulama* who were the *mujtahids* of *Shariah* or those who had the privilege to select the *imam*, who, it is well-known, were not necessarily those who were capable of doing *ijtihad*, or whether Razi refers to the entire *Ummah* by the term. Dr. Mohammad Ziauddin Al-Rayyis prefers the first of the above interpretations of the words of Razi, according to which it was essential for those comprising the *Ulul amr* to be *mujtahids*.[41]

Syed Mohammad Rashid Rida writes that Imam Nishapuri preferred the last of the above interpretations of *Ulul amr* by Imam Razi who had written that since this verse could not be applied to all the categories, it was clear that the entire *Ummah* could e deemed to be innocent and hence *Ulul amr* comprised those over whose choice there was unanimity among the *Ummah*.[42] According to Ibn Taimiyah the term *Ulul amr* refers to the *Umara* and the *Ulama*[43] Shaikh Mohammad Abduh says that after thinking for a long time he has reached the conclusion that *Ulul amr* means the institution of *Ahl al-hall wa al-aqd* which includes the *Umara*, the officials, the *Ulama* and the army commanders and includes all those tribal heads and leaders who were resorted to in dealing with matters of general welfare and essential services. Their decision was bound to be obeyed if all these reached a consensus on any matter. In this way Mohammad Abduh has extended the circle of *Ahl al-hall wa al-aqd* and does not confine it merely to the *Ulama*. Mohammad Abduh concludes by saying, "In my age *Ulul amr* means eminent *Ulama*, army leaders, Judges, big traders and farmers, those concerned with matters of general welfare, directors of institutions and business establishment, leaders of political parties, those well-versed in the Book of Allah, physicians and lawyers in whom the *Ummah* had trust and to whom it resorted to in resolving issues which confronted it."[44]

In the pronouncement of his cited above, Mohammd Abduh has not included officials among the *Ulul amr*. This appears to be his final opinion on the issue.

The chief disciple of Mohammad Abduh, Syed Rashid Rida has elucidated the above-mentioned pronouncement of his by saying that the term *Ulul amr* refers to those *Ahl al-hall wa al-aqd* who represent the power and authority of the *Ummah*.[45] Citing his teacher Mohammad Abduh in his Tafseer al Manar, Rashid Rida says that the term *Ahl al-Zikr* refers to *Ulul amr*, that is, scholars and thinkers concerned with the interests and welfare of the *Ummah*.[46] The author expresses himself in agreement with this. He writes that by *Ulul amr* was meant thinkers and respectable people who were aware of the interests of the *Ummah* and ways of protecting these interests and whose opinions were appreciated by the *Ummah*.[47] Rashid Rida adds that *Ahl al-Shura* are *Ahl al-hall wa al-aqd* (people at the helm of affairs) who elect the caliph and who are considered among other communities as representatives of the people.[48]

Abul Ala Maududi says that the expression *Ulul amr* refers to those who are capable of managing matters of common interest and those who have the power of deduction, that is, the ability to probe the reality of matters placed before them and to decide how to deal with the issues in hand in the light of the *Qur'ān* and the *Sunnah*. In other words, according to Maududi, two things are essential for those comprising the *Ulul amr*, namely participation in the affairs of the state and being *Ahl al-Zikr*, that is, ability to form correct opinion on matters in hand in the light of the Book of Allah and the *Sunnah* of the Prophet (SAW).[49]

Dr. Mahmood Fayyaz writes that according to verse 59 of *Surah al-Nisa*, the term *Ulul amr* means the officials but verse 83 of the Surah contradicts this interpretation because in this verse the expression *Ulul amr* is mentioned alongside the Prophet (SAW) as authorities that were to be obeyed by the faithful and hence it could not refer to mere officials of the state. Now the question arises as to who those persons were that comprised the *Ulul amr*. The *Qur'ān* indicates that these persons were the *Sahabah* the scholars, experienced people and experts whose opinion was generally accepted. It is these people who are referred to by the *Ulama* as *Ahl al-hall wa al-aqd*. Hence both the verses from *Surah al-Nisa* cited above refer to these groups since in both of them the same expression, *Ulul amr* has been used.[50] Shaikh Abdul Wahab Khallaf says that *Ulul amr* comprises both officials of the state as well as the *Ulama*.[51] While Shaikh Mohammad Abu Zahra avers that according to the *Tabiy'un* (followers of the *Sahabah* the term refers only to the *Ulama*.[52]

Shaikh Mahmood Shaltoot dismisses the entire controversy over the question by saying that *Ulul amr* means people with insight who have a perfect skill in contemplating issues placed before them and are well-known for their ability to comprehend the demands of expedience and the interests of the *Ummah*. He adds that problems of the *Ummah* are multidimensional, including as those of armed forces and defence, of law and order, of justice, finance and treasury as well as foreign affairs. Thus he says, there is a wide variety of dimensions and departments in everyone of which there are some individuals who are renowned for their farsightedness, maturity of thought and great services. He avers that it is these persons that constitute the Ulul amr and it is these people who are *Ahl al ijma*; consensus among them is decisive and compliance with this consensus is binding on the *Ummah.* Hence the term *Ulul amr* does not refer only to the *Umara* or officials of the state however high their status is, nor is it confined to the *faqihs* and the *mujtahids* since their understanding does not generally transcend scholarship of the *Qur'ān*, the *Sunnah* and the literature and they are usually not much conversant with affairs like those of war and peace, agriculture, trade, industry and politics, administration and management. Hence their position is like that of other *Ulama.* Then there are some who are skilled in a particular field, who are *Ulul amr* in their respective areas. They lay down the principles and rules and regulations in their respective spheres regarding matters on which the *Qur'ān* does not contain any injunction or details.[53]

Zaafir al Qasmi cites Dr. Mohammad Saeed Ramazan al- Booti to the effect that the *Ulul Amr* are those who are known as *mujtahids*, a term by which the *faqihs* and the *Ulama usool al-fiqh* mean *Ahl al-hall wa al-aqd.*[54] He adds that there are two main prerogratives of the *Ahl al-hall wa al-aqd.* First, their oath of allegiance to the person who is in their opinion, suitable for being a caliph confirms his selection to the post. Then the *Ahl al-hall wa al-aqd* can do *ijtihad* for taking decisions and making laws and their judgement has the status of *ijma.*[55] This means that, according to Dr. Ramazan, the term *Ulul amr* stands for *Ahl al-hall wa al-aqd* as for as the *Ulama* of *usool al-fiqh* are concerned. Since they are required to have the ability to do *ijtihad*, it is they who comprise the *Shura* too.

Such norms for the selection of the members of the *Shura* were followed during the period of the four Guided

Caliphs. These principles were difficult to follow later when caliphate was transformed into kingship and those who wielded state power distanced themselves from the common people of the *Ummah*. This also resulted in the *faqihs* and the *Ulama* started becoming isolated from the government and its affairs. As a result, books written on the issue of caliphate and in the discussions that took place on the question of the qualifications of *Ahl al-hall wa al-aqd* were watered down and it was no longer considered essential for people at the helm of affairs to possess learning that could enable them to do *ijtihad*. The *Ulama* concerned with the politics of the *Shariah* deemed it sufficient for a caliph to be a just, wise and farsighted Muslim having experience in the political and governmental affairs. Things went so far that even those who used the term *Ahl al-ijtihad* for those at the helm of affairs used the word *ijtihad* to mean insight and farsightedness in the affairs of the government. This was the logical outcome of changing conditions.

This was the reason why the connotation of the term *Ahl al-hall wa al-aqd* according to the *Ulama* of *Usool al-fiqh* was different from that of the *Ulama* of *Shariah*. The sense of this term became much broader and more comprehensive and all embracing, and the chiefs, the *Ulama* and representatives of different classes were included in the *Shura*.

From the above discussion it may be concluded that according to both the verses from the *Qur'ān* cited above the term *Ulul amr* means *Ahl al Shura* or *Ahl al-hall wa al-aqd* and that officials of state and the *amirs* are not included in the *Shura*. These verses connote that a decision arrived at by a majority of the members of the *Shura* is binding on the *Ummah*, and consensus among its members is final, compliance with which is essential for removing differences and ending disputes.

The following arguments can also be advanced in support of the Tafseer (interpretation) of the verses cited above[56]:

1. According to verse 59 of *Surah al-Nisa* obedience of the *amir*s is only proper when it is established that their judgement is just and that reasons advanced in support of their stand are based on the *Qur'ān* and the *Sunnah*. This means that these arguments would not go beyond the *Qur'ān* or the *Sunnah* and would not yield any new advantage. But if obedience to *ulul amr* means obligation to comply with decisions arrived at by consensus among the members of the *Shura* it would result in a new conclusion since it is often possible that there is consensus in the *Shura* on an issue which is not mentioned in the *Qur'ān* or the *Sunnah*.

2. If in the verses cited above the tem *Ulul amr* is construed to mean the *amir*s it would be necessary to add the stipulation to this that obedience to the *amir*s would be proper only if they are in the right. However, if a decision is that arrived at by consensus in the *Shura* or by a majority of its members, no such stipulation would be necessary since decisions of the *Shura* would be binding in every case.

3. Compliance or non-compliance with the actions and decisions of the *amir*s and the caliph would depend upon the *fatwas* (verdicts) of the *Ulama* who would decide whether or not they accord with the *Shariah*. This shows that the *Ulama* have the status of *Ulul amr* and hence it is much better to apply the term *Ulul amr* to the *Ulama*.

4. The *Qur'ān* uses the expression Ulul amr as a plural non which shows that it does not refer to the reigning sovereign but to members of the *Shura*.[57] It would not be proper to

use this plural noun for the caliphs as there would be only one caliph at a time.

5. Basically both the verses cited above are addressed to the Muslim contemporaries of the Prophet (SAW) and since no one culd be an *amir* or ruler during the life time of the Prophet (SAW), the expression *Ulul amr* obviously refers to the *Muhajirs* and the *Ansar* and prominent *Sahabah* whose opinion carried weight as they were the people whom the Prophet (SAW) himself consulted.[58]

6. The *Qur'ān* itself provides the interpretation f its verses. When one reads verse 59 of *Surah al-Nisa* in the light of its interpretation in verse 83 of the same *Surah* it becomes clear that the term *Ulul amr* refers to those who are consulted for solving problem relating to political, administrative, legislative and sociological affairs and it is these people who are deemed to be members of the *Shura*.

From the above discussion it may be concluded that the expression *Ulul amr* stands for *Ahl al-hall wa al-aqd* who are also members of the *Shura*. In this context Shaikh Ahmad Haridi says that the *Ulul amr* are persons belonging to the *Ummah* who are thinkers and leaders of public opinion who devote their minds to all aspects of life including those who reflect deeply on various matters and are proficient in different skills whom the *Ummah* recognizes and whose services in the realm of thought and scholarship and the results produced by their thinking are well-known to the entire community, which looks upon them as responsible persons, and whom the common people respect and trust.[59]

Modern Implications

From the above discussion on the selection of members of the *Shura* in the period of the Prophet (SAW) and of Four Caliphs and on the real meaning of the *Qur'ānic* verses cited above and the actual people these verses are addressed to, the question arises that if the Islamic system of *Shura* is implemented in the present day who would be its members and which classes of the people would be entitled to be elected to it. A majority of those who have given thought to this issue and have dealt with the Islamic system of *Shura* are of the opinion that as compared with the composition of modern parliaments those comprising the Islamic *Shura* would be eminent Muslim *Ulama*, masters of different skills, experts and experienced people, leaders of the army and of political parties.

In societies which have not attained sufficient progress in culture and civilization to be able to take recourse to elections to ascertain as to which individuals enjoy the confidence of the common people, their leaders, and eminent persons represent their respective areas through a natural method of selection. In this way, scholars, *faqihs* and individuals with insight are in the seat of power and they are popular among the common people who happily accept the ascendancy of such elite in the institutions of the state as well as in the society. This obviates the need for a formal election, since certain people emerge as representatives of the masses in a natural manner as a result of their deeds, services and capabilities so that even if formal elections are held it is these individuals who would be elected. In such a situation it is the leaders of the community, eminent personalities and scholars who would represent the common people in the *Shura*. However, a society which has advanced from its simple and natural state and has entered the phase of political and social progress, in which urban population has increased greatly, the geographical limits of which have been fixed, election have become indispensable to gain the acceptability and confidence of the people. As far as experts in different fields, skilled and experienced persons and scholars are concerned, in such a society they do not represent the people. Such individuals can only occupy the status of advisers in their respective fields of expertise. The basis of distinction between these two groups is the issue of representation.

It has been established above that during the period of the Prophet (SAW) and that of the Guided Caliphs members of the *Shura* really represented the people since they were the representatives of their respective communities and groups. They had the right to represent the people because of their learning and understanding of the *Qur'ān* and the *Sunnah*, ability, sincerity and experience and sacrifices in the cause of Islam and leadership of their tribes. It is true that at that time there were no formal elections in the modern sense of the term but in reality members of the *Shura* in the early years of Islam were the trusted and popular representatives of the people and were selected through the natural process of selection that prevailed at the time. This natural system of selection no longer exists in the present age, replaced as it has been with the process of formal election, so that the parliaments of today perform the functions that the *Shura* performed in the early period of Islam.

Abul Ala Maududi says that the conclusion that may be logically derived from a study of the period of the Guided Caliphs and even the practice of the Prophet (SAW) is that the *amir* ought not to consult every one or arbitrarily selected individuals but those who enjoy the trust of the common Muslims, in whose sincerity, good intentions and abilities people have faith and whose participation in the decision making process guarantees that these decisions would be implemented with the heartfelt cooperation of the people. Maududi adds that as far as the question of how to determine as to which individuals enjoy the trust of the people, the answer is that conditions in this respect are different from those that prevailed during the early years of

Islam. Hence, according to him in the conditions and exigencies of the present age all such possible and desirable measures can be adopted which can determine as to who are the individuals that enjoy the trust and confidence of the masses. The election process of today is one such method provided that those dirty tactics are not employed in elections which have made mockery of democracy in the present age.[60]

Qualification for the *Shura* Members

According to the tradition of the Prophet (SAW) a person whose advice is to be sought must be honest.[61]

Abul Hasan Ali Mawardi[62] says that three qualities are essential in a member of the *Shura*. They should be just, conversant with the affairs of the state, wise ad farsighted, while according to Imam Nawawi, they should fulfil the conditions necessary for being a witness, that is, they should be Muslims, free adherents of the *Shariah* and not charged with any misdeed.[63] It has been stated above that every member of the *Shura* ought to enjoy the confidence of the *Ummah* and should be acceptable to it.

According to a *Hadith*, the Prophet (SAW) once said that

من أشار علىٰ أخيه بأمرٍ يعلم أن الرشد في غيره فقد خانَهُ

if a person gives some advice to his brother about something knowing that the welfare of his brother lies in rendering some other advice, he is guilty of breach of trust.[64] There is another Hadith to the effect that

وإذا أراد الله بالأمير خيرًا جعل له وزيرَ صدقٍ إن نَسِي

ذكّرَهُ وَإن ذكر أعانَهُ وَإذا أرادَ بهِ غير ذَالك جعل له وزير

سُوءٍ إن نسى لم يذكره وَإن ذكر لَم يُعِنْهُ.

when Allah (SWT) intends to do good to *amir*, He bestows on him a righteous vizier who reminded him of his neglect and once he is remained of it, helps him and when Allah (SWT) does not wish for the welfare of *amir*, He gives him a wicked vizier who does not remind him of his neglect and does not help him even when he remembers what he has neglected.[65] Umar asks people to seek the advice of Allah-fearing persons in matters of religion.[65]

According to the above tradition and sayings it is incumbent upon a person whose advice is sought to tell what he considers to be the correct course of action. Once this idea is firmly entrenched in the mind of an adviser, he cannot give any misleading or wrong advice to anyone.

Honesty of an adviser also demands that he should not express his agreement for every step of the *amir* or caliph, irrespective of whether it is right or wrong, on the contrary, he ought to express his disapproval of the wrong decisions of the *amir* with sincerity.

Prophet Mohammad (SAW), once said to Kab bin Ujra: "May Allah save you from the mischief of the reign of foolish *amir*s." To the question of Kab as to what he meant by the expression 'reign of foolish *amir*s', the Prophet (SAW) replied:

قال رسول الله ﷺ لكعب بن عجرة يا كعب بن عجرة إنى أعيذك بالله من امارة السّفهاء، قال يا رسول الله وما امارة السفهاء؟ قال: أمراء يكونون من بعدى من دخل عليهم فصدّقهم بكذبهم وأعانهم علىٰ ظلمهم فليس منّى ولست منه و لن يرد علىٰ الحوض

> "After me, the reins of power will come in the hands of people who will not follow my practices and will not tread the straight path shown by me. A person who expresses himself in agreement with their wrong practices and participates in perpetrating cruelty will have nothing to do with me, nor would be able to be present by my side at the Cistern (tank) on the Day of Judgement."[67]

Maulana Maududi[68] has described two categories of qualifications for caliphate and membership of the *Shura*. The first of these are legal in nature which the election commission examines before deciding whether or not a person is eligible for the post, while the second one relates to qualities which the common people keep in mind while selecting, nominating or voting for a person.

According to him, there are four legal conditions for membership of the *Shura*:

1. Being a Muslim
2. Being a male
3. Being wise and mature
4. Being a citizen of *Dar ul Islam*

The above four qualifications entitle a person to be a caliph also.

Maulana Maududi says that other qualifications that electors seek in persons in order to select them and vote for them ought to be enshrined in the spirit of the entire body f the constitution of state, adding that the success of a constitution depends upon ability to create awareness among the common people so that they elect such persons only who have the qualities that accord with the spirit of the constitution. For elucidating this other category of qualifications, Maulana Maududi bases himself on the following sources:

إِنَّ اللّٰهَ يَأْمُرُكُمْ أَنْ تُؤَدُّوا الْأَمٰنٰتِ إِلٰى أَهْلِهَا

Allah doth command you to render back your trusts to those to whom they are due[69]

And

إِنَّ أَكْرَمَكُمْ عِنْدَ اللّٰهِ أَتْقٰكُمْ

"Verily the most honoured of you in the sight of Allah is he who is the most righteous of you."[70]

And

إِنَّ اللّٰهَ اصْطَفٰهُ عَلَيْكُمْ وَزَادَهٗ بَسْطَةً فِى الْعِلْمِ وَالْجِسْمِ

"He (the Prophet) said: Allah hath chosen him above you, and hath gifted him abundantly with knowledge and bodily prowess."[71]

and

وَلَا تُطِعْ مَنْ أَغْفَلْنَا قَلْبَهٗ عَنْ ذِكْرِنَا وَاتَّبَعَ هَوٰهُ وَكَانَ أَمْرُهٗ فُرُطًا

"Nor obey any whose heart We have permitted to neglect the remembrance of us, one who follows his own desires, whose case has gone beyond all bounds."[72]

and

مَن وَقّر صاحبَ بدعةٍ فقد أعانَ على هدم الاسلام

A person who respects innovators (in religious affairs) is a participant in the dismantling of Islam.[73]

And

إنا واللّه لا نولّى على عملنا هٰذا أحدًا سألَهُ أو حرصَ عليه

By Allah, we do not appoint any person to a post of our government who has applied for it or craves it.[74]

And

إنّ أخونكم عندنا مَن طَلَبهُ

According to us, the most dishonest person amongst you is one who himself desires to have a post.[75]

Amin Ahsan Islahi has refuted the assertion of those who opine that the *Shura* would comprise exclusively the *Ulama* and the *Faqihs*. According to him there are two stipulations for the membership of the *Shura* – being a leader of Muslims and having a deep understanding of the affairs of the state and political insight. He says that the accounts of the early Islamic period also show that only those persons were invited to the *Shura* who were the trusted leaders of the people and those who had insight in religious and worldly affairs. In this respect there was no discrimination between the old and the young. In his work *Kitab al Tafseer*, *Surah al-A'araf* Bukhari cites Ibn Abbas to the effect that consultative assemblies of Caliph Umar comprised learned people, both old and young. Caliph Abu Bakr called leaders and representatives of the Muslims.[76]

Adnan Ali Rida Nahwi considers three kinds of qualifications essential for membership of the *Shura*. The first of these, which he looks upon as basic qualities are faith and piety, learning, ability and capability which are indispensable in a member of the *Shura*. The second kind of qualities considered by him necessary in a member of the *Shura* are subsidiary ones, among which he lays especial emphasis on natural, human and moral qualities which should be taken into account only when a person has the basic qualities. The third kind of qualities needed by a person to be able to join the *Shura* are those of industry, perseverance for which a competitive spirit, experience skill, and judicious analysis have been greatly emphasised by him. According to him these qualities gradually mature and are perfected with age and shouldering of responsibilities but every member of the *Shura* is required to have their germs from the very beginning.[77]

In the opinion of Hamidul Ansari Ghazi every citizen of an Islamic state is entitled to be member of the *Shura* who follows the natural laws of Islam, is bestowed with average degree of learning and wisdom, is a well-wisher of the social system, and is indifferent to personal consideration of personal benefits and gains. Inshort, he should be trustworthy and ought to have sufficient power of thinking to be able to render shound advice.[78]

From the above discussion it appears that the *Ulama* and the researchers are of the opinion that officials of the state are entitled to be members of the *Shura*. However, in this context, Dr. Mahmood Fayyaz has raised a pertinent point which ought to be dealt with. He asks how some other person can rule in the presence of the Prophet (SAW). He adds that the term *Ulul amr* has been used in the *Qur'ān* as a plural, in which case it cannot mean anything other than members of the *Shura*. Shaikh Mohammad Abduh and Syed Mohammad Rashid Rida, too, have said the some thing.

In the light of the above discussion, qualities and qualifications required for being a member of the *Shura* may be summed up as follows:

1. He ought to follow the tenets of Islam and should have a high moral character.

2. He should have a perfect knowledge of the affairs of the state.

3. He ought to have the power of deduction side by side with knowledge of the Islamic *Shariah* to be able to understand the issues with which he is confronted and to render sound advice.

Mode of Selection

The mode of determining who should constitute the *Shura* is a controversial and fairly complicated issue. Many contemporary researchers consider formal election as the best method, while according to others a natural and gradual mode of selection is the most effective one. There are still others who opine nomination too as a proper device, and, in certain situation a desirable one, while some *Ulama* and intellectuals suggest a combination of the methods of formal election and nomination. All these schools of thought advance arguments based on the *Shariah* and history in support of their respective contentions, examination of which is necessary to arrive at the correct point of view with regard to the proper mode of selection of members of the *Shura*.

Formal Election

Those who advocate formal elections as the best method of constituting the *Shura* argue that the *Qur'ānic* injunction on the subject demands that the entire *Ummah* should participate in the selection of its members, so that the body enjoys the trust and confidence of the community and the cooperation of the community is ensured in the implementation of its decisions. But what about the mode of the election of the *Shura*? Should it be left to the consensus and *ijtihad* of every age, since there is no *Qur'ānic* pronouncement regarding it, nor is there any authentic precedent relating to it pertaining to the period of the Guided Caliphs. What was really practiced was that the *Shura* was elected with the will and consent of the entire *Ummah*. It is wrong to say that the Guided Caliphs did not know the method of election. The fact is that it is incumbent on every community to institute the *Shura* system in accordance with the prevailing conditions and contingencies. The procedure adopted in a particular period is not binding on the people of another period conditions and problems of which are entirely different.[79] If one examines the components, temperament and spirit of the Islamic system of *Shura*, the unescapable conclusion that he would arrive at would be that the way in which the Guided Caliphs implemented it was in conformity with the conditions that prevailed during the period. They followed a natural system of the selection of the *Shura* in such a manner that had general election been held in the present sense of the term none other than those selected by the Guided Caliphs would have emerged successful in these elections.

Another argument that the above-mentioned scholars advance in support of their contention that election is the method of constituting the *Shura* is that in the present complex and highly developed social system there is no device other than that of holding general elections to determine the collective opinion of the community and to establish the system of *Shura*. In their opinion this is the only method by which respective merits of the contending candidates can be correctly assessed.[80] Controverting those who favour the system of nomination to the *Shura* rather than election, these learned people say apart from the fact that *amir*s cannot on their own select persons who would be better and more suitable than those selected by the common people, it is most dangerous to give the ruler, however, just and pious he may be, the right to select his successor. They aver that just as Allah (SWT) has enjoined upon the faithful to conduct the affairs of the *Ummah* with mutual consultation, the establishment and composition of the *Shura*, too, ought to be done in such a manner that its members are elected by the people through a process of collective consultation.[81]

In this respect the stand of Maududi is absolutely clear. He is of the view that the method by which the opinion of the common people could be determined during the early period of Islam can no longer be applied in the present day, nor are there the same abstacles in the path of knowing the will of the people as there were in that period. So, he says, all those possible and desirable devices can be employed to determine as to which persons enjoy the trust and confidence of the people, keeping in mind the prevailing conditions and the needs of the present day, provided that those dirty tricks are not used in these elections which have made a mockery of democracy.[82]

Ameen Ahsan Islahi holds a similar view. He says that during the early years of Islam, since all those whose opinions carried weight were concentrated at one place, leadership of communities and tribes was determined by the demands of the prevailing social system. Moreover, he says, the territory of the Islamic state was also not very extensive and hence the system of *Shura* in it was most simple and elementary. Islahi says that at the present time conditions are very different and so modern method of general elections may be used with some essential reforms to constitute the *Shura*, and necessary laws can be adopted to determine the relationship between the *Shura* and ruler. He adds that doing so will not be against the injunctions of Islam.[83]

Evolution Theory

Another manner of constituting the *Shura* is the gradual and natural mode of election. This means that outstanding individuals automatically emerge in a society because of their merit and qualities. Qualifications required for people who would comprise the *Shura* would depend on the nature of the prevailing social system and people who gradually assume prominence would have these qualifications. In the capitalist system, gradual emergence of and respect and status enjoyed by an individual would depend upon his ability to make money and to multiply it several times. On the other hand, in a society of wicked people, those who are able to create mischief and disturbance would gradually become leaders of mischief makers. And in a religious and pious society individuals would automatically become prominent on the basis of complete adherence to their faith, and their piety and idealism, their ethical values and responsible behaviour would go on leaving their imprint on the society and their acceptability and popularity would gradually increase.

Authors holding the above-mentioned opinion have based their arguments, in especial, on the following authorities:

إِنَّ أَكْرَمَكُمْ عِندَ اللَّهِ أَتْقَاكُمْ

"Verily, the most honoured of you in the sight of Allah is (he who is) the most righteous of you."[84]

And

يَرْفَعِ اللَّهُ الَّذِينَ آمَنُوا مِنكُمْ وَالَّذِينَ أُوتُوا الْعِلْمَ دَرَجَاتٍ

> “”Allah will raise up to (suitable) ranks (and degrees), those of you who believe and who have been granted the knowledge.”[85]
>
> Umar bin Khattab says” “Acquire the knowledge of understanding of the faith before you get leadership (of the *Ummah*).”
>
> There is a famous saying “Your rulers have the standard of character according to that of you people.”

According to the above-mentioned scholars Islam has given due consideration to this law of gradual evolution of society. There are many instances in the history of Islam of slaves and persons from the lower strata of society becoming ministers, rich and wealthy people and *Ulama.* It is this law which plays a crucial role in determining who would be the people at the helm of affairs and the caliph, since these slaves and persons from the lower strata have automatically achieved prominence due to their high qualities and noble character and have occupied the highest position.

The centre of this gradual social evolution is the mosque of the locality in which *Ahl al-hall wa al-aqd* (people at the helm of affairs), *Ahl al rae* (those whose opinions carried weight), people with insight and the managing committee gather and discuss the problems of the locality. This assembly also looks after the needs and requirements of the area under its jurisdiction and people living there resort to it when faced with some difficulty. Thus mosque is the nucleus of a unit of such a natural mode of activity. The assembly of *Ahl al-hall wa al-aqd* (the people at the helm of the affairs) of a jami masjid is a larger unit comprising all the smaller units in a town. In this central mosque people of the whole town gather once a month where their problems are discussed from the pulpit and *Ahl al-hall wa al-aqd* (people at the helm of affairs) meet and tackle social and political matters. The imam of this jami masjid is the ruler of the town who is the leader of the people in religious as well as political affairs. In this way, the ruler of the place has an assembly of people at the helm of affairs at his disposal all the time to hold consultation with. Similarly the caliph, who leads the prayers in the jami masjid of the capital has the benefit of the different classes of people around him who are experienced persons, endowed with insight and skill and who are well-known and popular throughout the country. It is this naturally evolved assembly of the *Shura* which gives sound advice to the caliph of the time.[86]

This natural system of selection of the *Shura* was prevalent in the early years of Islam and, as a result of this system, able and deserving individuals achieved prominence and were appointed to high positions and comprised the *Ahl al-hall wa al-aqd* or the *Shura*. But now the number of problems has increased vastly, modern society suffers from different kinds of intricacies and progress in the fields of science and technology has made the society so complex that it is not possible to bring it back to its natural state. So the old methods are no longer valid. It is only in societies which are still simple and have not yet been affected by modern culture that the old system can be established.

Nomination

There are some scholars who regard nomination as a better form of selecting members of the *Shura*. In their opinion election under a democratic set up are replete with deficiencies and evil practices and hence they are not capable of constituting the *Shura* in a proper manner. They are of the view that the caliph or head of state should himself select people on the basis of their superiority over others as regard their abilities, experience and power of drawing right conclusions and in giving correct and sound advice on matter which they confront.[87]

These learned people and intellectuals are right when they recount a number of defects in the democratic process of election; but the system of nomination is likely to be accompanied by many more defects. It is beyond the capacity of a caliph to select good and suitable individuals and those enjoying the trust and confidence of the common people without holding a general election. Moreover, there is no guarantee of justice and rightfulness in making nomination to the *Shura*, since, however pious and devout a caliph may be, as compared with the judgement of the common people that of a single individual will be more likely to be faulty. In view of the importance of the *Shura* and its role in implementing the sound principles of the Islamic state, its composition cannot be left to the judgement of a single person.

Election Amidst *Mujtahids*

Some scholars have suggested that certain stipulations and qualifications may be laid down for the candidates for the membership of *Shura* before elections take place. That is to say, a person who obtains a degree and is recognised as a scholar in one of the fields of learning like *Shariah*, medicine, engineering, technology, agriculture, economics etc. which enables him to do *ijtihad* and draw logical conclusions, may be regarded as a *mujtahid*, provided he fulfils other conditions for doing *ijtihad*. According to these scholars, capacity for logical deduction will go on increasing with the passage of time and the number of members of a legislative assembly is usually small to obviate difficulties in the conduct of discussings and exchanges of opinion. They say when such a stage is reached general elections may be held for electing members of the *Shura* from among these *mujtahids* so as to ensure that those who are elected possess expertise, experience and deductive skill in different areas of learning. In this way, these scholars claim, through a general election both representatives of the people and experts in different fields will be present in the *Shura*. This process of election is not a unique or a rare one in modern democracies, since such a system is in force in a number of countries where elections are held in two stages, as a result of which experts get representation in the legislature and welfare of the common people is also ensured. Certain countries have prescribed some educational qualifications and financial standing for enrolment of people as voters while some other constitutions provide for sponsorship, that is, every candidate, has to be sponsored by a specified number of voters while there are still other constitutions, according to which candidates have to be nominated not by individuals but by institutions. If the above mentioned method is adopted, it would incorporate both a modern democratic process of election as well as basic features of the Islamic system of the selection of the *Shura*.[88]

However, the system of election stated above has been generally criticised very severely. Ability to read and write and to have some educationl qualifications ought not to be prescribed as conditions for being a voter and a candidate respectively. All the democratic states of today have rejected such a system. It is generally thought that acquiring skill and expertise in certain fields of learning and arts and ability to render sound advice in the affairs of the state are two different things and there is no essential corelationship between the two.

Hani Ahmad Dardiri suggests the following system of election which is similar to that mentioned above:

1. The ruler or the caliph should appoint an apex panel of persons who, in his opinion, has the ability to do *ijtihad* and

to draw logical conclusions, provided that the ruler or caliph is himself a *mujtahid.* Failing this, he should seek the advice and cooperation of a person who has the status of a *mujtahid* in nominating people to the panel.

2. The above-mentioned panel should conduct interviews with those who claim to have the ability to do *ijtihad* and then decide who among them are really capable of doing so.

3. Those who are considered by the apex panel able to do *ijtihad* may contest election for membership of the *Shura* from constituencies delimited by the ruler. These elections should be conducted by secret ballot so that the common people may select those among the *mujtahids* who, in their opinion, are more sober and have a greater awareness of their problems and interests.

4. The *majlis ijtihad* or *Shura* should comprise those who are elected through the above-mentioned process of election.

5. This *majlis ijtihad* should deliberate the other issues of organisation and establishment.[89]

The procedure suggested above is somewhat similar to the earlier one, since in this mode of election, too, the right to select the members of the panel eligible for being elected to the *Shura* is vested in the caliph and may be objected to on the same ground as that of the earlier viewpoint that vesting the right of nominating members to the panel in a single person would lead to dissentions and disturbances and that it is difficult to meet the demands of justice in selecting persons who are deemed capable of doing *ijtihad* and drawing logical conclusions from amongst millions of people, howsoever piously and justly the caliph may try to do so.

An analysis of the viewpoints mentioned above leads one to the conclusion that in the present age general election is the best way of constituting the *Shura* since this would ensure that the best and most excellent persons having high moral character are elected who enjoy the trust and confidence of the people and are popular among them and also to make sure that the common people cooperate with the *Shura* in implementing its decisions.

The Second Chamber

However, one problem that arises in following the above-mentioned procedure is that while those elected to the *Shura* under the system would enjoy the trust and confidence of the common people, it is not likely to result in the election of skilled or learned and scholarly people and those who are experts in different fields with wide experience since such persons would not be able to employ methods designed to seek popularity among the common people because of the indispensable demands of their respective fields of learning and expertise and their scholarly temperament. Thus, the *Shura* would be deprived of their services and representation. Researchers have suggested a number of ways of solving this problem to raise the standard of the *Shura* as well as to overcome the deficiency of the system of general elections like the institution of a second chamber and nomination of experts and learned people to the *Shura*.

Islamic Ethos Essential

But it should not be forgotten that such suggestions do not provide a radical solution of the problem. Weaknesses of the democratic system can only be removed by engendering political awareness, better use of mass media, and creating a more sound public opinion. Furthermore, the Islamic system of the *Shura* can only be implemented in an Islamic ethos, an ethos in which everyone has faith in the cardinal principles of the unity of Allah (SWT), the Prophet (SAW) of Islam and the Day of Judgement, is endowed with the qualities of piety and righteousness, in an atmosphere in which the spirit of cooperation pervades and where there is complete freedom of criticism and accountability side by side with the spirit of obedience to the ruler and sense of responsibility, an environment in which officials and responsible state functionaries have the feeling of the good and welfare of the people in their hearts, and are endowed with the high qualities, good intensions, wide learning and extensive experience.

It is in such an ambience that a truly Islamic *Shura* can function and can bless the world with its beneficent fruits. This is the reason why Islam lays stress first of all on moral rectitude and pays great attention to internal reforms rather than external ones. Only purity of faith and thought and sound character and action can make an Islamic state successful. If these things are overlooked, a lot of misunderstanding is created and the correct image of Islam is obliterated from the mind.[90]

Dr. Qutb Mohammad Tabeelah says that the deficiencies of the democratic system of elections can be gradually removed in the light of experiments and right conclusions drawn from these experiments, provided that there is freedom of criticism and questioning. He adds that, such an atmosphere of freedom and liberty does not disqualify a candidate who misuses this freedom while conducting his election campaign, ensnaring the masses in the web of pleasant and illusory dreams and employing modes and resources that wholly violate the teaching of Islam. Hence, in his opinion, side by side with the purity of aims and objectives, that of the methods and resources is also essential.[91]

Suggestions about benefiting from the experience of experts in different fields can only be implemented if the masses are keen on the enforcement of the *Shariah*, are anxious to remove un-Islamic practices and elements from the modern democratic systems and the constitution of the state expressly mentions that *Shariah* is the real source of legislation. It is necessary to have a detailed discussion on these suggestions in this light.

Suggestions to Improve

One of the suggestions relating to this is that the number of the members of the legislative assembly may be increased by amending the constitution so that the assembly comprises members directly elected by the people as well as a fairly large number of skilled people and experts in different fields nominated either by the elected members of the assembly or the government so that the legislative assembly has the benefit of the opinions of members who enjoy the faith and confidence of the common people as well as that of those who have special skills and expertise. In this way the *Qur'ān*ic injunction enjoining obedience to the *Ulul amr* would also be implemented.[92] Such a process of election-cum-nomination would bridge the gap between the old and the modern systems. It would be possible to benefit from the civilizational progress made in modern times and the goal of the formation of a Qurānic system would also be achieved.[93]

The above-mentioned suggestion is similar to that of the *Ulama* as well as the intellectuals in recent times. For example, when Faqihs and experts in Islamic *Shariah* could not get elected to the Egyptian parliament, a number of learned people suggested that a specified number of *faqihs* be nominated so that the opinions of experts in *Shariah* are taken into consideration in the process of decision-making by the parliament.[94] Shaikh Yusuf al Qaradhawi has also made a similar proposal. According to him, presence of people with ability to do *ijtihad* and draw logical conclusion in a legislative assembly is essential so that they keep an eye on the legislations under discussion and decide whether they are violative of the *Shariah* or in accordance with it.[95]

The greatest weakness in the above-mentioned suggestion is that the nomination of experts and those well-versed in *Shariah* by the government would militate against the confidence of the people in the legislative assembly since this would not be done with the consent of the *Ummah* and it is possible that in nominating of these persons the government is guilty of nepotism and favouritism, which would defeat the very purpose of such nominations.

Another weakness in the above-mentioned suggestion is that if decisions arrived at by legislative assembly by a majority are deemed by the *Shariah* scholars and experts to be against the *Shariah* it would lead to mutual opposition and this would endanger the very spirit of democracy. It would also mean decision being taken by the majority while the opinions of the *Shariah* scholars being considered merely as recommendations.

Still another suggestion in this context has been made by Zakaria al-Bari. He proposes the following procedure, based on the principle of *ijma* (consensus among the faithful), which is also practicable:

1. Conditions of eligibility of *mujtahids* and *ahl al-zikr* for membership of the *Shura* are to be laid down by the caliph but it should be kept in mind that only those pious and religious persons are selected who have the ability to do *ijtihad* and to draw logical conclusions. In his opinion, in the initial stage no other method is feasible. It is this apex

majlis al-ijtihad according to him, which should examine and evaluate the eligibility of candidates for the membership of the *Shura*.

2. Apart from the *mujtahids* there should also be advisers who are experts and learned in every field of knowledge and activity and experienced people who can be consulted whenever necessary to follow the Qurānic injunction to the effect that when knowledge is lacking the *ahl al-zikr* should be consulted.

3. It is the responsibility of every Islamic state, with the cooperation of other states, if possible, to remove the obstacles to Islamic solidarity.

4. In case of difference of opinion the majority should prevail as majority opinion is nearer to the rightful decisions.

5. It is the responsibility of the government to implement the will of the majority on all issues or collective interest so as to make it part of the law of the state. It is not practicable to use the method of *ijma* to find out the injunction of the *Shariah*, as enunciated by the *Ulama*. The best way of doing this would be to employ the method of collective legislation by the *Ahl al-hall wa al-aqd.*[96]

The above-mentioned proposal shows that the author wishes to give the power of legislation to the *majlis mujtahidin* instead of the parliament. But such a proposal would mean loss of confidence in legislation on the part of masses as it would deprive the community of Muslims of its share in state affairs, while the injunction of the *Qur'ān* is that the will of the people should prevail both in the election of the caliph as well as in managing the affairs of the state.

Another great defect in the above-mentioned proposal is that a *Shura* comprising experts in various fields and those with the ability to do *ijtihad* and draw logical conclusions would not be able to tackle political issues in a proper manner. This is so since temperament of those involved in research and specialisation would militate against their taking interest in coming to groups with the problems faced by the common people. During the early years of Islam there were *faqihs* who were experts in religious learning and also took interest in understanding and solving the problems of the common people. However, this is not possible in the present time. Earlier, the social system was most simple, more natural and free from the pollutions of the present age. Progress in the fields of culture and civilization has made the modern society most complex and complicated. Every field of learning today has a number of branches and every one of these branches has been subdivided into hundreds of branches. Interest in research and specialization is creating new and ever new problem. According to scholars, those who wish to obtain high academic degrees and devote their entire lives to this objective, find themselves more and mere estranged from social and collective affairs due to these conditions, as well to their temperament.[97] Hence it would be wrong to think that specialists in different fields have a greater ability to solve the problems of the people than others.

A third proposal that is put forward in this connection is that by a combination of the modern democratic system of elections and that of the Islamic system which ensures the advantages gained from the modern thinking and ideologies side by side with maintaining its Islamic spirit. In the opinion of the advocates of such a point of view it should be indispensable for a *mujtahid* of the present age to have been educated upto a specified level; and since providing facilities for education is the responsibility of the state in modern times, evidence of a particular kind may be specified by the state as essential in order that a person may be deemed to be a *mujtahid*. They add that it should be ensured that only such person should be declared eligible for membership of the *Shura* who possesses all of such qualifications and that incompetent persons should be kept out of the *Shura*. A consultative assembly should be constituted having people possessing such qualifications and all legislations ought to be placed before this assembly before being enacted so as to examine their compatibility with the *Shariah*. Such a procedure does not go against any of the modern democratic constitutions. Since elected assemblies have the right to consult experts and specialists so as to make up the deficiency in the list of its elected members because of the defeat of candidate with expertise and specialisations. This is the reason why modern government institute committee of experts in different fields.

Those who support the above suggestion say that by following such a procedure the process of evolution and progress would continue since, according to them, *Shariah* only enunciates basic precepts and principles, leaving the working out of details and subsidiary issues to man so that there is a lot of scope for detailed legislation in the interest of the welfare of the common people.[98]

The above-mentioned suggestion is understandable. However, membership of the *Shura* cannot be confined to *mujtahids* of the *Shariah*. This is because problems have become so complicated and life of the common people has become so complex that it is not possible to deny the need of the counsel of experts in other fields. Every problem that one confronts has a number of dimensions – religious, social, economic, psychological etc. and to take all these aspects of an issue into account, opinions of skilled and experienced people from every field of knowledge and activity is necessary.

Another suggestion relating to benefiting from the experience and expertise of experts is that since religious consciousness is on the increase among the common Muslims and there is a growing demand on their part to remodel social, communal and political institutions in the light of the *Shariah* and yearning for Islamisation of the aspects of the government is increasing, it is necessary that the constitution of an Islamic state should have the basic clause to the effect that Islamic *Shariah* is the fountain-head of all legislation. This is essential since till now constitutions of Muslim countries simply declare that Islam is its state religion. Addition of the above-mentioned clause to the constitution of an Islamic state would result in comprehensive guarantees for maintaining its Islamic character and would also ensure that the legislative assembly would not adopt a law which is repugnant to Islam. This would lead to a search for new procedures of legislation and ways would be found for the observance of Islamic *Shariah* without demolishing the existing political and social structure of the country and a gradual process of change would be evolved to avoid problem arising out of introducing amendments to the existing constitution and deletions from it and conditions of the country would change with the employment of a suitable strategy and sagacity alongwith faith. In the opinion of those who propose such a scheme, decisions of the *Shura*, which would be instituted in an Islamic state as a supplement to the elected parliament, would be binding and final. They make the following suggestions with regard to this *Shura*:

1. This assembly will comprise individuals who are equipped with high academic qualifications and armed with long period of specialised experience in their respective fields, like religion, law, economics, sociology and psychology. Experts in everyone of these areas will be

nominated to this assembly. This will be separate body, apart from the parliament.

2. The task of this assembly will be to examine and assess the rightfulness and suitability o all issues placed before it by the parliament.

3. Decisions of this assembly would be arrived at by a majority of votes.

4. These decisions of the *majlis al-Shura* will be binding on the parliament which will not have the authority to reject them since the constitution of the country will already have provided that Islamic *Shariah* is the fountain-head of the laws of the land. So the parliament, too, will be bound by it. If the parliament adopts a piece of legislation which goes against the spirit of such a clause of the constitution, it would be placed before the Supreme Court which would place the matter before the *majlis al-Shura*, the decision of which will constitute the law of the land. Even if the decisions of the *majlis al-Shura* are not deemed to be binding and final and are merely considered recommendatory, the legislative assembly will have to abide by them, since even the parliament has no right to violate the basic policy of the state.

5. Laws in force at the present time which are violative of the spirit of the *Shariah* can be declared ultra vires without causing harm to the welfare of the people. Decisions regarding such laws taken by the *majlis al-Shura* in the light of the *Qur'ān* and the *Sunnah* will be enacted and enforced by the parliament.

Scholars consider the above-mentioned proposal practicable as well as in consonance with the Islamic *Shariah*.[99] It also accords with the demands of modern times. This proposal entails the institution of a *majlis al-Shura* of the common people which will come into existence through a general election and a special *majlis al-Shura* which will have experts, scholars, specialists and *Ulama al-Shariah* which will be nominated by the caliph and will represent all the different fields of learning and skill. The task of the second *majlis* will be to examine and evaluate the decisions of the *majlis al-Shura* of the common people in the light of the Islamic *Shariah* and its decisions will be decisive and final. Thus there will be a bi-cameral *Shura* which will enjoy the trust and confidence of the common people and will also benefit from the learning, research and experience of specialists, scholars and skilled and experienced persons as well as *Ulama al-Shariah*.

NOTES AND REFERENCES

1. The *Qur'ān*, Āl-Imran: 159; al-*Shura*; 38.
2. The traditions that indicate that the persons with whom consultation was meant in the *Qur'ān*ic verse "*Shawirhum*" were Abu Bakr and Umar, were cited already. But this verse, as elaborated already, can not be confined to these two companions. Instead, the Prophet had consulted with other companions too and sometimes with the entire Muslims living in Madinah or participating in any battle.
3. Mansoor, Al-Mustashār Ali Ali, *Nazm al-Hukm wa al-Idarah fi al-Shariah al-Islamiah wa al Qawanin al-Wadhyiah*, Dar al-Fath, Beirut, 1971, p. 270; Abdur Rahman Abdul Khaliq, *Al-Shura fi Zill Nizam al-Hukm al-Islami*, *op. cit.*, p. 91; Abu Zahrah, Mohammad, *Al-Mujtama al-Insani fi Zill al-Islam*, *op. cit.*, p. 165; Abdul Majd, Ahmad Kamal, *Mauzuw al-Islam Dusturan*, Kitab al-Hilal, No. 250, Nov. 1971, (ed.) Ahmad Faraj.
4. Maududi, Abul Ala, *Islami Riyasat*, *op. cit.*, pp. 341-342.
5. Asad, Muhammad, *Principles of State and Government in Islam*, *op. cit.*, p. 53.
6. Islahi, Ameen Ahsan, *Islami Riyasat*, *op. cit.*, pp. 39-40.
7. Al-Maliji, Yaqub Muhammad, *Mabda al-Shura fi al-Islam ma al-Muqaranah bi Mabadi al-Dimiqratiyah al-Gharabiyah al-Nizam al-Marxi*, Muassasah al-Thaqafah al-Jameiyah, Alexandria, p. 147.
8. Mutawalli, Abdul Hamid, *Mabda al-Shura fi al-Islam*, *op. cit.*, p. 32.
9. Al-Maliji, Yaqub Muhammad, *Mabda al-Shura fi al-Islam*, *op. cit.*, p. 161.
10. Abdul Azim Mansoor has quoted in his article *I'itebarat al-Zaman wa al-Makan fi Shariah al-Islam' Majallah*

Minbar al-Islam, Vol. XI, No. 32, Nov. 1974 from al-Bidayah wa al-Nihayah that in the case of selection of caliph, Abdur Rahman b. Auf was so sensitive and responsible that he used to ask to the ladies in the houses, the students in the schools and to traders coming from the outside of Madinah to whom they deemed to be deserving to be caliph.

11. Maududi, Abul Ala, *Islami Riyasat*, *op. cit*., f.n. of pp. 343-344.
12. Abu Zahrah, Mohammad, *Al-Mujtama al-Insani fi Zill al-Islam*, *op. cit*., p. 165.
13. Al-Adawi, Ibrahim Ahmad, *Al-Nuzum al-Islamiyah: Muqawwamatuha al-Fikriyah wa Muwassasatuha al-Tanfiziyah fi Sadr al-Islam wa al-Asr al-Umayi*, Maktaba al-Anjlu al-Misriyah, 1972, p. 145.
14. Abu Zahrah, Mohammad, *Al-Mujtama al-Insani fi Zill al-Islam*, *op. cit*., p. 165.
15. Mansoor, Al-Mustashār Ali Ali, *Nazm al-Hukm wa al-Idarah fi al-Shariah al-Islamiah wa al-Qawanin al-Wadhyiah*, *op. cit*., p. 271.
16. Mutawalli, Abdul Hamid, *Mabadi Nizam al-Hukm fi al-Islam wa al-Muqaranah bi al-Mabadi al-Dusturiyah al-Hadithah*, *op. cit*., p. 685.
17. See, Fayyaz, Mahmood, *Al-Tarikh al-Islami, Asr al-Khulafa al-Rashedin*, p. 8.
18. Maududi, Abul Ala, *Islami Riyasat*, *op. cit*., p. 343.
19. See for example, Surah al-Nisa : 59, 3.
20. Qasmi, Zaafir, *Nizal al-Hukm fi al-Shariah wa al-Tarikh*, Dar al-Nafais, Beirut, 1974, Vol. 1, p. 232.
21. See, al-Mawardi, *Al-Ahkam al-Sultaniyah*, *op. cit*., pp. 5, 6.

22. Al-Bahi, Ahmad Abdul Munim, *Nizam al-Hukm fi al-Islam (Muhazarat)*, Al-Dirasat al-Ulya, Kulliyah al-Shariyah wa al-Qanoon, Jamea al-Azhar, p. 16.
23. *Ibid.*, p. 17.
24. Al-Rayyis, Muhammad Ziauddin, *Al-Nazriyat al-Siyasiyah al-Islamiyah, op. cit.*, p. 224.
25. Al-Fazili, Ahmad, *Nizam al-Hukm fi al-Islam, (Muhazarāt)*, Al-Dirasat al-Ulya, Qism al-Siyasah al-Sharyiah, Kulliyah al-Shariyah wa al-Qanoon, Jamea Al-Azhar, p. 90. From this legal decree of Hanafite school it is clear that the terms *Ulul amr* and *ahl al-Shura* connote the nobles and dignitaries of the *Ummah.*
26. Al-Bahi, Ahmad Abdul Munim, *op. cit.*, p. 19.
27. Al-Fazili, Ahmad, *Nizam al-Hukm fi al-Iṣlam*, *op. cit.*, p. 90.
28. Al-Bahi, Ahmad Abdul Munim, *op. cit.*, p. 19.
29. Al-Fazili, Ahmad, *Nizam al-Hukm fi al-Islam*, *op. cit.*, p. 90.
30. Al-Mawardi, *Al-Ahkam al-Sultaniyah*, *op. cit.*, p. 6.
31. Al-Rayyis, Muhammad Ziauddin, *Al-Nazriyat al-Siyasiyah al-Islamiyah, op. cit.*, p. 255.
32. The *Qur'ān*, 4: 59.
33. The *Qur'ān*, 4: 83.
34. Zamakhshari, Mahmood b. Umar, *Al-Kashshāf an Haqaiq e Ghawamiz al-Tanzil wa Uyoon al-Aqāweel fi Wajh al-Taaweel*, Dar al-Kitab al-Arabi, Beirut, Vol. 1, p. 523.
35. *Ibid.*, p. 540.
36. Ibn Kathir, Imaduddin Abul Fida Ismail, *Tafsir al-Qur'ān al-Azeem*, Dar al-Marefah, Beirut, 1969, Vol. 1, p. 516.
37. *Ibid.*, p. 518.

38. Tabrisi, Abu Ali b. Hasan, *Majma al-Bayan fi Tafsir al-Qur'ān*, Dar al-Kitab al-Labnani, Beirut, 1955, Vol. V, p. 138.

39. *Ibid.*, p. 174.

40. Razi, Fakhruddin, *Mafātih al-Ghaib*, (Al-Tafsir al-Kabir), *op. cit.*, Vol. III, p. 357.

41. Al-Rayyis, Muhammad Ziauddin, *Al-Nazriyat al-Siyasiyah al-Islamiyah*, *op. cit.*, p. 318.

42. Rida, Rashid, *Tafsir al-Manar*, *op. cit.*, Vol. V, p. 183.

43. Ibn Taimiyah, Taqiuddin Ahmad, *Al-Siyasah al-Sharyiah fi Islah al-Raaee wa al-Rayeeah*, *op. cit.*, p. 182; Ibn Taimiyah, *Al-Hisbah fi al-Islam*, al-Matbah al-Salafiyah, Cairo, 1387 A.H., p. 67.

44. Rida, Rashid, *Tafsir al-Manar*, *op. cit.*, Vol. V, p. 198.

45. Rida, Rashid, *Al-Kilafah wa al-Imamah al-Uzma*, p. 15.

46. Rida, Rashid, *Tafsir al-Manar*, *op. cit.*, Vol. IV, p. 25.

47. *Ibid.*, p. 203.

48. *Ibid.*, Vol. III, p. 11.

49. Maududi, Abul Ala, *Islami Riyasat*, *op. cit.*, pp. 464-465.

50. Fayyaz, Mahmood, *Al-Fiqh al-Siyasi Indal Muslimin*, Maktaba al-Khanji, Egypt, 1959, p. 14.

51. Khallaf, Abdul Wahhab, *Ilm Usool al-Fiqh wa Khulasah al-Tashree al-Islami*, Cairo, 1956, p. 15.

52. Abu Zahrah, Mohammad, *Al-Mujtama al-Insani fi Zill al-Isam*, *op. cit.* p. 182.

53. Shaltoot, Mahmood, *Al-Islam Aqidatan wa Shariatan*, *op. cit.*, p. 463.

54. Al-Qasmi, Zaafir, *Nizam al-Hukm fi al-Shariah wa al-Tarikh*, *op. cit.*, Vol. I, p. 235.

55. *Ibid*,

56. See for detail, Rashid Rida, *Tafsir al-Manasr*, *op. cit.*, Vol. V, p. 184.

57. Mutawalli, Abdul Hameed, *Mabadi Nizam al-Hukm fi al-Islam*, *op. cit.*, p. 210.

58. Rida, Rashid, *Tafsir al-Manar*, *op. cit.*, Vol. III, p. 11.

59. Quoted from Dr. Mahmood Hilmi, *Nizam al-Hukm al-Islami Muqarinan bi al-Nuzum al-Muwasirah*, Dar al-Fikr al-Arabi, Cairo, 1970, p. 68. The author has cited this opinion from, Shaikh Ahmad Haridi, *Muzakkirat Nizam al-Hukm fi al-Islam*, p. 108.

60. Maududi, Abul Ala, *Islami Riyasat*, *op. cit.*, p. 344.

61. Shakir, Ahmad Mohammad, *Umdah al-Tafsir an al-Hafiz Ibn Kathir*, Darul Maarif, Egypt, 1957, Vol. III, p. 64 ; Haithami, Nooruddin Ali b. Abu Bakr, *Majma al-Zawaid wa Manba al-Fawaid*, Darul Kitab al-Arabi, Beirut, 1967, Vol. VIII, p. 96.

62. Mawardi, Abul Hasan Ali, *Al-Ahkam al-Sultaniyah*, *op. cit.*, p. 6.

63. Al-Bahi, Ahmad Abdul Munim, *Muzakkirat Nizamul Hukm fi al-Islam*, *op. cit.*, p. 17.

64. Abu Dawood, *Al-Sunan*, Kitab al-Ilm, Bāb al-Tawaffi fi al-Futya.

65. *Ibid.*, Bāb Ittekhaz al-Vazir.

66. Abu Yusuf, *Kitab al-Kharaj*, *op. cit.*, p. 17.

67. Hakim, *Al-Mustadrak Ma al-Talkhees li al-Zahabi*, Maktaba al-Matbuāt al-Islamiyah, Halb, Vol. III, p. 480.

68. Maududi, Abul Ala, *Islami Riyasat*, *op. cit.*, pp. 347-350 (summarised).

69. The *Qur'ān*, 4: 58.

70. The *Qur'ān*, 49: 13.

71. The *Qur'ān*, 2: 247.

72. The *Qur'ān*, 18: 28.

73. Al-Tabrezi, Waleeuddin Mohammad bin Abdullah al-Khateeb, *Mishkat al-Masabih*, Vol. I, Kitab al-Iman, Bāb al-Ietisam bil Kitab was Sunnah.

74. Bukhari, *Al-Jame al-Sahih*, Kitab al-Ahkām; Ibn Hanbal, *Musnad*, Kitab al-Imarah.

75. Abu Daud, *Al-Sunan*, Kitab al-Imarah; Ibn Hanbal, *Musnad*, Vol. IV, No 393, 411.

76. Islahi, Ameen Ahsan, *Islami Riyasat*, *op. cit.*, pp 38-39.

77. Nahwi, Adnan Ali Rida, *Malāmih al-Shura fi al-Dawah al-Islamiah*, Matabi al-Farazdaq al-Tijariah, Reyadh, 1984, pp. 592-606.

78. Ghazi, Hamid al-Ansari, *Islam ka Nizam e Hukumat*, Lahore, p. 306.

79. Al-Maghribi, Mohammad Abdullah, *Nizam ăl-Hukm fi al-Islam*, Darul Fikr, Beirut, 1967, p. 84.

80. Asad, Mohammad, *Principles of State and Government in Islam*, *op. cit.*, p. 45.

81. *Ibid.*, p. 50.

82. Maududi, Abul Ala, *Islami Riyasat*, *op. cit.*, p. 344.

83. Islahi, Ameen Ahsan, *Islami Reyasat*, *op. cit.*, p. 38.

84. The *Qur'ān*, 49: 13.

85. The *Qur'ān*, 58: 11.

86. Al-Mashhad, Abdullah and Uwais Sayyed, *Buhuth fi Wazeefah al-Masajid fi al-Mujtama al-Muasir*, Paper presented in the 5th Islamic Conference of Majma al-Buhuth al-Ilmiyah, Feb. – Mar., 1970; Wasfi, Mustafa Kamal, *Al-Nizam al-Idari al-Islami*, 1974, pp. 68-158. ___________, *Al-Nizam al-Dusturi fi al-Islam Muqarinan bi al-Nuzum al-Muasirah*, Maktaba Wahbah, Egypt, 1974, pp. 72, 114-115; ___________, *Al-Sultah al-Shabiyah fi al-Islam*, 1969, pp. 22-23.

87. Uthman, Mohd. Raafat, *Reasah al-Dawalah, Fi al-Fiqh al-Islami*, dar al-Kitab al-Jamei, Egypt, 1975, p. 361.

88. Al-Eeli, Abul Hakim Hasan, *al-Hurriyat al-Ammah*, pp. 577-578; Al-Dardiri, Hani Ahmad, *Al-Tashree bain al-Fikrain al-Islami wa al-Dusturi*, Al-Biah al-Misriyyah al-Aammah, Egypt, 1976, p. 84.

89. Al-Dardiri, Hani Ahmad, *Al-Tasree bain al-Fikrain al-Islami wa al-Dusturi*, *op. cit.*, pp. 83-84.

90. For the study of foundations and prerequisites of Islamic *Shura* in detail, see, Nahwi, Adnan Ali Rida, *Malameh al-Shura fi al-Dawah al-Islamiyah*, *op. cit.*, pp. 79-190.

91. Tabeelah, Al-Qutb Mohd. al-Qutb, *Al-Islam wa Huquq al-Insān,* Dar al-Fikr al-Arabi, Cairo, 1976, p. 635.

92. As discussed already, the *Qur'ān*ic injunction enjoining obedience to the '*Ulul amr*' requires the formation of *Shura* comprising of *Ulama*, experts of various fields and politicians. Because the word '*Ulul amr*' necessarily includes these groups.

93. Khalfullah, Mohammad Ahmad, Al-*Qur'ān* wa al-Dawlah *Al-Kateb* Monthly, Egypt, Vol. 13, No. 148, July 1973, p. 80.

94. Tabeelah, Al-Qutb Mohd. al-Qutb, *Al-Islam wa Huquq al-Insān*, *op. cit.*, p. 635.

95. Al-Qaradhawi, Yusuf, *Al-Hulul al-Mustawradah wa Kaifa Janat ala Ummatena*, Muassasah al-Risalah, Beirut, 1971, pp. 77-78.

96. Al-Bari, Zakaria, *Usul al-Fiqh al-Islami*, Part I, 1971, pp. 83-84.

97. Uthman, Mohammad Fathi, *Ahl al-Hall wa al-Aqd man Hum, Majallah Al-Arabi*, Kuwait, July, 1980.

98. A-Tamāwi, Sulaiman Mohammad, *Al-Sultat al-Thalath fi al-Dasatir al-Arabiyah wa fi al-Fikr al-Siyasi al-Islami*

(Muqaranah), Dar al-Fikr al-Arabi, Cairo, 1973, pp. 307-309.

99. Hilmi, Mahmood, *Nizam al-Hukm al-Islami Muqaranan be al-Nuzum al-Muwasirah*, Dar al-Fikr al-Arabi, Cairo, 1970; Al-Ansari, Abdul Hamid Ismail, *Al-Shura wa Atharuha fi al-Dimiqratiyah*, *op. cit.*, pp. 263-264.

*****

5

PARTICIPATION OF WOMEN AND NON-MUSLIMS

Shura-Sharing Women

Participation of women in the *Shura* is an issue on which there is a great difference of opinion among contemporary *Ulama* and intellectuals. There is also much dispute over whether Islam bestows political rights on women and entitles them to take part in elections and referendums and to become members of legislative assemblies, or to be eligible for being head to the four walls of their homes, and their duty consists only of looking after the education and training of their children and serving their husbands, their being allowed to stir out of their homes only with the permission of their menfolk and in emergencies.

There are three distinct trends among the Muslim *Ulama* and intellectuals regarding these issues. According to one school of thought, women do not enjoy political rights and Islam enjoins on them to attend only to household tasks; their sphere of activity being absolutely different from and opposite of that of men. This was the opinion of earlier *faqihs* and some contemporary scholars agree with them.

Another opinion on the question is that while Islam allows women every political status except that of head of state but the conditions in the Muslim society are not yet congenial for and ready for according such rights to women. This opinion is held by a majority of contemporary *Ulama* and intellectuals.

The third viewpoint is that Islam does not deprive women of any political right. Those who hold this view think that this is a purely political and social problem which has nothing to do with religion. They say that it is for the *Ummah* to formulate a policy in this regard, keeping in mind the existing political and social exigencies and needs. According to these thinkers Islam does not stand in the way of this. This viewpoint has been put forward by some thinkers in modern times.

Antagonists' Approach

Those advocating the first of the three attitudes towards political rights of women cite the following verse in support of their stand:

اَلرِّجَالُ قَوّٰمُوْنَ عَلَى النِّسَاءِ بِمَا فَضَّلَ اللّٰهُ بَعْضَهُمْ عَلٰى بَعْضٍ وَّبِمَا اَنْفَقُوْا مِنْ اَمْوَالِهِمْ

> "Men are the protectors and maintainers of women, because Allah has given the one more (strength) than the other, and because they support them from their means."[1]

Concept of *Qawwām*

This verse means that men are protectors of women (*qawwām*), and not the other way round.[2]

These scholars say that the job of the legislative assemblies of today is not merely to enact laws. They control the entire political life of a country. They form and dissolve ministries, formulate policies, enforce law and order, tackle financial and economic problems and take decisions in matters of war and peace. So, in their opinion, the functions of these assemblies are not merely those of *faqihs* or *muftis* but to administer the entire country.[3]

The above argument is rebutted with the assertion that the verse cited above refers the family life and has no reference at all to the political life of a country. But this rebuttal is not sustainable since it has been accepted by the *Ulama* that absolute conclusions may be drawn from general statements. In this verse injunction on the role of men as protectors is an absolute one since there is no mention of the word 'home' in it and hence its meanings cannot be limited to family life. If the objection raised to such an interpretation of the verse, is accepted the question arises as to how one who has not been made a protector at home can be the protector of the whole country which is merely a collection of all the homes.[4]

This refutation does not have much validity since Islam recognises the capacities of women in other respects. For example, a lady can be made the guardian of an orphan; she can be given the charge of a trust and in a dispute where both parties are women, Islam deems it desirable for a lady to act as *Qazi*. This shows that superiority of men over women does not apply outside the sphere of family life and that the verse cited above is relevant only in this context.[5]

Gender-based Superiority

Another verse that is cited by those who are apposed to the idea of conferring political rights on women is as follows:

وَلَهُنَّ مِثْلُ الَّذِي عَلَيْهِنَّ بِالْمَعْرُوفِ وَلِلرِّجَالِ عَلَيْهِنَّ دَرَجَةٌ

"And women shall have rights similar to the rights against them, according to what is equitable, but men have a degree (of advantage) over them."[6]

Those who cite the above verse in support of their argument say that by the degree of advantage of men over women, it refers to the former being the protectors of the latter. According to them, application of this verse is not limited to the domestic sphere since the protection of a state involves a much greater degree of responsibility than that of a household. They wonder if it could be visualised that Allah (SWT) who does not deem a women fit to be the protector of her own household can make her the protector of a collection of hundred of thousands of households.[7] Such an interpretation of the verse cited from *Surah al-Baqarah* has been objected to on the ground that to a certain degree men have been considered superior to women and it is correct to say that they are protectors of women. But this verse has been revealed in the context of the issues of marriage and divorce and so it is related wholly to domestic matters and hence to tear it away from its background and context and apply it to the realm of politics is entirely unjustified.[8] According to the critics of the above-mentioned interpretation the 'degree' that is mentioned in the verse related to physiological and natural features which is indispensable for a society since no family system can work without any one being responsible for it, otherwise the system would disintegrate leading to anarchy everywhere.[9]

The third *Qur'ānic* verse that is cited to establish the superiority of men over women is as follows:

وَلَاتَتَمَنَّوْا مَا فَضَّلَ اللّٰهُ بِهِ بَعْضَكُمْ عَلٰى بَعْضٍ لِلرِّجَالِ
نَصِيْبٌ مِّمَّا اكْتَسَبُوْا وَلِلنِّسَاءِ نَصِيْبٌ مِّمَّا اكْتَسَبْنَ

> "And in no wise covet those things in which Allah hath bestowed His gifts more freely on some of you than on others: to men is allowed what they earn and to women what they earn."[10]

On the basis of this verse it is argued that men are superior to women and hence they are the guardians and protectors in all collective and social matters. This interpretation of the verse can be controverted by asserting that the superiority of men is confined to the management of family affairs since there is no mention in the verse of the superiority of men over women in absolute terms but in relation to inheritance, as is clear from the reading of the whole of this verse and the one following it which reads as follows:

وَلِكُلٍّ جَعَلْنَا مَوَالِيَ مِمَّا تَرَكَ الْوَالِدٰنِ وَالْأَقْرَبُوْنَ وَالَّذِيْنَ
عَقَدَتْ أَيْمَانُكُمْ فَاٰتُوْهُمْ نَصِيْبَهُمْ اِنَّ اللّٰهَ كَانَ عَلٰى كُلِّ شَىْءٍ
شَهِيْدًا

> "To (benefit) everyone, We have appointed sharers and heirs to property left by parents and relatives. To those, close, to whom your right hand was pledged, give them their due portion. For truly Allah is witness to al things."[11]

If verse 32 and 33 are read together it becomes clear that the difference that Allah (SWT) has established between men and women and the line of distinction that He has drawn between the two should not lead to the generation of an atmosphere of jealousy, rivalry, envy, resistance of struggle but one should pray to Him to bestow greater munificence since He would bestow as much as He would deem right and proper on the basis of His understanding and wisdom. In these verses there is no mention of political or collective matters, nor is there any talk of the superiority of men over women in national or social affairs.[12]

Delimiting the Sphere

Two other verses, both from *Surah Ahzab*, have been cited by the advocates of the exclusion of women from political rights. They are as follows:

وَقَرْنَ فِىْ بُيُوْتِكُنَّ وَلَا تَبَرَّجْنَ تَبَرُّجَ الْجَاهِلِيَّةِ الْاُوْلٰى

> "And stay quietly in your hoses, and make not a dazzling display like that of the former ties of Ignorance."[13]

And

وَاِذَا سَاَلْتُمُوْهُنَّ مَتَاعًا فَسْئَلُوْهُنَّ مِنْ وَّرَاءِ حِجَابٍ ذٰلِكُمْ
اَطْهَرُ لِقُلُوْبِكُمْ وَقُلُوْبِهِنَّ

> "And when ye ask (the prophet's spouses) for anything ye want, ask them from before a screen: that makes for greater purity for your hearts and theirs."[14]

Those citing these verses in support of their contention, claim that they delimit the sphere of activities of women so that they leave their homes only in emergencies and for short periods. If these citations apply to Muslim women other than the consorts of the Prophet (SAW) the question arises as to whether they are allowed to leave their homes embellished with cosmetics and ornaments in a coquettish manner and whether they are permitted to converse with strange males in a manner that arouses desire in their hearts for these men.[15] They say that it cannot be argued on the basis of these verses that the consorts of the Prophet (SAW) had some particular weakness of character because of which they were deemed to be incapable of shouldering responsibilities relating to matters outside their domestic sphere and that other women were considered superior to them.

The above mentioned arguments have been controverted by other scholars on the ground that these verses referred specifically to the consorts of the Prophet (SAW) and not to women in general, as is clear form the following words of the *Qur'ān*:

يٰنِسَاءَ النَّبِيِّ لَسْتُنَّ كَأَحَدٍ مِّنَ النِّسَاءِ إِنِ اتَّقَيْتُنَّ فَلَا تَخْضَعْنَ
بِالْقَوْلِ فَيَطْمَعَ الَّذِى فِى قَلْبِهٖ مَرَضٌ وَقُلْنَ قَوْلًا
مَّعْرُوْفًا وَقَرْنَ فِى بُيُوْتِكُنَّ وَلَا تَبَرَّجْنَ تَبَرُّجَ الْجَاهِلِيَّةِ
الْأُوْلٰى

> "O consorts of the Prophet ! Ye are not like any of the (other) women. If ye do fear (Allah), be not too complainant of speech, lest one whose heart is diseased should be moved with desire, but speak ye a speech (that is) just. And stay quietly in your houses, and make not a dazzling display, like that of the former times of Ignorance."[16]

These scholars assert that the injunction of the *Qur'ān* asking for something from behind the screen as meant for the Prophet's consorts and not for women in general. The whole of the verse containing this injunction is as follows:

يٰاَيُّهَا الَّذِيْنَ اٰمَنُوْا لَا تَدْخُلُوْا بُيُوْتَ النَّبِيِّ اِلَّا اَنْ يُّؤْذَنَ لَكُمْ
اِلٰى طَعَامٍ غَيْرَ نٰظِرِيْنَ اِنٰهُ وَلٰكِنْ اِذَا دُعِيْتُمْ فَادْخُلُوْا فَاِذَا
طَعِمْتُمْ فَانْتَشِرُوْا وَلَا مُسْتَاْنِسِيْنَ لِحَدِيْثٍ اِنَّ ذٰلِكُمْ كَانَ
يُؤْذِى النَّبِيَّ فَيَسْتَحْيٖ مِنْكُمْ وَاللّٰهُ لَا يَسْتَحْيٖ مِنَ الْحَقِّ
وَاِذَا سَاَلْتُمُوْهُنَّ مَتَاعًا فَسْئَلُوْهُنَّ مِنْ وَّرَاءِ حِجَابٍ ذٰلِكُمْ
اَطْهَرُ لِقُلُوْبِكُمْ وَقُلُوْبِهِنَّ

> "O ye who believe enter not the Prophet's houses, until leave is granted you, for a meal, (and then) not (so early as) to wait for its preparation: but when you are invited enter; and when you have taken your meal, disperse, without seeking familiar talk. Such (behaviour) annoys the Prophet; he is ashamed to dismiss you, but Allah is not ashamed to tell you the truth. And when ye ask (his ladies) for anything ye want, ask them from before a screen: that makes for greater purity for your hearts and for theirs."[17]

These scholars say that it is not something strange or unique that some special instructions are given to the consorts of the Prophet (SAW) which are not meant for other ladies. For example, while other ladies are allowed to marry again after the death of their husbands on the expiry of the period of *iddah*, the consorts of the Prophet (SAW) were not allowed to do so. In the same way, if the consorts of the Prophet (SAW) had done anything obscene, Allah (SWT) would have awarded much more severe punishment to them than He would give to other women for committing a similar sin.

Answering a question raised by Maududi, Dr. Abdul Hameed Mutawalli writes that the dignity and sobriety with which consorts of the Prophet (SAW) were asked to conduct themselves does not mean that they were required to be confined to their houses but to behave in a more respectable, dignified, sober and noble manner than other ladies which they were able to do by spending most of their time at home.[18]

Dr. Fuad Abdul Munim goes a step further and says that the injunction of sitting behind the screen did not apply to common Muslim women. He cites the following verse of the *Qur'ān* in support of his contention:

وَقُل لِّلْمُؤْمِنَٰتِ يَغْضُضْنَ مِنْ أَبْصَٰرِهِنَّ وَيَحْفَظْنَ فُرُوجَهُنَّ وَلَا يُبْدِينَ زِينَتَهُنَّ إِلَّا مَا ظَهَرَ مِنْهَا وَلْيَضْرِبْنَ بِخُمُرِهِنَّ عَلَىٰ جُيُوبِهِنَّ

"And say to the believing women that they should lower their gaze and guard their modesty, that they should not display their beauty and ornaments except what (must ordinarily) appear thereof, that they should draw their veils over their bosoms."[19]

In the preceding verse men, too, have been asked to lower their gaze and guard their modesty. This shows as in the Age of Ignorance, during the life of the Prophet (SAW), too, there was free mixing between the sexes and that women came out of their houses to procure the necessities of life without observing *hijab*. This is why Islam has asked both men and women to lower their gaze and has enjoined on women not to display blandishments but to cover their bosoms.[20]

One clear evidence of *hijab* not being practised during the life of the Prophet (SAW) is that once on the occasion of *Hijjatul wida*, al Fazal was sitting behind the Prophet (SAW) in the field of Mina when a woman came before him to get a *fatwa* from him on behalf of her father relating to *Hajj*. Al Fazal and that woman started looking at each other, whereas the Prophet (SAW) turned the face of Al Fazal to the other side.[21] This tradition does not mention any comment made by the Prophet (SAW) on the lack of modesty on the part of the woman but simply says that he turned the face of Al Fazal to another side. Likewise, the woman are not required to cover themselves when offering prayers or performing *Hajj*.

The *Sahabah* knew that injunction regarding *hijab* applied only to the consorts of the Prophet (SAW) and that it was not binding on other ladies. Once the Prophet

(SAW) sent one of his *Sahabah* to another city to fetch his wife from there; Prophet's consort gave permission to him to enter her room, the *Sahabi* said that it was not proper for any male other than the Prophet (SAW) to see his consorts.

Abu Bakr was greatly annoyed at the wedding of Ikramah bin Abi Jahl with Qateela since she was a slave-girl of the Prophet (SAW). Abu Bakr wanted to punish both by stoning them to death. However, Umar persuaded him not to do so saying that Qateela was not a consort of the Prophet (SAW) since he did not have any sexual relations with her nor did he bind her to observe *hijab*.[22]

Another argument that is advanced against the application of the injunction of *hijab* to common Muslim women is that they participated actively in the Battle of Hunain which took place in 19 A.H. while the verse cited above had been revealed in 5 A.H. This is another proof to support the contention that the injunction regarding *hijab* applied only to the Prophet's consorts: otherwise it is not conceivable that a woman should take part in a battle fully armed and observe *hijab* at the same time.

Even for the consorts of the Prophet (SAW) the injunction regarding staying at home was not an absolute one. Otherwise the Prophet (SAW) would not have taken them out for *Hajj* and *Umra* even after the above-mentioned verse had been revealed, nor would he have permitted them to participate in battles, and to go out to meet their parents or to visit the sick.[23]

Dr. Abdul Hameed Mutawalli says that Islam does not prevent women from doing any work so long as she observes the Islamic code of propriety and manners. It allows women to enter into contracts without seeking the permission of their husbands or legal guardians, which is not possible while maintaining privacy or staying at home, since for this it is indispensable for them to stir out of their houses, Islam does not bar them from going to the market place and mixing with men. Islam does not consider it necessary that the husband or a close relation of a women should act on her behalf as a *wakil* for entering into a contract with someone.[24]

Women Mentally Deficient

Those who advocate that women should be confined to their homes also cite Traditions of the Prophet (SAW) in support of their contention, apart from citing from the *Qur'ān*. In this connection, the first *Hadith* they cite is that once the Prophet (SAW) said

مارأيتُ من ناقصات عقلٍ ودينٍ أذهبَ للبِّ الرجلِ الحازمِ
من إحداكنّ.

that he had not seen anyone who was more deficient in mind and religiosity than women, who can impair the wisdom of even a sane person. This *Hadith* is interpreted to mean that man is perfectly wise and superior than women and that it is he who can be the protector of the society. If this *Hadith* is seen in its proper context it would be found that the Prophet (SAW) has himself elucidated these words of his. Some ladies asked him what he meant by saying that they were inferior in matters of wisdom and religion. He asked them whether or not it was true that the evidence of a woman is deemed to be less than half that of a man. When they replied in the affirmative, he said that this was the proof of the inferiority of their minds. He then asked them whether or not it is true that they did not perform *Salah* nor did they observe fasts when they were menstruating. When the ladies again replied in the affirmative, the Prophet (SAW) said that this showed that they were inferior in religious matters.[25]

قلن وما نقصان ديننا وعقلنا يا رسولَ اللّه؟ قال: "أليس شهادةُ المرأةِ مثل نصف شهادة الرجل؟ قلن: بلى قال: "فذالك من نقصان عقلها. أليس إذا حاضت لم تصلّ ولم تصم"؟ قلن بلى قال: "فذلك من نقصان دينها".

The above-mentioned *Hadith* makes it clear that the deficiency of women is limited only to the issue of giving evidence. In this connection the *Qur'ān* says as follows:

وَاسْتَشْهِدُوْا شَهِيْدَيْنِ مِنْ رِّجَالِكُمْ فَاِنْ لَّمْ يَكُوْنَا رَجُلَيْنِ فَرَجُلٌ وَّامْرَاَتٰنِ مِمَّنْ تَرْضَوْنَ مِنَ الشُّهَدَاءِ اَنْ تَضِلَّ اِحْدٰهُمَا فَتُذَكِّرَ اِحْدٰهُمَا الْاُخْرٰى

> "And get to witnesses, out of your men. And if there are not two men, then a man and two women, such as ye choose for witness so that if one of them errs, the other can remind her."[26]

The reason for this is that sentiments affect the rational and psychological life of women. However, this does not mean that man is superior to woman in absolute terms or that it is right to allege that women are mentally deficient. The real issue involved here is that women are less interested in financial matters and there is greater probability of their being wrong in such matters and so it is better that two women give evidence in such affairs. Had women been deemed to be absolutely deficient mentally their evidence would not have been acceptable at all. To this may be added the fact that, according to Islam, the evidence of a single woman is acceptable in matters specially concerned with womenfolk like births, suckling, lineage etc., while man is not considered worthy of evidence in such affairs.[27] In fact, in these matters women have much stronger power of recall than men so that evidence of a single woman is regarded as creditworthy. Mohammad Abduh writes that need for the evidence of two women in financial matters is not due to any basic mental deficiency in women but owing to the fact that they are less interested in such affairs. However, in domestic, matters, the mental capacity of women can be fully depended upon and their judgement in such affairs is deemed more trustworthy than that of men.[28]

Some *Ulama* have said that on the basis of the *Hadith* cited above, it cannot be contended that women are deficient in religious or rational matters. The Prophet (SAW) did not intend to declare women as mentally deficient but to point out to the emotions that are at work in their mind in specific situations and hence the Prophet's pronouncement should not interpreted in absolute terms but as somewhat like a metaphor.[29] So on the basis of this *Hadith*, it cannot be contended that women ought to be deprived of political rights, nor can any objection be raised to the authenticity of this *Hadith*.

Dr. Abdul Hameed Mutawalli cites a number of incidents from the history of Islam attesting to the wisdom and sagacity of women and wonders how it is possible that on the one hand Islam has given women a sense of self-respect and has accorded them a distinguished status in the society and on the other it deems them as mentally deficient. He asks how one's mind can accept this *Hadith* as correct and how, if the *Hadith* is considered to be right, it can be reconciled with the pronouncements of the *Qur'ān* in this respect.[30]

This objection of Dr. Mutawalli is not sustainable. This *Hadith* is correct and its interpretation is also correct. However it cannot be used to pronounce women deficient in wisdom and to deprive them of political rights. It can only be contended on the basis of this *Hadith* that in matters of trade, contractual and financial affairs Islam has taken into consideration the possibility of women going wrong and has made certain stipulation so as to safeguard their rights.[31] This is why Khalid Mohammad Khalid says that if certain deficiencies are removed, there will be no difference between the sagacity of men and that of women, as may be seen in the educational institutions including the universities of today where girl students excel their male counterparts in academic achievements. He says that people lend to remember the first part of the concerned *Hadith* but forget its concluding part. He asks that if the mental deficiency of women referred to in the *Hadith* meant that they were dull witted how is it that they are able to dominate their intellectual and sagacious male counterparts.[32]

On the issue of giving evidence, the author asks if the testimony of a husband would be acceptable in a case concerning his wife. He says that the reply of Imam Abu Hanifa to this question is in the negative even though the husband happens to be man. His next questions are whether the testimony of a villager would be deemed trustworthy for a person belonging to a town and whether the evidence of a father would be acceptable in a case concerning his son even though both of them are men and asks whether these men can be regarded as mentally deficient. He avers that answer to these questions is in the negative, since there are basically issues of *fiqh*, according to which the testimony of a woman is considered one half that of a man just as *fiqh* stipulates the testimony of four men in certain categories of cases.[33]

The following objections may be raised to the above-mentioned arguments:

1. Only the evidence of women is admissible in specific issues with which men cannot be familiar. This is because

such issues are of especial interest to women and hence their testimony relating to these matters is deemed to be authentic. On this basis it cannot be argued that women are perfect in wisdom and sagacity.

2. From the instances cited above it is clear that non-admissibility of evidence of men is limited to cases involving their kith and kin since they are not likely to be neutral in such cases. On the contrary, the testimony of women is not admissible on the ground that their attitudes are dominated by emotions. These two categories of issues are different from each other and an example from either of them cannot be applied to the other.

Hence it is contended that man has a superior status and this justifies his claim of superiority over his female counterparts.[34]

It had been argued that while it is correct to say that evidence tendered by women enjoys credibility and validity in specific matters relating to them since men are ignorant in such matters, it does not establish the deficiency of wisdom in women. Another argument that is advanced is that even if the evidence of a woman is deemed to have one half of the credibility compared with that of a man such a superiority of men over women is confined only to matters of evidence and it does not imply that men are superior to women in absolute terms nor it does justify the latter's being deprived of political rights. However, it can be established that men have greater rights in matters of evidence than women, but it cannot be argued that women have no political rights at all. It has further been argued that had this superiority of men over women been deemed sufficient to deprive women of their rights, such a principle would have had a general application, and a large segment of the population of men, too, would have been deprived of political rights.[35]

Ahādith Cited

Those who advocate that women should be deprived of political rights cite the following traditions of the Prophet (SAW) in support of their contention:

1. شاوروهنّ وخالفوهنّ

   Consult women but not heed their advice,

2. طاعةُ النّساءِ ندمةٌ

   Obedience women has to be regretted,

3. هلكت الرجال حين أطاعت النّساء

   Men have become victims of destruction whenever they have heeded women,

4. خالفُوا النّساءَ فإنّ فى خلافهنّ البركة

   Oppose women since opposing them brings blessing, and

5. لا يفعلنّ أحدكم أمرًا حتى يستشيرَ فإن لم يجد من يستشيرُه فليستَشِر إمرأةً ثم ليُخالِفها فإنّ فى خلافها البركةَ.

   None of you ought to do anything before consulting some one. If one does not find a man to consult he should consult a woman. But he should not heed her advice, since not heeding would bring him the blessings.

However, scholars of the *Hadith* literature have questioned the authenticity of the above-mentioned traditions. The first of these has been rejected as being a *marfu*.[36] The second one is *dhaeef* and Imam Saghani even considers it as a forged one. Though the third of these traditions has been accepted as *Sahih* by Hakim. Imam Zahabi has supported him in this respect. Zahabi himself has quoted Ibn Adi to the effect that it is a *dhaeef* tradition. The fourth *Hadith* has also been deemed to be *dhaeef* while the fifth one has been considered *munqate* and one of those to whom it has been attributed is Isa who has been judged as extremely unreliable by the author of *Tuhfah al-Ahwazi*,[37] while the author of *Fath al-Bari* in his comment on it says that the Prophet (SAW) used to consult Umm Salmah, which shows that it was proper to seek the opinion of educated and learned ladies.[38]

Scholars objecting to the bestowal of political rights on women cite another tradition of the Prophet (SAW) which says,

> وإذا كان أمراؤكم شراركم وأغنياؤكم بخلاءكم، وأموركم إلى نساءكم فبطن الأرض خير لكم من ظهرها.
>
> 'when the worst amongst you become *amirs*, when the wealthy in your midst become miserly and when your affairs are put in the charge of women, the belly of the earth would be better than its back'.[39]

These scholars aver that this *Hadith* prevents handing over the reins of the society of women and that conferring the right of vote on them and making them eligible to be candidates for the *Shura* are against the spirit of this *Hadith*. But this *Hadith* has been deemed to be *ghareeb* by Imam Tirmidhi on the basis of its wording, style and spirit.

Those supporting conferring political rights on women say that even if the *Hadith* is accepted as reliable it cannot be maintained that conferring political rights on women is the same thing as handing over the reins of the society to them. This is why Abd al-Mut'aal al-Sayeedi has said that handing over the reins of the society would be true only when the respective role of men and women are reversed, with womenfolk carrying on the activities of men and men performing the duties of women, managing the affairs of the kitchen and bringing up the children, and with women leaving their homes and managing the affairs of the state. He says that even if the situation is not absolutely changed but is somewhat near it, one would be justified in saying that the affairs of the society are in the hands of womenfolk. However, according to him, it would not be against the spirit of *Hadith* if alongside menfolk a few women take interest in some affairs of the state, since in such a situation, affairs of the state would be in the hands of men though a few women would be participating in their management. He says that the meaning of *Hadith* is absolutely clear. It is meant to make people beware of the situation when there is a complete reversal of the respective roles of the genders and all or most of the affairs are in the hands of womenfolk.[40]

Implications of the Hadith Negating the Political Role of Women

A well known *Hadith* which the *Ulama* and scholars cite as a decisive one in respect of the issue of the bestowal of political rights on women is worth being examined and analysed. Bukhari, Ibn Hanbal and Nasai cite a tradition of the Prophet (SAW) to the effect that when he heard that the Iranians had crowned the daughter of Kisra, he spontaneously said, that

لَن يُفلحَ قومٌ وَلّوا أمرهُم إمرأةً

> 'a nation would not be prosper which has handed over its affairs to a woman'.[41]

The *Ulama* assert that though this *Hadith* has been related as a piece of information it cannot be ignored since it cites the actual words of the Prophet (SAW), who is talking of the damage that is caused when a woman is appointed by a people to rule over them, and hence it would be advisable to avoid such a state of affairs. It is in the nature of a negative thing, though not a direct negative but a stylised and indirect one. It simply means that women should not be given the charge of all the responsibilities of the state except for those over which there is an agreement that they should be managed by them. They say that this is so since the word *amr* has been used in it which has a general application, according to which the appointment of women to the position of head of state, membership of judiciary and parliament and command of armies are all prohibited.[42]

The real ground for preventing women from occupying such positions is the fact that they are women. In this respect the term *imr'ah* (woman) has been mentioned clearly. However, advanced in education and learning unparalleled in wisdom and sagacity a woman may be, her being a woman is her real handicap, since being affected by sentiments and by contingencies and emergencies is her real weakness which enfeebles her power of understanding and undermines her determination.[43]

This argument has been rebutted even by those who are in favour of giving all political rights to women except the headship of the state as well as by those who even advocate conferment on them of the rights of being the head of the state. The first of these two groups says that the *Hadith* cited above only refers to the status of the highest *imamah* or head of state and it means that women ought not be made head of state but may be entrusted with other political posts and responsibilities. These scholars advance two arguments in support of their contention. The first of these is that in the *Hadith* referred to above, the word *amr* has been used which cannotes the post that includes all the affairs of the *Ummah* and this happens to be the highest post of *imamah* and the term does not refer to the membership of the judiciary, the ministry and command of the army.

This argument has been met by averring that a basic principle of *Usool al-Fiqh* is that a general statement is applicable to all cases, and includes every individual. For example, if a person says that his children have come, it would mean that a particular child of his has also come ad so has another particular child. In short his statement will include all his children. On the basis of this principle, the *Hadith* cited above implies a woman cannot have all the posts and political responsibilities one after another. In other words, this *Hadith* means that a nation would not prosper if it bestows the status of caliph or gives the responsibilities of a ministry or hands over the judiciary to a woman or makes her the commander of the army.

To apply the term *amr* to all the affairs of the state and then to confine these to *imamah* is the result of ignoring and dealing casually with *Usool al-Fiqh*. From what has been said above, the law of general application (*dalalah al-hukm al-aam*) is clear. So how can the *Hadith* referred to above be limited to the *imamah*.[44]

The following two arguments have been advanced to counter this refutation:

The generality of the individual (*mufrad*) related to the proper noun cannot be applied on all occasions if there is the possibility of being bound by any particular age. And such a possibility exists here. This means that women have not been excluded in absolute terms from any position of responsibility but that those responsibilities have been vested in them which they have the capacity to shoulder, and they have been exempted from the responsibilities the burden of which cannot be borne by them. It is another matter if there is any guidance in the matter from the *nass* (the text of the *Qur'ān* or the *Sunnah*) or any decision has been arrived at by *ijma.*[45]

The second argument advanced in this connection is that if it is accepted that a *mufrad* related to a proper noun may include the generality – as it is generally accepted in *Usool al-Fiqh* the injunction may be transformed from totality to particularity. For example, if some one says that men are holding a big rock, it does not mean that all the men are doing it but that a few men are doing so, though the general term *rijal* (men) refers to all men. In the same way, while the term *amr* connotes all affairs it has been used in the *Hadith* cited above particularly for the highest position of *imamah.*[46]

An another argument put forward by scholars who are in favour of political rights for women is that the *Hadith* cited above refers particularly to *imamah* or caliphate and its aim is to declare women eligible for being vested with particular responsibilities. According to these scholars this *Hadith* indicates that women are capable of shouldering all kinds of responsibilities except that of the caliph or the highest *imamah*, against which there is an injunction in this *Hadith*.

In Islam, there is a general principle of equality. The *Qur'ān* has enunciated the idea of the equality of rights and obligations between men ad women. However, if some thing has been said in the *nass*, it constitutes an exception to this general principle and confining the position of the head of state to men is an exceptional matter which does not come under the purview of any general principle.[47]

The scholars, who are in favour of bestowing of all political rights on women including that of the headship of the state, advance four arguments based on the *Hadith* under discussion in support of their contention, which are as follows:

1. This *Hadith* refers specifically to a particular incident. No general conclusion can be drawn from it.

2. It is based on *Khabr Wahed*(single channel).

3. This was a temporary injunction and hence it is not applicable to all ages.

4. This *Hadith* merely imposes restrictions on the despotic and arbitrary powers of women.

It would be worthwhile to analyse the above-mentioned arguments based on the *Hadith* under discussion and the objections that have been raised to these arguments in order to arrive at a correct interpretation of the *Hadith*.

Confined to Iranian Context

According to the scholars, the first arguments mentioned above, is related to a particular incident and hence the injunction contained in the *Hadith* can be applicable only to that incident. The Prophet (SAW) uttered these words when he heard that due to lack of male members of the royal family, the Iranians had crowned a princess. Earlier, when a messenger of the Prophet (SAW) had gone to the court of Emperor Kisra, he had torn his letter into pieces due to his arrogance and haughtiness. On hearing this the Prophet (SAW) had called upon Allah to tear the Iranian empire apart. Allah acceded to this curse from his favorite Prophet (SAW) and there arose such a situation that members of the royal family started fighting one another, with the result that none of its male members survived to shoulder the onerous responsibilities of the empire and people were compelled to hand over the reins of absolute power to the princess. It was such a situation that the Prophet (SAW) had said that a nation which makes a woman its head of state will never prosper. The comment of the Prophet (SAW) is related to this particular incident since the menfolk of Iran had been proved to be worthless and there was none amongst them who could take the reins of the government in his hands.

Whether or not an injunction based on a particular case has a general application is a controversial issue among the *fuqaha* (experts in jurisprudence). While Imam Ghazali says that a pronouncement based on a particular case should apply to all similar cases; other *mufrad* do not agree with him. Imam Ghazali says that conjecture regarding such a general principle can be applied to particular cases also and for this even a weak argument is adequate.[48]

It appears from the *Hadith* under discussion that it is meant to warn people that making a woman as head of a state militates against material welfare and that this statement has a particular relevance for the people of Iran, since their menfolk were incapable of shouldering the responsibilities of the head of state and hence this *Hadith* should be treated as referring to a particular case and ought not to be applied universally. In modern times, several nations have had women as their heady of state and they have been successful. However, even today if a nation reaches a stage when its menfolk are lacking in ability to shoulder the burden of the state and are compelled to accept a woman as their head of state, it can never flourish. This is so because management of affairs of a country depends upon the capacity and calibre of men and if men of a particular state are lacking in this capacity, women would be lacking in it even to a higher degree and disaster would be enevitable.[49]

Reliability of *Khabr Wahed*

Another argument advanced by those advocating the bestowal of all political rights to women is that the *Hadith* cited above is based on *khabr wahed.* It is derived from a single channel and it is unanimously held that such a *Hadith* is to be deemed *zann* even if it has been narrated by Bukhari. Abduh does not very often argue on the basis of a *khabr wahed* while Imam Abu Hanifah bases his arguments on famous traditions rather than on *khabr wahed.*[50] Hence, according to these scholars, this *Hadith* is not a definite to them, just as definite bases are required for *Salah*, *Saum*, Hajj, *Zakah* and other collective injunctions, a definite pronouncement is needed to deprive women of a particular right. The utmost that can be said on the basis of this *Hadith* is that the injunction contained in it is a *zann* which can be refuted with the employment of other arguments.[51]

The objection that has been raised to this argument is that though it is true that a *khabr wahed* is open to question, a part from the Khawarij and Mutazelah all other *Ulama* have accepted it since a *zann* which is preferable is sufficient as an argument in practical matters, and a large number of edicts of *Shariah* have their source in such traditions. They maintain that it is wrong to aver that Imam Abu Hanifah is against basing an argument on *khabr wahed.* The bulk of Hanafi *Ulama* as well the Shaafii, Maliki and Hanbali, all are of the opinion that it is obligatory to follow a *khabr wahed*, though they think that no definite conclusion can be drawn from it. Since knowledge about something does not necessarily mean that acting according to it is obligatory and in practical matters a preferable *zann* is enough. Besides, the *Ulama* of Zahiriyah and several *Ahl al-Hadith* scholars think that an injunction that deems acting upon it as obligatory also considers acting according to *Khabr Yaqini* too obligatory.[52] However, the propriety of acting on a *khabr wahed* and deeming preferred conjecture as adequate are applicable only to civil and criminal laws. Preferred conjecture cannot be deemed to be adequate in relation to constitutional issues which are concerned with the political system, the administrative machinery, freedom of individuals and their political rights. In such matters only a *Khabr Yaqini i.e., Sunnah Mutawātirah* or *mashhurah* can form the basis for a constitutional edict. While, the *Ulama* say that in regard to matters relating to *Masalih Mursalah* and issues concerning welfare of the common people *Khabr Yaqini* is essential, it will be indispensable in regard to edicts or a permanent nature.

The *fuqahā* deem acting according to *khabr wahed* as obligatory and it has been considered correct on the part of *qazis* to base their judgement on *khabr wahed* alone. This is an example of *qiyas an al-fariq* (illogical conjecture) since the *Hadith* that is under discussion cannot be the basis of pronouncing judgements (in individual cases) but for making a law. That is to say that in this case the status of the Prophet (SAW) is not that of a *qazi* but one of a legislator. In such a situation it is indispensable that a law is made on the basis of *khabr yaqini* and not on the basis of a *zann.* In judicial matters too, the evidence of a single individual is not deemed to be sufficient but for this two, and in some cases four witnesses are required. It is a principle of jurisprudence that the *hudud* in the doubtful cases cannot be implemented. This means that the authenticity of a *hadith* is essential for their implementation and constitutional laws are much more important than judicial cases. Hence in matters of the former much greater circumspection and certainty is needed that in other matters.[53] To sum up, it may be said that *khabr wahed* cannot be depended upon as the basis when a principle is being derived or a law is being enacted for which no guidance can be obtained from the *Qur'ān*. However, a *khabr wahed* can be the basis of argumentation to be elucidated some point or to make a general statement apply to specific cases. However, in case of a constitutional issue it is essential for the *Sunnah* to be *Mutawātir*. This distinction between the two sets of issues is nothing new since it is an established principle of *fiqh* that in matters of codes of beliefs (*aqaid*) *Sunnah Mutawātirah* is essential and no principle can be based on a *khabr wahed*.[54]

To the above-mentioned arguments the objection that has been raised is that the *fuqaha* do not attach much significance to constitutional issues and legal details but these have also been deemed by them as subsidiary sets of beliefs, and hence though the condition of *tawatur* has been imposed, such condition does not apply to subsidiary laws and orders and this is so since according to them, the importance of constitutional laws is no greater than that of civil and criminal laws.

Non-Universality of Hadith

The third argument is that there are two kinds of injunctional traditions. While some of them have been employed for deriving general laws, others are in the nature of temporary pronouncements which do not have general application and universality. The *fuqaha* say that if circumstances establish that particular pronouncements have been made or actions taken by the Prophet (SAW) as the Messenger of Allah and were meant to be made into laws, such pronouncements and actions would have the status of permanent laws like pronouncing something as *halal* (permissible) and *haram* (prohibited). However, they say that things uttered or actions taken by him as head of state or leader of Muslims do not have the status of general laws since these were based on existing contingencies, like deploying armies, appointing *qazis*, entering into agreements, management of financial affairs and other such matters which belong to the second categories of *ahadith.* In the same way, these *fuqaha* say, a general law that the Prophet (SAW) pronounced as a *qazi*, too, ought not to be deemed as universal and immutable.[55] Some *Ulama* also hold that if it is established by definite evidence that in such and such matter the Prophet (SAW) had taken into consideration a certain attitude of the people at that particular time, it too would not have a general and everlasting application.[56] In other words, according to these scholars, the *Hadith* in which the Prophet (SAW) has said that the nation which has handed over its affairs to a woman would not prosper, cannot be deemed to have a general and permanent application since he had made this pronouncement not as the messenger of Allah and a preacher but as a head of state and the leader of his people. Again, they say that from the background of this *Hadith* it is clear that it has been uttered under specific circumstances, when, owing to the prevailing political conditions, internal disturbances and mutual dissensions it was not possible for men to handle the reins of the government of Iran. Hence, they say that with a change in circumstances this utterance of the Prophet (SAW) would not be applicable.

Dr. Salahuddin Dabbus has rebutted the above-mentioned argument as follows:

1. Those demanding *Tawātur* of *Hadith* for the implementation of constitutional injunction and laws and wish to limit the applications of *ahādith* to specific circumstances and cases go against the principle derived by the *fuqahā* that the *ahādith* shall apply universally irrespective of the reasons behind their utterance. If the

wordings are couched in general terms, they shall have a general application.

2. The fact that a constitution is the product of specific circumstances and times does not mean that the *Hadith* under discussion has a limited application. Because though the constitutional laws are limited by the prevailing conditions and demands of the age such a limitation is not necessarily applicable to revealed laws.

3. Taking the circumstances and demands of the time into consideration cannot be confined merely to constitutional laws but can also apply to commercial, criminal and civil and all other matters, such an approach would render the entire *Shariah* severely limited in its application.[57]

The above-mentioned objections leveled by Dabbus have been met with the following observations:

1. One of the principles of *fiqh* is that if something has been said in general terms is should have a general application, and there should be no need to look for any specific reason for it. But this principle is not a definite and unchangeable one, since there are many actions of the Prophet (SAW) that are the products of specific times and circumstances and hence no *mujtahid* can ignore these considerations.[58] Moreover, even the principles of *fiqh* are not deemed to be definite now. Many contemporary scholars are openly saying that *ijtihad* is required even in respect of these principles. Need is being felt to derive new *Usool al fiqh* in the light of the *Qur'ān* and the *Sunnah* in the present age of progress in science and technology. Even Shaukāni wrote a book entitled *Irshad al-Fuhūl ila Tahqeeq al-Haqq min Ilm al-Usool* suggesting deletions from and additions to these principles. There is much scope for correction, amendment and addition in *Usool al-fiqh*. Dr. Yusuf al-Qaradhawi has written that many

principles of *fiqh* require greater elucidation. He has also pointed out to the necessity of reviewing the division of the *Sunnah* into legal and non-legal elements and has suggested the need for a doctoral project on the subject in view of its importance.[59]

2. In reply to another argument of Dabbus it has been said that taking the conditions and times into consideration has not been characteristic of man-made law only but Muslim *fuqahā* have also kept these in mind Imam Qarafi has written that actions taken by the Prophet (SAW) as head of state cannot be made general laws since these were done in specific set of conditions.[60] For example, the Prophet (SAW) has ordained that a person who has killed some one in a war will get the belongings of the person killed. This *Hadith* cannot be the basis of a common law since it is among political laws which depend upon the contingencies and demands of every age.[61] Hence, Imam Kāsāni has written that these words of the Prophet (SAW) were uttered to persuade people to participate in *Jihad* and is not a universally applicable law which cannot be uttered. It is possible that the Prophet (SAW) had said this while addressing a particular community. So, no general principle can be derived from this *Hadith.*[62] There has been a controversy over this *Hadith* only due to the difference among the *fuqaha* on whether this pronouncement was made by the Prophet (SAW) as a messenger of Allah and a preacher or as a head of state and political leader.[63] On the basis of this *Hadith* the *fuqaha* have held that a Muslim who kills a *kāfir* (non-believer), or a *Mushrik* (polytheist) would not be the owner of the belongings of the person who has been killed. It is for the *imam* to legislate in this matter keeping in mind the welfare of the *Ummah* and the demands of the time.

Another *Hadith* of this kind is that

مَن أحيا أرضًا ميتةً فهى لَهُ

"a person brings a dead piece of land to life will be its owner."

According to Abu Hanifah, this can only be done with the consent of *imam* since the Prophet (SAW) had ordained it as a head of state and leader of the Muslims, while Imam Mālik and Imam *Shafi'i* accept this *Hadith* as the basis of a common law and consider the approval of the *imam* or head of state in this respect unnecessary, since both of them believe that the Prophet (SAW) had ordained it as a preacher.

There is a similar controversy over the *Hadith* under discussion, attributing the failure of a nation which makes a woman its head of state as to whether the Prophet (SAW) made this pronouncement as the head of state or as the messenger of Allah. A majority of *Ulama* hold that he had said this as a Prophet (SAW) and hence this utterance has the status of a general law and it is obligatory to follow it, while some contemporary scholars are of the opinion that it was a political pronouncement which had been made by him as a head of state and hence no general principle can be based on it, and that this *Hadith* cannot be universally applied.[64]

3. In reply to the third objection it has been said that the fact that demands of circumstances and time are taken into consideration in the laws of other faiths does not nullify the *Sunnah* and the sources of Islamic *Shariah*. The *fuqaha* have held that the orders that were issued by the Prophet (SAW) as an *imam*, head of state and *qazi* and the pronouncement he made in the light of his experience and personal opinions cannot be deemed to be universal laws which have to be enforced in all ages. This principle of *fuqāhā* does not negate the Islamic *Shariah*. While talking

about certain pronouncements of the Prophet (SAW) the *fuqāhā* have made it clear that these had been made keeping the circumstances and the demands of the time in mind but in spite of this they have not pronounced any *fatwa* nullifying the *Shariah*.

This matter may be looked at from another angle, that of the proportion of verses relating to the injunctions of *Shariah* out of the total number of verses in the *Qur'ān*. But of 6000 *Qur'ān*ic verses only 200 relate to injunctions of *Shariah* and of these 200 verses, too, very few are concerned with constitutional laws. It may also be seen that while the *Qur'ān* deals in detail with injunctions related to observances (*ibādāt*), punishments (*hudūd*) and public affairs (*muamalāt*), the same is not true of constitutional matters.[65] This is because constitutional laws are to a very great extent conditioned by the circumstances in which they are enacted and enforced. It should be kept in mind that this entire discussion is about *Hadith* relating constitutional matters of a permanent nature on the basis of which permanent constitutional measures have to be adopted which are obligatory in every age. The discussion is not about constitutional laws which are not of a permanent nature but are concerned with details, elucidations and explanations.

If there is a correct procedures, laws can be made temporarily by subsidiary time-bound constitutional articles. The *Sunnah* made many such laws like these on lost camels, prohibiting women from praying in the mosques, triple divorce being treated as final, non-acceptance of the evidence one's father or husband, acceptance of bail in murder cases by mistake etc.[66] In the same way, if specific procedures are followed in adopting constitutional measures, there would be no danger of the entire *Shariah* becoming invalid.[67]

Check on Arbitrary Power

The fourth argument advanced by those who are in favour of the bestowal of all political rights on women is that the *Hadith* under discussion prevents people from handing over absolute power in the hands of a woman and this would be possible only when all kinds of political rights are bestowed on her and she becomes an absolute ruler heading a tyrannical regime and when there is none among men to challenge her absolute and tyrannical rule and that she runs the administration without consulting sagacious and farsighted men and things come to such a pass that the woman starts dealing with all or most matters in a dictatorial and arbitrary manner.[68] They add that a single man or woman head of state simply cannot have all the reins of power in his or her hands in any government which is based on the Islamic system of *Shura* and in which decisions are taken by a majority within the confines of the *Shariah*, since in such a system the real power vests in the representatives of the people and their legislative bodies. They say that the *Hadith* under discussion does not apply to such a case.[70] In modern times the head of state in the cabinet system of government has only a nominal status and in practice the real power is in the hands of others. There is a lack of centralization in religious and political affairs in the system that prevails in Muslim countries in the present age and *Khilafah* today does not have the connotation it once had, since earlier the *Khalifah* managed all the affairs of the state directly.

Distinction between religious and political powers and the above-mentioned system of government prevailing in Muslim countries are not in consonance with the spirit of the Islamic *Shariah* since Islam does not believe in this kind of secularism nor does it advocate the concept of duality of the spiritual and temporal aspects of life.

According to the *Qur'ān*, the Prophet (SAW) was invested with all the religious and political powers. According to Islam, a caliph should not have only political sagacity and a grasp of administrative affairs but he is also a protector of religion and *Shariah.* His duties include propagation of the faith, waging of Jihad against the enemies of Islam, establishment of the basic pillars of Islam, protection of the rights of Muslims etc.[71] However it would not be correct to consider these duties and powers as being tantamount to a theocratic system.[72]

According to these scholars, it is not necessary to exclude women from shouldering the responsibilities of caliphate if the true spirit of the Islamic system of government is prevailing and the principles of the *Shura* are being observed. However, it is no longer proper to burden a woman with the responsibilities of the caliphate since the system of government that has been in existence in Muslim countries after the period of *al-Khulafa al-Rashidūn* and the manner in which this system started departing from the Islamic system of *Shura*, this is no longer valid as it would militate against the *Hadith* under discussion.

History also Disapproves

Those who are against the bestowal of political rights on women base their third argument of *Ijma* (consensus) and historical evidence. According to them, during the entire period of the history of Islam women have been kept away from participation in political affairs. They say that nowhere in the Islamic history is there any example of a woman being given any political responsibility. Ladies during the early years of Islam, especially the consorts of the Prophet (SAW) were adorned with the gifts of education and culture but they never offered themselves for any political position, nor did the Muslim society of the time ask them to tread the thorny path of politics. Had the *Qur'ān* or the *Sunnah* allowed this, both men and women would not have ignored it. Ladies did not join the special assembly of *Saqifah bani Sāedah* nor did they participate in the ceremony for offering allegiance to caliphs. A large number of assemblies of the *Shura* were held during the period of the Prophet (SAW) and that of the *al-khulafa al-Rashidūn* but there is no evidence of participation of women in any of them.[73]

Ibn Qudāmah says that women are suitable neither for the highest *imamah* (caliphate) nor for the posts of provincial governors. Therefore, neither the Prophet (SAW) nor any of the *al-khulafa al-Rashidūn* nor those who succeeded them appointed any woman was a *qazi* or a governor. Had this been deemed proper the entire history of Islam would not have been bereft of a single instance of any precedent in this respect.[74] Consequently, there have been a consensus that an indispensable condition for the post of *imamah* is that one should be a male.[75]

Some scholars have challenged such inferences from the *Ijma* and the history of Islam. They cite several instances of the participation of ladies in political affairs during the early years of Islam. Some of these are as follows:

1. Caliph Umar appointed Shifā bint Abdullah as a superintendent of the market which was undoubtedly a position involving public relations.[76]

2. An outstanding example of the participation of women in political affairs is the role Āisha (consort of the Prophet) played in the Battle of *Jamal*. She was practically the leader of the caravan of three thousand people which marched from Makkah to Basrah demanding punishment to those who were responsible for the assassination of caliph

Uthman. During this campaign, she dealt with religious and political matters also. Fro example, when the question arose as to whether Talha should lead the prayers or Zubair should do so, she ruled that this duty should be assigned to Abdullah b. Zubair. She also wrote letters to the people of Basrah and to Ahnaf b. Qais, which establishes that the leadership of the campaign was in her hands. And when Abu Bakrah who is also a narrator of the *Hadith* under discussion, which is supposed to exclude women from the position of head of state reached in the presence of Āisha at that time he spontaneously said that the consort of the Prophet (SAW) was issuing commands and was wielding the real power in the campaign and that the *Hadith* was against a lady doing so. This shows that people knew that on that occasion the leadership of the campaign was in the hands of the consort of the Prophet (SAW).[77]

This argument based on the role of Āisha in the Battle of *Jamal* has been countered with the contention that it was not her purpose to wage a Jihad, nor did she leave her home to lead the army, and that her sole aim was to avenge the wrongful assassination of caliph Uthman. It was with this aim in view that she had stepped out her home and this action was not related to public relations or for shouldering any political responsibility which involved the use of her personal authority and power.

However, this objection is not tenable since Āisha did not stir out of her home only to seek vengeance for the murder of caliph Uthman but for leading an army in order to correct deviations and to re-establish the *Shura* system and she wielded power in real terms. It was on realizing the authority that she wielded that Abu Bakrah had said that Allah had saved him from getting involved with the sedition (*fitnah*) since the Prophet (SAW) had said that a nation could not prosper which had handed over its affairs to woman. Since Abu Bakr̄ah saw with his own eyes that Āisha was wielding power, he did not participate in the Battle of *Jamal*.[78]

3. There are a large number of instances of the participation of women in the affairs of the *Ummah* in the history of Islam, like the role played by them in the second allegiance of Aqabah, and the political activities of Fatimah (daughter of the Prophet) during the caliphate of Abu Bakr. History also records on instance of a lady objecting to a ruling by caliph Umar related to the payment of bridal dower (*sadaq*). Women also took part in debates and discussions held in mosques which were counterparts of modern parliaments. In this respect the role played by Nāilah, wife of caliph Uthman is well-known.

4. It is also not correct to say that ladies did not participate in or were not invited to consultative assemblies. It is fairly well-known that the Prophet (SAW) often consulted Umm Salmah and there is evidence establishing that the second caliph included women among those whom he consulted.[79] Abdur Rahman b. Auf held consultations with women too on the issue of caliphate after the martyrdom of caliph Umar. Ahmad Shauqi al-Fanjari says that the Prophet (SAW) invited ladies also to participate in the assemblies of the *Sahabah* which he convened before taking part in a battle.[80]

5. It is claimed that there is a consensus (*ijma*) among the *Ummah* against making a lady head of state. However, the question arises as to what the scholars mean by the term *ijma*? If they mean by it the *ijma* of the *Sahabah*, then they are wrong since there is no evidence in the history of Islam to the effect that the *Sahabah* had taken any such decision at any of their assemblies. Nor is there any mention in the accounts of the *Sirah* of the Prophet (SAW) that any *Sahabi* had made any such pronouncement and other *Sahabah* had

put a seal of confirmation on it with their silence so that it could be termed a silent consensus (*ijma al-sukut*). If it is contended that according to the *Hadith* under discussion a woman ought not to be made head of state nor should she be vested with any political responsibility the contention can be countered by saying that there was a difference of opinion regarding this even during the period of the *Sahabah*, an example of which is the marching out of Āisha as the head of a large army. This shows that there was no *ijma* nor was there any commonly accepted practice in the matter.

If someone says that in practice the *Sahabah* were against this and they did not assign the responsibilities of public affairs to women and that there was no *'urf 'aam* (commonly accepted practice) in the matter, it can be contended that there are instances in the history of Islam indicating that women were appointed to posts relating to public affairs; and even if it is conceded that the *Sahabah* did not assign positions relating to political and public affairs to women this does not negate its propriety and it can not be called *ijma*. It is possible that in that age there was a preponderance of menfolk or that women were not interested in assuming responsibilities or the society of the time had a special temperament due to which there was continual warfare and it was not deemed necessary for women to enter the field of action.

If it is contended that though there was no *ijma* during the period of *Sahabah* the *fuqaha* who came after them had put a ban on appointing women to position connected with public affairs through *ijma*. It will raise many pertinent questions like whether it was possible for an *ijma* to be held with the participation of all the *Ahl al-Ijtihad* and *fuqaha* whether the works of all of them are available to religious scholars to lay claim to *ijma* and whether there exists no possibility of there being any group of *fuqaha* who held the opposite view whose opinions are not available and whether the pronouncements of such *fuqaha* on the issue have been compiled. The utmost that may be contended is that in view of the conditions and demands of their times many *fuqaha* had made pronouncements against the participation of women in public affairs and that such pronouncements can be overruled in view of the changed conditions, and demands of the present day.[81]

Above the arguments of those scholars have been discussed who try to establish that women cannot be deprived of political rights on the basis of citation from the *Qur'ān*, the *Hadith* or reference to *Ijma* and Islamic history. Arguments advanced in favour of their contention as well as the rebuttal of the objections raised to it have also been dealt with in detail.

Protagonists' Approach

Now a discussion can be taken up on the stand taken up by another group of scholars who hold that women can be appointed to every public office except that of the head of state and that Islam is not opposed to it. Views of some scholars can also be taken up who are of the opinion that the social conditions of the present day are not suitable for bestowing political rights on women, holding that Islam has raised women to the great heights of honour, and the modern society has not reached the stage in which women could be bestowed political rights.

Concept of Qur'ānic Equality

This group of scholars have cited the following verses of the *Qur'ān* in support of their contention:

1. وَلَهُنَّ مِثْلُ الَّذِي عَلَيْهِنَّ بِالْمَعْرُوفِ

"And women shall have rights similar to the rights against them, according to what is equitable."[82]

These scholars claim that this verse indicates the equality of rights and duties between the sexes. However, it may be contended against interpretation of the verse that it has been revealed in the context of divorce and is aimed at elucidating the mutual rights of the consorts and hence it cannot be cited in support of the contention that women ought to be given political rights.

2. وَلَقَدْ كَرَّمْنَا بَنِي آدَمَ

"We have honoured the children of Adam."[83]

According to scholars advocating conferment of political rights on women, this verse shows that men and women are equal since the word '*bani*' includes both the sexes and that respect for women demands that they ought to be given all those rights that are enjoyed by men. This argument has been countered by contending that if for some reason women are deprived of certain political rights, it does not affect their honour at all.

3. وَالْمُؤْمِنُونَ وَالْمُؤْمِنَاتُ بَعْضُهُمْ أَوْلِيَاءُ بَعْضٍ يَأْمُرُونَ بِالْمَعْرُوفِ وَيَنْهَوْنَ عَنِ الْمُنْكَرِ وَيُقِيمُونَ الصَّلَوٰةَ وَيُؤْتُونَ الزَّكَوٰةَ وَيُطِيعُونَ اللَّهَ وَرَسُولَهُ

"The Believers, men and women, are protectors one of another, they enjoin what is just and forbid what is evil, they observe regular prayers, practice regular charity and obey Allah and His messenger."[84]

This verse has been interpreted to mean that men and women are both partners in the management of political and social affairs of the community and cooperate with one another in exercising all the powers of legislation, justice, administration and enforcement of injunctions and interdictions come under the heading of *amr bil mārūf wa nahy anil munkar* (enjoining the just and forbidding the evil) whether such duties are performed through legislation and *ijtihād*, through judicial pronouncement or through administration and enforcement of laws.[85]

The objection that can be raised to the above contention is that it is not an indispensable condition of *amr bil mārūf wa nahy anil munkar* that there is complete equality between men and women in every degree and stage since it is not possible to have complete equality even among men in this respect, and hence this verse cannot be interpreted to mean absolute equality between the sexes in the matters of holding public offices.[86]

يَـٰٓأَيُّهَا ٱلنَّاسُ إِنَّا خَلَقْنَـٰكُم مِّن ذَكَرٍ وَأُنثَىٰ وَجَعَلْنَـٰكُمْ

4. شُعُوبًا وَقَبَآئِلَ لِتَعَارَفُوٓا۟ إِنَّ أَكْرَمَكُمْ عِندَ ٱللَّهِ أَتْقَىٰكُمْ

"O mankind, We created you from a single (pair) of a male and a female, and made you into nations and tribes, that ye may know each other (not that ye may despise each other). Verily the most honoured of you in the sight of Allah is (one who is) most righteous of you."[87]

and

يَـٰٓأَيُّهَا ٱلنَّاسُ ٱتَّقُوا۟ رَبَّكُمُ ٱلَّذِى خَلَقَكُم مِّن نَّفْسٍ وَٰحِدَةٍ

وَخَلَقَ مِنْهَا زَوْجَهَا وَبَثَّ مِنْهُمَا رِجَالًا كَثِيرًا وَنِسَآءً

"O mankind, severe your Guardian-Lord who created you from a single person, created of like nature his

> mate and from them twain scattered (like seeds) countless men and women."[88]

These two verses show that a woman is a human being in all respects, and, as such, she is entitled to every right and can shoulder every responsibility and that the only factor enabling both men and women to shoulder responsibilities is that both of the sexes are rational and intellectual beings.[89]

In his commentary on these verses, Mohd. Izzat Darwazah writes that the *Qur'ān* has clearly enunciated equal responsibilities, both religious and worldly, to men and women in the fint of these verses which shows that Allah treats both the sexes as equals.[90] Thus He says,

وَمَا خَلَقَ الذَّكَرَ وَالْأُنْثَىٰ إِنَّ سَعْيَكُمْ لَشَتَّىٰ فَأَمَّا مَنْ

أَعْطَىٰ وَاتَّقَىٰ وَصَدَّقَ بِالْحُسْنَىٰ فَسَنُيَسِّرُهُ لِلْيُسْرَىٰ

> "By the creation of male and female, verily (the ends) ye strive for are diverse. So he who gives (in charity) and fears (Allah) and (in all sincerity) testifies to the Best, We will indeed make smooth for him the path to bliss."[91]

It has been contended that though these verses indicate equality of the sexes, they do not appear to relate to political rights since there is no mention of such things in them at all. What these verses emphasise is that there should be no discrimination between human beings and that equality and justice should prevail in the society and hence it can not be held on the basis of these verses that men and women are equal as regards their rights relating to the appointment to public offices and the enjoyment of political rights.[92]

Queen of Saba – A Model

1. In the words of the Queen of Saba, the *Qur'ān* says:

قَالَتْ يٰۤاَيُّهَا الْمَلَؤُا اَفْتُوْنِيْ فِيْۤ اَمْرِيْ مَا كُنْتُ قَاطِعَةً اَمْرًا حَتّٰى

تَشْهَدُوْنِ قَالُوْا نَحْنُ اُولُوْا قُوَّةٍ وَّاُولُوْا بَاْسٍ شَدِيْدٍ وَّالْاَمْرُ

اِلَيْكِ فَانْظُرِيْ مَاذَا تَاْمُرِيْنَ قَالَتْ اِنَّ الْمُلُوْكَ اِذَا دَخَلُوْا قَرْيَةً

اَفْسَدُوْهَا وَجَعَلُوْۤا اَعِزَّةَ اَهْلِهَاۤ اَذِلَّةً وَكَذٰلِكَ يَفْعَلُوْنَ

"Ye chiefs, advise me in (this) my affair, no affair have I decided except in your presence." They said, "We are endued with strength, and given to vehement war, but the command is with thee, so consider what thou wilt command, "She said, "Kings, when they enter a country, despoil it and make the noblest of its people its meanest. Thus do they behave."[93]

It has been argued on the basis of these verses that women are endowed with deep insight, understanding, farsightedness and courage and that they are sagacious in the handling of political affairs, that they have a grasp of the rise and fall as well as ups and downs of governments and go to the bottom of matters and adopt correct strategies irrespective of the avowal of loyalty by the administrative and the military personnel. These verses aver that women comprehend the intricacies of politics and are well-versed in the manner in which a ruler should deal with the affairs of state.[94]

The above-mentioned argument may be countered with the contention that the *Qur'ān* simply relates the story of the Queen of Saba and that her mention is not intended to affirm the validity of otherwise of her pronouncement and that even if this shows that a lady was once the head of a state it has been mentioned only as a story, since this fact relates to the pre-Islamic era whereas there are explicit pronouncements in the *Qur'ān* and in the *Hadith* against a woman being head of state.

Historical Evidences

Scholars advocating bestowal of all political rights to women except that of head of state cite the following incidents of Islamic history too besides giving citations from the *Qur'ān*, in support of their contention.

1. They say that by conferring on a woman the right of giving safe conduct to people in times of war and peace, the Prophet (SAW) had bestowed all political rights on women. They cite the incident of Umm Hāni giving safe conduct to a non-believer (*kāfir*) after the conquest of Makkah, whereas her brother Ali b. Abi Tālib wanted to kill him. When Umm Hāni approached the Prophet (SAW) about it, he supported her stand, saying "O Umm Hāni, I too shall give safe conduct to a person to whom you have done so."

Those who hold the opposite view contend that pronouncement made by the Prophet in his capacity as a leader of the Muslims cannot be deemed to have general application. They add that the right of giving asylum is not a political right on the basis of which conferment of political rights on women may be justified.

2. The Prophet (SAW) accepted that allegiance of a delegation of the Ansar which included two ladies. Alongwith other members of the delegation these ladies, too, were party to the political agreement that was arrived at binding them to protect Islam and the Prophet (SAW) at all costs. According to those who are in favour of the bestowal of political rights to women, this shows that women too enjoyed political rights according to Islam.[95]

This contention has been countered with the statement that there was a difference between the oaths of allegiance to the Prophet (SAW) offered by men and women. Since while the former undertook to protect Islam and to participate in Jihad, the latter promised to abide by the moral and ethical precepts of Islam, and to obey the Prophet (SAW) as was done after the conquest of Makkah. They add that the *Qur'ān* also confirms this in the following verses:

يٰٓأَيُّهَا النَّبِيُّ إِذَا جَآءَكَ الْمُؤْمِنٰتُ يُبَايِعْنَكَ عَلٰٓى أَن لَّا يُشْرِكْنَ
بِاللّٰهِ شَيْـًٔا وَلَا يَسْرِقْنَ وَلَا يَزْنِينَ وَلَا يَقْتُلْنَ أَوْلَادَهُنَّ وَلَا
يَأْتِينَ بِبُهْتَانٍ يَفْتَرِينَهُ بَيْنَ أَيْدِيهِنَّ وَأَرْجُلِهِنَّ وَلَا يَعْصِينَكَ
فِي مَعْرُوفٍ فَبَايِعْهُنَّ وَاسْتَغْفِرْ لَهُنَّ اللّٰهَ إِنَّ اللّٰهَ غَفُورٌ رَّحِيمٌ

> "O Prophet When believing women come to thee to take the oath of fealty to thee, that they will not associate in worship any other thing whatever with Allah, that they will not steal, that they will not commit adultery (or fornication), that they will not kill their children, that they will not utter slander, intentionally forging flashood, and that they will not disobey thee in any just matter – then do thou receive their fealty, and pray to Allah for the forgiveness (of their sins), for Allah is oft-Forgiving, Most Merciful,"[96]

Two arguments have been advanced against each above-mentioned objection:

A) On the occasion of the conquest of Makkah no oath for the defence and military support was required. Those who embraced Islam at that time were not asked for the kind of oath of allegiance. Both men and women who entered the fold of Islam were required to declare their firm faith in Allah (SWT) and His Prophet (SAW) and to abide by the decisions of the Prophet (SAW). It is true that women embracing Islam were asked to swear to the things mentioned in the verse quoted above. This is why Hind bint Utbah pointed out to the Prophet (SAW) that the oath women were being asked to take was different from that which was being administered to men.

B) In spite of the difference between the oaths that men and women were required to take while embracing Islam it cannot be argued that women did not have any political rights. The very fact that women were among those who were required to take oath of allegiance to the Prophet (SAW) is enough to show that they had political rights. Women were not asked to swear to wage Jihad since this is primarily an obligatory injunction (*fard al-kifāyah*) for menfolk. There is nothing in the *Qur'ān* or the *Sunnah* to prevent women from offering allegiance. On the contrary, the verse cited above makes it clear that women were included among those who took oat of allegiance to the Prophet (SAW). From the *Sirah* of the Prophet (SAW) it is learnt that both men and women of Makkah used to gether at Dar Arqam. It is true that later women were excluded from offering allegiance. In the opinion of a scholar, the reason of this was that the age of the Guided Caliphs was that of continual warfare. There were regular clashes with the enemies of Islam and struggle for the expansion of the faith. All the times, either there was some war or preparations of a war were going on. Abu Bakr had to face two bloody wars and his successor was continually busy with making conquests. Obviously it was not the task of women to participate in battles. However, they took part in giving drinking water to the injured and in bandaging their wounds. The temper of the society of that time was warlike and militant and this had a great impact on the lives of the people, so that even a matter like that of oath of allegiance could not escape being affected by it. This is why ladies do not appear to have been administered *bai'ah* (oath of allegiance) at the time.[97]

3. The Prophet (SAW) consulted Umm Salmah, one of his consorts on the occasion of the signing of the Peace Treaty of Hudaibiyah. This ought to be used as an evidence of the participation of ladies in political affairs.

This argument can be countered by saying that while the above incident shows that women cannot be deprived of the right to vote, it does not establish that women can be appointed to public offices or asked to shoulder political responsibilities.

The Consensus

The group of scholars advocating full participation of women in political affairs bases its arguments on *ijma* and the continuous practices of Islamic history. According to them, women participated in public affairs during the period of the Guided Caliphs in proportion to their attainments in learning and insight, though there are very few instances of their participation in the propagation of the faith, in holy wars and the defence of Islam. After the demise of the Prophet (SAW), Fatimah, his daughter, played an active role in politics and prevented her husband from offering allegiance to the First Caliph. When a *Shura* assembly was held in the mosque both men and women participated in it. One instance of this is the fact that a women opposed the stand taken by Caliph Umar on the issue of the payment of bridal dower (*Sadāq*) and that none of the *Sahabah* present on the occasion objected to this. This silence on their part is an evidence of an *ijma* justifying the participation of women in public affairs.[98]

As states above, Āishah, consort of the Prophet (SAW), took an active part in politics to the extent of heading an army. Again, Nāilah wife of the Third Caliph used to advise her husband in administrative affairs and this has been testified by him. Her role in the campaign against Ali became more prominent when she sent the blood stained shirt of her husband to Muawiah in Syria and more than fifty thousand people gathered there to demand avengement and punishment for the assassins of the third Caliph. Those supporting Ali, too, included women who were not less active than their male counterparts in conducting *jihad* and fighting for the defence of Islam, and were ready to support his forces with money and food supplies and administering drinking water to the injured.[99]

According to those who argue in favour of rights by women, the above-mentioned instances from the history of Islam show that Islam gives women the right to participate in public and political affairs, to take part in the process of elections, to be members of the *Shura* and to shoulder every political responsibility except that of the head of state.

Grounded Realities

There is also a group of scholars who recognize that in principle a woman can be appointed to any public office except that of the head of a state and that Islam does not stand in the way of this but they feel that there are certain practical problems due to which Muslim women have been rendered incapable of using their political rights in modern times.

These scholars say that the first difficulty that Muslim women of today face is that it is indispensable for the enjoyment of political rights they are able to concentrate all their energies and efforts on shouldering political responsibilities. This is so since this involves mixing with strange men and traveling alone. These thinkers are of the opinion that in such a situation it would be better for Muslim women to attend to their domestic responsibilities and not to take the risk of going beyond Islamic restriction applying to them. Dr. Mustafa Sibāi expresses his extreme hostility to the idea of women being burdened with political responsibilities in the following words:

"I declare most clearly that the stand of Islam on the issue of interest taken by women in political affairs is that of utter repugnance and disgust. I do not consider it *haram* (prohibited) for women nor do I hold that women do not have the capacity to solve political problems, but my stand is based on the social evils that result from this which would lead to a blatant violation of Islamic injunction and code of conduct."[100]

The second obstacle in the way of enjoyment of political rights by women, according to these scholars, is that moral standards prevailing in modern times are not those that are required by Islam, only in the presence of which women can exercise their political rights keeping in mind in every respect the teachings and code of conduct of Islam. During the early years of Islam, according to these scholars, participation of women in public affairs was proper since the entire society was psychologically prepared for it. But as a result of a radical change in the entire society it is not possible for women to take full part in politics and at the same time to practice the Islamic injunctions and laws.[101]

The solution to the first of these problems posed by the scholars is that respect for the Islamic injunction and code of conduct should be practiced and care should be taken that there is no departure from Islamic teachings. This was the method that was used during the period of the caliphate and it was in view of this that Samra bint Muhaik Asadiyah performed the function of *amr bil maruf wa nahy anil munkar* (ordering the good and forbidding the bad) and wherever there was any violation of Islamic laws by any trader or businessman he was whipped by her. It was due to this that Khaulah bint Thālabah criticized the second Caliph in public in the interest of the *Ummah.* This never led to any public disturbance or upheaval in the society of the time and there was no violation of Islamic teachings. So these scholars wonder why there should be any such dangers today. Observance of Islamic laws is one thing and participation of women in political activities is another and there is no reason why these two should be mixed up. While women are allowed by Islam to participate in political affairs, they have also to follow the Islamic *Shariah.* If women are prevented from participating in politics, it does not follow that they would necessarily abide by the Islamic *Shariah.* In the same way their participation in political activities would not lead to violation of Islamic teachings on their part.[102]

Talking about the second hurdle in the way of the participation of women in politics, some scholars say that it is essential for the enforcement of any specific ideology and way of life that the ethical, social and political conditions prevailing in a particular society are congenial for this. So, according to them, for a proper application of the laws of Islam, a specific environment and a special social system are required, without which no Islamic law can be enforced. They say that it is the responsibility of every individual to contribute his mite to the creation of such an atmosphere and the entire Muslim community is answerable to Allah (SWT) in this respect. However, they say that the important point is that lack of congenial atmosphere cannot be put forward as an excuse for not enforcing Islamic injunctions and women cannot be deprived of their political rights pending the creation of suitable social conditions and necessary changes in the environment. According to these scholars, the participation of women in politics itself, if it is in keeping with Islamic injunctions and code of conduct, can contribute to the creation of a proper social atmosphere.[103]

Secular Approach

On the issue of the participation of women in politics, there is a third school of thought according to which it is not at all an issue concerning religion or *fiqh* but a wholly social and political one which can be tackled taking into consideration the prevailing political and social conditions and the demands of justice and equity. The exponents of this approach assert that there is no definite injunction in Islam against the participation of women in politics, this being purely a matter of *ijtihad*.

Elucidating this point of view, Dr. Abul Hamīd Mutawalli says that it would be wrong to seek the solution of the problem in religious beliefs or in the principles of *fiqh* and Islamic injunctions. He says that this issue cannot also be resolved by following the Western countries blindly or by thinking along the line of those according to whom conferment of political rights on women signifies progress. He adds that it would also be wrong to find a solution on the basis of the temperament of women, their natural attitudes, basic responsibilities and domestic pre-occupations, since such an approach to the issue is an attempt to enter the field of psychology. Dr. Mutawalli concludes by saying that a correct solution of the problem lies in treating the issue as a social and political one and to look for its solution in the light of the prevailing political, economic and social conditions, keeping in mind the common practices and trends of the people, and their likes and dislikes and the requirements of justice and equity.[104]

The greatest weakness of this point of view is that it is based on a secular approach. In spite of treating the issue as a political, moral and social one, no Muslim would accept any solution which goes against the basic principles and moral precepts of Islam. This issue cannot be discussed only in view of the demands of the time since Islam has set out specific principles and procedures even on political, social and economic matters which are binding on all Muslims. This is why the stand of most *Ulama* and scholars is that though the issue of political rights for women is undoubtedly a political and social one, its solution must be found in Islamic principles and procedures which may be derived from the *Qur'ān* and the *Sunnah*. Another point that ought not to be overlooked is that according to Islam the basic duty of a woman is managing her domestic and family affairs, and that relations between husband and wife are those of mutual cooperation and understanding, so that the two should assist other in fulfilling their respective obligations. However, this does not at all mean that women are incapable of performing other duties. The truth is that woman is most suitable for running the house and bringing up children but she can also render services in political and social fields. The following principles have to be observed for a better domestic management and a stable relationship between men and women:

(i) In principle, men have to shoulder the responsibility of supporting a family economically. It is not incumbent on a woman to take up a job or to struggle for livelihood, though it is permissible for her to do so. Leaving her home to earn money is not her duty. However, if she does so, her family should feel obliged to her for this.

(ii) Islam has specified the respective shares of men and women in inheritance and this has been done in view of the economic responsibilities of men.

(iii) Islam has formulated several injunctions relating to honour and respect that is due to women and has laid down several rules of conduct which have to be observed by women if they enter public life.

From the detailed discussion given above, it may be concluded that Islam has conferred political rights on women and that the arguments advanced by the *Ulama* and scholars who hold this view are stronger than those of their opponents. However, whether or not a woman can be head of state is a controversial matter and on this issue there are great differences of opinion among the *Ulama* and the scholars. The dominant trend among them is that the texts of the *Qur'ān* and the *Sunnah* the evidence of Islamic history and the larger interests of the *Ummah* do not allow a woman to be head of state, though Islam does not forbid women from exercising their rights to vote, participating in a referendum, being eligible for the membership of the *Shura* or participating in other political activities. Further, to some *Ulama*, participation of women in political activities is *wajib kifāyah* (obligatory collectively) because it relates to *amr bil maruf wa nahy anil munkar* (ordering the good and forbidding the wrong).[105]

The Case of Non-Muslims

Whether or not a *dhimmi* or non-Muslim citizen is eligible for the membership of the *Shura* has been a major controversial issue among Muslim scholars, especially in modern times. While one group of *Ulama* and scholars not merely thinks that the participation of non-Muslims in the *Shura* is not only not violative of the principles of Islam but considers it indispensable in view of the demands of the modern times, another group holds a contrary view and looks at it as something which is against the principles of Islam. There is a third school of thought, proponents of which willy-nilly considers conferment of the rights of non-Muslims to be members of the *Shura* as advisable but with certain reservations and on some conditions.

Non-Muslims were Later Accommodated

According to the first group of thinkers, the *fuqaha* had confined the membership of the *Shura* to Muslims in the early period of Islam when participation of non-Muslims to this body was deemed to be illegal. This was due to certain social, political and religious reasons. The Jews and the Christians were hostile to Islam and were busy in hatching conspiracies against the Islamic movement. They could not tolerate the successes achieved by Islam. This is why, the

Prophet (SAW) and the Guided Caliphs excluded them from their consultative assemblies. But conditions have changed now. By consulting non-Muslims on matters not relating to religious affairs, like industry and trade, science and technology, maintenance of law and order etc., their experience and expertise can be utilized. These thinkers are of the opinion that if an assembly of the *Shura* has a majority of Muslims and functions wholly under the influence of the principles of Islam, there is no harm in having non-Muslims as its members.[106]

They say that after the age of the Guided Caliphs when non-Muslim subjects of Islamic states started living peacefully, identifying their aspirations with those of the Muslims, caliphs initiated consulting them on non-religious issues and even acted according to their advice. According to these thinkers since the *Qur'ān* does not clearly question the propriety of holding consultation with non-Muslims, this policy of their exclusion from consultative assemblies ought to be looked upon as a temporary one and in the modern age they should be given all rights of voting and being consulted whenever necessary.[107]

Ideological Obstacles

The second group of scholars holds that non-Muslims ought not to be considered eligible for the membership of the *Shura*. They advance the following arguments in support of their contention:

1. The Islamic state is one that is based on certain principles and only those can be entrusted with the responsibility of running the government in it who believe in these principles. How can those people who do not believe in these principles or are not satisfied with them be included among those who are entitled to advise or criticize the government?[108]

This argument holds good for a non-Muslim being made head of an Islamic state but cannot be applied to their entitlement for the membership of the *Shura* since this assembly will have an overwhelming majority of Muslims and hence it would abide by the *Qur'ān* and the *Sunnah*. Non-Muslims who may not have embraced Islam can be treated as loyal citizens of the state once when they take the pledge to abide by the constitution of the state. In such a situation how can they influence the entire assembly of the *Shura* on becoming its members and how can they make it go against Islamic laws or the interests of the Islamic state?

2. The *Qur'ān* asks the faithfuls clearly to obey Allah, His Prophet and those among themselves who are the *Ulul amr*.[109] This shows that public offices can only be given to those who are Muslims.[110]

The term *Ulul amr* has been discussed above. If this expression is taken to mean government officials, as some interpreters of the *Qur'ān* hold, the above-mentioned argument is not valid, since the highest office to which the term *Ulul amr* may be applied is that of the head of state. It cannot include the assembly of the *Shura*. Hence the *Qur'ān*ic verse concerned cannot be validly cited against the conferment of the right of non-Muslims to be members of the *Shura*. And if this argument is accepted, what difference can a few non-Muslim members make in view of the overwhelming majority of Muslim members in the *Shura*. So the condition of obedience to Muslim *Ulul amr* can be fulfilled in spite of the presence of some non-Muslims in the *Shura* where decisions are arrived at by majority of votes and the decisions of the *Shura* are binding on everyone. In such circumstances *Ulul amr minhum* means a majority of Muslims in the *Shura*.[111]

3. A third verse of the *Qur'ān* is also cited against conferment of the right of the membership of the *Shura* on non-Muslims, which is as follows:

يَـٰٓأَيُّهَا الَّذِينَ ءَامَنُوا لَا تَتَّخِذُوا بِطَانَةً مِّن دُونِكُمْ
لَا يَأْلُونَكُمْ خَبَالًا وَدُّوا مَا عَنِتُّمْ قَدْ بَدَتِ
الْبَغْضَآءُ مِنْ أَفْوَاهِهِمْ وَمَا تُخْفِي صُدُورُهُمْ أَكْبَرُ

> "O ye who believe! Take not into your intimacy those outside your ranks: They will not fail to corrupt you. They only desire your ruin: rank hatred has already appeared from their mouths, what their hearts conceal is far worse."[112]

Another verse that is cited in this connection is as follows:

يَـٰٓأَيُّهَا الَّذِينَ ءَامَنُوا لَا تَتَّخِذُوا الْيَهُودَ وَالنَّصَـٰرَىٰٓ
أَوْلِيَآءَ بَعْضُهُمْ أَوْلِيَآءُ بَعْضٍ وَمَن يَتَوَلَّهُم مِّنكُمْ
فَإِنَّهُ مِنْهُمْ إِنَّ اللَّهَ لَا يَهْدِي الْقَوْمَ الظَّـٰلِمِينَ

> "O ye who believe! Take not the Jews and the Christians for your friends and protectors: They are but friends and protectors to each other. And he amongst you that turns to them (for friendship) is of them. Verily Allah guideth not a people unjust.":[113]

The above verses are taken by this group to mean that Muslims have been asked to desist from seeking the help of non-Muslims, confiding in them or appointing them to positions of authority.

Addressing the Belligerents

Rebutting the above arguments, those who are in favour of non-Muslims being members of the *Shura* say that the first of these verses refers to the pagans whose hostility to Islam had become absolutely clear and about whom it was well-known that they would start hatching conspiracies against Islam at the first available opportunity. However, they say that if the non-Muslims are peaceful and if there is no evidence of their hostility to and hatred for Islam and they are not using hypocrisy and deception to work against the faith, there is no harm in making use of their experience, talents and advice, especially when they belong to the same country alongwith their Muslim brethren, have common interests and are confronted with common dangers. In such a situation of peace and mutual confidence non-Muslims can be appointed to public positions.[114]

These scholars say that the second verse cited above refers to the hypocrites who were in league with the pagans and passed on the secrets of the Muslims to them.[115] According to an account, when the Muslim forces were facing an adverse situation during the Battle of Uhud some hypocrites started thinking of siding with the Jews while others began to think of extending their hands of friendship to the Christians. It was on this occasion that this verse was revealed, which prevented the hypocrites from taking such steps.[116]

Constitutional Measures

According to the third group of scholars, representation of non-Muslims in the *Shura* is not proper from a strictly Islamic point of view, but it is possible to find ways of doing so if the constitution of the country provides as follows:

(i) That the parliament of the country shall not have the power to make any law that goes against the *Qur'ān* or the *Sunnah*.

(ii) That the *Qur'ān* and the *Sunnah* shall be the primary sources of legislation for the country.

(iii) That the person who would have the authority to give final assent to a legislation shall be a Muslim.

In the opinion of those scholars a separate representative assembly may be constituted to represent non-Muslims instead of their being made members of the *Shura*. This, they say, would enable them to meet their requirements and to project their point of view regarding the administration of the country. These scholars add that membership as well as voting right in such an assembly can perform the following functions:

(i) The right to suggest the adoption of and making amendment to personal laws of non-Muslims, which would be enacted after getting the assent of the head of the state.

(ii) To give free expression to their complaints, objections and suggestions regarding the administration of the country and the decisions of the *Shura*.

(iii) To ask questions relating to matters of interest of their communities as well as to conditions prevailing in the country in general. A representative of the government should be deputed to this assembly of non-Muslims to answer their questions.

Those advocating the participation of non-Muslims in political affairs in an Islamic state say that either of these methods may be adopted to enable them to do so.[117]

From an analysis the points of view of the above-mentioned schools of thought, it can be concluded that if circumstances demand, ways can be found to give representation to non-Muslims in the assembly of the *Shura*. In this way it would also be possible to learn about the problems and difficulties faced by non-Muslim minorities and to get their advice and suggestions relating to the affairs of the country. This would also inculcate in these minorities a sense of loyalty to the country and its constitution. Then participation in the affairs of the country would at the same time generate in them a sense of discipline and obedience. This would not injure the spirit of Islam, since all legislation would be enacted on the basis of the *Qur'ān* and *Sunnah* and there would be a majority of Muslims in the *Shura* and decisions would be taken by a majority of votes. In such a situation there is no need to bar non-Muslims from voting on matters relating to *Shariah* or the election of the head of the state,[118] since they will only have to elect a Muslim and discussion on matters would be in keeping with the Islamic constitution. On the other hand, their loyalty to the country cannot be ensured if they are not allowed to participate in the political process of an Islamic country.

NOTES AND REFERENCES

1. The *Qur'ān*, 4: 34.
2. Abdul Hameed, Ibrahim, *Nizam al-Qaza fi al-Islam*, Jamea Al-Azhar, Kulliyah al-Shariah wa al-Qanun, p. 30.
3. Maududi, Abul Ala, Islami Reyasat, *op. cit.*, pp. 506-507.
4. *Ibid*, p. 507.
5. Abdul Hameed, Ibrahim, *Nizam al-Qaza fi al-Islam*, *op. cit.*, p. 30.
6. The *Qur'ān*, 2: 228.
7. Maududi, Abul Ala, *Islami Reyasat*, *op. cit.*, p. 508.
8. Mutawalli, Abdul Hameed, *Mabda al-Shura fi al-Islam*, *op. cit.*, p. 862.
9. Shaltoot, Mahmood, *Al-Islam: Aqeedah wa Shariah*, *op. cit.*, p. 176.
10. The *Qur'ān*, 4: 32.
11. The *Qur'ān*, 4: 33.
12. Al-Ansari, Abdul Hameed Ismail, *Al-Shura wa Athruha fi al-Dimiqratiyah*, *op. cit.*, p. 268.
13. The *Qur'ān*, 33: 33.
14. The *Qur'ān*, 33: 53.
15. Maududi, Abul Ala, *Islami Reyasat*, *op. cit.*, p. 508.
16. The *Qur'ān*, 33: 32-33.
17. The *Qur'ān*, 33: 53.
18. Mutawalli, Abdul Hameed, *Mabadi Nizam al-Hukm fi al-Islam*, *op. cit.*, p. 874. The author has quoted this interpretation of the Qur'ānic verse under discussion

from the exegesis of Aalusi *e.g. Rooh al-Maani*, Vol. 22, p. 9.

19. The *Qur'ān*, 24: 31.

20. Ahmad, Fuad Abdul Munim, *Mabda al-Musawāt fi al-Islam wa al-Muqaranah bi al-Dimiqratiah al-Hadithah.* Muassasah al-Thaqafah al-Jameyiah, Egypt, 1972, p. 216.

21. The author has cited this Hadith from the *Sahih of Bukhari* Vol. II, p. 163.

22. Ahmad, Fuad Abdul Munim, *Mabda al-Masawat fi al-Islam, op. cit.*, p. 216.

    The author has cited these instances from the following sources:

    Ibn Sad, *Tabaqat*, Vol. VIII, p. 143, Tabari, *Tarikh*, Vol. III, p. 261.

23. Mutawalli, Abdul Hameed, *Mabda al-Shura fi al-Islam, op. cit.*, p. 876; _______, *Mabda Nizam al-Hukm fi al-Islam, op. cit.*, p. 889. The author has quoted Dr. Mahmood Salam Zanati from his book *Ikhtilāt al-Jinsain Indal Arab* as follows: It is historically proved that the system of *hijab* and unmixed society was not familiar to the Arabs equally in the period of *Jahiliyah*, prophethood or of Guided Caliphs. This system was first introduced by the Umayyads and was popularized in the period of Abbasids. The mixed society was a familiar one before the advent of Islam. The woman was free to make some commercial contracts with the gents. The ladies used to come to literary market of 'Ukāz; recited their poems and discussed with the men. They also participated in the battles. Islam retained the same system providing certain norms and moral values. That is why the women were free to participate in all the collective and societal works during the period of prophethood, *Khilafah Rashidah* and in the initial period of Umayyads too.

24. Mautwalli, Abul Hameed, *Mabadi Nizam al-Hukm fi al-Islam, op. cit.*, p. 875.

25. For detail see, Qastalani, *Irshad al-Saari li sharh Sahih al-Bukhari*, Dar al-kitab al-Arabi, Beirut, Vol. 1, p. 347.

26. The *Qur'ān*, 2: 282.

27. For a detailed study see; Al-Jauziyah, Ibn Qayyim, *Al-Turuq al-Hukmiyah fi al-siyasah al-Sharyiah*, Al-Mussasah al-Arabiyah li al-Tabaah wa al-Nashr, Cairo, 1961, p. 92.

28. Mahmood Shaltoot has quoted the statement under consideration of Mohammad Abduh and has discussed in detail. See, Sahltoot, Mahmood, *Al-Islam: Aqidah wa Shariah, op. cit.*, pp. 261-262.

29. Al-Ansari, Abdul Hameed Ismail, *Al-Shura wa Athruha fi al-Dimiqratiyah, op. cit.*, p. 273.

30. Mutawalli, Abdul Hameed, *Mabadi Nizam al-Hukm fi al-Islam, op. cit.*, p. 882.

31. Mohammad Ajlooni (*Kashf al-Khifa wa Muzeel al-Albas amma Ishtahara min al-Ahadith ala Alsinah al-Nass*, Dar Ihya al-Thuras al-Arabi, Beirut, 1351 A.H., p. 27) has cited a Hadith narrating that the Prophet (SAW) had consulted Umm Salmah on the occasion of Peace Treaty of Hudaibiyah. He wonders how was she consulted if the women were deemed by the Prophet (SAW) as mentally deficient.

32. Khalid, Khalid Mohammad, *Al-Dimiqratiyah Abadan*, Dar al-Kitab al-Labnani, 1974, p. 240.

33. *Ibid*, pp. 242-243.

34. Al-Ansari, Abdul Hameed Ismail, *Al-Shura wa Athruha fi al-Dimiqratiyah, op. cit.*, pp. 275-276.

35. *Ibid*, p. 276.

36. Al-Albani, Mohammad Nasiruddin, *Al-Ahadith al-Zaeefah wa al-Maudhuah*, Damascus, second edition,

1384 A.H., Vol. I, No. 430., all the five *ahadith* quoted in the text are discussed by al-Ansari, Abdul Hameed Ismail, *op. cit.*, p. 76.

37. See for detail, Al-Albani, *op. cit.*, No. 430, 435, 436; Mubarakpuri, Mohammad Abdur Rahman bin Abdur Rahman, *Tuhfah al-Ahwazi bi Sharh Jame al-Tirmizi*, ed. Abdur Rahman Mohd. Usman, Maktaba Salafiyah, Madinah, second edition, Vol. VI, p. 544.

38. Asqalani, Ibn Hajar, *Fath al-Bari li Sharh al-Bukhari*, *op. cit.*, Vol. VI, p. 275. Ajlooni, Ismail Mohammad, *op. cit.*, pp. 3, 37, No. 1529, 1648.

39. Mubarakpuri, Mohammad Abdur Rahman bin Abdur Rahman, *Tuhfah al-Ahwazi bi Sharh Jame al-Tirmizi*, *op. cit.*, Vol. VI, p. 544; Al-Khateeb, Waliuddin, *Mishkat al-Masabeeh*, Damascus, 1961, Vol. II, p. 695.

40. Al-Sayeedi Abdul Mutaal, *Min Ayna Nabda*, Maktaba Al-Khanji, Egypt, p. 112.

41. Shaukani, Mohammad bin Ali, *Nail al-Awtar Sharh Muntaqa al-Akhbar Min Ahadith Sayyid al-Akhyar, Mustafa al-Babi Halbi, Egypt, 1969, Vol. VIII, p. 273.*

42. Abdul Hameed, Ibrahim, *Nizam al-Qaza fi al-Islam (Muhazarāt)*, Qism al-Siyasah al-Sharyiah, Al-Dirasāt al-Ulya, Kulliyah al-Shariah wa al-Qanoon, Jamea Al-Azhar, Egypt, p. 85.

43. Al-Fazili, Ahmad, *Nizam al-Hukm fi al-Islam*, *op. cit.*, p. 58.

44. Utwah, Abdul Aal, *Nizam al-Qaza fi al-Islam*, Qism al-siyasah al-Sharyiah, Al-Dirasat al-Ulya, Kulliyah al-Shariah wa al-Qanoon, Jamea Al-Azhar, Egypt, 1973, p. 18.

45. Abdul Hameed, Ibrahim, *Nizam al-Qaza fi al-Islam*, *op. cit.*, p. 32.

46. *Ibid*, p. 33.

47. Mutawalli, Abdul Hameed, *Mabadi Nizam al-Hukm fi al-Islam, op. cit.*, p. 878.

48. Al-Ghazali, Abu Hamid, *Al-Mustasfa min Ilm al-Usool*, Maktabah al-Jundi, Cairo, p. 335.

49. Al-Sayeedi, Abdul Mutaal, *Min Ayna Nabda, op. cit.*, pp. 110-111.

50. Mutawalli, Abdul Hameed, *Mabadi Nizam al-Hukm fi al-Islam, op. cit.*, p. 877.

51. Al-Sayeedi, Abdul Mutaal, *Min Ayna Nabda, op. cit.*, p. 111.

52. Al-Nabhan, Mohammad Farooque, *Nizam al-Hukm fi al-Islam*, Kuwait, 1974, pp. 315, 324. The author also has referred Hasbullah, *Usool al-Tashree al-Islami*, pp. 43-49.

53. Mutawalli, Abdul Hameed, *Mabadi Nizam al-Hukm fi al-Islam, op. cit.*, p. 189; __________, *Azamah al-Fikr al-Siyasi*, Egypt, 1970, p. 75.

54. Mutawalli, Abdul Hameed, *Mabadi Nizam al-Hukm fi al-Islam, op. cit.*, pp. 191-201. The author also has referred Abu Zahv, *Al-Hadith wa al-Muhaddithun*, p. 121; Al-Ghazali, *Al-Mustasfa, op. cit.*, Vol. 1, p. 138.

55. See, Shaltoot Mahmood, *Al-Islam: Aqeedah wa Shariah, op. cit.*, p. 521; Mutawalli, Abdul Hameed, *Azamah al-Fikr al-Siyasi, op. cit.*, p. 68. They have referred Abdul Wahab Khallaf, *Usool al-Fiqh*, p. 44; Mohammad Mustafa Shalbi, *Al-Fiqh al-Islami bain al-Misaliyah wa al-Waqiyiah, Majallah Al-Huqooq*, Vol. IX, No. 1-2, 1959-1960, p. 130. All these scholars have quoted to and depend upon Imam Qarafi Maliki, *Al-Ihkam fi Tamyeez al-Fatāwa min al-Ahkam wa Tasarrufaat al-Qazi wa al-Imam*, pp. 86-108.

56. Mutawalli, Abdul Hameed, *Mabadi Nizam al-Hukm fi al-Islam, op. cit.*, p. 69. The author has referred Abdul Wahab Khallaf, *Masaadir al-Tashree al-Islami*,

Majallah Al-Qanoon wa al-Iqtisād, April-May, 1955, p. 259.

57. Dabbus, Salahuddin, *Al-Khalifah: Tawliyatuh wa Azluh* (*Dirasah Muqaranah*), Muassasah al-Thaqafah al-Jameyiah, Egypt, p. 274.

58. Abul Majd, Ahmad Kamal, *Muajahah ma Anaasir al-Jamud*, Majallah *Al-Arabi*, Kuwait, May, 1977, p. 19.

59. Al-Qaradhawi, Yusuf, Nazarāt, *Majallah Al-Muslim al-Muasir*, Beirut, April 1975, No. 1-2, pp. 136-138.

    To study it in detail, please see: Wasfi, Mustafa Kamal, *Imkān al-Ijtihad fi Usool al-Fiqh*, *Majallah Al-Muslim al-Muasir*, *op. cit.*, p. 131; Abus Saud, Mahmood, *Majallah Al-Muslim al-Muasir*, *op. cit.*, pp. 122-123; Abu Majd, Kamal, Muajahah me Anaasir al-Jamud, *Majallah Al-Arabi*, *op. cit.*, p. 18.

60. See for detail: Ahmad, Fuad Abdul Munim, *Mabda al-Musawaat fi al-Islam ma al-Muqarana bi al-Dimiqratiyah al-Hadithah*, Muassasah al-Tahqafah al-Jameyiah, Egypt, 1972, p. 74. The author has quoted following sources in his support: Al-Qarafi al-Maliki, *Al-Ihkam fi Tamyiz al-Fatawa min al-Ahkam*, *op. cit.*, pp. 24-25; Abdul Baasit, Badr al-Mutawalli *Muzakkirah fi Tarikh al-Tashree*, 1967, p. 52; Al-Shaikh Taj, *Al-Siyasah al-Sharyiah*, 1953, p. 21; Shaltoot, Mahmood, *Al-Islam: Aqidah wa Shariah*, *op. cit.*, p. 509.

61. Al-Ansari, Abdul Hameed Ismail, *Al-Shura wa Athruha fi al-Dimiqratiyah*, *op. cit.*, pp. 291-292.

62. Al-Kāsāni, *Al-Badaye*, Vol. VII, p. 115 quoted from Ahmad Al-Faazili, *Nizam àl-Hukm fi al-Islam*, *op. cit.*, p. 9.

63. Mutawalli, Abdul Hameed, *Mabadi Nizam al-Hukm fi al-Islam*, *op. cit.*, p. 65.

64. *Ibid*, p. 65. The author has quoted: Mohd. Mustafa Shalbi, *Taaleel al-Ahkam*, p. 389.

65. Umar Abdullah has done a significant work on the verses of the Qur'ān relating to the various injunctions. For a detailed study of this, see his book *Al-Urf fi al-Fiqh al-Islami*, p. 98.

66. Al-Namir, Abdul Munim, *Ala Abwab Taqneen al-Shariah, Al-Ahraam*, Ist April, 1978.

67. These specific procedures to adopt the constitutional measures are clearly defined by Yusuf al-Qaradhawi in his book *Fiqh al-Zakah*, Muassasah Al-Risalah, Beirut, 1973, Vol. I, p. 230.

68. Al-Sayeedi, Abdul Mutaal, *Min Ayna Nabda, op. cit.*, pp. 111-112.

69. *Ibid*, p. 112.

70. Mutawalli, Abdul Hameed, *Mabadi Nizam al-Hukm fi al-Islam, op. cit.*, p. 887.

71. To understand the religious duties of a Khalifah see: Al-Tamavi, Sulaiman, *Al-Sultaat al-Thalath*, Dar al-Fikr, Beirut, 1973, pp. 368-370.

72. Abduh, Mohammad, *Al-Islam wa al-Nasraniyah ma al-Ilm wa al-Madniyah*, Maktabah Mohd. Ali Sabih, Egypt, 1954, pp. 59-61.

73. This was the fatwa of the Egyptian committee consisting of Ulama of Jamea Al-Azhar, See for detail, Al-Fazili, Ahmad, *Nizam al-Hukm fi al-Islam, op. cit.*, p. 56.

74. Ibn Qudamah, Muaffiquddin, *Al-Mughni*, Dar al-Kitab al-Arabi, Beirut, 1972, Vol. X, p. 127.

75. Utwah, Abdul Aal, Nizam al-Qaza fi al-Islam, *op. cit.*, p. 13.

76. Ibn Hazm, Mohammad bin Ahmad b. Sayeed, *Al-Muhalla*, Maktabah al-Jumhuriyah al-Arabiyah bi al-Azhar, Egypt, 1970, Vol. X, p. 631.

77. For a detailed study of the activities of women in the history of Islam, see: Al-Zarkali, *Al-Aalam*, Vol. I, p. 279.

78. Al-Sayeedi Abdul Mutaal, *Min Ayna Nabda*, *op. cit.*, p. 108.

79. Al-Tamawi, Sulaiman Mohammad, *Umar bin Khattab wa Usool al-Siyasah wa al-Idarah al-Hadithah*, Dar al-Fikr al-Arabi, Beirut, 1969, p. 137.

80. Al-Fanjari, Ahmad Shauqi, *Maqal al-Marah al-Muslimah fi Mayaadin al-Qitaal*, *Majallah al-Arabi*, Kuwait, No 198, May, 1975.

81. Dr. Ibrahim Abdul Hameed has well discussed the point why the ladies were appointed on the posts of *qazi* in Islamic history and that when participation of women in military and political affairs has been proved in the history, they can in the first stage be appointed as *qadis*. See the author, *Nizam al-Qaza fi al-Islam*, *op. cit.*, p. 33.

82. The *Qur'ān*, 2: 228.

83. The *Qur'ān*, 17: 70.

84. The *Qur'ān*, 9: 71.

85. Ahmad, Fuad Abdul Munim, *Mabda al-Musawat fi al-Islam ma al-Muqaranah bi al-Dimiqratiyah al-Hadithah*, *op. cit.*, p. 196.

86. *Ibid*, p. 229.

87. The *Qur'ān*, 49: 13.

88. The *Qur'ān*, 4: 1.

89. Bint al-Shaati, Aisha Abdur Rahman, *Al-Mafhum al-Islami li Tahreer al-Marah*, A lecture delivered in Umm Darman University in 1966-67. Quoted from, Ahmad, Fuad Abdul Munim, *Mabda al-Musawat fi al-Islam*, *op. cit.*, p. 197.

90. Darwazah, Mohammad Izzat, *Al-Marah fi al-Qur'ān wa al-Sunnah*, Al-Maktabah al-Asriyyah, Beirut, 1968, p. 29.

91. The *Qur'ān*, 92: 3-7.

92. Ahmad, Fuad Abdul Munim, *Mabda al-Musawat fi al-Islam*, *op. cit.*, p. 230.

93. The *Qur'ān*, 27: 32-34.

94. Shaltoot, Mahmood, *Al-Qur'ān wa al-Marah*, *op. cit.*, p. 87.

95. Ahmad, Fuad Abdul Munim, *Mabda al-Musawat fi al-Islam*, *op. cit.*, p. 223.

96. The *Qur'ān*, 60: 12.

97. Al-Qasmi, Zaafir, *Nizam al-Hukm fi al-Shariah wa al-Tarikh*, Dar al-Nafaaes, Beirut, 1974, p. 278.

98. Ahmad, Fuad Abdul Munim, *Mabda al-Musawat fi al-Islam*, *op. cit.*, p. 201.

99. *Ibid*, p. 203.

100. Al-Sibai, Mustafa, *Al-Marah bain al-Fiqh wa al-Qanoon*, Al-Maktabah al-Asriyah, Damascus, 1962, p. 62.

101. Al-Khauli, Al-Bahi, *Al-Marah bain al-Bait wa al-Mujtama*, *op. cit.*, p. 144.

102. Ahmad, Fuad Abdul Munim, *Mabda al-Musawat fi al-Islam*, *op. cit.*, p. 234.

103. Mutawalli, Abdul Hameed, *Mabadi Nizam al-Hukm fi al-Islam*, *op. cit.*, p. 898.

104. *Ibid*, pp. 898-909.

105. Al-Ansari, Abdul Hameed Ismail, *Al-Shura wa Athruha fi al-Dimiqratiyah*, *op. cit.*, p. 320.

106. Ahmad, Fuad Abdul Munim, *Mabda al-Musawat fi al-Islam, op. cit.*, p. 143; Ameer Ali, *The Spirit of Islam*, Idara Adabiyat Delhi, 1978, pp. 272-273.

107. Al-Eili, Abdul Hakeem Hasan, *Al-Hurriyat al-Aammah fi al-Fikr wa al-Nizam al-Siyasi fi al-Islam: Dirasah Muqarnah, op. cit.*, p. 431.

108. Maududi, Abul Ala, *Islami Riyasat, op. cit.*, p. 523 ; Asad Muhammad, *Principles of State and Government in Islam, op. cit.*, pp. 39-40.

109. The *Qur'ān*, 4: 59.

110. Maududi, Abul Ala, *Islami Riyasat, op. cit.*, p. 348; Asad Muhammad, *op. cit.*, p. 40.

111. Al-Ansari, Abdul Hameed Ismail, *op. cit.*, p. 323.

112. The *Qur'ān*, 3: 118.

113. The *Qur'ān*, 5: 54.

114. Ahmad, Fuad Abdul Munim, *Mabda al-Musawat fi al-Islam, op. cit.*, p. 139; Rashid Rida, *Tafseer Al-Manar, op. cit.*, Vol. IV, pp. 83-84, Al-Maraghi, Ahmad Mustafa, *Tafseer al-Maraghi*, 1965, Vol. IV, p. 45.

115. Al-Qurtubi, Abu Abdullah Mohammad b. Ahmad al-Ansari, *Al-Jame li Ahkām al-Qur'ān*, Dar al-Kutub al-Misriyah, 1938, Vol. VI, p. 216.

116. Al-Aalusi, Abul Fazl Shahabuddin Syed Mahmood, *Rooh al-M'aani, op. cit.*, Vol. VI, p. 156.

117. Maududi, Abul Ala, *Islami Riyasat, op. cit.*, pp. 598-599.

118. Most of the Ulama and Muslim intellectuals have unnecessarily emphasized while discussing the validity of membership of non-Muslims to the *Shura*, on the point that if it becomes unavoidable to include non-Muslims to the *Shura*, they must not be given the right to vote while there is any discussion on Shariah or the election of the head of state is going on. See for detail, Rahman, Gauhar, *Islami Siyasat*, Ram Pur, 1982, p. 315; Islahi, Ameen Ahsan, *Islami Riyasat, op. cit.*, p. 50.

COMPLEMENT: Public Roles of Women

There are religious and historical considerations concerning the inclusion of Muslim women in the public sphere. The *Qur'ān* addresses women as individuals who are responsible for their moral individuality. It states that no individual, regardless of sex, will be forced to bear hardship beyond his or her capacity (2: 233, 2: 286); that each person is responsible for his/her own account (6: 164, 40: 17, 20: 15); and that any good deed returns to the one who performs it (2: 272).

The *Qur'ān* further associates the call for women's individual piety with communal participation in public good, as indicated in verse 33: 53. This verse invites human beings to display their individual and communal virtues for the public good. It also establishes a common obligation for both men and women to endow themselves with the ethical qualities, such as chastity, truthfulness, and patience, which work at both personal and communal levels.

Whereas the *Qur'ān* provides the general principles governing a woman's participation in public life, concrete examples of how they actually participated can also be found in the early history of Islamic civilization. Muslim women in early Islam had numerous public roles in such different fields as the economy, education, religion, and the military. For example Khadija bint Khuwaylid (d. 619), the Prophet's first wife, was renowned among the Quraish for her business acumen.

During a war time, Muslim women participated in the military, Muhammad (SAW) used to bring his wives to the battlefields. 'Āisha bin Abu Bakr (d. 678) accompanied the Prophet (SAW) to the wars and learned many military skills, such as initiating pre war negotiations between combatants, conducting and ending wars. It should come as no surprise that the Prophet's contemporaries and companions entrusted her military ability to restore justice and communal good. At the Battle of the Camel, in 656, she led a force of 13,000 soldiers against the Caliph Ali (d. 661) after he failed to punish murderers of Uthman (d. 656). Muslim history is replete with the tales of many other Muslim women warriors such as Husayba (of the Battle of Uhud in 625) Umm 'Umara (of the Battle of 'Uqraba in 634), al-Khansa (of the Battle of Qadisiyah in 636), and Hind bint 'Utba and Huwayra (of the Battle of Yarmuk in 637).

Women have also played important roles in the field of religious knowledge. 'Āisha was one of the most authoritative sources in the transmission of the Prophetic tradition. Hafsa, another Prophet's wife preserved the original collection of the *Qur'ān*. And Fatima, the Prophet's youngest daughter, played an equally important role in the transmission of the Prophetic tradition.

In the following pages is given an account of those prominent women discussed in the chapter as those who played socio-political roles in the early Islamic history or in the classical ancient period as referred in the *Qur'ān*.

Bilqis

Saba may reasonably be identified with the Biblical Sheba (I Kings X 1-10). It is in detail referred to in the *Surahs* of the *Qur'ān* called after its name 34: 15-20, and *al-Namal* 27: 20-44. It was a city in Yemen, said to have been three days' journey (say 50 miles) from the city of San'a. A recent German explorer Dr. Hans Helfritz, claims to have located it in what is now Hadhramaut territory. The famous dam of Maarib made the country very prosperous, and enabled it to attain a high degree of civilization. The

Queen of Sheba therefore rightly held up her head high until she beheld glories of Prophet Sulayman.

The Queen of Sheba (by name Bilqis in Arabian tradition) came apparently from Yemen, but she had affinities with Abyssinia and possibly ruled over Abyssinia also. The Habasha tribe (after whom Abyssinia was named) came from Yemen. Between the southern coast of Yemen and the north-eastern coast of Abyssinia, there are only the Straits of Bab al-Mandab, barely twenty miles across. In the 10th or 11th century B.C. there were frequent invasions of Abyssinia from Arabia, and Sulayman's reign of 40 years is usually synchronised with B.C. 992 to 952. The Sabaen and Himyarite alphabets, in which we find the south-Arabian pre-Islamic inscriptions, passed into Ethiopic, the language of Abyssinia. The Abyssinians possess a traditional history called "The Book of the Glory of Kings" (*Kebra Nagast*), which has been translated from Ethiopic into English by Sir E.A. Wallis Budge (Oxford, 1932). It gives an account of the Queen of Sheba and the only son Menyelek I, as founders of the Abyssinian dynasty. This was provided not only with the abundance of spices and gems and gold but with sciences and arts and perhaps the spiritual possibilities which made the Queen accept the religion of Unity and Truth as mentioned in the holy *Qur'ān*. The ancient religion of the people of Saba consisted in the worship of the heavenly bodies, the sun, the planets, and the stars. Possibly the cult was connected with that of Chaldaea, the home land of Abraham. Yemen had easy access to Mesopotamia and the Persian Gulf, by way of the sea, as well as with Abyssinia. That accounts for the Christians of Najran and the Jewish dynasty of Kings (*e.g.* Zu Nuwas d. 525 A.D.) who persecuted them in the century before Islam, - also for the Christian Abyssinian governor Abraha and his discomfiture in the year of the Prophet's birth, say 570 A.D. Jewish-Christian influences were powerful in Arabia in the sixth century of Christian era.

The character of Queen Bilqis, as disclosed in the holy *Qur'ān*, is that of a ruler enjoying great wealth and dignity, and the full confidence of her subjects. She does nothing without consulting her council, and her council are ready to carry out her commands in all things. Her people are manly, loyal and contented, and ready to take the field against any enemy of their country. But their Queen is prudent in policy, and is not willing to embroil her country in war. She has the discrimination to see that the Prophet Sulayman is not like ordinary kings who conquer by violence. Perhaps in her heart she has a ray of the divine light already, though her people are yet pagans. She wishes to carry her people with her in whatever she does, because she is as loyal to them as they are to her. An exchange of presents would probably establish better relations between the two kingdoms. In Bilqis, we have a picture of womanhood, gentle, prudent and able to tame the wilder passions of her subjects and more important she demonstrates herself as grateful – after the truth is discovered and unveiled – and; acknowledges her own mistakes freely and frankly; and heartly joins with the Teacher Sulayman in the worship of God, the source of all truth and knowledge. The holy *Qur'ān* very beautifully narrates the episode in the following verses:

وَتَفَقَّدَ الطَّيْرَ فَقَالَ مَالِيَ لَا أَرَى الْهُدْهُدَ أَمْ كَانَ مِنَ الْغَائِبِينَ ۝
لَأُعَذِّبَنَّهُ عَذَابًا شَدِيدًا أَوْ لَأَذْبَحَنَّهُ أَوْ لَيَأْتِيَنِّي بِسُلْطَانٍ مُبِينٍ ۝
فَمَكَثَ غَيْرَ بَعِيدٍ فَقَالَ أَحَطْتُ بِمَا لَمْ تُحِطْ بِهِ وَجِئْتُكَ مِنْ سَبَإٍ
بِنَبَإٍ يَقِينٍ ۝ إِنِّي وَجَدْتُ امْرَأَةً تَمْلِكُهُمْ وَأُوتِيَتْ مِنْ كُلِّ شَيْءٍ وَلَهَا
عَرْشٌ عَظِيمٌ ۝ وَجَدْتُهَا وَقَوْمَهَا يَسْجُدُونَ لِلشَّمْسِ مِنْ دُونِ اللَّهِ
وَزَيَّنَ لَهُمُ الشَّيْطَانُ أَعْمَالَهُمْ فَصَدَّهُمْ عَنِ السَّبِيلِ فَهُمْ لَا يَهْتَدُونَ

○ أَلَّا يَسْجُدُوا لِلَّهِ الَّذِي يُخْرِجُ الْخَبْءَ فِي السَّمَٰوٰتِ وَالْأَرْضِ
وَيَعْلَمُ مَا تُخْفُونَ وَمَا تُعْلِنُونَ ○ اللَّهُ لَا إِلَٰهَ إِلَّا هُوَ رَبُّ الْعَرْشِ
الْعَظِيمِ ○ قَالَ سَنَنظُرُ أَصَدَقْتَ أَمْ كُنتَ مِنَ الْكَٰذِبِينَ ○ اذْهَب
بِّكِتَٰبِي هَٰذَا فَأَلْقِهْ إِلَيْهِمْ ثُمَّ تَوَلَّ عَنْهُمْ فَانظُرْ مَاذَا يَرْجِعُونَ ○
قَالَتْ يَٰٓأَيُّهَا الْمَلَؤُا إِنِّي أُلْقِيَ إِلَيَّ كِتَٰبٌ كَرِيمٌ ○ إِنَّهُ مِن سُلَيْمَٰنَ وَإِنَّهُ
بِسْمِ اللَّهِ الرَّحْمَٰنِ الرَّحِيمِ ○ أَلَّا تَعْلُوا عَلَيَّ وَأْتُونِي مُسْلِمِينَ ○
قَالَتْ يَٰٓأَيُّهَا الْمَلَؤُا أَفْتُونِي فِي أَمْرِي مَا كُنتُ قَاطِعَةً أَمْرًا حَتَّىٰ
تَشْهَدُونِ ○ قَالُوا نَحْنُ أُولُوا قُوَّةٍ وَأُولُوا بَأْسٍ شَدِيدٍ وَالْأَمْرُ إِلَيْكِ
فَانظُرِي مَاذَا تَأْمُرِينَ ○ قَالَتْ إِنَّ الْمُلُوكَ إِذَا دَخَلُوا قَرْيَةً
أَفْسَدُوهَا وَجَعَلُوا أَعِزَّةَ أَهْلِهَا أَذِلَّةً وَكَذَٰلِكَ يَفْعَلُونَ ○ وَإِنِّي مُرْسِلَةٌ
إِلَيْهِم بِهَدِيَّةٍ فَنَاظِرَةٌ بِمَ يَرْجِعُ الْمُرْسَلُونَ ○ فَلَمَّا جَاءَ سُلَيْمَٰنَ قَالَ
أَتُمِدُّونَنِ بِمَالٍ فَمَا ءَاتَىٰنِۦَ اللَّهُ خَيْرٌ مِّمَّا ءَاتَىٰكُم بَلْ أَنتُم بِهَدِيَّتِكُمْ
تَفْرَحُونَ ○ ارْجِعْ إِلَيْهِمْ فَلَنَأْتِيَنَّهُم بِجُنُودٍ لَّا قِبَلَ لَهُم بِهَا
وَلَنُخْرِجَنَّهُم مِّنْهَا أَذِلَّةً وَهُمْ صَٰغِرُونَ ○ قَالَ يَٰٓأَيُّهَا الْمَلَؤُا أَيُّكُمْ
يَأْتِينِي بِعَرْشِهَا قَبْلَ أَن يَأْتُونِي مُسْلِمِينَ ○ قَالَ عِفْرِيتٌ مِّنَ الْجِنِّ
أَنَا ءَاتِيكَ بِهِۦ قَبْلَ أَن تَقُومَ مِن مَّقَامِكَ وَإِنِّي عَلَيْهِ لَقَوِيٌّ أَمِينٌ ○ قَالَ
الَّذِي عِندَهُ عِلْمٌ مِّنَ الْكِتَٰبِ أَنَا ءَاتِيكَ بِهِۦ قَبْلَ أَن يَرْتَدَّ إِلَيْكَ طَرْفُكَ
فَلَمَّا رَءَاهُ مُسْتَقِرًّا عِندَهُ قَالَ هَٰذَا مِن فَضْلِ رَبِّي لِيَبْلُوَنِيٓ ءَأَشْكُرُ
أَمْ أَكْفُرُ وَمَن شَكَرَ فَإِنَّمَا يَشْكُرُ لِنَفْسِهِۦ وَمَن كَفَرَ فَإِنَّ رَبِّي غَنِيٌّ
كَرِيمٌ ○ قَالَ نَكِّرُوا لَهَا عَرْشَهَا نَنظُرْ أَتَهْتَدِي أَمْ تَكُونُ مِنَ الَّذِينَ
لَا يَهْتَدُونَ ○ فَلَمَّا جَاءَتْ قِيلَ أَهَٰكَذَا عَرْشُكِ قَالَتْ كَأَنَّهُ هُوَ
وَأُوتِينَا الْعِلْمَ مِن قَبْلِهَا وَكُنَّا مُسْلِمِينَ ○ وَصَدَّهَا مَا كَانَت تَّعْبُدُ مِن

دُوْنِ اللّٰهِ اِنَّهَا كَانَتْ مِنْ قَوْمٍ كٰفِرِيْنَ ۝ قِيْلَ لَهَا ادْخُلِي الصَّرْحَ
فَلَمَّا رَاَتْهُ حَسِبَتْهُ لُجَّةً وَّكَشَفَتْ عَنْ سَاقَيْهَا قَالَ اِنَّهٗ صَرْحٌ مُّمَرَّدٌ
مِّنْ قَوَارِيْرَ قَالَتْ رَبِّ اِنِّيْ ظَلَمْتُ نَفْسِيْ وَاَسْلَمْتُ مَعَ سُلَيْمٰنَ لِلّٰهِ
رَبِّ الْعٰلَمِيْنَ ۝

And he (Sulayman) took a muster of the birds; and he said: "Why is it I see not the Hoopoe? Or is he among the absentees? I will certainly punish him with a severe penalty, or execute him, unless he bring me a clear reason (for absence)".

But the Hoopoe tarried not far: he (came up and) said: "I have compassed (territory) which thou hast no compassed, and I have come to thee from Saba with Tidings true. "I found (there) a woman ruling over them and provided with every requisite; and she has a magnificent throne. I found her and her people worshipping the sun besides God: Satan has made their deeds seem pleasing in their eyes, and has kept them away from the Path – so they receive no guidances, (kept them away from the Path) that they should not worship God, who brings to light what is hidden in the heavens and the earth, and knows what ye hide and what ye reveal. God! – there is no god but He! – Lord of the Throne, Supreme!"

(Sulayman) said: "Soon shall we see whether thou hast told the truth or lied! Go thou, with this letter of mine, and deliver it to them: then draw back from them, and (wait to) see what answer they return."

(The Queen Bilqis) said: 'Ye chiefs! There is – delivered to me – a letter worthy of respect. It is from Sulayman, and is (as follows): "In the name of God, Most Gracious, Most Merciful: "Be ye not arrogant against me, but come to me in submission (to the true religion)."

She said: "Ye chiefs! Advise me in (this) my affair: no affair have I decided except in your presence."

They said: "We are induced with strength, and given to vehement war: but the command is with thee; so consider what thou wilt command."

She said: "Kings, when they enter a country, despoit it, and make the noblest of its people its meanest, thus do they behave. But I am going to send him a present and (wait) to see with what (answer) return (my) ambassadors."

Now when (the embassy) came to Sulayman, he said: "Will ye give me abundance in wealth? But that which God has given me is better than that He has given you! Nay it is ye who rejoice in your gift! Go back to them and be sure we shall come to them with such hosts as they will never be able to meet: we shall expel them from there in disgrace, and they will feel humbled (indeed)."

He said to his own men: "Ye chiefs! Which of you can bring me her throne before they come to me in submission"? Said a powerful jinn: "I will bring it to thee before thou rise from thy council: indeed I have full strength for the purpose, and may be trusted".

Said one who had knowledge of the Books: "I will bring it to thee within the twinkling of an eye! "Then when (Sulayman) saw it placed firmly before him, he said: "This is by the grace of my Lord! – to test me whether I am grateful or ungrateful! And if any is grateful truly his gratitude is (a gain) for his own soul; but if any is ungrateful, truly my Lord is Free of all Needs, Supreme in Honour."

He said: "Transform her throne out of all recognition by her: let us see whether she is guided (to the truth) or is one of those who receive no guidance."

So when she arrived, she was asked, "Is this thy throne?" She said "It was just like this; and knowledge was bestowed on us in advance of this, and we have submitted to God".

And he diverted her from the worship of others besides God: for she was (sprung) of a people that has no faith.

> She was asked to enter the lofty Palace: but when she saw it, she thought it was a lake of water, and she (tucked up her skirts), uncovering her legs. He said: "This is but a palace paved smooth with slabs of glass." She said: "O my Lord! I have indeed wronged my soul: I do (now) submit (in Islam), with Sulayman, to the Lord of the worlds." (*al-Namal*, 27: 20-44)

'Āisha (614-678)

'Āisha bint Abu Bakr was the favourite wife of the Prophet Muhammad (SAW) and a significant religious and political figure in early Islam. The daughter of Umm Ruman and one of the Companions Abu Bakr, she married the Prophet at a young age. Her intelligence, beauty, and spirited personality are well recorded in historical sources.

The *hadith* tradition records a unique level of intimacy shared by the Prophet and 'Āisha. They bathed in the same water, he prayed while she lay stretched out in front of him, he received revelation when they were under the same blanket, and he expressed a desire to be moved to 'Āisha's chamber when he knew his death was approaching. Affection and playfulness also characterised their relationship. They raced with each other and enjoyed listening to the singing of Ethiopian musicians together. The Prophet related that when 'Āisha was pleased with him, she would swear "By the God of Muhammad", and when she was annoyed with him, she would swear "By the God of Abraham". She regularly engaged the Prophet on issues of revelation and religion. Recognising the intelligence and perceptiveness, he told the Muslims "Take two-thirds of your religion from al-Humayra," the term of affection referring to the rosy-cheeked 'Āisha.

A scandal once surrounded 'Āisha, who was mistakenly left behind during a carvan rest stop on an expedition with the Prophet. She returned to Madinah escorted by a young man who had found her waiting alone. Amid the ensuing gossip and speculation about 'Āisha's fidelity, one of the Prophet's companions Ali, advised the Prophet to divorce her. Finally a *Qur'ān*ic revelation exonerated her of all suspected wrongdoings, proclaiming her innocence. This same revelation established the punishment for false accusations of adultery:

إِنَّ الَّذِينَ جَاءُو بِالْإِفْكِ عُصْبَةٌ مِّنكُمْ لَا تَحْسَبُوهُ شَرًّا لَّكُم بَلْ هُوَ
خَيْرٌ لَّكُمْ لِكُلِّ امْرِئٍ مِّنْهُم مَّا اكْتَسَبَ مِنَ الْإِثْمِ وَالَّذِي تَوَلَّىٰ كِبْرَهُ
مِنْهُمْ لَهُ عَذَابٌ عَظِيمٌ ۝ لَوْلَا إِذْ سَمِعْتُمُوهُ ظَنَّ الْمُؤْمِنُونَ
وَالْمُؤْمِنَاتُ بِأَنفُسِهِمْ خَيْرًا وَقَالُوا هَٰذَا إِفْكٌ مُّبِينٌ ۝ لَوْلَا جَاءُو
عَلَيْهِ بِأَرْبَعَةِ شُهَدَاءَ فَإِذْ لَمْ يَأْتُوا بِالشُّهَدَاءِ فَأُولَٰئِكَ عِندَ اللَّهِ هُمُ
الْكَاذِبُونَ ۝ وَلَوْلَا فَضْلُ اللَّهِ عَلَيْكُمْ وَرَحْمَتُهُ فِي الدُّنْيَا وَالْآخِرَةِ
لَمَسَّكُمْ فِي مَا أَفَضْتُمْ فِيهِ عَذَابٌ عَظِيمٌ ۝ إِذْ تَلَقَّوْنَهُ بِأَلْسِنَتِكُمْ
وَتَقُولُونَ بِأَفْوَاهِكُم مَّا لَيْسَ لَكُم بِهِ عِلْمٌ وَتَحْسَبُونَهُ هَيِّنًا وَهُوَ
عِندَ اللَّهِ عَظِيمٌ ۝ وَلَوْلَا إِذْ سَمِعْتُمُوهُ قُلْتُم مَّا يَكُونُ لَنَا أَن نَّتَكَلَّمَ
بِهَٰذَا سُبْحَانَكَ هَٰذَا بُهْتَانٌ عَظِيمٌ ۝ يَعِظُكُمُ اللَّهُ أَن تَعُودُوا لِمِثْلِهِ
أَبَدًا إِن كُنتُم مُّؤْمِنِينَ ۝ وَيُبَيِّنُ اللَّهُ لَكُمُ الْآيَاتِ وَاللَّهُ عَلِيمٌ
حَكِيمٌ ۝ إِنَّ الَّذِينَ يُحِبُّونَ أَن تَشِيعَ الْفَاحِشَةُ فِي الَّذِينَ آمَنُوا
لَهُمْ عَذَابٌ أَلِيمٌ فِي الدُّنْيَا وَالْآخِرَةِ وَاللَّهُ يَعْلَمُ وَأَنتُمْ لَا تَعْلَمُونَ ۝
وَلَوْلَا فَضْلُ اللَّهِ عَلَيْكُمْ وَرَحْمَتُهُ وَأَنَّ اللَّهَ رَءُوفٌ رَّحِيمٌ ۝

"Those who brought forward the lie are a body among yourselves: think it not to be an evil to you: on the contrary it is good for you: to every man among them (will come the punishment) of the sin that he earned, and to him who took on himself the lead among them, will be a Penalty grievous.

> "Why did they not' bring four witnesses to prove it? When they had not brought the witnesses, such men, in the sight of God (stand forth) themselves as liars!
>
> "Were it not the grace and mercy of God on you in this world and the Hereafter, a grievous penalty would have seized you in that ye rushed glibly into this affair.
>
> "Behold, ye received it on your tongues and said out of your mouths things of which ye had no knowledge; and ye thought it to be a light matter, while it was most serious in the sight of God.
>
> "And why did ye not, when ye heard it, say? – "It is not right of us to speak of this: Glory to God! This is most serious slander!"
>
> "God doth admonish you, that ye may never repeat such (conduct), if ye are (true) believers. And God makes the signs plain to you: for God is full of knowledge and wisdom.
>
> "Those who love (to see) scandal published broadcast among the believers, will have a grievous penalty in this life and in the Hereafter: God knows and ye know not.
>
> "Were it not for the grace and mercy of God on you, and that God is full of kindness and mercy, (ye would be ruined indeed). (al-Nūr, 24: 11-20)

In the lifetime of the Prophet she, together with his other wise, was referred to as "Mother of the Belivers". She is known to have transmitted approximately 1210 traditions (*hadith*), only 300 of which are included in the canonical *hadith* collections of Bukhari and Muslim. She is said to have transmitted *hadith* to atleast eighty five Muslims, as well as to have corrected inaccuracies in the *hadiths* reported by some of the male-companions.

After the death of the Prophet (SAW) she was critical of the third caliph, Uthman, but also called his killers to accountability during the caliphate of Ali. Together with the companions Zubair and Talha, she mobilised opposition to Ali, culminating in the Battle of Camel (656 A.D.). The name of the battle reflects the centrality of 'Āisha's role in the conflict, seated on her camel in the middle of the Battlefield. This struggle over succession marked the development of a major civil war (called *fitna*) in Islam, which ultimately contributed to one of the most significant religious and political divisions in the Muslim world. The representations of 'Āisha in subsequent Shi'ite and Sunni polemics reflected some of the historical antagonisms between the two. Traditions hold that she was consulted on theological, legal and other religious issues, and was also known for poetic skills. She is buried at Jannat al-Baqī' in Madinah.

Sukayna (671-737)

Sukayna was the nickname (*Laqab*) of the granddaughter of Fatima (the daughter of the Prophet) and Ali bin Abi Talib. Her full name is variously given as Umayma (according to al-Kalbi) or Amina (according to al-Isbahani) bint Husayn. Her mother was al-Rabāb bint Imra al-Qays al-Kalbiyah, a poet, whose father was the reputed military leader of the Kalb.

Having lost both her father and husband (Abdullah bin al-Hazan bin Abi Talib) at Karbala, Sukayna moved to Madinah, where she acquired a taste for intellectual matters from her mother. In 686 A.D. she married Mus'ab b. al-Zubayr (d. 691), who was killed fighting for his brother Abdullah b. al-Zubayr, the acknowledged caliph in Madinah and Iraq. Then, after a couple of marriages which ended in divorce, she finaly wed Zayd b. Umar, the grandson of Uthman b. Affan. She died as his widow at the age of sixty seven.

A member of the *ahl al-bayt*, Sukayna nevertheless had the reputation of a *barza*, a woman who is never veiled, entertains men at home, and is recognised for her judgement and sound reasoning. Her bold integrity was expressed politically in her opposition to the Ummayyads, and socially in her marriage contracts, wherein she insisted on her freedom from marital control and demanded the monogamy of her intended husband. Though it was to a hairstyle – *al-turrah al-Sukayniyya* – that she gave her name, Sukayna was, importantly, a lover of the arts. According to Abu Zinad (d. 747), Jarir (d. 728), and Farazdaq (d. 727) were two famous poets whose skills she encouraged, and Ibn Surayj (d. 744), one of the great singers of the Hijazi school, considered himself her protégé, and set many of her verses to music.

Khadija bint Khuwaylid (d. 620)

The first wife of Muhammad (SAW) was a daughter of Khuwaylid of the Quraish family of Abdul 'Uzza. The authorities are unanimous in saying that when she made the Prophet's acquaintance and took him into her service she was well-to-do merchant's widow who was carrying on business independently. She had been twice married previously and had children of both marriages. The one husband was a Makhzumi, the other a Tamimi, Abu Hala, whose real name is variously given; but this Abu Hala is also mentioned by others among the followers of the Prophet, which – if both stories are true – would make Khadija a divorced woman. When she discovered the brilliant qualities of her young employee, she proposed marriage to him; according to the generally accepted story, her father was dead by this time, according to another, still alive and opposed to the marriage, so that she only obtained his consent. Most authorities make Muhammad (SAW) twenty-five at this time and Khadija forty. None can doubt the essential accuracy of the tradition, for the alteration in the Prophet's circumstances has witness borne to it in the *Qur'ān* (93:8) and the fact that he was content with one wife so long as Khadija lived may be related to her superior social position. Her wealth must have been a great help to him during his struggle and her death, after she had probably suffered considerable losses through the hostility of the great merchants, contributed to make his position still less endurable. But her personality seems to have been of even greater weight with her husband; in any case tradition draws a very attractive picture of the moral support which she afforded him during the excitement and agitation of the first revelation. That Warqua b. Nawfal was her cousin must have helped to make her sympathetic to the Prophet's mission. Imam Bukhari has quoted a *hadith* narrated by "Āisha, the mother of the faithfuls. The *hadith* is lengthy but it highlights very beautifully the sympathetic and supportive role played by Khadija in strengthening the missionary movement of Islam:

> Narrates 'Āisha, the mother of the faithful believers: the commencement of the Divine Revelation to Allah's Prophet was in the form of good dreams which came true like day light, and then the love of seclusion was bestowed upon him. He used to go in seclusion in the cave of Hira where he used to worship (Allah alone) continuously for many days before his desire to see his family. He used to take with him the journey food for the stay and then come back to (his wife) Khadija to take his food likewise again till suddenly the Truth descended upon him while he was in the cave of Hira. The angel came to him and asked him to read. The Prophet (SAW) added, "The angel caught me (forcefully) and pressed me so hard that I could not bear it any more. He then released me and again asked me to read and I replied, 'I do not know how to read. Thereupon he caught me again and pressed me a second time till I could not bear it any more. He then released me and again

asked me to read but again I replied, "I do not know how to read (or what shall I read)?' Thereupon he caught me for the third time and pressed me and then released me and said, "Read in the name of your Lord, who has created (all the exists), has created man from a clot. Read and your Lord is the Most Generous" (96: 1-3) Then Allah's Apostle returned with the Revelation and with his heart beating severely. Then he went to Khadija bint Khuwaylid and said, "Cover me! Cover me!" They covered him till his fear was over and after that he told her everything that had happened and said, "I fear that some thing may happen to me." Khadija replied

كلّا وَاللهِ ما يُخزِيكَ اللهُ أبدًا إنّك لَتصِلُ الرّحم، وتحمِلُ الكَلّ

وتَكسِبُ المعدومَ وتَقرِي الضّيفَ وتُعينُ على نوائبِ الحَقّ

"Never! By Allah, Allah will never disgrace you. You keep good relations with your Kith and Kin, help the poor and the destitute, serve your guests generously and assist the deserving calamity – afflicted one."

Khadija then accompanied him to her cousin Warqua bin Nawfal bin Asad bin Abdul 'Uzza, who during the pre-Islamic period became a Christian and used to write the writing with Hebrew letters. He would write from the Gospel in Hebrew as much as Allah wished him to write. He was an old man and had lost his eye sight. Khadija said to Warqua, "Listen to the story of your nephew, O my cousin!" Warqua asked, "O my nephew! What have you seen?" Allah's Apostle described whatever he had seen. Warqua said, "This is the same one who keeps the secrets (angel Gabriel) whom Allah had sent to Moses. I wish I were young and could live up to the time when your people would turn you out." Allah's Apostle asked, "Will they drive me out?" Warqua replied in the affirmative and said, "Anyone (man) who came with something similar to what you have brought was treated with hostility; and If I should remain alive till the day when you will be turned out then I would support you strongly." But after a few days Warqua died and the Divine Revelation was also paused for a while. (*Sahih al-Bukhari*, Chapter I, *Hadith* No. 3)

Fatimah Zahra (605-633)

Daughter of Muhammad (SAW) and his first wife Khadija, born at Makkah probably about the year 605 A.D. She was brought to Madinah after the migration by Ali or Zayd bin Haritha, and married to Ali after the battle of Badr. Her sons Hasan and Husain were most probably born in A.H. 4 and 5 respectively. There were also two daughters of the marriage, Zainab and Umm Kulthum, the latter born in the last year of Fatimah's life. Apart from these facts, the historical details for her life are scanty. After the conquest of the rich oases of Northern Hijaz, the Prophet allotted to Fatimah, as to each of his wives, an annual allowance of 85 loads of wheat. She is said to have accompanied him on the expedition in which Makkah surrendered (A.H. 8) and on the "Farewell Pilgrimage", and was present at his death. After Abu Bakr was elected as the *Khalifah*, she remained implacably hostile to him, either because of her feud with "Āisha, or because Ali had been passed over, or because Abu Bakr refused to allow her claim to inherit the oasis of Fadak, on the plea that it was the private property of her father. But before the close of the same year (11/633) she died. She appears to have suffered from poor health during the greater part of her life.

It may appear surprising that the earliest sources contain so little information about her, and that too so confused. Even among the traditionists she is rarely cited; in Ibn Hanbal's compilation, her *musnad* occupies only one page against the 250 devoted to 'Āisha. For the other daughters of the Prophet (SAW), however, there is even less; while in contrast to them, a considerable biographical literature grew up around her at a later date. The explanation of these facts is largely to be sought in the sectarian disputes of the first and second centuries of the *Hijra*. Eighteen *hadiths*, however, are ascribed to her and the senior companions like Ali, Hasan, Husain, 'Āisha, Umm Kulthum, Umm Raf'i , Anas bin Malik have received them from her.

In the eyes of the Shia, Fatimah represents "The embodiment of all that is divine in womanhood, - the noblest ideal of human conception". Her birth was miraculous, her union with Ali decided by divine decree. Having been the person most dear to the Prophet (SAW), she was carried off by grief for his death. Later Sunni literature also, following its general tendency, has been influenced by these Shi'i traditions, and without going to the same lengths, has progressively enhanced the position of Fatimah in the Prophet's household. The Sunnis do not reject the *hadiths* in which she is declared to be "queen of the women of paradise next Maryam, daughter of Imrān"; they give her the enigmatic epithet *batul* "virgin".

Khaulah bint Th'alabah

Khaulah belonged to the Khazraj tribe of Madinah and was the wife of Aus bin Samit, the brother of 'Ubadah bin Samit the chief of Aus tribe. Though in Islam, Aus divorced her by an old pagan custom: the formula was known as *Zihar*, and consisted of the words "Thou art to me as the back of my mother". This was held by pagan custom to imply a divorce and freed the husband from any responsibility for conjugal duties, but did not leave the wife free to leave the husband's home, or to contract a second marriage. Such a custom was in any case degrading to a woman. It was particularly hard on Khaulah, for she loved her husband and pleaded that she had little children whom she had no resources herself to support and whom under *Zihar* her husband was not bound to support. She urged her plea to the Prophet (SAW) and in prayer to God. Her just plea was accepted, and this iniquitous custom, based on false words, was abolished. In a quick response to Khaulah, following verses were revealed:

قَدْ سَمِعَ اللّٰهُ قَوْلَ الَّتِى تُجَادِلُكَ فِى زَوْجِهَا وَتَشْتَكِىٓ إِلَى اللّٰهِ
وَاللّٰهُ يَسْمَعُ تَحَاوُرَكُمَا إِنَّ اللّٰهَ سَمِيعٌ بَصِيرٌ ۝ اَلَّذِينَ يُظٰهِرُونَ
مِنكُم مِّن نِّسَائِهِم مَّا هُنَّ أُمَّهٰتِهِمْ إِنْ أُمَّهٰتُهُمْ إِلَّا الّٰئِى وَلَدْنَهُمْ وَإِنَّهُمْ
لَيَقُولُونَ مُنكَرًا مِّنَ الْقَوْلِ وَزُورًا وَإِنَّ اللّٰهَ لَعَفُوٌّ غَفُورٌ ۝

> "God has indeed heard (and accepted) the statement of the woman who pleads with thee concerning her husband and carries her complaint (in prayer) to God: and God (always) hears the arguments between both sides among you: for God hears and sees (all things). If any men among you divorce their wives by *Zihar* (calling them mothers), they can not be their mothers except those who gave them birth. And in fact they use words (both) iniquitous and false: but truly God is one that blots out (sins) and forgives (again and again). (al-Mujadalah 58: 1-2)

This unprecedented event of a she-companion being heard and accepted immediately by the divine revelation became very popular and prestigious in favour of Khaulah. Ibn abi Hātim and Baihaqi both related that at some time Umar along with some companions were going to somewhere. Amid the road a woman checked Umar and started talking in detail. Umar used to listen her uninterruptedly and patiently. One of the companions complained: O leader of the faithfuls, you made these Quraishite leaders stood along the road for the sake of an old woman! Umar replied: Do you known who was that woman? She was Khaulah bint Th'alabah whose complaint was heard from beyond the seven skies; by God! If she would have stopped me for the whole night I would do so; I excuse her only at the time of prayers.

Ibn Abdul Barr in his account *al-Isti'ab* has narrated the event differently. He related from Qatādah that when Khaulah met Umar on his way he offered salutation to her. She after responding in the proper way used to address him in a derogative way saying: "Surprising! O Umar, there was a time when I saw you in the market of Ukāz; you were called 'Umayr; used to pasture the goats and sheeps. No more time passed and you were recognised as Umar. After some time you were selected as *amir al-muminin.* Always do fear from Allah and take care of the subjects. Remember one who fears from the divine punishments, treats with even the ordinary man as his relative; and who fears from the death may lose the same which he tries to keep safe." On seeing this, Jarud Abdi, one of those accompanied with Umar, spontaneously reacted: O woman! You have insulted *amir al-muminin* beyond the limits. Umar said: "Let her continue; do you know who this lady. She was heard from above the seven skies, Umar must hear her preferably." Imam Bukhari also has narrated a similar event.

Shifa bint Abdullah (d. 24/640 approximately)

Shifa, the daughter of Abdullah and Fatimah bint Wahb Makhzumi, the wife of Abu Hashmah Adawi embraced Islam before migration and was allotted by the Prophet (SAW) in Madinah a house in which she resided with her son. According to *Usud al-Ghabah*, she was one of the wise and learned ladies. She related the traditions from the Prophet (SAW) not less than twelve. Those who received the traditions from her included his son Sulayman and two grandsons (Abu Bakr and Uthman), Abu Salmah, Hafsah and Abu Ishaq. Ibn S'ad has quoted that Umar used to prefer her opinion and take into account while dealing with the issues and sometimes he entrusted her with the charge of supervising the market.

Umm Salmah (596-681 A.D.)

Hind Makhzumi, popularly known with the nickname Umm Salmah, the daughter of Suhayl (Abu Umayyah) and 'Atikah bint 'Āmir was flourished in a luxurious atmosphere; her father was a generous wealthy leader of Makkah and was known as *Zād al-Rākib* since he used to support financially all the members of caravan while travelling. She embraced Islam along with his husband Abdullah bin Abdul Asad known as Abu Salmah; first migrated to Abyssinia and then alone to Madinah and thus became the first migrant among the ladies. When his husband died in 4 A.H. she accepted the marriage offer of the Prophet on her terms and conditions and was remarried with him in the last days of the same year and thus included among the mothers of the faithfuls, she was counted among the highly learned, courageous, wise and enthusiastic women. Not less than 378 traditions are narrated by Umm Salmah who are included in the third rank of traditionist companions. Abu Hurairah and Ibn Abbas were no more independent of her expert learning. Marwan bin Hakam, the personal secretary of the third caliph used to consult her again and again and declared. "How can we dare to ask others while the Prophet's consorts are alive."

Umm Salmah participated in numerous wars. She accompanied the Prophet (SAW) in the Peace Treaty of Hudaibiyah. According to Bukhari, the Prophet after concluding the treaty with the Quraishite leaders instructed his companions thrice to slaughter the animal and untie the dress of *ihram* but in vain; none moved forward to do so since some clauses of the treaty were considered by the Muslims as unpleasing and they consequently were aggrieved and depressed. The Prophet entered the residence and make a complaint to Umm Salmah. She advised him to slaughter the animal publicly and shave himself in order to untie the *ihram* dress. The Prophet accepted her advice and all the companions seeing him rushed to follow him. This advice of Umm Salmah to be offered to the Prophet (SAW) indicates her expertise in human psychology. Imam al-Haramayn al-Juwaini used to say that this farsightedness and sound thinking was unprecedented in the entire history of women.

Umm Salmah participated in the battle of Khaybar also. In 9 A.H. in the case of *īla* confronted between the Prophet (SAW) and his consorts, Umar as a relative came to Umm Salma – after he warned his daughter – turned into – the Prophet's consort Hafsa – and talked about the seriousness of the case. Umm Salmah roughly responded: "Very surprising O Ibn Khattab! You interrupted every thing; you wish even to interrupt the private affairs of the Messenger of God and his consorts!" The answer was straightforward and silenced Umar. Late in the night the news mistakenly flashed that the Prophet (SAW) had divorced his consorts. In the early morning Umar rushed to the Prophet (SAW) and repeated the story. When he quoted Umm Salmah, the Prophet (SAW) smiled. She died in the age of 84 and was buried in *Jannat al-Baqī'*.

Umm Hāni (d. after 40/661)

Fakhitah, popularly known by her nickname (*Laqab*) Umm Hāni, was the daughter of Abu Tālib, the uncle of the Prophet (SAW). Her mother was Fatimah bint Asad and thus Ali, Jafar and Umm Hāni were the real brothers and sister. She married with Hubayrah bin Amar and embraced Islam in A.H. 8 when Makkah was captured. She provided asylum to two of her pagan relatives and it was sanctioned by the Prophet (SAW) inspite of Ali's opposition. His husband flew at the eve of the conquest of Makkah to

Najrān. According to Tirmidhi she died after the death of Ali; while *Tahzib* provided a different version that she departed during the caliphate of Muawiyah.

Umm Hāni narrated forty six traditions of the Prophet (SAW). Those who received the traditions from her included: Jad'ah, Yahya, Harun, Abu Murrah, Abu Sālih, Abdullah bin Abbas, Abdullah b. Harith b. Naufal, Ibn Abi Laila, Mujāhid, 'Urwah, Abdullah b. 'Ayash, Sh'abi, 'Ata, Muhammad bin Uqbah. Umm Hāni frequently visited the Prophet (SAW) and asked about various issues. Once she made a query from him of the meaning of the Quranic verse no. 29 of the chapter *al-'Ankabût*.

Umm 'Umārah (d. after 12/633)

Nasībah, popularly known by her nickname (*Laqab*) Umm 'Umārah, belonged to Najjār, a clan of Khazraj tribe of Madinah was the daughter of K'ab bin Amar. She was first married with Zayd bin 'Asim and then Arbah b. Amar, accompanying whom she participated in the allegiance of the Valley (*Aqabah*) that included 73 men and two women. She participated wholeheartedly in the Battle of Uhud and fought bravely against the pagans. Watering the Muslims injured in the battlefield she defended the Prophet (SAW) herself when the situation reversed and turned into Muslim defeat. She used to protect him by her sword and arrow when attacked by the pagans. The Prophet himself has related that I saw her in the battlefield of Uhud defending me against my right and left. A Makkan soldier accessed to the Prophet (SAW) uninterruptedly and Umm 'Umarah checked him and she was injured. According to some accounts she killed a pagan in the same battle. She participated in the treaty of Hudaibiyah, battle of Khaybar and also in the conquest of Makkah. During *riddah* wars, she participated accompanying her son Habib in the battle of Yamamah under the leadership of Khalid bin Walid. His son was killed in the battle and she took a pledge that either Musaylimah would have killed or she would have lost her life in the way of God. She then plunged in the battlefield with a sword in her hand and received twelve injuries on her body and finally one hand of her was cut off. Musaylimah also was killed.

Hind bint 'Utbah (d. 14/635)

Hind was the daughter of 'Utbah, the most respectable among the leaders of Quraish, was first married with Fākih bin Mugheerah Makhzumi and finally with Abu Sufyan b. Harb, the famous leader of Umayyah tribe. She, her father and husband all opposed the Prophet (SAW) teeth and nails. She accompanying her husband provoked the Makkan pagans to take revenge for the mass killings in the Badr and the fanatic pair led the pagan army in the battle of Uhud. She demonstrated inhuman and cruel way of taking revenge from the dead bodies of the Muslims after having garlanded in her neck the pieces of the deads. She hired an expert military man, Wahshi, the slave of Jubayr bin Mut'im to kill Hamzah bin Abdul Muttalib who had already killed her husband in the battle of Badr. Hind took revenge from Hamzah in the way that she cut off the stomach of his dead body and tried unsuccessfully to digest his lungs. This hurted the Prophet unthinkably but he did not loose his patience being benevolent to the whole world.

Hind, at the eve of the conquest of Makkah, embraced Islam in a dramatic way. She being veiled offered her pledge to the Prophet (SAW) in public but with certain arguments and in a rough style. The dialogue run between Hind and the Prophet was as follows:

Hind: O messenger of God, on what teaching you do take pledge from us?

The Prophet: Do not associate anyone with God.

Hind:	We accept it though you did not take this pledge from the men.
The Prophet:	Do not steal.
Hind:	I take something secretly from the wealth of my husband, I do not know whether it is legal or not.
The Prophet:	Do not kill your generation.
Hind:	We fostered them infants; you killed them youngs; let they and you understand each other.

Inspite of this rough dealing the Prophet overlooked her. This benevolent dealing of the Prophet imprinted heavily on her mind. She spontaneously cried: "O messenger of God! Your tent was the most detested one in my eyes; now it is the dearest one to me." She then rushed to her residence and made the idols in to pieces and commented: "We were deceived by you!"

During the period of Umar's caliphate, Hind and her husband Abu Sufyan both participated with full enthusiasm in the battle of Yarmuk in 15/636 against the Byzantines. According to *Usud al-Ghabah* she inherited self-respect, egoistic trend, farsightedness and intelligence. According to Ibn S'ad she died during the caliphate of 'Uthman, while some accounts record it as happened during Umar's caliphate.

Khansā bint Amar (d. 24/645)

Tumādhir, popularly known as Khansa, bint Amar belonged to the clan Sulaym of Qays tribe of Makkah; was first married with Rawāhah bin Abdul 'Uzza and then with Mirdas bin Abu 'Āmir. She embraced Islam in her old age in Madinah along with her fellows after the migration. The Prophet (SAW) heard her reciting her poetry and enjoyed.

During the caliphate Umar she participated in the battle of Qadisiyah along with her four sons. She addressed them in the battlefield inciting for jihad and sacrificing their lives for the sake of Islam. She said: "My dear sons! You have embraced Islam and opted migration eagerly; otherwise you were in no way of burden on your homeland, nor your country was affected by any famine (that would have compelled you to leave your birth place)! Nonetheless you took your older mother and put her to Persia. By God! You held the purest blood in your veins; I never deceived your father nor ever insulted or defamed your maternal uncle. You know very well that this world is lasting and fighting against the pagans is rewarding and a pious duty. God proclaims: "O ye who believe! Persevere in patience and constancy; vie in such perseverance, strengthen each other; and fear God; that ye may prosper" (3: 200). So prepare for fighting after you get up in the morning and fight in the battlefield for the last moment." All the young sons of Khansa moved to the battle in the next day enthusiastically and were martyred. She after receiving the news thanked God. These martyrs were Abdullah and Abu Sharjrah from the first husband and Zayd and Muawiyah from the next one.

Khansa was a distinguished poetess and in elegies she was treated unequal. The author of *Usud al-Ghabah* has commented that "all the experts of poetry are unanimously agreed that no poetess may be equated with her from the pre-or-post Khansa." Laila al-Akhyaliyah (d. after 704) was counted by the experts of poetry as the chief of all the poetesses; Khansa, however, was exempted from this categorisation. In the market of pre-Islamic 'Ukāz she was graced with the title of *artha al-Arab* (the most distinguished poetess of elegy throughout Arabia) written on the banner being installed on the front door of her tent. When she recited her poetry to Nābigha Dhubyāni the greatest poet of the period he was surprised and remarked spontaneously: "Had I not heard (A'asha Qays) Abu Basīr (d. 629) I would have recognised you the greatest poet of the world."

Khansa used to compose only few lines in the initial stage. Her brothers Sakhr and Mu'awiyah were killed in the tribal clashes and this provoked her to compose lengthy elegies full of emotions and psychological sentiments. The following poetic line of her is very famous:

وَإِنَّ صخرًا لتأتمّ الهداة به   كأنّه علم في رأسه نارٌ

"Sakhr is proudly followed by the stalwarts,
as he seems a mountain on the top of which
a light is twinkling."

Here poetic collection is a bulky one and is translated in to French also.

Nāilah bint al-Farāfisah

Nāilah, the daughter of al-Farafisah bin al-Ahwas al-Kalbiyah was the wife of the third Islamic Caliph Uthman bin Affan and a poetess and orator, of bold and courageous nature. During the period of rebellion against her husband she advised him to call Ali bin Abi Talib and consult him. When the anarchists attacked Uthman she defended him; she spontaneously called her servant Rabāh for help but in vain. In this attempt her fingers cut off. After the murder of her husband she composed few liens of elegy mourning about his personality and character. She delivered a firing long speech in the mosque publicly provocating for revenge. She then wrote all the details and also despatched the blood-stained shirt of Uthman and her torn fingers to Mu'awiyah who ruled in Syria. After the disorder was over and the situation normalised Mu'awiyah sent to her the marriage message that was refused.

*****

6

FUNCTIONS OF *SHURA*

Jurisdiction of *Shura*

There are no specific limits to the scope of the *Shura* or the matters which ought to be placed before it for consultation in the *Qur'ān* and the *Sunnah*.[1] The injunctions in the holy *Qur'ān* relating to the *Shura* indicate that this body can deal with all affairs of the Muslim community and every aspect of its life. Thus it may be said that all public affairs of the Muslim *Ummah* can, rather should be, the subject of consultations. However, there are two limitations on the scope of the *Shura*. The first is that it cannot take decisions on issues regarding which injunctions exist in the *Qur'ān* or in the *Sunnah*, except when its purpose is only to interpret the injunctions or to enforce them. Obviously, this could happen only in the period subsequent to that of the Prophet (SAW), for during his time the Prophet (SAW) himself was the authority for their interpretation and enforcement.

The second condition is that when an issue is referred to the *Shura*, it is precluded from reaching a decision contradicting a legislative injunction in the holy *Qur'ān* or in the *Sunnah.*[2] In the event of being such a contradiction, following the opinion of the *Shura* is prohibited.[3]

It is more compatible with the Islamic method of legislation to exclude certain matters from the purview of the *Shura*. Daily administrative matters which occupy the executive and administrative branches of a state, due to their nature and need for quick decisions, cannot be brought before *Shura* except when they are related to important issues or to problems which affect entire personnel in these branches.[4]

Combination of Legislature and Executive

The principle of "Consultation among themselves" underlying the creation of *Majlis al-Shura* naturally includes the *amir* for, having been elected by the community as head of the state, he must be regarded as its foremost representative in all matters pertaining to community affairs. More than this by virtue of his being the focal point of all *amr* in an Islamic polity, the *amir* cannot merely be an ordinary member of the *majlis*, but must be its leader, duty bound to guide its activities and to preside – either personally or through a nominee – over its deliberations. This stipulation, implies that in a state, which is subject to the authority of a Divine Law, there can be no radical separation of the legislative and executive wings of the government.[5] This constitutes a most important Islamic contribution to political theory.[6]

Scholars assert that the head of the state and its *majlis al-Shura* performs both legislative and executive functions. In modern democracies, a sharply drawn separation of powers between the legislatures and the executive is considered to be the only effective safeguard against a possible abuse of authority by the executive. This western principle of government has certain merits. According to it, the legislature controls the functioning of executive and thus prevents it from exercise its powers in an irresponsible manner. However, equally undoubtedly, a government as a whole – including both its executive and legislative aspects – is more often than not greatly hampered by this radical separation of functions, and is thus obviously at a disadvantage compared with an autocratic government. Islam is as uncompromisingly opposed to autocracy as any of the western democratic polities could conceivably be, but in this matter Islam follows a middle way, avoiding the disadvantages of either of these systems and securing to the Muslim community the advantages of both. By integrating the executive and the legislative wings of the government through the instrumentality of the *amir* it is possible to overcome this duality of power, which, western countries so often places the executive and the legislature in opposition to one another, in modern democracies and, at times, makes parliamentary government unwieldy or even ineffectual. But this gain in efficiency in an Islamic state is not achieved at the cost of relinquishing the principle of popular control over the activities of the government. Indeed, any possible tendency toward autocracy on the part of the executive is checked at the very outset by the transaction of all governmental activities, executive as well as legislative, must be an outcome of consultation among the accredited representatives of the community.

In logical pursuance of this principle of interdependence, one may conclude that the decision arrived at by *majlis al-Shura* through a majority vote are not of a merely advisory character to be accepted or rejected by the executive at its discretion – but are legally binding on it.

As has been discussed in the previous chapters, during the period of the Four Caliphs the Arab society had preserved its tribal structure to a large extent and the leaders of the tribe and clans possessed the right to speak and act on behalf of their respective groups. Had the caliphs insisted on elections, those very chieftains would have been elected. Hence, none of the Guided Caliphs saw any reason for changing the method by which the *majlis* came into being. Nowadays clan leadership has lost its erstwhile importance. Consequently there is no longer any way of ascertaining the opinion of the community except by means of a popular vote.

This applies not only to the method by which the *majlis* is to come into being, but also to the terms of reference under which it would work and the position which it would occupy a modern Islamic state.

One may conclude from the history of the periods of the Prophet (SAW) and the Four Guided Caliphs that there was total collaboration between the executive and the legislature. However, Islamic chronicles indicate that the legislature cannot overrule the *amir*. He is not bound to seek prior consent of the *Shura* in day to day administration. In this connection scholars refer to the verse of the holy Qur'ān.

فَإِذَا عَزَمْتَ فَتَوَكَّلْ عَلَى اللَّهِ

"And when you have decided upon a course of action, place your trust in Allah",[7]

Which has been interpreted to mean that although the *amir* is bound by the temporal legislation enacted by the *majlis* and by its decisions on major questions of policy, the manner in which he translates these decisions and directives into action is left to the discretion of the executive over which he presides. Though the *majlis*, is empowered to frame the temporal laws on the basis of which a country is to be governed, to formulate major policies to be pursued, and, in general, to supervise the activities of the government, it is not entitled to interfere with the day to day working of the executive.[8] It is generally agreed that the *amir* must possess executive powers to the fullest extent. An office of head of state shorn of real powers and reduced to a mere figure-head is obviously redundant according to the Qur'ānic injunction which enjoins in the Muslims' to be obedient to the *Ulu al-amr* (those who hold authority), which is a corollary of their obedience to Allah (SWT) and His Prophet (SAW).[9]

Concentration of Power

However, even if full executive powers are conceded to the *amir* the question remains as to whether those powers (and functions resulting from them) are to be vested in him alone, or whether he should exercise them in partnership, as it were, with a cabinet of ministers representing major parties in the *majlis al-Shura*, their tenure being dependent on this body's vote of confidence. There exists no explicit pronouncement, in the *Shariah* in either of these matters. Nevertheless, from the wordings of many authentic traditions it appears that the Prophet (SAW) envisaged the concentration of all executive responsibilities in the hands of one person as being most suitable for Islamic polity. Here are some of these traditions:

مَن أطاعني فقد أطاع اللّٰه ومَن عصاني فقد عصا اللّٰه،
ومن يطع الأميرَ فقد أطاعني ومَن يعص الأميرَ فقد
1. عصاني وإنّما الإمام جُنّةٌ يُقاتَل من ورائِه ويُتّقى به.

"He who obeys me obeys Allah (SWT); and he who disobeys me, disobeys Allah (SWT); and he who obeys the *amir*, obeys me, and he who disobeys the *amir*, disobeys me. Behold, the leader (*al-Imam*) is but a shield from behind which the people fight and by which they protect themselves."[10]

ألا كلكم راع وكلّكم مسئول عن رعيته فالإمام الذى على
2. النّاس راع وهو مسئولٌ عن رعيّته.

"Verily, each of you is a shepherd, and each of you is responsible for his flock. (Thus) the leader (*Imam*) who is placed over the people is a shepherd responsible for his flock."[11]

من بايع إماما فأعطاه صفقة يده وثمرة قلبه فليطعه إن
3. استطاع فإن جاء آخر ينازعه فاضربوا عنق الآخر.

"He who has pledged allegiance to an *imam* giving him his hand and the fruit of his heart, shall obey him if he can (*i.e.* as long as he is not ordered to commit a sin), and if another person tries to usurp the *imam's* rights, smite that other person's neck."[12]

These and similar sayings of the Prophet (SAW) are entirely in keeping with his more general command that whenever a group of Muslims is engaged in any work of common interest, one man should be chosen from among them as *imam* to lead the others.[13] Nevertheless, one might argue that even a government on the European parliamentary pattern, a council of ministers deriving its mandates from the people and directly responsible to the legislature and ultimately to the people would not necessarily be against the principle of one man leadership of an Islamic state, where the cabinet is headed by the *amir*, who combines in his person the twin functions of head of the state and of Prime Minister. Commonsense, however, says that such an arrangement would render the position of the *amir* highly anomalous. On the one hand, he is supposed to be head of the executive in his own right, by virtue of a popular election, on the other he has to share his executive responsibilities with a group of ministers individually responsible to the legislature. Thus it would be the parties represented in the *Shura*, and not the *amir*, who would be the ultimate fount of all executive power in the state. Apart from the fact that such an arrangement would militate against the Islamic concept of leadership, it would inevitably result in the government policy being always dependent on a compromise or, rather, on an unending series of compromises between various, sometimes conflicting, party programmes, and never being able to attain that single-mindedness and inner continuity so essential for an Islamic state.[14]

The principle of compromise between opposing party programmes may be necessary (and sometimes even morally justifiable) in communities which are not animated by any definite ideology and are, therefore, bound to subordinate all political decisions to the people's changing views as to what may be the right course of action under the given circumstances. But it is certainly out of place in an ideological Islamic state, in which the concepts of 'right' and 'wrong' have definite connotations and cannot possibly be made dependent on mere expediency. In such a state, both legislative and administrative policies must at all times be expressive of the ideology on which the community has agreed beforehand, and this can never come about if the government is obliged to subordinate its day to day activity to considerations of fluctuating party politics. This, of course, does not preclude the existence of parties in an Islamic legislature. If freedom of opinion and criticism is recognised as the citizens' inherent right, the people must be accorded the freedom to group together for the purpose of propagating certain sets of views as to what would be the policy of the state on this or that question, provided these views do not run counter to the ideology on which the state is based, the parties thus constituted must have the right to argue put forward their respective viewpoint, within and outside the *majlis Shura*. However, this freedom to form parties and to propagate their programmes should not be allowed to interfere with the administration of the government.

Islamic Presidentialism

In view of all this, it would seem that a 'Presidential' system of government would correspond more closely to the requirements of an Islamic polity than a 'parliamentary' one. As a matter of fact, the very term *Wazir* (minister) which the Prophet (SAW) has used connotes a person who helps the head of the state to bear his burden. The Prophet (SAW) says:

وإذا أراد الله بالأمير خيرًا جعل له وزير صدق إن نسي ذكره وإن ذكر أعانه وإذا أراد به غير ذالك جعل له وزير سوء إن نسي لم يذكره وإن ذكر لم يعنه.

> "If Allah means well with the *amir*, He provides for him a trustworthy assistant (*wazir*) to remind him whenever he forgets, and to help him whenever he remembers. And if Allah does not mean it well with him, He provides for him a bad assistant, who does not remind him whenever he forgets and does not help him whenever he remembers."[15]

The Qur'ānic injunction '*amruhum Shura baynahum*' makes the transaction of all major governmental business directly dependent on consultation. The *Shura* is required to give its verdict on all important policy issues as well as evolve temporal laws under which the country is to be governed. But in practice the matter is not so simple.

Scholars of political science are aware of the fact that it is not the legislative assembly but the executive branches of government that 'make' most laws in a modern state. As a rule, any major item of legislation entails a great deal of expert preparation and research, a thorough knowledge of social and economic issues involved, and, finally, considerable legal acumen in the formulation of the laws that are to be enacted. It is obvious that such an accumulation of expert knowledge and technical ability cannot be expected of an assembly of persons elected on the basis of a wide suffrage; for the electorate is, naturally, concerned only with the individual merit of the candidates, and is not in a position to assess each candidate's technical qualifications for law-making. Moreover, the parliament, comprising a comparatively large number of representatives, would not be capable of studying preparing and drafting any elaborate legislation. Consequently the work of research, preparation and drafting new laws becomes, in modern states, the responsibility of the executive. It is in the executive departments of government that most of the major legislative bills are expertly prepared by civil servants who have been trained specially for this purpose, and are only then placed before the legislative assembly for discussion, possible amendment and final adoption. Such a procedure might be entirely satisfactory from the Islamic point of view so far as popular consent is concerned, for no legislative measure can become law unless and until it has been thoroughly discussed in the *Shura*. However, popular consent alone does not constitute the beginning and the and of all Islamic requirements with regard to legislation: the principle of *Shura* categorically demands that all governmental activity should be a direct outcome of consultation. But such a practice would hamper the executive at every step, thus destroying its freedom of action. This would not be a problem in an

Islamic *Shura* comprising technical experts. As has been discussed in one of the previous chapters, there should be a quota, fixed for the experts in *Shariah* in modern law technically experienced persons from all fields, as well as those who are familiar with law-making technicalities in the *Shura.* These persons would be nominated or selected by the *amir* or *Shura* itself. In this body the principle of consultation would be followed.

In all modern parliaments special committees are constituted to deal with particular problems of government. It is before these committees that the executive has to justify its policies. However, the approval or disapproval of a parliamentary committee is usually on *ex post facto* verdict on the policies of the executive. In Islamic *Shura* no such problem is likely to arise because the legislative and executive powers are in one hand. The head of the state, and through him the *Shura*, is solely responsible for all legislative and executive functions to the people.

Compare with Parliamentarism

In view of all this, it would appear that a presidential system of government would correspond more closely to the necessities of Islamic state than a parliamentary form in which the executive powers are shared by a cabinet jointly responsible to the legislature. Modern parliament[16] and Islamic *Shura* differ from each other in the following respects:

1. In modern parliamentary systems the executive is divided into two parts – real and nominal (a Prime Minister being head of the government and the Monarch or President acting as head of state). Usually the monarch occupies his throne by hereditary title whereas a president is elected by the parliament. It does not mean that the head

of state fills a purely formal or decorative office. Constitutional monarchs still have important prerogatives.

In Islamic *Shura* system, on the contrary, there is no division of executive at all. All the powers are vested in the caliph or head of state and through him in the *Shura*. Any conception of nominal head of state is non-existent here, The head of the state has to be selected or elected by the consent of the people and he is only responsible to the people.

2. It is in the very nature f the parliamentary system that there are two distinct offices and that the head of the government is appointed by the head of the state. Though the head of the state is bound by the outcome of parliamentary elections and must appoint head of the party which is a clearly victor. But this is the situation only where one party or a stable coalition has obtained an absolute majority of seats. But in many parliamentary democracies, especially those which have a multi-party system it is possible that no party gets absolute majority. In such cases, in selecting the Prime Minister who can best obtain a working majority the patronage of the head of the state may tilt the balance in favour of the leader of a particular party.

In the *Shura* system of Islam, there is no room for a head of the state who has little say in the day to day political affair and who is merely supposed to receive ambassadors and decorate ceremonial occasions. Islamic system, does not allow expenses incurred in such decorative office. Secondly, a one-man rule is preferable and more close to the spirit of Islamic polity, the head of the government must be elected by the people and should have the faith and trust of the public and this is possible only through a countrywide general election.

3. An interesting feature of parliamentary democracies is its process of law making. Everyone knows that the work of research, preparation, and drafting of new legislation is the responsibility of the executive. It is the executive wing of the government whose experts prepare most of the legislative bills and thus only in exceptional instances the elected assembly is associated with the current activities of the executive in a way that would fully correspond to the injunctions of *Shura*. In the *Shura* system all administrative policies and legislative enactments must be decided on consultation with the chosen representatives of people from beginning to end, while in a parliamentary system conflict between the cabinet and the elected members of the legislative is a common phenomenon. This is against the very spirit of Islamic *Shura*.

4. A distinctive characteristic of parliamentary democracies is that when the head of the government becomes dissatisfied with his assembly, he asks for its dissolution by the head of the state. In the pre-parliamentary monarchies of Europe the monarch could, if. was dissatisfied with his assembly, dissolve one or more houses in the hope of securing a more pliable group of representatives after a fresh election. Today when the executive is divided, it is still the head of state who dissolves the parliament, but he does so only on the request of the head of the government.

In the *Shura* system the head of the state has no power to dissolve the assembly. The members of the *Shura* may be removed from their offices not by the head of state, but, by the people who have elected them provided (i) they have lost the confidence and trust of the people (ii) they are going against the clear-cut teachings of Islam (iii) or they are no more loyal to the state.

5. One important feature of the parliamentary system is the process of the election of the head of the state. In many countries the monarch is the head of state who occupies his throne by hereditary title, while in other countries the head of state is the president who is elected by the legislature.

In the Islamic political system, neither hereditary posts are justified nor can the president be chosen without the consent of the people. He must be appointed through a general election directly or indirectly. The Four Guided Caliphs occupied their posts after public allegiance was ascertained in their favour. Some of them, of course, were nominated by the outgoing caliph, but they were declared as head of state only after general allegiance in their favour as ascertained.

6. A parliamentary government, though directly responsible to the legislature, is only indirectly responsible to the electorate. The government as a whole is not directly elected by the voters but is appointed indirectly from amongst the representatives whom they elect to the Assembly. It is true that members of the government, like other members of legislature must be elected. However, they do so not as members of the government but as candidates for the legislature in the ordinary way. The responsibility for transforming them, once they are elected, into ministers, rests with the Prime Minister alone, and while the monarch selects the Prime Minister.

In the *Shura* system, the Executive is dependent on a popular vote or consent and the caliph or President in the political system, is elected by the whole body of electors. He owes his position not, as in parliamentary government, to the Assembly. Between two general elections and after that too, he can speak to the voters and masses directly, not indirectly through an assembly as is the case with the parliamentary system. In *Shura* system, the electorate, therefore bears a double responsibility. The Voters elect representatives from their constituency to the *Shura* and also elect the caliph or the President as both head of the executive and head of the state.

In view of differences between the parliamentary democracies and Islamic *Shura* discussed above, it may be concluded that the Islamic system of *Shura* is distinct from the parliamentary system. Nevertheless there are a few similarities between these two systems. For example, in both the systems, legislature is the focus of power in the state. The fusion of executive and legislative powers in both the systems are responsible for the overriding ascendancy of legislature in the political order. It is the stage on which the drama of politics is played out. It is the focus of nation's ideas. It is the school where future political leaders are trained. In both the systems, the legislature is the focal point of the nation's political interest, and the centre of the political system.

In both the systems, legislature or *Shura* as a whole has a status that is superior to that of the executive. This superiority is strictly a governmental notion affecting relations between the two branches of the government. It is compatible with the belief that in a very real sense it is the electorate which is ultimately supreme (In Islamic *Shura*, however, this supremacy, is subordinated to that of the *Shariah*).

Compare with Presidential System

There is no doubt that the Islamic *Shura* system differs from the parliamentary democracies in its spirit and structure. In most respects the two systems stand on opposite poles. But it will not be correct to say that the *Shura* system is a true copy of the presidential form of government, and that there is no sharp distinction between the two. The fact is that the two systems, irrespective of some of their similarities, differ on certain crucial points:

1. In contrast to the Islamic *Shura* in which authority is exercised by a collective institution, the presidential government tends to be centred round an individual. There is a famous story relating to Abraham Lincoln's (1809-65) meeting with his cabinet. He put a proposal before it and then took a vote in which he alone supported his suggestion. He then remarked: "Noes 7, Ayes 1, The Ayes have it." His cabinet did not consist of members of the Congress nor could they introduce any bills in the Congress. The American President is not bound to act upon the advice of his cabinet and can override it even if its advice is unanimous.

In the *Shura* system, members of the cabinet are compulsorily members of legislature too. The caliph or President acts in the consultation of the cabinet and the legislature. He is bound to act according to the advice of the majority of the members of the *Shura*.

2. The American President enjoys veto power over the bills passed by the Congress. It is a negative power of the President to prevent the Congress from encroaching upon the executive authority. No bill passed by it can become law without the signatures of the President. The President is given ten days to reject or approve a bill or resolution passed by both the Houses. If he signs the bill it becomes law immediately. If he does not take any action on it, it becomes law automatically at the expiry of ten days (Sunday and holidays excepted) even without the signature of the President, provided the Congress is in session. The President can veto a bill (within ten days) and send it back to the Congress for reconsideration. Then the Congress is authorised to pass the bill again with a two-thirds majority. The President cannot exercise his veto power for the

second time. Sometimes the veto of the President can become absolute also. If the President does not take any action on the bill and before the expiry of ten days the Congress adjourns, the bill is killed. In the closing days of the session the Congress passes many bills and sends them to the President who kills many of them simply by pocketing them. President Roosevelt (1858-1919) of U.S.A. nullified 631 bills passed by the Congress (371 by vetoing and 230 by pocketing them).

In the *Shura* system of Islam, the President/Amir is bound to consult with the *Shura* on important policy matters, and act accordingly. He enjoys no veto power over the bills passed by the *Shura*. As discussed earlier, according to some researchers, Abu Bakr used veto power against the opinions of the companions regarding the war against the apostates, and for despatching Usama army. They cite the instance of Umar too who used this power in regard the distribution of land after the conquest of Iraq. But, as stated above in detail, the cases were not understood properly.

3. Though the American President wields legislative powers when he signs or vetoes bills sent to him by Congress or when he sends a message to the Congress and calls the attention of the Congress towards the affairs of the state, yet the presidential system is based on principle of the 'separation of powers'[17] with checks and balances, which was popular in the eighteenth century and was advocated by two eminent writers in particular, namely John Locke (1632-1704) and Montesquieu (1689-1755). John Locke, writing at the end of the seventeenth century, suggested that the long conflict between British Monarch and the Houses of Parliament would best be resolved by the separation of the King as Executive from the two Houses as legislature, each body having its own sphere. In 1721,

Montesquieu a French writer, pronounced himself in favour of the separation of the executive, legislative and judicial powers. In the American Presidential system a clear distinction is drawn between the three branches of the polity. All the legislative powers are vested in the Congress while the President, who is the head of the Executive, is neither related nor responsible to the legislature.

In the *Shura* system of Islam, there is no separation of legislative and executive powers. In this system all the powers re coordinated. The head of state takes active part in the adopting of all legislative measures. He may discuss, initiate, persuade and argue on any matter with the *Shura*, as the Four Guided Caliphs did. Likewise, the *Shura* shares in executive authority when it discusses policy matters and ratifies treaties and confirms appointments. In this system, the term 'separation of powers' is irrelevant.

4. In the Islamic *Shura*, the same persons may belong to both the executive and legislative branches of government, while it is obligatory in presidential system for the personnel of the two branches to be separate. Neither the President nor his colleagues may sit in the legislature. In the Islamic *Shura* system, members of cabinet may be members of the legislature also. There is no convention or law whereby the members of the assembly are not eligible for office in the administration and vice-versa.

In spite of these difference, both the systems (*Shura* and presidential) have certain common features:

1. In both the systems the executive is not divided and the head of the state is elected by the people. An undivided executive obviously requires that there is no delineation of the respective functions of head of state and the government. It is a feature of both the systems that both

the head of the executive and the assembly are selected by the people.

2. In both the systems, the Executive is bound to abide by the constitution. He may not be dependent on the legislative Assembly for his political survival but he is very much dependent on its good-will for the furtherance of state policies. The budget, foreign policy programmes, senior appointments – all require its acquiescence. If there is no agreement, the assembly may decide to take no action. However, it cannot remove the head of the state.

3. In both the systems the head of the state is not empowered to dissolve the legislature, and, therefore, the former is not in a position to coerce the latter. In the United States, President Eisenhower (1890-1969) declined for some time to take issue in 1954 with Senator Mc Carthy on the grounds that a Senator's conduct was primarily the responsibility of the Senate, not of the Executive. In 1957, after the suicide of the Canadian Ambassador to Egypt, the President was unable to assure the Canadian people that congressional committees would in future exercise more discretion since he was not responsible for the behaviour of the Senate.

After the battle of Uhud in which the Prophet Muhammad (SAW) fought against the Makkan pagans outside Madinah against his own will and the Muslims were defeated, no action was taken to dissolve the assembly. Instead, the Qur'ān asked him to continue the process of consultation with it.

French Model more Compatible

Some scholars view that a presidential system of government, especially the one practiced in the United States, corresponds closely to the requirements of the Islamic polity.[18] But the French system of presidential government would be perhaps, more close to Islamic *Shura* than the

American one. After a thorough study of both the presidential systems, one may reach the conclusion that the Constitution of Fifth Republic in France is a mixture of parliamentary and presidential systems of government and is, therefore closer to spirit of Islam. The following are some of the common features of the French and the Islamic political systems.

The French President is not as powerful as his counter part in America. Though he is vested with enormous powers by the constitution, still he is to perform many functions on the advice of the Council of Ministers. It is the Council of Ministers that appoints the Councillors of the state, the Grand Chancellor of the Legion of Honour, Ambassadors and Envoys Extra ordinary, Master Councillors of the Audit office, prefects, representatives of the government in the overseas territories, general officers, Rectors of academic institutions and directors of Central Administrations. The Council exercises some authority in the financial sphere too. Moreover, though there does not exist any close relationship between the Council of Ministers and the legislature, the Council is responsible to the legislature for all its actions and policies. It is clearly written in the Constitution that "The Premier, after deliberation by the Council of Ministers, may pledge the responsibility of the government to the National Assembly with regard to the programme of the government, or with regard to a declaration of general policy, as the case may be. The National Assembly may question the responsibility of the government by the vote of a motion of censure."[19]

Members of the French National Assembly can influence the working of ministers by asking them questions and by criticising their performance. In case the National Assembly passes a vote of no – confidence against the Council of Ministers, they have to resign.[20] These are some of the features that show that the French President has less powers than the American ad since the former has to consult the Council in many matters. He has some influence upon legislature too. In the *Shura* system of Islam, the President/Amir is head of state and head of Government both, but he is bound to act according to the decisions of the *Shura* in all the policy matters and the legislature plays a vital role in the political system.

In the *Shura* system, the President or Caliph has the power to conduct referendum on any executive or legislative problem for which there is no guidance in the Qur'ān or the *Sunnah*, by-passing the *Majlis al-Shura*. The case of the captives of Hawazin during the period of the Prophet (SAW) may be cited as an example here. In this case, the Prophet of Islam consulted his companions in general and when they could not reach any unanimous decision, the Prophet said, "We do not know who is ready to withdraw and who is not." Then he called the representatives of the people and it was decided to release the prisioners.[21] Sçholars are of the opinion that consultation by the Prophet (SAW) with the masses in this case provides justification for referendum if the situation requires it.[22]

The manner of the selection of Uthman as Caliph has already been cited. In this case, Abdul Rahman b. Awf who was authorised to select the caliph, took the advice of every Muslim living in Madinah. He went from door to door and consulted even with women and also with traders coming from outside Madinah. Some writers have cited this instance in support of holding referendum.[23] This power is vested in the President of France also. He has the power to conduct referendum over the propriety or otherwise of the bills. The Constitution of Fifth Republic especially provides that holding of referendum is a personal privilege of the President and this does not need even the counter-signature of Prime-Minister.[24] It is entirely upto the President to elicit or refuse to elicit the opinion of the common people over a bill or a treaty through a referendum. Bills over which referendum may be conducted include those relating to the organization of public authorities, seeking approval of a community agreement or proposing to authorise the ratification of a treaty, which without being contrary to the Constitution would affect the functioning of institutions.[25] Article II of the French Constitution which contains these provisions categorically enjoins that the President, at the suggestion of the government during parliamentary sessions or on a joint motion of the National Assembly and the Senate may submit for referendum all measures enumerated above. But, on all three occasions when the provisions of this Article were invoked, the initiative invariably came from the President and not from the government or Parliament. The President invoked this Article in 1962 and claimed that it empowered him to submit directly to the people amendments to the constitution, ignoring the procedure prescribed in Article 89.

Though democracy, both as a consent and a system, goes back to ancient times in the western history, thought and philosophy and is a natural extension of the materialistic philosophy that regards man as a physical entity whose value is measured in pragmatic terms only, based on his usefulness to the state and society and hence it cannot be compared with the Islamic system of *Shura*. Though there are some apparent similarities between the western democracies and the overall spirit of the *Shura*, the former has certain un-Islamic elements that would completely distort the true image of Islam if the two are found to be completely similar. Although the *Shura* aims at choosing proper leadership, establishing checks and controls over the rulers and arriving at discions to be accepted, appreciated and supported by the people, it is not the same thing as democracy. By definition, the *Shura* derives from a philosophical perception which is essentially different from that of democracy. This difference lies in the notion of justice as a concrete fact of existence which man arrives at through his own nature and divine revelation, and which he endeavours to attain irrespective of his personal desires and interests.[26]

However, for the sake of a modern understanding sometimes comparison is necessary and here one has to speak in the language of others to clarify matters. It may, therefore, be concluded that the *Shura* system is closer to the Presidential system of the Fifth Republic of France than to other Western democratic polities.

NOTES AND REFERENCES

1. The *Qur'ān*, 3: 159.
2. Audah, Abdul Qader, *Al-Islam wa Awdha una al-Siyasiyah*, Beirut, 1967, p. 158, Uthman, Abdul Karim, *al-Nizam al-Siyasi fi al-Islam*, Beirut, 1968, p. 35.
3. *Ibid*, see for details: Abu Zahrah, Shaikh Muhammad, *Al-Madahib al-Siyasiyah al-Islamiyah*, pp. 37, 38. Also see what al-Qurtubi has related about Abu Abdullah b. Khuwaiz Minda, a Maliki jurist, concerning the dominance of the *Shura* in *Tafsir al-Qurtubi*, Vol. 4, p. 250, Cf. Tafsir al-Tabari, Vol. 7, p. 345.
4. El-Awa, Muhammad S., *On the Political system of the Islamic state*, Indiana, 1980, pp. 90-91.
5. In support of this, it is pertinent to quote the second Caliph of Islam who put before members of his advisory committee both legislative and executive issues. For legislative cases one may see the problems put before them such as those of punishment for drinking and the disposition of the land conquered in Iraq during his rule, while for executive affairs his appointments of provincial governors, his consultation about problems of military organization, land revenue, provincial and national administration and like matters.
6. Asad, Muhammad, *The Principles of State and Government in Islam*, *op. cit.*, p. 51.
7. The *Qur'ān*, 3: 159.
8. Asad, Muhammad, *The Principles ` of State and Government in Islam*, *op. cit.*, pp. 57-58.
9. The *Qur'ān*, 4: 59.
10. Al-Bukhari, Muhammad b. Ismail, *al-Jame-al-Sahih*, Kitab ạl-Jihad, Kitab al-Ietisam, Kitab al-Imarah.

11. *Ibid*, Kitab al-Jumuah, Kitab al-Janaiz.
12. Muslim, *Al-Jame al-Sahih*, Kitab al-Imarah, Abu Daud, *Sunan*, Kitab al-Fitan.
13. Most of the authentic traditions to this effect have been quoted and analysed by Muhamad bin Ali al-Shawkani in his classical work *Nayl al-Awtar*, Cairo, 1344 A.H., Vol. IX, pp. 157-158.
14. Asad, Muhammad, *The Principles of State and Government in Islam*, *op. cit.*, pp. 59-60.
15. Abu Daud, *Al-Sunan*, *op. cit.*, Kitab al-Imarah.
16. Parliamentary system means, here, the British one because it is the British system which has provided an example for a great many other countries. But this is not to imply that the British parliamentary system should be taken as the model and that others are, deviations from the norm. See for detail, Douglas V. Verney, *Analysis of Political Systems*, Routledge and Kegan Paul Ltd., London, 1959, pp. 17-56.

    Dr. Verney has made an interesting comparative study of parliamentary and presidential systems. According to him, the parliamentary system can best be understood on following grounds:

    i) The assembly becomes a parliament.

    ii) The executive is divided into two parts.

    iii) The head of state appoints the head of government.

    iv) The head of government appoints the ministry.

    v) The ministry or government is a collective body.

    vi) Ministers are usually members of the parliament.

    vii) The government is politically responsible to the assembly.

    viii) The head of government may advise the head of state to dissolve the parliament.

ix) The parliament as a whole is supreme over its constituent parts, government and assembly, neither of which may dominate the other.

x) The government as a whole is only indirectly responsible to the electorate.

xi) The parliament is the focus of power in the political system.

The author has given eleven features of presidential system, too, for the sake of comparison:

i) The assembly remains an assembly only.

ii) The executive is not divided but is a president elected by the people for a definite term at the time of assembly elections.

iii) The head of the government is head of state.

iv) The president appoints heads of departments, who are his subordinates.

v) The president is sole executive.

vi) Members of the assembly are not eligible for office in the administration and *vice versa*.

vii) The executive is responsible to the constitution.

viii) The president cannot dissolve or coerce the assembly.

ix) The assembly is ultimately supreme over the other branches of the government and there is no fusion of the executive and legislative branches as in a parliament.

x) The executive is directly responsible to the electorate.

xi) There is no focus of power in the political system.

17. Though some scholars assert that the term 'separation of powers' is an inadequate and misleading description of the

theory underlying presidential government, yet the term is commonly used in all the academic works of constitutional discourses. According to scholars presidential and parliamentary governments do differ over the separation not of powers but of institutions and persons. See for detail, Apter, E. David and Eckstein, Harry, (editors), *Comparative Politics*, Princeton, N. Jersey, 1963, pp. 184-85.

18. Asad, Muhammad, *op. cit.*, pp. 61, 62.

19. Article 4(a) of the *Constitution of the 5th Republic of France*.

20. Article 50,

21. Ibn Hisham, *op. cit.*, Vol. IV, pp. 135-36;

    Waqidi, *op. cit.*, Vol. III, pp. 950-52.

22. Al-Hulw, Majid Ragheb, *Al-Istifta al-Sha'bi Bain al-Anzemah al-Wadhyiah wa al-Shariah al-Islamiyah*, Maktaba al-Manar al-Islamiyah, Kuwait, 1980, pp. 41-42.

23. Keelani, Abdur Rahman, *Khilafat wa Jumhuriyat*, Lahore, 1985, pp. 67-68 ; See the case in detail, Ibn Kathir, *Al-Bidayah wa al-Nihayah*, Vol. VII, p. 147.

24. Article 19 of the *Constitution of the 5th Republic of France*.

25. Article 11 of the *Constitution of the 5th Republic of France*. For the relevant discussion see, Pickles, Dorothly, *The Fifth Republic*, New York, 1960; Williams, Philip, *Politics in Post-war France*, London, 1958, Litterdale, D.W.S., *The Parliament of France*, London, 1951.

26. See for detail, Abu Sulayman, Abdul Hamid, Islamization of knowledge with Special Reference to Political science, *American Journal of Islamic Social Sciences*, U.S.A., Vol. 11, No. 2, 1985, pp. 263-89.

*****

CONCLUSION

Any attempt by present-day Muslims to seek the establishment and enforcement of *Shariah* as their supreme law is bound to be confronted with immense obstacles and difficulties in respect of contemporary political sciences. Political science is a social field of study which has not hitherto drawn the attention of Muslim scholars. Since there has been a dichotomy between the intellectual and political leadership in the history of Islam, the adverse effect of which on the direction of Islamic studies is dominated by unsystematic methods of though.[1] Consequently, any vision could not be developed lending to organization of Muslim *Ummah* based on Islamic *Shariah*. Even the most important social/political institution of *Shura* could not be explained to the people.

Shura is one of the most misunderstood concepts in the field of Islamic Political thought. Many scholars consider it no more than a system of autocracy, whereas the orientalists view it as a despotic way of government. These misconceptions result from the concentration of Muslim political scientists debating merely technical situations as to who will qualify to be a caliph; who should be his successor; the performance of allegiance; the obligation upon the ruler to follow *Shariah*: and the duty of the masses to obey him. But they failed to fathom the core of the political and organizational operation, the factors and forces affecting its structural stability and the regulations that determine the choice and define the role of political and social cadres which are bound with the responsibility of handing over authority from one leader to another and from one generation to the next. Equally important is the ability of these cadres to supervise the manner of decision-making, the manner in which the leadership exercises authority and the limits it should not exceed. The urgent need for these fundamental checks and controls totally escaped the attention of the writers in this disciplines.[2] An examination of the system during the period of *Kilafah Rashidah* and insight into the manner in which it functioned has to be cautious and specialised. The objective researcher will certainly realize the significance of *Shura* and its practice during the Four Caliph's period. There was no place for any form of despotism. The cases cited by the scholars in favour of a non-democratic system in the Islamic history, if be studied in a comprehensive systematic and organized way, will be sufficient to prove the just opposite view. The issues in which the Prophet (SAW) did not seek any consultation or he did not agree with his companions, were resolved through revelation. And if Abu Bakr, for example, could not implement the majority opinion regarding *Riddah* wars, it was not due to any despotic or arbitrary attitude. Instead, the caliph quoted the *Hadith* in his support and the issue, thus, did not remain under the jurisdiction of *Shura*. It is well established fact that only those cases may be put to the *Shura* regarding which there is no clear-cut guidance in the text of the *Qur'ān* and the *Sunnah*. If any verse the *Qur'ān* or any text of the *Sunnah* is found concerning any problem, there will be no consultation at all.

After a close study of the Islamic history especially that of the Prophet (SAW) and Four Caliphs, one has to conclude that decisions of the majority of the *Shura* would be binding upon the caliph/*amir*/head of state, though he is not bound to consult on day to day administrative problems. The best available method to select the better candidates for membership of the

Shura is a general election and the *Shura* would be bi-cameral consisting of the representatives elected directly by the people and of the experts both of *Shariah* and worldly affairs nominated or selected by the *Amir* or the *Shura* itself.

The history supports and the texts of the *Qur'ān* and the *Sunnah* do not contradict that the women may be permitted to contest the election of *Shura* if it is deemed necessary and Islamic ethics and moral values are not violated. *Dhimmis* may also be granted the permission to be member of the *Shura* provided the constitution clearly declares that only a Muslim would be the head of state and all the parliamentary laws would be subordinate to the basic sources of Islamic *Shariah*.

It may be pointed out that though the comparison between Islamic and non-Islamic systems and use of foreign political terminologies in Islamic studies is not desirable, yet Islamic *Shura*, if compared, would be more closer to the presidential system rather than the parliamentary one. And if the constitution of presidential countries be studied comparatively, the Fifth Republic of France would have more similarities to Islamic *Shura* rather than the Constitution of America or any other country practicing presidential system.

The main theme of this work is the need for giving a practical and applied shape of *Shura* system in the modern world of systematic theories and political conceptions. The first prerequisite in this process is to have a clear idea of the reality of classical Muslim political thought. After going into details one may reach to the point that classical political studies are no more than a handful of personal reflections on Islamic constitutional law, administration, biographies and laws regulating war and peace. The scholars have pointed out certain shortcomings in these studies as follows:

(a) There are scarcely any analytical studies in the field of Islamic political thought.

(b) There is no effort to trace the nature and significance of issues brought about by political phenomena in Islamic history.
(c) There is no attempt to distinguish between the original and alien elements, or the permanent and ephermeral elements in the system.
(d) The historical factors which actually influenced the foundations of the *Ummah*, its experiences and interactions with other nations have been totally ignored.
(e) The studies conducted both locally and internationally about Islamic systems of government and the lessons to be learnt from the actual application of these systems are also inadequate.[3]

Ibn Taimiyah (1263-1328 A.D.) has written voluminously and almost on and every aspect of Islam. His political ideas and theories are scattered through out his precious writings. His books *Minhaj al-Sunnah, al-Siyasah al-Shariyah, al-Hisbah fi al-Islam, and Kitab al-Ikhtiyarat al-Ilmiyah* have notable and marvellous discussions on political theory. He is regarded one of the very few original and distinguished political thinkers in Islam. However, his works represent a confused political thinking. For example, he has advocated for *Shura* being compulsory for a caliph on the one hand.[4] But, on the other this vision was destroyed by another very visible idea, that of *Ahl al-Shaukah* (the people of power), that is people who held the real power to decide the form and the policy of the state. The term was basically used to support the Mamluks who were fighting against the Crusaders and the Mongols. According to him, *Ahl al-Shaukah* are all those persons who, irrespective of their profession and station in life, command the respect and obedience of the community. Ibn Taimiyah writes: "So the *Khilafah* is not conditioned by any thing except the support of the *Ahl al-Shaukah*; and as regards the common people by whose arms the state comes into being they are only the means by which the purposes of the *Ummah* are realised."[5]

Thus, in his view, the common people do cooperate in achieving the fundamental aims of the state, but so far as the institution of caliphate is concerned it is only the *Ahl al-Shaukah* who count. No doubt, Ibn Taimiyah was a sincere Muslim scholar but he converted the idea into a principle of the *Shariah* and sanctified potentially the principle of "Might is right".[6]

Similarly Ibn Taimiyah advocated the status quo, however tyrannical and unjust it be, so that the enforcement of *Shariah* might not be hampered or stopped. The object of this theorisation was to prevent criticism of the government and root out all tendencies of political rebellion. Naturally such attitude from religious scholars provides great self-confidence and courage to tyranny and repression. It is true that Ibn Taimiyah's support to Mamluks was of vital importance in the context of defence of Islam in those times. But this theory that rebellion cannot be justified as a right of the people under any condition is certainly questionable to the reason or the *Shariah*.[7]

This is only an example to explain the confusing thinking inherited by classical political thinkers and hence failing to help more regarding the process of revivalism. The reforms one should strive to achieve require the Islamization of political science because without proper insight into the field, the reconstruction of the Ummah and the preparation of cadres for leadership are impossible. This basically in the field of theorization, can be done by holding research on all the contemporary problems in the light of basic guidelines of the *Qur'ān* and the *Sunnah* coping with the modern challenges confidently.

*****

NOTES AND REFERENCES

1. This intellectual deficiency may be exampled with the reference of the most popular jurist namely Ibn Rushd Qurtubi (1126-1198). He has described the confusion originated from the assumption that Abu Bakr's prohibition against cutting trees during the Riddah wars was not in conformity with the Sunnah of the Prophet (SAW) who, during his campaign against the Banu Nadhir, burnt down their date-trees. This confusion will whither away if we adopt a realistic and comprehensive approach because it is necessary to deal each problem in the context of its specific requirements in time and place. The Prophet (SAW) adopted a specific method against Banu Nadhir when Madinah had very little power and limited resources while the enemy forces were able to fight out any seize no matter how long it lasted. Consequently, the Prophet (SAW) ordered the Muslims to cut down the date-trees to reduce the will of Jews to stay in Madinah and enjoy their properties. Abu Bakr, during his caliphate, acted adversely, to prove the moral superiority of Islam and Muslims. The Roman and Persian armies practiced all forms of atrocities especially in Iraq and Syria where they oppressed the inhabitants. Abu Bakr planned to act in a manner that would clearly demonstrate the fundamental moral and ethical differences between the Muslims and non-Muslims.
2. Abu Sulayman, Abdul Hamid, Islamization of knowledge with special Reference to Political Science. *American Journal of Islamic Social Sciences*, U.S.A., Vol. 2, No. 2, 1985, p. 281.
3. *Ibid*, pp. 288-89.
4. Ibn Taimiyah, *Al-Siyasah al-Sharyiah*, *op. cit.*, p. 158.
5. Ibn Taimiyah, *Minjah al-Sunnah*, *op. cit.*, Vol. IV, p. 232.
6. Khan, Qamaruddin, *Political Thought of Ibn Taimiyah*, *op. cit.*, Preface, p. III-IV.
7. Fahad, Obaidullah, Ibn Taimiyah Ki Siyasi Fikr, *Islam Awr Asr Jadeed*, Vol. 21, No. 1, January, 1989, pp. 87-89.

*****

GLOSSARY OF ISLAMIC TERMS

'Ahd: pl. 'uhūd; 'joining together'; a contract; a written designation of succession left by a caliph from the tie of the Umayyad Caliph Abdul Malik onwards. As a *Qur'ān*ic term, it denotes God's covenant with men and His Commands, the religious engagement and contracts. In law it is generally restricted to political enactments and treaties; land which had capitulated before conquest was known as *'ahd* land.

Āhād: Sing. *Wahed*, These are the traditions which were transmitted during the first three generations of the Muslims by one to four transmitters only. The Muslim Jurists differed among themselves about the legal significance of Ahad. Imam Malik did not consider all the *Ahad* traditions which were not backed by the practices of the companions and the *Tabiyun*. Abu Hanifah accepted some of them and rejected others. In cases of intricate legal problems he declined them unless they are supported by circumstantial evidence and basic Islamic principles. But Shafi'i preferred the *Ahad* traditios to *Qiyas* in all cases.

***Ahl* al-hall wa al-aqd:** 'Those who are qualified to unbind and bind'; term for the representatives of the Muslim community who act on its behalf in appointing and deposing a caliph or other rules.

Akhbāriyya: In Twelver shi'ism, those who rely primarily on the traditions, *akhbar* of the *imams* as a source of religious knowledge, in contrast to the *usuliyya*, who admit a larger share of speculative reason in the principles of theology and religious law.

Asma al-Rijal: Names of the men, applies to the life and character of the narrators of *hadith* as discussed by the traditionists in order to check their veracity. All the reporters who suspected of making forgery in their reports were declared as unreliable. This huge literature did not differentiate between the high and the low, or between the rulers or their officials and the common people. The distinguished specialists and critics of these reports generally disassociated themselves from the state officials, from the partisans in the civil war.

Darura: and *idtirar* 'necessity'. In law it has a narrow meaning what may be called the technical state of necessity (resulting from certain factual circumstances which may oblige an individual to do some action forbidden by the law), and a wider sense: to describe the necessities and demands of social and economic life, which the jurists had to take into account in their elaboration of the law which was otherwise independent of these factors. The legal schools agree that prohibitions of a religious character may be disregarded in cases of necessity and danger, while most of the offences committed under the rule of necessity are excused without any form of punishment. However, murder, the amputation of a limb, and serious wounding likely to cause death, irrespective of the circumstances, are never excused. The term in its wider sense signifies practical necessity, the exigencies of social and economic life. It takes into consideration the existence of rules and whole institutions in Islamic law while reasoning by strict analogy would have condemned.

Faqih: pl. *fuqaha*; in its non-technical meaning it denotes any one possessing knowledge and understanding. In law it became the technical term for a specialist in religious law and in particular its derivative details, *furu*. In older terminology, however, it as opposed to *'alim* denotes the speculative, systematic lawyer as opposed to the specialist in the traditional elements of religious law.

Fard or Faridah: Literally something which has been apportioned, or made obligatory; as a technical term in Islamic law it is a religious duty or obligation, the omission of which will be punished and the performance of which will be rewarded. *Fard 'ayn* is the individual duty such as ritual prayer, fasting, etc. *Fard Kifayah* means the collective duty, the fulfillment of which by a sufficient number of individuals excuses others from fulfilling it, such as funeral prayer, holy war, etc.

Fāsid: In law, a legal act which does not observe the conditions of validity *stricto sensu* required for its perfection; vitiated and therefore null. Only in the Hanafid school of law is *fasid* distinct from *batil*, which there denotes a legal act which lacks one of the elements essential for the existence of any legal activity.

Faskh: In law, the dissolution of any contractual bond whatever, effected, as a rule, by means of a declaration of intention pronounced in the presence of the other contracting party, or by judicial process. The term is to be distinguished from *infisakh* which comes about without the need of any declaration or judicial decree. Dissolution of marriage open to the wife or her relatives is by way of *faskh*, while the dissolution of marriage by man is *talaq*.

Fatwa: A *fatwa* (pl. *fatawa*) is an advisory opinion issued by a recognized authority on law and tradition in answer to a specific question. Fatawa can range from single-word responses (e.g., 'Yes'. 'No', or 'Permitted') to book-length treatises. Although typically focused on legal matters, *fatwa*, termed a *mufti* – whose authority derives from his knowledge of law and tradition – has functioned independently of the judicial system, indeed often privately. While court rulings rely on the sifting of evidence and conflicting testimonies, *muftis* assume the facts presented by their questioners, which, obviously, can bias the answer. Moreover, a *fatwa* differs from a court judgement, or *qada*, not only in its wider potential scope for instance, although *ibadat* are essential part of Islamic law, they transcend the jurisdiction of the courts – but also because the *qada* is binding and enforceable, "performative", while the *fatwa* is not. Instead, it is "informational", and, while decisions of *Shariah* courts usually pertain only to the specific cases they adjudicate, thus setting no legal precedents, *fatawa* are very often collected, published and cited in subsequent cases.

Gharib: Literally strange, uncommon. In philology it means rare, unfamiliar expressions, and frequently occurs in the titles of the books, mostly such as deal with unfamiliar expressions in the *Qur'ān* and *hadith*. In the science of tradition it means a *hadith* from only one companion, or from a single man at a later stage, to be distinguished from *gharib al-hadith* which applies to uncommon words in the text, *matn*, of traditions.

***Hadith*:** Primarily means 'new' as opposed to *qadim* 'old'. From this followed the use of term for a piece of news or report. In Islamic literature the reports with regard to the sayings, and doings of the prophet and the events occurred and were not noticed by the Prophet (SAW) positively or negatively *(taqrir)* were called *hadith*.

Hanafid School: The oldest sunni juristic school founded by Abu Hanifah (80-150 AH) in Kufah and codified together with the collective efforts made by his forty disciples, was first edited and systematized by Muhammad bin Hasan Shaybani and Abu Yusuf, the two prominent students of the founder. The hanafids relied after the *Qur'ān*, the Sunnah, the sayings of the companions, on *qiyas*, the individual reasoning as the principle of legislation. Among the distinguished hanafid sources the following are very important: *al-Jami al-Saghir, al-Jami al-Kabir, Ziyadat, Mabsut, al-Siyar al-Saghir, al-Siyaar al-Kabir*, all the six by Muhammad bin Hasan Shaybani; *Haruniyat, Kaisaniyat, Ruqiyyat* all the dictations of the some author; *kitab al-Mujarrad* by Hasan bin Ziyad: *Kitab al-Amali* ascribed to Abu Yusuf.

Hanbali School: This is the fourth juristic school among the Sunni Muslims and is founded by Ahmad bin Hanbal (780-855 AD) the famous traditionist and scholar of *fiqh*. The founder was a close student of Shafi'i and took keen interest in the science of traditions. He compiled the encyclopedia of *hadith* entitled *al-Musnad.* The School flourished in Baghdad (Iraq) and spread later on in other parts of the Muslim world. He was severely tortured and persecuted on the issue of the 'creation of the *Qur'ān* by the Abbasid Caliph Mamun. The school basically emphasized upon the *Qur'ān*, the Sunnah, the sayings and fatawa of the companions, the *mursal* and *dhaeef hadiths* and *Qiyas* as the sources of Islamic law strictly in the order. About '*ijma* Ibn Hanbal used to say that instead of claiming any *'ijma* it should be pronounced that no dispute in the case is recorded. In order this school kept the principle of *Istishab* on the first and the principles of *masalih mursalah* and *sadd dharai* on the second and third. The scholar who compiled in detail the juristic opinion and *fatawa* of the founder was Abu Bakr Khallal who edited the said work into 200 parts; it was summarized by Abul Qasim Umar bin Husain Kharqi (d. 334 AH) in his *Kitab al-Mukhtasar* that became so popular as 300 commentaries on it were prepared throughout the history. The next source is *al-Mughni* by Ibn Qudamah al-Maqdisi (d. 620 AH) in to twelve volumes; it was well appreciated by the scholars of other schools of law also. Some other sources are also important like *al-Muharrir fi al-Fiqh* by Majduddin Abul Barakat (d. 652 AH); *al-Qawaid al-Nūraniyah al-Fiqhiyah* by Ibn Taimiyah (d. 828 AH); *al-Furu* by Muhammad bin Muflih al-Maqdisi (d. 762 AH); *al-Iqna'* by Sharfuddin al-Maqdisi (d. 960 AH); *Kashshaf al-Qina 'an Matn al-Iqna'* by Mansur bin Yunus al-Buhuti (d. 1051 AH) and so on.

Hukm: pl. Ahkam: decision, judgement. In philosophy it means the judgement or act by which the mind affirms or denies one thing with regard to another, and thus unites or separates them. In grammer it means the specific activity of a word, the proper function which the world performs at the basic position, *martabah*, in which it is placed. In law *al-ahkam al-khamsah* applies to the five qualifications *fard* (obligatory), *mustahabb* (recommended), *mubah* (indifferent), *makruh* (reprehensible) and *haram* (forbidden), by one or the other of which every act of man is qualified.

Ilm al-Dirayah: The criticism of the content and text (*matn*) of *hadith* because the genuineness of the *Isnads* is no proof of the actual genuineness of the text of the tradition to which they are attached. According to *muhaddithun*, even if *Isnad* is faultless, the text may be a forgery. The following principles, in this context may be laid down; (b) a tradition should not be against the dictates of reason and natural laws and common experience; (c) the traditions containing disproportionately high rewards of insignificant good deeds or disproportionately severe punishments for ordinary sins must be rejected; (a) A tradition must not be contrary to the other traditions which have been already accepted by the authorities on the subject as authentic and reliable. Nor should it be contrary to the text of the Quraan or the accepted basic principles of Islam; (d) the traditions containing the excellent virtues of the various chapters of the Qur'ān should not be generally accepted as reliable; (e) the traditions containing the excellence and praises of persons, tribes and particular places should be generally rejected; (f) the traditions which contain detailed prophecies of the future events with dates must be rejected; (g) and the traditions containing such remarks of the Prophet (SAW) as may not be in keeping with prophetical position, or such expressions as may not be suitable to him, should be rejected.

Ilm al-Jarh Wa al-Tadil: The science of criticism of the reporters of *hadith*. This science forms a very important part of *asma al-rijal*.

Ilm al-Riwayah: The criticism of the *Isnad*, its origin and earliest application to *hadith*, and its development and the origin and development of biographical literature in connection with it, and other connected matters are discussed in this science. The principles of criticism in this science may be summarized as follows: (i) Every *hadith* must be traced back to its original reporter through a continuous chain of transmitters, whose identity, unquestionable character and high quantities of head and heart must have been established. (ii) Every *hadith* reporting an event which took place every now and then in the presence of a large number of people, must have been originally reported by several narrators.

Irsāl: 'Sounding forth'; technically, the utterance of a report lacking the bridle or restraint of adequate formal attestation. It normally refers to a report from successor about the Prophet (SAW) which fails to name the companion intermediary.

Isnad: The experts of *hadith* and sincere scholars tried their best to check the forgeries and established certain principles for the sake of criticizing the forged reports and of establishing the true ones among them. They made it imperative for the reporters to give the name of the narrators through whom they received the reports. This chain of narrators is known as the system of *Isnad.*

Istihsan: Arbitrary personal opinion, a method of finding the law which for any reason is contradictory to the *qiyas*, reasoning by analogy. The reason may be a text, an *ijma* (consensus), an emergent need and interest or an stronger *qiyas*. Abu Hanifah, Ahmad bin Hanbal and Malik uphold this as a secondary source of Shariah but Shafi'i negates it and treats it an original legislation contradictory to Shariah. Most of the jurists think this principle as one providing comfort, simplicity and relax to the common people, safeguarding Figh from rigidity and exaggeration of reasoning and protecting the objectives of Shariah in every phase of history by the exercise of *ijtihad*.

Istishab: Literally 'accompanying one'; in Islamic Figh one of the secondary sources of Shariah and the principle by which a given judicial situation that had existed previously was held to continue to exist as long as it could not be proved that it had ceased to exist or had been modified. Among the classical jurists Shafi'ites and Hnbalites accepted it as a general principle of legislation. To them, for example, a missing man would be treated legally an alive one and all the ordinances related to an alive man would be applied to him; his wife would remain in his marriage, his property would be undistributed and he would be treated a partner in inheritance etc. But the Hanafids and Malikids have accepted *Istishab* only in terms of defending a man, not affirming him. In the cited case, for example, the missing man would have his rights as a husband and as a property owner but would receive no share from the inheritance.

Istislah: 'Seeking the public interest'. In Islamic law it designates one of the secondary sources for legislation; keeping in view the *masalih mursalah*, the interests of community that have no argumentative grounds both positively and negatively the otherwise usual method of deduction is applied. Among the jurists Malikids rely on it most; the Hanbalites count it in the *qiyas*, not an independent source and Hanafids also consider it. In applying this principle three conditions are to be observed: (i) the interest must be realistic and actual not imaginary; (ii) it should not be personal, that must be common (iii) and the interest must not be contradictory to any *ijma* or text-based ordinance.

Jafari school is based on the traditions reported by *Ahl bait*. After the *Qur'ān*, the traditions (of *Ahl bait*) and sayings of imams (relted to *Ahl bait*) are main sources of law. In the secondary sources reason and *ijma* are placed. Najaf and Qumm have been the main centres of Jafari school in the history. Among its sources following are important: (i) *al-Kafi* by Abu Jafar Muhammad bin Yaqub al-Kulayni (d. 329 AH); (ii) *Man La Yahduruhu al-Faqih* by Muhammad bin Ali bin Babwayh al-Qummi (d. 381 AH); (iii) *al-Istibsar* and *Tahzib al-Ahkam* both by Abu Jafar Tusi (d. 460 AH); (iv) *Sharai al-Islam* by Hilli Jafaar bin Hasan (d. 676 AH); *Tazkirah al-Fuqaha* and *Qawaid al-Ahkam* by Jamaluddin Hasan bin Yusuf Hilli (d. 726 AH).

Jami/Jame: Those collections of *hadith* which contain traditions relating to all the various subject matters. The *Sahih* of Bukhari as well as that of Tirmidhi come under this category.

Malikid School: The second juristic school in chronological order, founded by Malik bin Anas (93-179 AH) in Madinah. Among his teachers are the muhaddithun arid jurists like Abdur Rahman bin Hurmuz, Ibn Shihab Zuhri, Jafar Sadiq, Muhammad bin Yahya Ansari, Rabiah bin Abdur Rahman, and among his contemporaries are Abu Hanifah, Sufyan Thawri, Laith bin Sad, Awzai, Abu Yusuf and among his students are Shafi'i, Abdullah bin Mubarak, Muhammad bin Hasan Shaybani. Malik opposed the Abbasid governor of Madinah on the issue of forced divorce declared by him ultravires and was tortured. This school was a combination of both *riwayah* and *rai*. Being a prominent *muhaddith* Malik himself compiled *Kitab al-Muatta*, the first book of traditions on the one side and founded a juristic school based on common objectives of Shariah and the public interests on the other. The school relied mainly on the reports and *fatawa* of the companions of Madinah and counted the practice of people of Madinah as *ijma* and preferable to *Khabr Wahed* in case of any clash between the two. *Masalih mursalah* and *sadd dharai* were important juristic principles to deduct the ordinance in the newly confronted situations. Among the basic sources of Malikid school the following are important: *Kitab al Muatta* by Malik bin Anas; *al-Mudawwanah al Kubra* edited by Asad bi Furat through the dictations taken from Ibn Qasim, the prominent Malikid student, and some corrections were added in that by Ibn Suhnum later on; *al-Wadhihah* by Abdul Malik bin Habib; *Utbiyah* by Muhammad bin Abu Bakr; *Muaziyah* by Muhammad bin Muazi. Among the prominent disciples of Malik are: Abdullah bin Wahb, Abdur Rahman bin Qasim, Ashhab bin Abdul Aziz and Abdul Malik Ibn Majshun.

Maqtu: 'Broken off'; used as a *hadith* in whose *isnad* a gap is detectable so that it does not reach its putative source, normally the Prophet, in an unbroken connection. Some use *munqati* as a synonym of *maqtu* but the former term is more commonly used of any break at any point in the *isnad*.

Mardud: A rejected tradition, more particularly a tradition from a weak transmitter which contradicts what authorities transmit.

Marfu: 'Raised', used as a *hadith* which involves the Prophet's authority.

Mashhur: is a tradition which being transmitted originally in the first generation by two, three or four transmitters, was later on transmitted on its authority by a large number of transmitters in the next two generations. Such *hadith* is also known as *mustafid*.

Maslaha: pl. *masalih*, the Islamic concept of public interest or welfare. In law the term in the sense of 'general good' and 'public interest' is used as a basis for legal decisions.

Matn: 'The back' or 'the body', the substantive content of any *hadith*, whether oral or written.

Maudu/Mauzu: A *hadith* that is forged and fabricated and declared by the authorities as unreliable on the basis of *riwayah* or *dirayah* criticism; as the *hadith* reported by Abu Harayrah alone that the Prophet used to recite *Bismillah* loudly in all his prayers, or the *hadith* reported by Abu Bakr alone that at the time of the call for the prayers the Muslims kissed their thumbs when the prophet's name was recited. These were rejected by *muhaddithun* because these are reported by a single companion whereas the events reported took place several times every day in the presence of a large number of Muslims. Or the *hadith* cited by Bukhari, that Adam is height was sixty yards, has been criticized by Ibn Hajar Asqalani on the basis of the measurement of the homesteads of some of the ancient nations, which do not show that their inhabitants were of an enormous height. The *hadith* reported by some traditionists that 'he who loved, kept clean and died, is a martyr' has been declared by Ibn al-Qayyim as forged and baseless. He says that even if the *Isnad* of this *hadith* were so bright as the sun, it would not cease to be wrong and fictitious.

Mauquf: 'Halted', a reported which stops short of reaching the Prophet and thus involving the authority of a companion or later figure.

Mubah: Licit, authorized, one of the five juridical qualifications of human acts; indifferent, neither obligatory or recommended, nor forbidden as reprehensible.

Munkar: pl. *munkarat, manakir:* 'unknown, objectionable'; in the science of tradition, a tradition whose transmitter is alone in transmitting it and differs from one who is reliable, or is one who has not the standing to be accepted when alone. When one says of a transmitter *yarwil manakir* 'he transmits the *munkars*', this does not involve the rejection of all his traditions; but if he is called *munkar al-hadith*, they are all to be rejected.

Munqati: See *maqtu*.

Mursal: In the science of *hadith*, a tradition in which a successor quotes the Prophet (SAW) directly, that is, the name of the companion is' lacking in the *isnad*. *Mursal al-Sahabi* is a tradition in which a companion describes some event involving the Prophet (SAW) at which he/she could not possibly have been present.

Musalsal: Literally strung together. In the science of tradition the term is applied when the transmitters in an *isnad* use the same words, or are of the same type, or come from the same place. *Musalsal al-half* is a tradition in which each transmitter swears on oath. *Musalsal al-ayd* and *al-musalsal fi al-akhdh bi al-ayd* is a tradition in which each transmitter gives his hand to the one to whom be transmits the tradition.

Musannaf: are those large collections of *hadith* in which the traditions relating to most or all the various topics are put together and arranged in various books or chapters dealing with a particular topic.

Musnad: This term (literally 'supported') was coined for such traditions as were supported by a complete uninterrupted chain of authorities *(Isnad)* going back to a companion who related it from the Prophet (SAW) himself. But later on the term came to be used in the general sense of a reliable and authoritative tradition. Technically, it is, however used for those collections of *hadith* in which they are arranged according to the names of the final authorities by whom they are related, irrespective of their subject matter. Such are the *Musnads* of Abu Dawud Tayalisi (d.204/809), Ahmad bin Hanbal (d. 233/847), Abdullah bin Muhammad bin Abi Shaybah (d. 235/849), Uthman bin Abi Shaybah (d. 237/851), Abu Khaythamah (d. 234/844) and others.

Mustadrak: are such collections of *hadith* in which the compiler having accepted the conditions laid down by any previous compiler, collects together such other traditions as fulfill those conditions and were missed by the previous compiler. To this class belongs the Mustadrak of al-Hakim who collected together such *hadith*s as fulfilled the conditions laid down by Bukhari and Muslim and were not included by them in their *Sahihs*.

Mutawātir: This is a tradition which has been transmitted throughout the first three generations of the Muslims by such a large number of transmitters as can not be reasonably expected to agree on a falsehood. There is a difference of opinion about the number of the transmitters necessary for it during each of the first three generations. Some authorities fix it at seven, some at forty, some at seventy and some at a much higher number. Imam Suyuti has collected together such a traditions in his book *al-Azhār al-Mutanathirah fi al-Akhbar al-Mutawātirah.*

Muttasil: 'Connected up'; having an unbroken *isnad.*

Naskh: The generic title of a number of theories concerned with apparent conflict of *Qur'ān*ic verses, or of *Qur'ān* with *hadith* or of one *hadith* with another. Three main applications of this principle will be found in the literature on the sources of law: alleged omissions from the *Qur'ān* based on the interpretation of verses that appear to refer to the possibility of the Prophet's 'forgetting', the alleged abrogation of certain *Qur'ān*ic verses, or of certain *hadiths*; the claim that certain rulings of the law originated in verses allegedly revealed, but since 'withdrawn' from the *Qur'ān*ic Texts. Shah Waliullah of Delhi, India claimed only the three verses as being abrogated; while Hameeduddin Farahi and his disciple Ameen Ahsan Islahi negated the idea of any abrogation in the *Qur'ān* exclusively.

Rāwi: A transmitter of reports, written or oral.

Rāy: 'View' the considered, judicious opinion of a qualified scholar. Later, the term was used pejoratively to imply 'mere opinion', as opposed to adherence to *hadith.*

Sadd Dharāi: In Islamic Shariah, it is one of the secondary sources of legislation; a method of reasoning to the effect that, when a command or prohibition has been decreed by God, everything that is indispensable to the execution of that order or leads to infringement of that prohibition must also, as a consequence, be commanded or prohibited. Umar, the second caliph, for example, prohibited praying near the tree under which *bayat ridhwan* took place at the eve of Hudaibiyah treaty (06/627) so that it might not lead to any undue worship, or the tree night not be turned into any sanctuary.

Sahaba: Singular Sahib or Sahabi, the companions of the Prophet dating from the first conversions (at Makkah in 610 and Madinah in 621) until the death of Anas bin Malik (91/710 or 93/712). In earlier times the term was restricted to those who had been close to the Prophet (SAW). Later it also included those who had met him during his life time, or who had seen him even if only for quite a short time. After the *Qur'ān* and the Sunnah of the Prophet the Companions are the sources of Islamic Shariah. The sayings of the companions as the source sometimes explain the text of the *Qur'ān* or *hadith* and sometimes add to Islamic law. These sayings are categorized into three: (i) those sayings that must not be based on reasoning; these form an authoritative argument unanimously; (ii) those sayings which have no contradiction among the companions also constitute authentic since it seems an *ijma* (iii) and the sayings which are contradictory to any other saying of the companions; by Malik and Ibn Hanbal it also constitutes a source while Abu Hanifah says that in case of lacking any guidance in the *Qur'ān* and Sunnah he is free to opt any saying of the companion. Shafi'i is reported to have not accepted it as a source but the modern scholars like Abu Zahra has approved for Shafi'i the otherwise.

Saheefah: These are such collections of *hadith* as were written down by some companions during the life time of the Prophet (SAW) or their followers in the next generation. Such kind of *Saheefah* was collected by Abu Hurayrah and taught and handed down by him to his student Hammam bin Munabbih, and is now edited and published by Dr. Hamidullah. The most important, however, is the *Saheefah* collected by Abdullah bin Amr bin al-'Aas who gave it to the title of *al-Sadiqah*.

Sahih: 'Of sound health'; the highest grade of *hadith* in whose *isnad* figure the highest grade of transmitters.

Shafi'i School: The juristic school found by Muhammad bin Idris Shafi'i (150-204 AH) as an outcome of the experiences he gained from the different schools prevailing in the Muslim world like his teacher Malik bin Anas; Muhammad bin Hasan Shaybani the hanafid jurist; Umar bin Abi Salmah the pupil of Awzai; Yahya bin Hassan the pupil of Laith bin Sad and became a synthesis of all the good features of Islamic Law. The school started in Makkah crossed the regions of Madinah and Iraq and flourished to the full zenith in Egypt. This is mostly based on the individual opinion and fatawa of the companion Abdullah bin Abbas. Shafi'i preferred *hadith* to *qiyas* and defended the value and status of *hadith* in legislation and opposed the two principles of *Istihsan* and *Istislah* and delimited the *qiyas*. One of the distinctive features of the school is the codification, formulation and systematization of the principles by the founder himself who travelled across the Muslim world, popularized his school and organized his circles of followers. Among the sources of Shafii school the following are important *Kitab al-Umm, Kitab al-Risalah* both by the founder; *al-Mukhtasar* by Yusuf al-Buwaiti; *al-Mukhtasar* by Ismail al-Muzni; *al-Muhazzab* (6 volumes) by Abu Ishaq Shirazi (d. 476 AH); *al-Wajeez* by al-Ghazali (d. 505 AH); *al-Majmu Sharh al-Muhazzab* (17 volumes) by Abu Zakariya Nawawi (d. 676 AH); *Minhaj al-Talibin* by Nawawi; *Hashiyah Qalyubi, Tuhfah al-Muhtaj 'ala Sharh al-Minhāj* by Ibn Hajar al-Haythami; *Mughni al-Muhtaj ilā Sharh al-Minhāj* by Shamsuddin Sharbini (d. 977 AH) and *Nihaayah al-Muhtaj ila Sharh al-Minhāj* by Shamsuddin al-Ramali.

Shiah School: Literally means 'a partisan' and comes from *Shiat Ali* (the party of Ali). The latter comprised a small circle, originally fewer than a dozen men, who advocated the candidacy of Ali for caliphate as opposed to Abu Bakr and then Umar and Uthmaṇ. The Shia'h Muslims are different from the Sunni majority on the issues like caliphate, *imamah, ijtihad*, Shariah arguments, religious doctrines and so on. To this group the door of *ijtihad* is ever open. It believes in the four basic sources of legislation; the *Qur'ān*, the *Hadith*, reason and *ijma*; only those traditions are authentic which are reported by the family of the prophet (*Ahl Bait*); *Ijma* is defined as the consensus of their ulama on any saying of their 'innocent' imam (*m'asum*); the religious obligations incumbent on every Muslim are six: *salah,* *saum, hajj, zakah, khumus* and *jihad.* Shiah themselves are divided into three principal groups. The largest division by far, Twelve-Imam Shi'ism, also called 'Twelver's (*Ithna Ashariyah*), has been the official religion of Persia since the Safavid dynasty came to power in 907/1501. The second group, Zaidis, are also called "Five-Imam Shiites" are concentrated in India. These groups each contain further sub divisions, and in some cases have given rise to offshoots. As a school of jurisprudence the first two became popular; the first as Jafari school as to have ascribed to Imam Jafar Sadiq (80-148 AH) and the second as Zaidi school as to have ascribed to Zayd bin Ali (80-122 AH). Ismailis could not be popularized as any juristic school; they, however, rely in jurisprudential issues on *Da'aim al-Islam* by Qadi Numan bin Muhammad Tamimi Maghribi (d. 363 AH).

Sihah Sittah: The Six authentic collections of *hadith* which are as follows:

(i) *al-Jami al-Sahih* by al-Bukhari
(ii) *al-Jami al-Shih* by Muslim
(iii) *Kitab al-Sunan* by Abu Dawud
(iv) *Kitab al-Sunan* by Nasai
(v) *Kitab al-Sunan* by Tirmidhi
(vi) *Kitab al-Sunan* by Ibn Majah

Sunan: Those collections of traditions that contain *Ahadith al-Ahkam* (Legal traditions) only and leave out those traditions which relate to historical and other matters, are known as *Sunan* as that by Abu Dawud (d. 889AD), Ibn Majah (d. 887AD), Nasai (d. 915AD), Baihaqi (d. 1066 AD) etc.

Sunnah: Originally means precedent and custom but is used by the Muslims as a term for the doings and practices of the Prophet. The distinction from the word *hadith* is, somehow, theoretical.

Tadlis: Fraud; dissembling by giving the impression of being able to report from a person whom one has not however met, or if having met him, not heard from him what one purports to transmit as being his words. It is also used of disguising the name of an informant, with the probable intent to mislead. One who practices *tadlis* is a *mudallis*.

The first two have been generally accepted as authentic since, the life time of their compilers. The third and fourth were first recognized as authentic by Ibn Hazm (994-1063 AD). After some time the *Jami* of Tirmidhi was added to the above four books and the five books together were given to the distinguish hed title of *al-Usul al-Khamsah*. Ibn Majah's Sunan was added to the five books of *hadith* first time by Abul Fadl Muhammad bin Tahir (d. 505/1113). A century after the death of Ibn Tahir Ibn Majah's *Sunan* was again recognized as one of the six collections of *hadith* by Abdul Ghani (d. 606/1203), Ibn al-Najjar (d. 643/1245), Ibn Taimiyaah (d. 652/1254), Najibuddin bin Sayqal (d. 672/1273), Shamsuddin al-Jazari (d. 711/1311) and al-Mizzi (d. 742/1341). It means that from the seventh century onwards the six books have been generally recognized by the Muslim world as the most reliable collections.

Thiqah: Entirely trustworthy and reliable as a transmitter.

Urf wa Ādat: Custom, customary law. Where Islamic Shariah has no text from the *Qur'ān*, Sunnah, or ijma, customary law prevails provided the custom must not be harmful or against the nature. Two conditions are mentioned by the jurists in this regard: (i) the custom must prevail and dominate the society; the practice of few people does not form the *'urf;* (ii) at the time of legislation the custom is practiced; any custom in advance can not constitute the '*urf*. The discretionary judgements based on *'urf* would be changed with the change of *'urf* as scholars have clarified.

Zahiri School: A school of law which never gained a significance and is now extinct. It was begun by disciples of Dawud bin al-Khalaf al-Isfahani called al-Zahiri (the literalist; 204-241/809-855 or 297/910). He had been himself a disciple of Shafii but he rejected completely the doctrine of analogy (*qiyas*), and the opinions of any but the closest of the Companions, and insisted upon a strictly literal interpretation of the *Qur'ān* and the Sunnah. The objection to analogy went so far as even to forbid searching for the reasons for a religious law. Ibn Hazm (384 AH-

456 AH) in Spain was a Zahiri, as were a number of Sufis including Ibn Arabi. This surprising fact leads one to conclude that the literalism of the *Zahiris* was not simply a desire for simple solutions. Their literalism did not stop at the letter, but rather took it as a point of departure, as an intensification of the apprehension of the Divine Reality. It is Dawud Ibn Khalaf who reports the traditions: "he who loves with unrequited love and remains chaste, dies a martyr". This ambience of heroic lyricism seems as aspect o the absoluteness of the Zahiri stand. The Zahiris claim that: We describe God as he describes Himself". Dawud composed many books on *Fiqh* as *Kitab Ibtal al-Taqlid*, and *Kitab Ibtal al-Qiyas*. Among the works of Ibn Hazm, *al-Muhalla (12 volumes)* and *al-Ihkam fi Usul al-Aahkam* are important.

Zaidi school tilts to some extent to Hanafid school in the principles of deduction, individual reasoning, ijtihad and in issuing *fatawa* according to research made by Abu Zahra of modern Egypt. The Shia scholars generally nullify the beliefs of Zaidis and do not deal with their jurisprudential issues. Among the Zaidi *mujtahids* Hasan bin Salih bin Hayy (d. 168 AH), Hasan bin Zayd bin Ahmad (d. 270 AH), Qasim bin Ibrahim Alavi his grandsons Hadi Yahya and Abu Jafar Muradi are notable. The oldest sources about the school are *al-Majmu* as have ascribed to Zayd bin Ali himself and *al-Raud al-Nadhir Sharh Majmu al-Fiqh al-Kabeer* by Sharfuddin Husain bin Ali Ahmad Haimi (d. 122 AH).

GENERAL GLOSSARY

Aathar	Ahaadith, plural of athar, but usually reserved for a report from the companions.
Adālah	Abstinence from cardinal sins and avoidance of minor one; impartial judgement, Justice.
Ahl al-Ahwā	The term was applied by orthodox theologians to those Muslims whose religious tenets in certain details deviate from the general ordinances of the Sunni confession.
Ahl al-bayt/al-bait	Literally the people of the house, viz., the family of the Prophet. The term has been interpreted variously; the current orthodox view is based on a harmonizing opinion, according to which the term includes the *ahl al-'abā* (the Prophet, Ali, Fatimah, al-Hasan and al-Husayn) together with the wives of the Prophet; among the Shia the term (which they call by preference '*itra*) is limited to the *Ahl al-Kisā'* and their descendants.
Ahl al-Dhikr	The men of message. The Qur'ān (16:43) applied the term to those men

	who are wise, intelligent and God-fearer, are qualified to have an opinion in religious matters.
Ahl al-Fatwa	Those Muslim scholars whose opinions are regarded as authoritative.
Ahl al-Hadith	The scholars of hadith, *muhaddithun*, applies also to a Muslim sect that follows hadith without any explanation and rational interpretation and does not follow any juristic school of thought.
Ahl al-Ijma	Those who form the consensus.
Ahl al-Ijtihad or *Mujtahidoon*	Those who possess the qualification of Ijtihad.
Ahl al-Kisā	The people of the cloak, viz., the Prophet and his daughter Fatimah, his son-in-law Ali, and his grandsons al-Hasan and al-Husayn, whom the Prophet sheltered under his cloak.
Ahl al-Kitab	People of the Book namely Jews and Christians
Ahl al-Nazar	Those who apply reasoning, a term probably coined by the Mutazilites to denote themselves; later it came to mean careful scholars who held a sound, well-reasoned opinion on any particular question.
Ahl al-Rae	Those whose opinion carried weight, who are entitled to give opinion on legal and political matters and who use individual reasoning.
Ahl al-Shaukah	Those who hold the real power to decide the form and policy of the state.
Ahl al-Shura	The members of Consultative Assembly.
al Baqarah (Surah)	The Cow, the secod chapter of the Qur'ān.
Āl Imrān	The Family of 'Imrān (the father of Moses), the 3rd chapter of the Qur'ān, the title is referred to in its verse no. 33 where the story leads the readers from the Mosaic dispensation to the miracles

	connected with the birth of Jesus and his ministry.
al-Ahzāb	Confederates, 33rd chapter of the Qur'ān entitled with the reference of its verse no 20 emphasizing on the historical unholy confederacy against the Prophet made by the Makkan Quraish, the Jews of Banu Nadīr and Banu Quraiza, and the Ghatfan tribe of Bedouin Arabs from the interior in 5 A.H.
'Asr	The prayer in afternoon.
al-Hashr	Gathering or Banishment, 59th Chapter of the Qur'ān with reference to its verse no. 2 discussing mainly the story of the expulsion of the Jewish tribe of Banu Nadhīr in Rabí I A.H. 4.
al-Hijābah	Office of gatekeeper to Holy Kabah
Al-Hukm al-aamm	The common application of any juristic injunction
al-Imārah	Maintaining discipline in the sacred house of Kabah. This was the trust of Abbas bin Abdul Muttalib in pre-Islamic Arabia.
Al-Khilafa al-Rashidah	The period of the first four caliphs in the history of Islam.
Al-Khulafa al-Rashidun	The first four Caliphs who ruled the Islamic state after the death of the Prophet; Four Rightly-Guided Caliphs namely, Abu Bakr, Umar, Uthman and 'Ali.
(al-) Livā	Its synonym is *rāyah* meaning flag, banner and standard interchangeably. In the military traditions of Arabia keeping the national or tribal standard in a campaign, or on the battle field was a great honour, and generally a respectable family or clan was entrusted with this function. In the Makkah oligarchy the privilege of holding the tribal standard was permanently enjoyed by the clan of Abd al-Dār of Quraish who kept it in all

the battles in the pre-and-post Islamic periods, when the Prophet sent his first expedition under the command of his uncle Hamzah towards *Sīf al-Bahr* he also appointed a standard-bearer, following the time-honoured custom of the Arabs. Since the Islamic army was drawn from various tribes, there were several standard-bearers, representing each of them. Therefore it was quite natural that this office retained its tribal character throughout the period of the Prophet.

al-Mustaliq (- Banu) — A clan of Khuzā'ah tribe that planned and prepared to attack Madinah in 5 A.H. The Prophet marched and encamped in Muraisee'i; the leader of the enemy force Harith bin Abi Zarar flew from the field but the local inhabitants still stood and fought unsuccessfully. Among the prisoners of war there was also Juwairiyah, the daughter of the leader who later on willingly accepted Islam and got married with the Prophet.

al-Rifādah — Hosting the pilgrims. This function in the pre-Islamic period involved a tax which the Quraish paid from their own property to Qusay bin Kilab who used it to provide food for those pilgrims who, during their stay in Mina, did not have the means to obtain provisions. This was first established by Qusay bin Kilab. By the time the Prophet had been called to his mission, this post had reached to the descendents of Abd Manāf.

al-Sidānah — Office of custodian. The *sādin* was the servant of Kabah and the house of idols, who managed and cared of it and held the keys of the temple. This office was

	held by Abd al-Dar bin Qusay bin Kilab in the pre-Islamic period.
al-Siqāyah	Water Services to Pilgrims. Noble service to supply of water and other drinks (especially raisins soaked in water) to pilgrims was entrusted to Abbas bin Abdul Muttalib in *Jahiliyah* and early Islamic period. The *siqayah* of water was due to its scarcity and the edemand for it and the *siqayah* of drinks was a gesture of hospitality to guests of the sacred House of Allah.
al-Taubah	Repentance, Ninth Chapter of the Qur'ān with reference to its verse 104, also known as *Barāat* (Immunity), the opening word of the Surah.
Aman	Safe conduct or pledge of security.
Amīr	Commander, governor, prince; a person invested with command, and more specially military command. *Amīr al-hajj*: the leader of the caravan of pilgrims to Makkah. *Amir majlis*: the master of audiences or ceremonies. Under the Saljuqs of Asia Minor this was one of the highest dignitaries; under Mamluks this had charge of the physicians, oculists and the like. *Amīr ul muminīn*: the commander of the believers; adopted by Umar b. al-Khattāb on his election as caliph, the title was employed exclusively as the protocollary title of a caliph until the end of the caliphate as an institution.
Amr	Affair, the polity
Amr bil Maroof	Ordering good
Anarchy	A state of disorder due to lack of government or control. Origin from Greek *an*-'without'+*arkhus* 'ruler'.
Ansar	Madinite Muslims who received the Muhajirs wholeheartedly and helped the Prophet with their lives and property.

Anthology	Origin Greek anthos 'flower'. A collection of poems or other pieces of writing or music.
Aqabah	Name of the valley situated between Mina and Makkah where the first covenant (known as *Ba'yat al-Nisa*) between the Prophet of Islam and the twelve Madinaite pilgrims occurred in the eleventh year of the Prophethood. The next year in the thirteenth year of Prophethood 72 Madinaite pilgrims on the same place took the pledge on the hands of the Prophet to defend him at any cost. This is known as *Bay'at al-harb*.
Aqāid	Pl. of aqidah, the religious beliefs
Areef	Battalion commander
Arkān	The main parts of the daily prayer.
Arqam, (Dār)	Arqam ibn Abd Manāf (d. 55/675) belonged to the tribe Makhzum from the Quraish clan, companion of the Prophet. His house at Safa hill was the centre of Islamic preaching in Makkah; Umar embraced Islam here. Arqam attended all the sights with the Prophet who appointed him also the collector of Zakah. He died in Madinah.
Ashraf	Nobels of the Community.
Autocracy	Origin from Greek *autos* 'self'+*Kratos* 'power'. A system of government in which one person has total power.
Aws	An Arab tribe that resided permanently in Madinah in the pre-Islamic period. They embraced Islam later on.
Azān	The word *azān/adhān* along with its abridged accompaniment, the *iqāmah* is an oral rite linked to mosques, daily prayer, sacred identity and birth rites. The *azān* and the *iqāman* are usually called outside and inside mosques,

respectively: The former signals prayer times, and the latter the beginning of congregational prayer. The *azān* given in public signals the presence of Islam, and gives members of a largely descentralized faith a sense of belonging. The *azān* functions as a disjuncture between the sacred and the profance, between the Friday prayer, for instance, and the world of trade. It also distinguishes Islam from other religions: when Muslims needed some means to announce the prayer, they asked for a horn, a Christian symbol, but were providentially directed to the *azān*, instead. Finally, the *azān* is chanted into the right ear of a newborn and the *iqāmah* into the left ear.

Azm Determination

Badr Badr lies 125 kilometres to the South of Madinah. It became famous in Islamic history due to the first major encounter between the Muslims and the Quraish of Makkah after the migration that took place in this place on 19th Ramadan 02 A.H./Friday 17th March 623 A.D.

Bait ul Māl The 'fiscus' or treasury of the Muslim state. The notion of public as distinct from private ownership and the idea of properties and monies designed to serve the interests of the communities is said to have been introduced; first by Umar bin al-Khattab; coupled with the institution of the *Dīwan*, it marks the starting point of the *baitul māl* as state treasury. Previously the term designated the depository where money and goods were temporarily lodged pending distribution to their individual owners. In the administration of the later caliphate, the term *makhzan* seems to have almost

	replaced the *baitul māl*, which reflects the proportionate increase of presentations in kind and the diminution of fiscal receipts in hard cash.
Bay'ah	The process in which Muslims had accepted the nominated or elected caliph as their legitimate ruler; community confirmation to the selected caliph by the consultative assembly.
Bismika Allahumma	In your name, O Allah.
Bismillah al-Rahman al-Rahim	In the name of Allah, Most Gracious, Most Merciful.
Colonialism	The practice of acquiring control over another country, occupying it with settlers and exploiting it economically.
Conquest/Fath (of Makkah)	The Peace treaty of Hudaibiyah concluded in 628 A.D. between the Muslims and the Makkans for ten years was basically a no-war pact. In the meantime in a fighting between beduins Quraish took sides against a group allied to the Muslims and that was genuinely taken by the Prophet as a breach of the Hudaibiyah treaty. In January 630, therefore, at the head of an army of 10000, he invaded Makah, meeting almost no resistance. The Kabah was purified of idols and in the course of the following weeks, almost all the Makkans accepted Islam.
Dalalah	The juristic argument
Dar al-Harb	Areas of land that are out of Muslim control; enemy land and territory.
Dar al-Islam	The Islamic land governed by Muslims and its inhabitants; Islamic territory.
Dar al-Nadwah	Assembly house in Makkah, where the Quraysh used to assemble in the pre-Islamic period for consultation and deliberation.
Dhimmi	Non Muslim citizen residing in an

	Islamic state who is granted full protection and citizenship rights and at the same time is exempt from military duties and obligations.
Fard 'Ayn	Individual religious obligation in Islam
Fard al-Kifāyah/wājib al-Kifāyah	A collective religious duty in Islam that may be performed by an individual or group representing the whole population of a town.
Fiqh	Islamic jurisprudence, comprehension specifically of the *Qur'ān* and *Hadith*, technically the branch of learning concerned to understand and relay the revealed law.
Fiqhi	Relating to Fiqh
Fiqhi	Relating to *Fiqh*.
Fitnah	Disorder, mischief, persecution
Fuqaha	Plural of Faqih
Ghatfān	One of the oldest northern tribes of Arabia who first fought against the Prophet of Islam in the battle of Ahzāb then entered to Islamic fold in 629 A.D. but apostated after the death of the Prophet. Khalid bin Walid successfully persuaded them to re-inter Islamic society. They supported Aisha at the eve of the battle of Camel in 656 A.D.
Ghayr matlu	Un-recited, the traditions of the Prophet
Ghusl al-Janābah	The major ablution necessary to renew the ritual purity following menstruation or sexual intercourse.
Hadd	Pl. *hudūd*: hindrance, impediment, limit, boundary, frontier. In the Qur'ān it is used (always in the plural) to denote the restrictive ordinances or statutes of God. In law it has become the technical term for the punishments of certain acts which have been forbidden or sanctioned by punishments in the Qur'ān and have thereby some crimes against religion. The punishments are the death penalty,

	either by stoning or by crucifixion or with the sword; the cutting off of the hand and/or the foot; and flogging with various numbers of lashes, their intensity depending on the severity of the crime. In theology *hadd* in the meaning of the limit, limitation, is an indication of finiteness, a necessary attribute of all the created beings but incompatible with God. In scholastic theology, philosophy and metaphysics it is a technical term for definition, *e.g. hadd haqiqī* that which defines the essence of a thing and *hadd lafzi*, that which defines the meaning of a word.
Hakimiyah	Sovereignty of God
Halal	Lawful, legal
Haram	Prohibited, unlawful
Hawāzin (bin Mansur)	Pre-Islamic grandfather from Adnān chief clan. His children founded various clans and tribes as Thaqīf, Bạkr, 'Aamir, Nasr, Káb, Kilāb Jádah etc. They fought against Quraysh in Ukāz; entered to Islamic fold after the battle of Hunayn.
Hazm	Farsightedness
Hijāb	Veil, cover, curtain. In Islamic literature the term applies to cover the face of a woman, which is controversial. According to the majority of Islamic scholars and jurists unveiling the face is lawful for an woman.
Hijjatul wida	The last pilgrimage in the life of the Prohet of Islam performed in March 632 A.D. The Prophet led the caravan from Madinah of 30 thousand men and women. In this he delivered his famous sermon in Arafāt and declared the Islamic charter of human rights consisting of universal brotherhood, equality, the rights to women etc.

Hijrah Migration

Hudaibiyah A place on the road from Jaddah to Makkah just outside the Haram (restricted precinct) about ten miles from Makkah. Known in Islamic history due to the peace signed between the Quraish and the Prophet at the same place. Here the Prophet stopped and awaited the outcome of events when prevented from making the pilgrimage by the Makkans. The truce was later on concluded between the two parties in 628 A.D. for a no war pact for ten years.

Huffāz al-Qur'ān Those who learnt the *Qur'ān* by heart, pl. of hāfiz.

Hujjah A Qur'ānic term meaning both proof and presentation of proof. It is applied to a conclusive argument attempting to prove what is false as well as what is true; dialectical proof. In Shia theology it refers to that person through whom inaccessible God becomes accessible, and sometimes to any figure in a religious hierarchy through whom an inaccessible higher figure became accessible to those below. In its more specialized meaning it referred to a particular function within the process of revelation, sometimes identified with the role of Salman as witness to Ali's status as caliph. Among the Ismāilis it is a rank in the hierarchy, coming under the Bāb. The Hujjah concluded the *dáwah* and was one of the greater *dā'is*, of whom there were twelve, or occasionally twenty-four. Each seems to have been in charge of a district.

Hunayn A valley between Makkah and Taif (Saudia). The leader of Hawāzin tribes Malik bin Awf al-Nasri, after the conquest of Makkah, fought in 08/630 against the Prophet of Islam in this Valley and was badly defeated. Muslim army received a lot of booty there. The routed enemy took refuge in Taif which was besieged unsuccessfully; but the Muslim victory persuaded the desert tribes to accept Islam and shortly thereafter the rebel tribes and Taif also surrendered and entered Islam.

Ibādah — Submissive obedience to a master, and therefore religious practice, corresponding, in law, approximately to the ritual of Muslim law; the religious acts which bring the creature into contact with his creator, while its counterpart, Mu'*āmalāt*, signifies relations between individuals.

Ibādāt — Religious obligations

Ibādāt badaniyah — Physical obligations made in the religion

Iddah — "Number". The interval of time which a woman must observe after divorce or the death of a husband, before she can remarry. It's purpose is to determine the paternity of possible offspring but also, in the case of divorce which has not been pronounced three times, to provide a space of time in which a reconciliation may take place. The duration of *Iddah* is three months or three menstrual periods in the case of divorce, and four moths and ten days in the case of the death of the husband.

Ihrām — The pilgrim's dress consisting of two pieces of unseamed white cloth.

Ijma al-Sukut — A consensus not verbally declared but practiced and not openly opposed.

Ijtihādi — Relating to *ijtihād*

Ikhtiyār — Choice. In philosophy it means free preference or choice option, whence power of choice, free will. In law it has

	meaning of opinion freely stated. In treatises on the *imāmah*, where the term has the meaning of choice or election, it is customary to contrast the *ahl al-Ikhtiyār* with the *ahl al-nass*, the supporters of the free election with the supporters of textual determination.
Ilm	Knowledge
Ilm al-Hadith	The Islamic discipline dealing with the knowledge of *hadith*.
Imam	The caliph, the leader, the ruler.
Imr'ah	Woman
Infaq	To spend one's wealth for the pleasure of Allah.
Ismah	Innocence
Istifta al-Sh'abi	referendum
Istikhāra	The concept which consists of entrusting God with the choice between two or more possible options, either through piety and submission to His will, or else through inability to decide oneself, on account of not knowing which choice is the most advantageous one. The divine voice in the midst of performing two *rakats* of a supererogatory prayer is expressed.
Istikhlāf	Succession, nomination by the caliph as his successor
Ithna Ashariyyah	The main school of theology of the Shiite who believed in the twelve Imams.
Jagir	Rent-free estate.
Jamal/Camel (the battle of)	The battle fought between Ali, the fourth caliph on the one side and Talha, Zubayr and Aisha on the other in 36/656, Known with al-Jamal (Camel) because Aisha leading the opposition forces was riding on a camel.
Janābah	Sexual intercourse with woman
Jihad	The Holy war in the way of Allah.
Jumu'āh	Friday

Kafir	Non-believer
Kalimah al-Tauheed	Affirmation of faith in the oneness of Allah.
Katib al-Wahy	Scribe of the revelation.
Khalifah	Successor of the Prophet.
Khandaq (the battle of)/Ahzāb/Trench	The Prophetic battle in which the Quraish and their allies from Ghátfan, Banu Murrah, and Ashjá tribes under the leadership of Abu Sufyān with a provocation from the Jews of Quraydha and Banu Nadhir surrounded Madinah city. Salman al-Farasi suggested the Prophet to dig a trench around the city to defend it. The joint front of enemies returned back unsuccessfully to Makkah in 05 A.H./627 A.D. It is also known as the battle of Ahzāb.
Khawarij	One of the oldest Muslim sects rebelled first against Ali the fourth Caliph of Islam who had accepted the principle of arbitration (*tahkīm*) in the battle field of Siffīn (37/657) and then fought against Muawiyah too. One Khāriji Ibn Muljam later on killed Ali while he was performing the afternoon prayer. Khawārij later on organized themselves into a militant socio-religious organisation and were always busy in plotting conspiracies and rebellions against the mainstream Muslims. Among its dignitaries were Tirmah bin Hakim, Dhahhak bin Qays Shaybani, Qatari bin al-Faja'h etc.
Khaybar	A fortified place in the north-east of Madinah, where the Jewish tribes resided. They continued their hostilities against the Muslims with greater vigour and zeal. The noble Prophet after a siege of twenty days and a hard struggle in the 7th year of *hijrah* conquered them and

	compelled them to live therein on certain conditions. The victory was referred to in the Qur'ān 33:27 and 48:19.
Khazraj	The Yamanite tribe that migrated after the breakthrough of Maārib Dame from the South of Mesopotamia to Madinah region. They later on spread over the whole region till Khaybar and Tayma in the 5th century. After embracing Islam they defended the Prophet against Quraish wholeheartedly.
Kisra	Kisra II Parvez, the Sassanid King (590-628), accessed to throne with the help of the Byzantine Emperor in 591 A.D., occupied Jerusalem in 614, was defeated later on by Herculius and was killed in the prison.
M'utazilah	The classical Muslim sect as opposed to Asharites, founded by Wāsil bin Ata (d. 748 A.D.) and Amar bin Ubaid (d. 761 A.D.) who departed from the circle of al-Hasan al-Basari (642-728). They mainly depended on logic, reasoning and rational approach in the religio-philosophical issues. They believed in and propagated the five basics: i) *tawhid* (oneness of God), ii) *adl* (justice), iii) *al-manzilah bain al-manzilatayn* (that a Muslim committing a severe crime is no more a *mumin* but he does not turn into a *Kafir* also; he rather keeps himself by this act on the place between the two places), iv) *w'ad wa w'aeed* (all the rewards and punishments are correct), and v) *amr bi al-maroof wa nahy an al-munkar* (ordering good and forbidding wrong). They believed in the *Qur'ān* as a created entity (*makhluq*).
Madinah	The epithet of *al-Munawwarah*, 'the radiant' is usually added to the name of this city. Originally it was called

'Yathrib', a name with pagan connotations, and became known as *Madinah al-Nabi* 'the city of the Prophet' after the *hijrah*. It was an oasis of the dates from its palm groves. It is situated in the midst of volcanic hills around a small plain called the *manakhah* (from *nikh*, the command to make a camel kneel) where caravans to the city would stop and camp. The two Arab tribes Aws and Khazraj, and several Jewish tribes resided there before migration.

Madni Surah — The Qur'ānic chapter revealed in or around Madinah

Maghāzi — A term which signifies in particular the expeditions organized by the Prophet of Islam in the Madinan period. In a broader sense, it refers to the Prophet's general biography and background.

Majlis — a term meaning a meeting place, meeting assembly, a reception hall (of a caliph, high dignitary or other personage) and a session which is held there, a hall in which a professor's courses are given or a judge's sentences delivered, or further where the debates of an assembly take place; it assumed the modern connotation of parliament in the 19th century, as the concept of parliamentarism became wide-spread. Among the Ismailis it referred to a formal session of religious instruction, the place of it, and also to the lecture or sermon read in it by a *dā'i* to the faithful. Among the Indian *Shi'īs* it is especially used for the shi'iī mourning assemblies held during Muharram to commemorate the tragedy of Karbalah. Majlis Shura is historically the name given to

	extraordinary *adhoc* consultative assemblies in the Ottoman Empire, laking place between the Russo-Ottoman war of 1768-1774 and roughly, the abolition of the Janissaries in 1826.
Majlis al-Ijtihād	The Council that is entitled to individual and collective reasoning within the Islamic paradigm
Majlis al-Mujtahidin	The Council of those who perform *ijtihād*.
Majlis al-Mujtahidin	Assembly of mujtahids
Majlis al-Shura	*Consultative Assembly.*
Majlis al-Shura	The Consultative Assembly, the parliament.
Makkah (al-Mukarramah)	Wrongly written as Mecca also. The Blessed. For thousand of years it has been a spiritual centre. Ptolemy, the 2nd century Greek geographer mentioned it calling 'Makoraba'. The Dravidian Puranās also speak of an ancient holy place there dedicated to the god of wisdom. Originally it was called Bakkah (narrow) a description of the site between the mountains that press upon the city and valley of the Holy Palaces (The Qur'ān 3:96). Of visible monuments that date back to ancient times exists today only the Kabah, which has been rebuilt several times. The landscape surrounding the city is of a striking aridity, as if of immeasurable age. It is nature reduced to its bare foundations, evoking the limitless and the invisible. The Qur'ān called Makkah the "uncultivated" valley; and indeed, its inhabitants have always depended upon commerce for their livelihood. The Quraish of the Kinānah tribe, who descended from an ancestor called Fihr, had inhabited Makkah for several centuries before the revelation of Islam.

entering into commercial agreements with surrounding countries and financing caravans to carry trade-goods. The Qur'ān mentions the "Winter and the Summer Caravan" (106:2) which sometimes numbered thousands of camels, the great incense trade of the Yemen was routed through Makkah.

Makki Surah — The Qur'ānic chapter revealed in Makkah

Manbij — A city in Syria near Halb, was known as Mabbuk in the classical period, a centre of war operations in the Roman period. Here the Emperor Herculius snatched the cross wood from Persia in 630 A.D.

Maruf — Just and right (Known to the people).

Masjid — Mosque

Masjid Nabawi — The Prophetic Mosque in Madinah is the second most venerable mosque in Islam after *al-Masjid al-Harām* at Makkah. This was first supported by the trunks of standing palm trees that had grown there, and the Prophet himself worked on its construction. Then it was enlarged and decorated by Umayyad Caliph Walid bin Abdul Malik and al-Mahdi. The present extension was made by the Mamluks, the Ottomans and in modern times by King Abdel Aziz al-Saud (d. 1969 A.D.).

Matlu — Recited, the Holy Qur'ān

Minjaniq — The catapult, this and the *dabbābah* were two engines of siege which were designed for direct attack on the walls of the forts and fortresses in order to compel the besieged either to surrender or to fight in the open field. The *dabbābah* was a movable tower built in several stages or stories on each of which were stationed a number of men able to make their onslaught simultaneously at different levels. Those below were armed with pick and drills while the others used bows and arrows both to protect their own men and to inflict damage on the defenders on the walls. It is notable that at least the one *dabbābah* used in the Tāif expedition, was made of the cowskins. Most of these weapons were captured as booty in the Prophetic expedition against the Jews of Khaybar.

Muakhāt — Brotherhood established after the migration by the Prophet among the Muhajirs and Ansar.

Muamalāt — Transactions

Mubalaghā — In grammar is used to denote the intensive meaning of a number of morphemes and synthagmas. Most consistently it is applied to the intensive marticiples of the forms fa'*ūl*, *fáál* etc. In literary theory it came to mean pyperbole, intensification. Qudāma. (337/948) uses it to denote a very specialized type of emphasizing in which a poetic idea is rounded out by a pertinent little exaggeration at the end of the line.

Mufrad — In grammar it denotes the singular, usually when applied to the simple noun, in opposition to the dual and plural forms. In morphology, it means simple, as opposed to *Murakkab* 'compound', and designates a noun made up of a single element. In syntax it means 'in isolation' as opposed to *mudāf* 'in annexation' and designates a noun which is not followed by a determinating complement. In lexicography, more often used in the plural *mufradaat* and denotes the words taken in isolation in the lexicon.

Mufti — One who is authorised to pronounce

	legal verdicts.
Muhaddith	Pl. muhaddithūn, the scholar of hadith
Muhājir	Pl. *muhajirūn*: Literally one who migrates. In Turkey and Ottoman lands it was used for refugees and the victims of the population exchanges in the early years of the Republic; by 1933 the term was replaced by the neologism *gocmen*. In India it has been used to describe those Muslims in the Indo-Pak subcontinent who migrated from their homes in order to protect their religion and to safe-guard their interests as Muslims, the first group leaving in the early decades of 20th century and the second group in 1947. In early Islam the plural *muhajirūn* stands for the Emigrants, those Makkan Muslims who emigrated from Makkah to Madinah either just before Muhammad (SAW) himself or in the period up to the conquest of Makkah in 08/630.
Muharram	The first month of Islamic calendar.
Mujtahid	The scholar who performs *ijtihād*
Mulukiyah	Kingship, monarchy
Mushrikun	Those who attribute partners or associates to God.
Mut'ah	Temporary marriage lawful in Shiites but prohibited in Sunnis.
Nāfilah	Pl. nawāfil: In theology, supererogatory work; those works which are supererogatory in the plain sense, in contradistinction to other works which have become a regular practice, *sunnah muakkadah*.
Nahr	Sacrifice of animals at the eve of *hajj*
Nahrawān (the battle of)	(38/658) Following the battle of Siffīn (37/657) and the arbitration which followed, a group receded from the followers of Caliph Ali and became

known as *Khawarij*. They embarked on a military campaign taking Madain. Ali attacked them at Nahrawān and annihilated all but a handful. In revenge he was assassinated by a surviving Kharjiite, Ibn Muljam.

Nahy an al-Munkar — Forbidding wrong

Nass (Pl. nusus) — Text of the *Qur'ān* or Prophet's sayings.

Nihāwand — A city in the South of Hamzān (Iran). Here the famous war of Islam under Numan bi Muqarrin against Persian army under General Firozān occurred in 22 A.H./642 A.D. Numan was killed and the battled was led then by Huzaifah bin al-Yamān and was won. Afterwards the last Sassanid Yazdagird fled into Khurāsan and then to Merv where he was killed by one of his satraps.

Parliament — (from old French *parlement*; Latin *parliamentum*), the original Legislative Assembly of England, Scotland or Ireland and successively of Great Britain and the United Kingdom; legislatures in some countries that were once British colonies are also known as Parliaments. The British Parliament consists of the sovereign, the House of Lords, and the House of commons. Here the real executive powers are vested with the Prime Minister.

Presidentialism — The theory or system of government in which president is treated as the chief executive. He is the chief of state, but his actual power varies from country to country; the presidential office is charged with great powers and responsibilities in the United States and some other countries, but the office is weak and largely ceremonial in Germany and in many countries.

Qādi — Judge, a representative of authority,

invested with the power of jurisdiction. In theory, the head of the community, the direct or indirect delegate, *nāib*, the delegate retaining the power to do justice in person. The objective being the application of the law, which is essentially religious, the function of the judge is a religious one. In theory, his competence embraces both civil and penal cases, and includes the administration of mosques and pious endowments. His competence in penal matters, however, is restricted to the very few crimes envisaged by the law, their repression being currently undertaken by the police. In Indo-Pak subcontinent the term is now applied to the man of formal religious knowledge assigned on behalf of waqf authorities, the duty of delivering the sermon at the eve of the marriage ceremony and then fulfilling the documental requirements in this regard.

Qādi 'askar, judge of the army, an institution dating from the 2nd/8th century. Under Salahuddin Ayyubi the institution was called *qādi Lashkar*. The position began to lose its importance after the middle of the 10th/16th century, when power passed into the hands of the grand *mufti* of Istanbul. It was finally abolished under the Turkish Republic. *Qādi al-Jamāáh* was the title which Abdur Rahman gave, between 138/755 and 141/758, to the *qādi* of the Spanish territory already conquered, until then known as *qādi al-Junūd*, *qādi* of the military district. Later it became an institution similar to that of the *qādi al-qudat*. *Qādi al-qudat* 'the judge of

	judges'; the highest position in the system of the judicial organization of the Islamic state, which, when combined with the institution of the *wizara*, was the highest step under the authority of the caliph.
Qādisiyah	A place near Kufah in the west of Najaf (Iraq), where the famous war of Islam under the command of Sád bin Abu Waqqās during the caliphate of Umar, was fought against the Iranian army under general Rustum and Persia was defeated in 15 A.H./636 A.D. This opened the doors of Persian Empire to Islam. The legendary Persian war flag, the *Drafsh-i-Kavianeh*, made of leather and precious stones was captured.
Qasr	Palace
Qawwām	The guardian, the protector, the custodian
Qiyās	Analogical reasoning used in Islamic jurisprudence first by Abu Hanifah; after the *Qur'ān*, hadith, and consensus it is the fourth source of Islamic Shariah *Muhaddithun* opposed it and declared it invalid.
Quraish	One of the powerful tribes of Makkah. The name comes from the root to 'bite' (*qarasha*), whence also the word for the shark, 'the biting fish' (*qirsh*), sometimes thought to be the 'totem' of the tribe. Possibly Quraish was the nickname of Fihr, the ancestor of the tribe, whose other name was al-Nadr. This was settled in Makkah by an ancestor of renown called Qusayy who displaced the previous inhabitants, the Khuza'ah. The clans who lived in the immediate vicinity of the Kabah, in the lowest part (*al-Batha*) of Makkah, were known as *Abtahi* or *Bitahi* or as *Quraish*

al-Bitah.* Less illustrious families who lived further out, were known as *Quraish al-Zawāhir*. The location of Makkah on important caravan routes across the peninsula, and the prestige of the Kabah in the pre-Islamic period gave it a considerable advantage as a trading city with the result that the Quraish became one of the richest and most powerful tribes. This gave them claims to be an aristocratic pre-eminence. The Prophet himself was of the Banu Hashim clan of the Quraish.

R.A. — *(Abbrev.)* radia Allahu 'anhu, 'Allah may please with Him'.

Rabiul Awwal — The third month of Islamic calendar

Rak'at — A single cycle of actions and words, different combinations of which constitute ritual prayer at various hours in a day.

Referendum — Origin Latin, 'something to be referred', A direct vote by the electorates of a country on a single political issue.

Riddah wars (Harb al-Riddah) — Riddah literally means apostasy, especially from the faith. It is historically the name given to the defection of the Arab tribes after the death of the Prophet. At this time several so-called false prophets rose into prominence as al-Aswad 'Ansi in South Arabia, Tulayha Asadi in Central Arabia, Musaylimah in Yamamah etc. Abu Bakr fought uncompromisingly against all these leaders and those also who declined to pay *Zakah* to Islamic state.

Ru'sa — Plural of rayis, the head of state.

S.A.W. — Abbrev. *Sallallahu 'alaihi wasallam*: Peace, greetings and blessings of Allah be upon him.

S.W.T. — Abbrev. *Subhanahu wa Ta'āla*: Allah

	the Praised and Exalted
Sabā	A state in the south Yeman, mentioned in Old Testament and in Arab, Greek and Roman writings, was a great centre of trade, commerce and held a prominent culture. One of its ruler the Queen Balqees is admirably mentioned in the *Qur'ān*.
Sabab	Pl. Asbāb. 'Cause', the specific historical situation claimed to have led to the revelation of a particular Qur'ānic verse, or the institution of a given ruling by the Prophet.
Sadāq	The bridal dower
Sahabi	Singular of *Sahabah*, companion of the Prophet
Sahih	This name is given to the utterly faultless Hadith in which there is no weakness either in regard to the chain of transmission (*Isnad*) or in regard to the text (*Matn*) and in which there is no tendency to contradict any established belief of Islam.
Sahihain	The two authentic compilations of hadith e.g. al-Jami al-Sahih of Bukhari and that of Muslim who have incorporated in their compilations the *Sahih ahādith*. These are counted as the first two of the six authentic compilations of hadith (*Sihāh Sittah*).
Salah	The daily prayers; one of the five pillars of Islam.
Saqīfah bani Saa'edah	Roofed passage in Madinah ascribed to Banu Sā'idah. The name of the assembly of Madinan Muslims, became famous in the Islamic history because of the decision taken at the spot about the critical question of leadership after the death of the Prophet.
Saum	Fasting
Separation of Powers	Division of the legislative, executive and

(Theory)	judicial functions of government among separate and independent bodies. Such a separation, it is argued, limits the possibility of arbitrary excess by government. The first modern formulation of the theory was that of the French writer Montesquieu in De *L'esprit des Lois* (1784), although the English philosopher John Locke had earlier argued that legislative power should be divided between king and parliament.
Sh'abān	Eighth month of Islamic Calender.
Shahādah	The Islamic confession of faith, one of the five pillars of Islam, in law, testimony.
Shari'ah	Often translated as "Islamic Law", it is better understood as the path of correct conduct that God has revealed through his messengers, particularly the Prophet Muhammad (SAW). The earliest sources indicate its meaning as a "way of belief" either Muslim or non-Muslim, and it was used to translate the word *Torah* into Arabic. Jurists tend to prefer the term *fiqh* in their books on jurisprudence, leaving *Shariah* as a general term. Intention (*niyyah*) to fulfil one's duty to God is often as important as the act itself, and every action should be conceived as worshipping God. This focus on God extended to a medieval institutionalization of the *Shariáh* that limited human authority. Even today, there is no central authority for matters of Islamic law in Sunni Islam (some Shi'ites have developed authority structures), and Muslims may seek advice from a number of different authorities (*muftis*) before making up

their mind. Further, actions are assigned one of five "*Shariah* values" (*ahkām*); between required and forbidden are: recommended, indifferent, and disapproved. These valuations have led some to describe *Shariah* as ethics rather than as law. Arguably postcolonial legal institutions have utterly changed the Muslims' relationship to *Shariah*, both by codifying the law and by replacing *Shariah* courts. *Shariah* in Western discourse has come to signify Islam as moribund or authoritarian, perhaps reflecting Christian presumptions of a distinction between law and gospel. Rhetorical use is also found among Muslim intellectuals, some of whom urge a "return" to *Shariah* focusing primarily on issues of public dress and ritual conduct, but also invoking the idea of the *Shariah* as a total way of life.

Shawwal — The tenth month of the Islamic calendar

Shia — The Shiite community of Muslims

Shura — Consultation; consultative assembly; in modern Arabic literature it denotes the parliament introduced in various Muslim countries due to influence of western political thought, though the term is originally Qur'ānic but on the Muslim countries there is no impact of the Islamic polity recognized and appreciated in the Qur'ānic paradigm.

Siege — Origin old French *sege* 'a seat' a military operation in which enemy forces try to capture a town or building by surrounding it and cutting off its supplies.

Sirah — Biography of the Prophet

Siyar — Juristic source for Muslim law of nations.

Sultān — The king, the power

Sunan — Singular *Sunnah*, compilations of hadith

	made by different scholars like Ibn Majah (d. 887), Nasai (d. 915), Abu Dawud (d. 889), Baihaqi (d. 1066) etc.
Sunni	Mainstream Muslims, followers of the Sunnah of the Prophet
Surah	The chapter of the *Qur'ān*
Surah al-Aárāf	The Heights, the 7th chapter of the Qur'ān. The title is derived from its verse nos. 46 and 48.
Surah al-Fath	The 48th Qur'ānic chapter, the title derived from its first verse. The Surah described the peace treaty of Hudaibiyah as a 'manifest victory' while some of the items of the treaty not being reciprocal were objected in the Muslim camp. This treaty as history testified, led to the conquest of Makkah and the sweeping away of the autocracy.
Surah al-Nisa	The Women, the third chapter of the Qur'ān; the title derived from its verse No. 19. The Surah also emphasizes on the rights of women that must be recognised in marriage, property, and inheritance and they should be held in honour and dignity (verses 15-42 and 62).
(Surah) al-Shura	Consultation, 42nd chapter of the Qur'ān, the title is derived from its verse no. 38.
Taabein/Tabiyūn	The followers of the Sahabah.
Tabuk	A place about 500 Kilometers to the north of Madinah. The Holy Prophet marched with 30,000 men towards it in 630 A.D. as a precautionary measure to meet the Romans who were planning to attack the Islamic capital with the assistance of the chiefs of Ghassān, Lakhm and Jazm but the enemy did not arrive. The Prophet stayed there for about 20 days and made peace with tribal chiefs in that region.

	about 20 days and made peace with tribal chiefs in that region.
Tafsir	Exegesis
Takbir	Repetition of the manufactory formula in the prayers.
Taqlid	The term refers to the "following" or "imitation" of a legal expert by a non-expert. In Sunni Muslim Law, in both its classical and modern manifestations, *taqlid* is generally viewed negatively. It is the activity that the legally unaccomplished (called *muqallid*) are forced to perform. As they have no legal qualifications, they must merely obey the interpretation of the law put forward by the *mujtahid*. *Taqlid* in the Sunni traditions was, however, not always used with negative connotations. The theory of *ijtihād* developed within the Sunni tradition, with grades of *ijtihād* from absolute *ijtihād* (*ijtihād mutlaq*) to *ijtihād* within the school (*ijtihād fi al-madhhab*) to partial *ijtihād*. A more sophisticated theory of *taqlid* accompanied these developments. A scholar might be viewed as *muqallid* to the founding *imām* of the *madhhab* (since a jurist would not normally claim that his *ijtihād* was superior to that of the *imām*), but was a *mujtahid* with regard to jurists of lesser rank within the school. *Taqlid* was, therefore, a recognition of the importance of the *madhhab* tradition as both a legal identity and as setting the broad parameters within which a jurist might operate.
Tarāwīh (Salat al-)	'Singular *tarwīha*, Literally: refreshment, relaxation. In religious context it denotes the supererogatory prayer consisting of eight *rakats* to Ahl al-Hadith and twenty *rakats* to Hanafids,

	performed just after *salah al-Isha* (prayer in the night) during the whole month of Ramadān.
Tawakkul	Reliance on God
Tawātur	A form of transmission of the traditions which consists of the affirmation of the report by persons/narrators so large (7 or 25 or 70) as logically to exclude any possibility of fraud or lying. This is superior to all other channels and is just next to the Qur'ān.
Tawīl	Interpretation that goes beyond the letter of a text in search of the spirit of the ordinanće. Contrasts with *tafsir* (in most cases) interpreting precisely what is in the text its *zāhir*.
Tawkil	Representation in transactions
Thābit	'Firm'; said of one who is a competent transmitter of precisely what he heard.
Uhud	On the western outskirts of Madinah, it is a volcanic hill with a plain stretching before it. The battle was fought here between the Muslims and the Makkans in 625 A.D./third years of *hijjrah.*
Ulama al-Shariah	The Scholars of Islamic Law
Ultra vires	Origin Latin 'beyond the powers', beyond one's legal power or authority.
Ulul amr	Those who hold authority and power.
Umara	The plural of Amir.
Umayyads (Banu Umayyah)	The descendants of Umayyah bin Abd Shams, founder of one of the clans of Quraish. The name was given to dynasty founded by Muawiyah bin Abu Sufyān, who ruled Islam from their capital, Damascus 661-750 A.D. When Abbasids replaced them they transferred their dynasty to Spain and ruled there 756-1031 A.D. from their new capital Qurtubah. They number 16; most popular among them were Abdur

	Rahman I al-Dākhil (756-788), Abdur Rahman III al-Nāsir (912-961) who was entitled as *amir al-mūminīn* and occupied the strongest and most influential position among the rulers of the middle age.
Ummah	Muslim community.
Umrah	The lesser pilgrimage or visit to Makkah, which may be performed at any time, its ceremonies take place entirely within the precincts of the Grand Mosque of Makkah and require a little over an hour to accomplish. It is comosed of the seven circumambulations of Kabah (*tawāf*), followed by a prayer of two *rakat* facing the space between the Black Stone and the door of the Kabah known as *al-Multazam*, the drinking of the water of Zamzam and finally the ritual walking between the hills of Safa and Marwah seven times.
'Umum Balwā	A difficulty or danger that affects the whole society; in Islamic law such a situation is taken into consideration as the common necessity or demand and causes some relaxation or excuse in Islamic ordinances.
Urf aamm	Common practice
Ushr	Taxes levied on cultivated land owned by Muslims amounting to one-tenth of the products.
Ushur	Taxes levied on foreign commodities accounting to one-tenth of the price.
Usool al-Fiqh	Roots of jurisprudence. According to Sunnis the bases of Islamic Law are four: *Qur'ān*, *Hadith*, *Qiyas* and *Ijma*. Ijtihad is the extrapolation from these principles to specific cases. The Hanbalites and Ahl Hadith generally limit *ijma* to the generation of companions and *tabiyūn*. The Twerver

	Shiites add the teachings of their Imams to Sunnah and admit the *ijtihad* of qualified temporary religious authorities.
Usul	Source and method of classical Muslim jurisprudence *i.e. Qur'ān, Sunnah, Qiyas, Ijma* and other rules and measures of Ijtihad.
Uswah	Model
Uthmaniyah/Ottomans	Also called Orsmanlis, established first their Sultanate (1326-1516 A.D.) and then independent caliphate (1516-1924) were a clan of the Ghuzz branch of Turks, descended from a chieftain called Ertoghrul, whose son Uthman founded a principality in Asia Minor. This principality turned gradually into the most powerful Caliphate in history.
Wahy	Revelation
Wakīl	A representative, an individual who is delegated some power in transactions on behalf of some other.
Wazir	Minister.
willy-nilly	adv. Whether one likes it or not, without direction or planning. Origin later spelling of 'will I, nill I', 'I am willing, I am unwilling.
Yarmūk	One of the tributary streams from the river of Jordan that flows between Ajlum and al-Balqā. The battle fought between Islamic army under Khalid bin Walid and the Byzantine army that numbered in fifty thousand on the bank of the same river in 636 A.D. is know as Yarmuk battle. The war concluded in the occupation of the Byzantine Empire.
Yathrib	The old name of Madinah
Zakah	Alms tax, a tax imposed on Muslims by the *Shariah* and non-Muslims are exempted from it.
Zann	Speculation as opposed to *Yaqin*
Zuhr	Noon Prayer

BIOGRAPHICAL NOTES

Khalid, Mohammad Khalid (b. 1920)

Egyptian writer and essayist. Bron in Sharqiyyah Province, he graduated from al-Azhar in 1947 with an Almiyah degree from the Faculty of Shariah and then acquired a diploma in teaching form the same. He worked as a teacher of Arabic language and then in the Cultural Bureau of the Ministry of Culture. He later became a supervisor in the Department for the Publication of the Heritage. He has written more than thirty books as well as articles on religious and political issues in the newspapers ad magazines such as *al-Sharq al-Awsat* (London), *al-Muslimun, al-Musawwar, al-Ahrām* and *al-Wafd.*

His first book *Min Huna Nabda* (From Here We start, 1950) was confiscated because of the objections raised by al-Azhar and then released by order of the Cairo district court. He expressed his secular views along with the Islamic references in other books also written in the 1950s and early 1960s, such as *Muātinūn La Riáāya* (citizens, not the subjects, 1951), *Ma'an ala al-Tarīq – Muhammad wa al-Masīh* (Altogether on the road: Mohammad and Christ, 1958), *al-Dimiqratiyah abadan* (Democracy for Ever, 1953). In his book *al-Dawlah fi al-Islam* (The Government in Islam, 1981) the author revised his secular approach and advocated a semi-Islamic view on the theory of governance in Islam. He now realised that Islam has a civic and religious mission and calls for a state that should apply the Islamic principles – liberty, *shura* and parliamentary democracy. His first unrevised approach was evaluated in Islamic perspective by the Ikhwan-oriented scholar Mohammad al-Ghazali in his book *Min Huna Nálam* (From Here We Know).

Qutb, Sayyid (1906-1966)

Literary critic, novelist, poet, Islamic thinker and most famous Egyptian activist of twentieth century, exceeded in reputation even the founder of *al-Ikhwan al-Muslimun*, Hassan al-Banna (1906-1949). His passionate writings contain powerful images of the maladies of contemporary Islamic societies and an idealization of the faith through the words of the Qur'ān and Sunnah. In 1948 he was despatched to the United States by the Ministry of Education in which he was employed, to study western methods of education. He spent about three years abroad, leaving America in 1950. This trip to America marked a transition from literary and educational pursuits to intense religious commitment. He in 1953 joined the Ikhwan and was appointed editor of its weekly organ. Due to his uncompromising attitude toward the *jahili* system, he was arrested and tortured in jail frequently. In 1965 he was detained on the charges of terrorism and sedition. In controvertible evidences against Qutb were apparently not presented as his revolutionary tract, *M'aālim fi al-Tariq* (Milestones 1964) did not explicitly call for armed overthrow of the state. Rather it urged resistance by turning away from existing society ad creating a model *ummah* which eventually would establish true Islam. Despite great international pressure the government executed Qutb and two colleagues on 29 August 1966.

Qutb regarded the leadership of Muslim societies which he disapproved, and the societies that went along with them, to be living in a state of *Jahiliyah* which can be considered anything that is inimical to Islam. He thought of Islam as a comprehensive way of life. Islam thus provides model solutions to all aspects of human existence. In his most sustained work

Khasāis al-Tasawwur al-Islami wa Muqawwamātuh (characteristics of Islamic Ideology and its components, 1962) he elaborates Islam's revolutionary image in detail. One of his socio-political program is the organicism and connotations of corporatism which he calls *al-tajamm'u al-haraki* (dynamic concrescence). His notions of Islamic social justice were well discussed in his famous book *al-Adālah al-Ijtima'yiyah fi al-Islam.* His Quranic commentary *Fi Zilāl al-Qur'ān* is treated as the masterpiece of Arabic literature.

Maududi, Sayyid Abul Āla (1903-1979)

Islamic ideologue, politician, the most prominent revivalist thinker of the modern Muslim world. His interpretative reading of Islam has contributed greatly to the activists from Morocco to Indonesia. Jama'at Islamic (founded by him in 1941), the organisation that has embodied his ideology over the course of the past six decades, has played a significant role in the history and politics of Pakistan, India, Bangladesh, Sri Lanka and the South Asian communities, of the Persian Gulf states, Great Britain and North America. After the collapse of the Khilafat Movement of India in 1924, he became suspicious of Indian National Congress's manipulation of nationalist sentiments to serve Hindu interests. He opposed the Indian nationalism and counted it as against the religion of Islam and its teachings of universal Ummah in his book *Muttahidah Qaumiyat Awr Islam.* In his work *al-Jihād fi al-Islam*, he explained systematically Islamic response to war, peace, violence and other issues related to international law and relations without offering any apology. After the partition of India in 1947, he divided *Jamā'at Islami* into independent Indian and Pakistani units and himself migrated to Lahore to assume the leadership of the *Jamā'at.* He did much here to mobilise public opinion for the cause of Islam, pushing the Ulama to demand an Islamic Constitution. Between 1948 and 1950 he was imprisoned for refusing to lend religious legitimacy to the government's military campaign in Kashmir. In 1954 he was again imprisoned, and this time sentenced to death, for his role in instigating the disturbances against the Ahmadiyah in Punjab in 1953-54. His sentence was later commuted and he was released from prison in 1955: He was incarcerated on two other occasions; in 1957 and again in 1967 for challenging the regime of Ayub Khan.

Throughout his years of activism and Islamic struggle Maududi continued to produce an impressive number of articles, pamphlets and books. His Quranic translation and commentary *Tahfīm al-Qur'ān* (6 volumes) begun in 1942 and completed in 1972 is one of the most widely read Quranic *tafsirs* in Urdu. His writings constitute an interpretative reading of Islam that sought to mobilise faith for the purpose of socio-political action. His ideological perspective has been influential in the unfolding of revivalism across the Muslim World. The counters of Islam's discourse with socialism and capitalism were first defined by him, as was much of the terminology associated with Islamic revivalism, including 'Islamic revolution', 'Islamic state', 'Islamic Ideology' and 'Theo-democratic Khilāfah'.

Maududi's vision was dialectic in that he saw the battle between Islam and *Jahiliyah* (paganism) – both the West and the Hindu culture of India – as the central force in the historical progression of Muslim societies. This struggle would culminate in an Islamic state, which would in turn initiate broad reforms in society, thereby erecting an Islamic order. In his conception, Islamic revolution was to unfold within the existing state structures rather than after their destruction. He disapproved the use of violence in promoting the cause of Islam and defined the ideal Islamic state as 'democratic caliphate'.

Abduh, Muhammad (1849-1905)

Abduh, the most influential reformer ad jurist of the nineteenth century, was born in the Nile River delta in the northern Egypt and received a traditional Islamic education in Tanta. He graduated from Al-Azhar University in Cairo in 1877, where he taught for the nest two years. It was during this period that he met Jamaluddin Afghani, whose influence upon Abduh's thought over the next decade would be profound. When Afghani was expelled from Egypt in 1879, Abduh was also briefly exiled from Cairo to his native village. He returned to Cairo the following year to become editor of the official government gazette, *al-Waqāi al-Misriyya* and began publishing articles on the need for reform in the country. When the British occupied Egypt following the 'Urabi Revolt of 1882, Abduh was sentenced to three years' exile for assisting the nationalists. He lived briefly in Britain before joining Afghani in Paris, where the two would publish the highly influential journal *al-'Urwa al-Uthqa*. He returned to Beirut following the journal's demise in 1884. In this period Abduh first met Rasid Rida who would become his chief biographer and most distinguished disciple. In 1888, following a rethinking of his revolutionary ideas he was allowed to return to Cairo. He became a member of the newly created administrative board for al-Azhar University in 1895. In 1899, he was appointed a member of the Legislative Council, and more importantly became in the same year the grand mufti of Egypt. In this new position Abduh championed reforms that he saw necessary to make Shariah relevant to modern problems. He advocated the institution of *ijtihad* (individual reasoning) in producing a vibrant civilization and creatively interpreting the Qur'ān and *hadith*. To him the jurists must consider public welfare *maslahah* over dogma when rendering judgement. The legal opinions (*fatāwa*) he wrote for the government and individuals on such issues as polygamy, divorce, and the status of non-Muslims before the import of his reformist attitudes. During the last years of his life, Abduh collaborated with Rashid Rida in publishing the journal *al-Manār* founded by Rida in 1898. The most systematic presentation of Abduh's approach to Islamic reform is found in his essay *Risālah al-Tawhīd*. In opposition to European positivist philosophers, he argues that reason and revelation are separate but inextricably linked sources of ethics.

Shaltut, Mahmood (1893-1963)

He was an Egyptian religious scholar, jurist and reformer of al-Azhar in Cairo. Born in a farming village of lower Egypt Shaltut distinguished himself as a student in the principal religious institute of Alexandria and later at al-Azhar. He became an instructor of Islamic jurisprudence at al-Azhar in 1927. The following year,, Muhammad Mustafa al-Maraghi was appointed *Shaykh al-Azhar* (rector), and Shaltut immediately emerged one of his ardent supporters. When conservative opposition forced al-Maraghi out of office the following year, Shaltut continued pressing for reform. Because of his opposition, he was dismissed from al-Azhar in 1931. Upon al-Maraghi's re-appointment as rector in 1935, he returned as a senior official in the faculty of Islamic law. Following service in various committees and conferences inside and outside al-Azhar, Shaltut was appointed *Shaykh al-Azhar* in 1958. During his tenure, Shaltut oversaw a modernization of the school's curriculum in theology and law, and addition of new faculties, including medicine. His influence, however, was undermined, when the Nasser government imposed direct state control over al-Azhar in 1961. The progressive bent of Shaltut's thought is best exemplified in his condemnation of Islamic sectarianism and his appointment of scholars of Shi'ite *fiqh* at al-Azhar.

al-Sibā'i, Mustafa (1915-1964)

Born in Homs, Damascus in 1915, Sibai went to Egypt in 1933, to study at the University of al-Azhar, where he was influenced by the Egyptian *al-Ikhwan al-Muslimun* (The Muslim Brotherhood). In 1949 he completed his Ph.D. dissertation entitled "The Position of *Sunnah* in Legislation". Charged with subversion by the British government in 1934 and 1940, he was eventually deported to Palestine. He questioned the economic and cultural reliance of Muslim states on either the United States or the Soviet Union, feeling that Muslims should assert their independence from Western influences. He advocated social reform based both on Marxist theories and traditional Islamic thought and strongly believed in the idea of universal Islamic solidarity. He discussed the rights of women under Islamic law in an article published in 1962. A noted author and scholar of *fiqh* and *Sunnah*, he also edited the journal al-*Manār, al-Muslimun* and *Hadhārat al-Islam.* Being an activist, Sibai had forged by 1946 a merger between different Islamic groups to form the *Ikhwan al-Muslimun* (Muslim Brotherhood) in Syria and was elected its general supervisor (*al-Murāqib al-'āmm*). Until the Brotherhood's suppression by the Shishakli regime in 1952, Sibai worked to strengthen his movement, which he conceived not as a *jam'iyah* or political party but as a *ruh* (spirit) seeking to raise public consciousness to achieve comprehensive Islamic reform. He was also distinguished educator and administrator at the University of Damascus. His most important contribution of Islamic thought was his book *Ishtirakiyat al-Islam* (The Socialism of Islam) in which he urged the Islamic notions of socialism. This created an uproar because of its opposition to capitalism, its association of Islam with socialism, and its ostensible support of Nasser's ideology at a time when the Egyptian Brotherhood was suppressed.

Khalafullah, Mohammad Ahmad (b. 1916)

Contemporary Islamic modern thinker. Born in Sharqiyah Province in Lower Egypt, he attended traditional Islamic schools, a government school, and then Darul Uloom, followed by the Faculty of Arts at the Egyptian (later Cairo) University, from which he graduated in 1939. he completed his M.A. in 1942, with a thesis on *"al-Jadal fi al-Qur'ān"* (Polemic in the *Qur'ān*), later published as *Muhammad wa al-Quwā al-Mudāddah* (Muhammad and the Forces of Opposition), and then joined the University faculty as a tutor. In 1947 he presented a doctoral dissertation on the *Qur'ān* to the Faculty of Arts which stirred up considerable controversy and was not sustained, so he resigned from his University position in 1948. This dissertation was published after revision in 1951 under the title *al-Fann al-Qisasi fi al-Qur'ān al-Karim* (The Art of Narrative in the *Qur'ān*) and has been reprinted several times since. He gained his doctorate in 1954 with a thesis on *Abu al-Farj al-Isbahāni.* He worked for many years in the Ministry of Culture, becoming undersecretary for planning in this Ministry. Since retirement he has been active in the Egyptian Committee for Asian-African Solidarity and has been vice-President of the National Progressive Unionist (*Tajamm'u*) party. He is Chief editor of magazine *al-Yaqzah al-Arabiah* (Arab Awakening), has written many articles on the *Qur'ān* and Islam for popular periodicals, such as *Ruz al-Yusuf*, and has written a large number of books, including works on modern reformers such as Abdullah al-Nadim and Abdur Rahman al-Kawakibi, and works on Islamic topics, such as *al-Qur'ān wa Mushkilāt Hayatina al-Mu'āsirah* (The *Qur'ān* and Our Contemporary Problems), *al-Qur'ān wa al-Dawlah* (The *Qur'ān* and the State), and *al-Islam wa al-'Urubah* (Islam and Arabism). He is treated as a liberal scholar who argues that Arab socialism is consistent with Islam; fixed prohibition and commands can be established only by a very clear text of the *Qur'ān*, and in social matters *maslahah* (the Muslim welfare) generally takes precedence over *nass*.

Al-Ghazali, Mohammad (1917-2001)

Born in 1917, al-Ghazali was an Egyptian Islamic thinker who was educated as a jurist at al-Azhar University, Cairo, and held prominent positions with the Ministry of Awqāf and the Mosques Department. During his early career he sided with the Muslim Brotherhood until he separated himself from the Organization in the 1950s. Al-Ghazali wrote over forty books that are considered to be very important in the field of modern legal studies and theology. In (Islam and Political Despotism) *al-Islam wa al-Istibdād al-Siyasi* and (Prejudice and Tolerance in Christianity and Islam) *al-T'assub wa al-Tasāmuh bayn al-Masihiyah wa al-Islam* he advocated the variety of ways in which religion could be a source of social justice and promote peace in the modern world. As a scholar al-Ghazali is known for an independent, well-balanced approach to jurisprudence, and he cited Islamic texts in favour of gender equality, greater political participation, environmental awareness, and human rights. He is critical of modern Muslim scholars who focus too much on pedantic details of adhering to rituals and not enough on governance, finance, ethics and moral philosophy. He is critical of radical and neoconservative scholars who failed to understand the comprehensive nature of religion and he refused to recognise their myopic views of faith. He felt they were poorly trained scholars who purposely select esoteric *hadiths* and *Sunnah* accounts to argue their point and further their political agendas.

Rida, Rashīd (1865-1935)

Rida was the most prominent disciple of Mohammad Abduh, and one of the most influencial scholars and jurists of his age. He was born near Tripoli, in present-day Lebanon. His early education consisted of training in traditional Islamic subjects and a brief, disenchanting exposure to the secular curriculum of the Ottoman government school in Tripoli. His reformist views began to form in 1884-85 when he was first exposed to

Jamaluddin Afghani's and Abduh's journal *al'Urwa al-Wuthqa* (the firmest grip). In 1897 he left Syria for Cairo to collaborate with Abduh. The following year he launched al-Manar, first weekly and then a monthly journal comprising Quranic commentary (begun by Abduh, continued by Rida, but never completed) and opinions on pressing legal, political and social issues of the day. Like Abduh, Rida based his reformist principles on the argument that the *Shriah* consists of *ibadāt* and *m'uāmalāt*. Human reason has little scope in the former and the Muslims should adhere to the dictates of *Qur'ān* and *hadith*. The Laws governing *m'uāmalāt* (social relations) should conform to Islamic ethics but on specific points may be continually reassessed according to changing conditions of different generations and societies.

Al-Maraghi, Mustafa (1881-1945)

Egyptian reformist and rector of al-Azhar (1928-29 and 1935-45). Shaykh Mustafa al-Maraghi is the link between the reforms of his mentor Muhammad Abduh and such subsequent leaders of al-Azhar as Mustafa Abd al-Rāziq, Abdul Halim Mahmud and Mahmood Saltut; the last, his professed disciple, later transformed al-Azhar by compromising with the secular nationalist regime of Gamal Abdul Nasser. He was described by his contemporaries as a unique man of strong character and leadership abilities. Maraghi's dismissal by King Fuad in 1929 caused a revolt among the Azhari Ulama that resulted in the dismissal of seventy of them. As a reformer he believed in Islam's flexibility and ability to adapt to the needs of modernity. He called for social, legal and educational reforms and pursued an aggressive campaign-begun by Abduh and finished by Shaltut – to integrate the modern sciences into al-Azhar's curriculum. To that end he organised committees to reform the University's regulations and curriculum and created a supervisory department for research whose responsibilities included publishing and translation. He called for the exercise of *ijtihād*, reinterpretation, and opposed *taqlid*. He worked for the reconciliation of different schools of law and cooperated with the Agha Khan in setting up Islamic educational and research associations to arbitrate between various schools and strengthen ties among them. He also waged a campaign against Christian missionaries and the schools they opened in Egypt, which he felt were compromising Islam and undermining Islamic society. He also participated in international religious conferences, where he asked for recognition of the equality of all religious groups.

Islahi, Ameen Ahsan (1906-1997)

One of the most accomplished students of the renowned Quranic scholar Hamiduddin Farahi (d. 1930).. He was born in Bamhore, a village in Azamgarh, India. After his initial education, he was admitted to Madrasatul Islah, from where he was graduated in 1341/1922. he started his career as a journalist, writing for several newspapers. In 1344/1925 he met Farahi, and at the latter's suggestions came to Sarai Mir in order to study with him. From 1344/1925 until Farahi's death five years later, Islahi lived in close association with Farahi, and mastered the latter's approach to the *Qur'ān*. With his teacher he studied not only the *Qur'ān* but also philosophy, political science and other subjects. After Farahi's death, Islahi studied *Hadith* with Muhammad Abdur Rahman Mubarakpuri (1283 or 84 – 1354/1866 or 87-1935), one of the great scholars of *Hadith* in India. After returning to Sarai Mir he managed for the publication of Farahi's works and published a journal *Al-Islāh* (Reform). In 1359/1940, Abdul 'Āla Maududi (1321-1400/1903/1979) founded the *Jamaat Islami* and Islahi soon joined it as a regular member. In the Jamā'at he became a key figure and always held distinguished positions. In the mid-1950s, following serious differences, he resigned from the Jamā'at. In 1378/1958 Islahi founded the Tanzim Islami, but the venture did not prove successful. Since then he was mainly engaged in private scholarly work. The chief product of this phase is *Tadabbur e Qur'ān*, parts of which were first published in the monthly *Mīthāq*. After the completion of *Tadabbur* in 1400/1980, he established in Lahore a study circle in which instruction on the *Qur'ān* and *Hadith* was to be imparted in accordance with Farahi-Islahi approach. His other books include" *Mabādi Tadabbur Qur'ān, Tazkiyah Nafs, Dāwat e Din Aur Uska Tariq e Kār, Islami Qanūn ki Tadwin, Mabādi Tadabbur Hadith, Islāmi Riyāsat, Haqiqat Tawhid, Haqiqat Shirk, Haqiqat Taqwa* etc.

Ḥamidullah, Muhammad (Dr.) (1908-2002)

He was born in Hyderabad, obtained his degree of Alimiyah from Madrasah Nizamiyah in 1924, B.A. from Usamnia University and LL.B. and M.A. also from the same. He was awarded D.Phil by the Boun University in 1932 and honorary D.Litt. by the Sorbonne University. In 1938 he returned to Readership in Islamic International Law at the Osmania University. Following the collapse of Hyderabad state in 1948 he migrated to Paris. He took up an assignment with *Centre Nationale de la Recherche Scientifique* in 1954, which ended in 1978. During this period he taught in the several other universities in Turkey and Germany. He wrote extensively across a wide spectrum of Islamic disciplines including the translation of the *Qur'ān*, *Hadith*, *Seerah*, *Fiqh*, Islamic International Law, Islamic history and Arabic epigraphy. He wrote over a hundred books and over 1000 articles in several languages, including French, German, English, Arabic, Turkish, Persian and Urdu. He knew 22 languages including Thai, which he learnt at the age of 84. He is the only scholar in the world to have translated the *Qur'ān* in three European Languages: French, English and German. English translation was partly published from South Africa in 1960. The German translation, though complete, remains unpublished. His most important contribution to Islamic studies is his French translation and commentary of the Holy *Qur'ān* published in more than 30 editions and is very popular. His another work 'Introduction of Islam" is rendered into 22 languages. Some of his English publications include: *'The Battlefields of the Prophet Muhammad', 'The First Written Constitution in the World', 'Sahifah Hammam bin Munabbih', 'Muhammad Rasulullah', 'The Muslim Conduct of State', 'The 1400th Anniversary of the Completion of Islam', 'Emergence of Islam: Lectures on the Development of Islamic Worldview', Intellectual Tradition and Polity'* etc.

al-Aqqād, Abbās Mahmud (1889, Aswān, Egypt – 1964 Cairo)

Egyptian journalist, poet and literary critic who was a prolific writer and an innovator of 20th century Arabic poetry and criticism. Born in modest circumstances, al-Aqqād continued his education through reading when his formal schooling was cut short. He supported himself throughout most of his career by writing. An outspoken political commentator, he was imprisoned for some months in 1930-31 for remarks opposing the government. In 1942, with the advance of German troops, he sought refuge in Sudan as a precaution against German reprisals for his attacks on Adolf Hitler. His literary works included poems; a novel, *Sarāh* (1938), based on one of his own romances; and critiques of classical and modern Arabic authors. His essays show the influence of 19th century English practitioners of the form, particularly Thomas Carlyle. Al-Aqqād devoted much thought to religion and politics and his works include studies of the philosophy of the *Qur'ān*, of social and political philosophy, and biographies of various Muslim rulers known as '*Abqariyyāt*'.

'Audah, Abdul Qādir (d. 1374/1954)

One of the distinguished judges of Shariah courts at Egypt. He was among the prominent leaders of *al-Ikhwan al-Muslimun*. In response to his severe criticism to Egyptian government he was imprisoned by Gemal Abdul Nasser on the charges of plotting conspiracy to kill him in 1954 and was sentenced to death alongwith some other Ikhwan leaders. His books include : *al-Islam wa Awdhāa'una al-Siyasiyah* (Our Political Systems and Islam), *al-Tashr'i al-Jinãi al-Islami* (The Criminal Law of Islam), *al-Māl wa al-Ḥukm fi al-Islam* (The Finance and Polity in Islam) and *al-Islam bayna Jahl e Abnāihi wa 'Ijze Ulmaihi* (Islam between the Ignorance of Its Followers and withdrawal of its Scholars).

Asad, Muhammad (1900-1992)

Asad, who emerged as one of the towering personalities among the Muslim intellectuals of the twentieth century, a reverted Jew named Leopold Weiss was born on 12th July 1900, in the town of Lvov (Lemberg) in Eastern Galicia, then a part of Habsburg Empire. At the age of 22 he became a correspondent for the *Frank furter Zeitung* one of the most prestigious newspapers of Germany and Europe. In this position he travelled extensively in the Muslim countries between the Libyan desert and snow-covered peaks of Pamirs, between the Bosphorus and the Arabian Sea and in 1926 when he was in the Berlin subway embraced Islam; his wife Elsa also a few weeks later accepted this new religion. In 1927 both left for Makkah and spent almost six years in Arabia where they were warmly welcomed by the King Abdul Aziz Ibn Saud (d. 1953). His academic knowledge of classical Arabic- made easier by his familiarity with Hebrew and Aramaic – was further enhanced by his wide travels and public contacts. To study Muslim culture further east such as those of India, Eastern Turkestan, China and Indonesia, he departed for India in 1932. After the creation of Pakistan in 1947, Asad migrated to Pakistan to head the Middle East Division in the Foreign Ministry, here he capped his diplomatic career by serving as Pakistan's Minister Plenipotentiary to the United Nations but he resigned this position in 1952. He left New York also in 1955 and after some time he finally settled in Spain where he breathed his last in February 1992.

Asad's writings on Islam and Muslims extend over half a century, from the 1920s to the 1980s. His writings include: *Unromantisches Morgenland* (1925); *Islam at the Crossroads* (1934); *Sahih al-Bukhari: The Early years of Islam* (1935-38) (an annotated translation); *The Road to Mecca* (1954); *The Principles of State and Government in Islam* (1961); *The Message of the Qur'ān* (1964-1980) an interpretation of, and a commentary on, the Muslim Holy Book; and *This Law of Ours and Other Essays* (1987). Between 1946 and 1947 he also brought out a journal, *Arafāt: A Monthly Critique of Muslim Thought.* His first book was written in German Language and carried his original name Leopold Weiss. He wrote this book with Elsa, between March and October of that year he had visited Palestine, Transjordan, Syria, Egypt, Turkey as well as Malta. The book is illustrated by 59 photographs. His talent as a young writer in particular his powerfully evocative yet lyrical descriptions of countryside, moods and people is surprising. His Quranic interpretation and commentary *The Message* represents *magnum opus* of his works. A critical study of this work is made by Adbul Majid Khan in his Ph.D. thesis entitled "*A Critical Study of Muhammad Asad's The*

Message of the Qur'ān (1980), submitted in the Department of Islamic Studies, A.M.U., in 2005.

Tabātabāi, Muhammad Husayn (1903-1981)

Known to his contemporaries as 'Allama Tabatabai, one of the foremost Quranic commentators and traditional Persian philosophers of the twentieth century. Born to a well-known family of Shi'ite scholars of Tabriz in 1321/1903 he carried out his early studies in the city of his birth, and when some twenty years old, he set out for Najaf, Iraq, to persue some advanced studies in the juridical as well as philosophical sciences, reaching the highest level of *ijtihād* in both domains. It was also at this time that he underwent special training and was initiated into the inner dimension of Islam associated in Shi'ite circles with *irfān* (gnosis). In 1934, he returned to Tabriz, where he began to teach, but he did not become nationally known until the communist domination of the Iranian province of Azerbaijan forced to him to come to Tehran and Qom at the end of World War II. He spent the rest of his life in Qom with some days of each month being spent in Tehran. He devoted his time completely to teaching and writing and died in Qom in 1981.

At once a great teacher, saintly presence, and prolific writer, Tabatabai wrote a large number of works. Some of his works, some written in Arabic and others in Persian, deal with the *Qur'ān* and especially religious maters, the most important of which is the voluminous *al-Mizān*, written originally in Arabic and translated into Persian mostly under Tabatabai's direction. Among his religious works are *Qur'ān dar Islam* and *Shiah dar Islam* both of which have been translated into English. A second category includes his numerous philosophical works, ranging from his major philosophical opus, *Usul Falsafah-yi ri'alism*, to his last philosophical writings, *Bidayat al-Hikmah* and *Nihayat al-Hikmah*. Finally, there are the works dealing with current religious and philosophical debates, of which the most significant is *Musahabat ba Ustad Kurban*, containing some of his discussions with the French philosopher and Islamist, Henry Corbin.

al-Sharqawi, Mahmood (d. 1391/1971)

An Egyptian literary figure who administered al-Maktabah al-Azhariyah for a long time as librarian and assisted in the preparation of some of its indexes. A number of publications are credited to him. This includes: *al-Mujtama al-Arabi; Rihlah ma' Ibn Batutah*; *al-Undulus wa Ifriqiyah* and *Indonesia al-Mu'āsirah.*

Al-Sayeedi, Abdul Mut'aal (1313- after 1377/1894 – after 1958)

A reformist scholar belonged to Azhar, Egypt, was born in a village Kafr al-Najba of Daqhaliyah. His father died when he was an infant of one month only, and was educated and fully supported by his mother. He was graduated from Jam'i Ahmadi in 1336 A.H. and started his teaching career from the same institution and then was appointed as a teacher in the Faculty of Arabic Language at Azhar University in 1368 A.H. He wrote a number of books all published. His works included: *Naqd Nizam al-Talim al-Hadith li al-Azhar; Al-Ilm wa al-Ulama wa Nizām al-Talim; Fi Maidān al-Ijtihād; al-Waseet fi Tarikh al-Falsafah al-Islamiyah; al-Mujtahidun fi al-Islam; Tarikh al-Islah fi al-Azhar; al-Qur'ān wa al-Hukm al-Ist'imāri; al-Qadāya al-Kubra fi al-Islam; Limādha anā Muslim; al-Siyasah al-Islamiyah fi 'Ahd al-Nubuwah* and *al-Nazm al-Fanni fi al_Qur'ān* etc.

Haykal, Mohammad Husain (1305-1376/1888-1956)

He in original, Muhammad bin Husain bin Sālim Haykal, has been reputed internationally in modern Arabic journalism. A historian belonged to *al-Majm'a al-Lughawi*, a distinguished politician of Egypt born in the village Kafar Ghanam of Daqhaliyah, was graduated from the Law College Cairo in 1909 and received his Ph.D. in law from Sorbonne University, France in 1912. He initiated an office for Lawyers in Mansurah. Most of his writings were published in *al-Jareedah.* He supervised as editor in Chief the daily *al-Siyasah* (turned into weekly later on) and taught the subject of civil law in the Egyptian University. In politics he was a member of Dastur Party supporting S'ad Zaghlul and his party. He was given the portfolio of education minister two times and the chairmanship of the Senate (1945-

50). His books include: *Hayat Muhammad; Fi Manzil al-Wahy; Thawrat al-Adab*; *al-Siddique Abu Bakr*; *al-Faruque Umar* (2 Volumes); *Asharatu Ayyām fi Sudan*; *Waladi*; *Tarājim Sharqiyah wa Gharabiyah*; John Jock Rousseau; *Zaynab*; *al-Ambraturiyah al-Islamiyah.* He died in Cairo. His most popular work, however, was his *Hayat Muhammad* (The Life of Muhammad) which was translated into English by Islamil Raji al-Faruqi in 1976. In his book the author examined all the extant Sirah and *hadith* literature with the eye of an objective, scientific and critical scholar. He weighed the evidence for every claim previously made against the trustworthy source-evidence and daringly reported only what such evidence warranted. His object, which he realised admirably in this work, was two fold: first, to put in the hands of contemporary Muslim, a biography which reveals the career of the Prophet in the full light of historic reality; second, to bring out the essence of Islam as exemplified in the life of the greatest Muslim, to show the relevance of Islam to modern life, and to contrast the Islamic message with the claims of modern western ideologies.

Khallāf, Abdul Wahāb (1305-1375/1888-1956)

Abdul Wahab bin Abdul Wāhid Khallāf, an Egyptian jurist, was the teacher of Islamic law in the Law College, an inspector for sometime in the Shariah Departments and one of the members of the prestigious academy *Majm'a al-Lughah al-Arabiyah.* Born in the village Kafr al-Zayat, graduated from Shariah College, Cairo in 1912 and taught in the same in 1915. In 1935 he was appointed as assistant lecturer for Shariah in the Law College of Cairo University, then as lecturer and worked till 1948. He died in Cairo. His books included: *Ahkām al-Waqf fi al-Shariah al-Islamiah; Nur min al-Qur'ān al-Karim; Ilm Usul al-Fiqh; Nurun ala Nur; al-Siyasah al-Shar'yiah; Tarikh al-Tashri al-Islami; al-Ijtihad wa al-Taqlid; Ahkam al-Mawarith; al-Ahwal al-Shakhsiyah* etc.

Enāyat, Hamid

Hamid Enayat was a professor of Political Science from Tehran University, where he was the chairman of the Department of Politics from 1971 to 1976. He also taught Islamic Political

Thought and Institutions at Khartoum University, Sudan. Before his death, he was a fellow of St. Antony's College and used to lecture on Modern Middle Eastern History at Oxford University in 1980. In addition to translating into Persian numerous basic works in his field, such as Aristotle's Politics and Hegel's Reason in History, this scholar of Iranian origin, has also written a number of books in Persian, and articles in English on political and ideological trends in the Muslim world. His most important work, however, is his *Modern Islamic Political Thought (The Response of the Shi'i and Sunni Muslims to the Twentieth Century)* published in 1982 by The Macmillan Press Ltd. This book describes and interprets the major political ideas among Muslims particularly those expressed by the Egyptians and Iranians – but also a few writers and thinkers in Pakistan, India, Lebanon, Syria and Iraq. The introduction of the book outlines the way in which traditional heritage has affected the development of modern ideas, and made them cogent and appealing to a modern but also religious-minded audience. This is followed by a study of the political differences between the two main schools, Shi'ism and Sunnism, and especially on the two-fold process of conflict and concord between them. The main intention is to show that the relationship between the two had been slowly changing in recent times, and least in the realm of political doctrines, from confrontation to cross-sectarian fertilisation. This approach later re-emerges, at several other points of the book, with more examples of the implicit or explicit convergence between the two. The remaining chapters of the book are devoted to two basic themes and their ramifications: the concept of the Islamic state from the time it was received after the abolition of the caliphate in Turkey in the twenties till the late seventies, and the Muslim response to the challenge of the alien, modern ideologies of nationalism, democracy and socialism.

al-Albani, Nāseruddin (1331-1420/1914-1999)

The most authentic traditionist (*muhaddith*) of the modern world Abu Abdur Rahman Muhammad Nāseruddin, son of Nuh Nijati al-Albani, popularly known as 'Allama Albani', was born in a village of Ottoman Albania. His father, a graduate of Shariah Institute of Ottoman Astana (now Istanbul) was a source of religious knowledge and guidance in his homeland, and migrated to Syria and permanently settled down in Damascus. Shaykh Albani completed his education from his father and his scholar-friends as Shaykh Sayeed Burhani, Shaykh Mohammad Mubarak. He initiated his professional career as watch repairer. He started delivering lectures two times in a week emphasising on strict adherence to *hadith* as opposed to the sayings of jurists and founders of various schools. Later on he was appointed as lecturer of *hadith* in Jamiah Islamiah, Madinah in 1381 A.H. and he resigned his post in 1383 A.H. Due to political and sectarian oppositions he used to move from Damascus to Oman, then to Beirut and United Arab Emirates and finally back to Oman. He was honoured by the King Khalid bin Abdul Aziz of Saudi Arabia as a member of Upper Council of Madinah University in 1395 A.H. and was graced with the King Faisal Award in 1419 A.H. For the purpose of reform and revival of pure Islamic teachings he travelled across the Muslim world and fully attended the seminars, conferences, public meetings and academic debates, all for the sake of reviving the true Islamic approach toward the Holy *Qur'ān* and *hadith.* These lectures, legal decrees and sermons are recorded in more than seven thousand cassettes and are estimated to be compiled in more than forty volumes, perhaps under the supervision of *Dar al-Ma'ārif*, Reyadh.

Being the most distinguished *muhaddith* of the modern world, who edited, compiled and critically evaluated the *hadith* literature. His academic endeavours exceeded the hundred; only some have got published, the others are preserved in the form of manuscripts. Shaykh Albani was treated by the scholars as the walking encyclopaedia of *hadith* criticism. His books included: *Irwa al-Ghalil fi Takhrij Ahadith Manār al-Sabil; Ahkam al-Janāiz wa Bid 'auha; Sifat Salāt al-Nabi; Nasb al-Majāniq fi Nasf Qissat al-Gharaniq; Adāb al-Zafāf fi al-Sunnah al-Muttahhirah; Ghāyat al-Marām fi Takhrij Ahadith al-Halal wa al-Haram; Tahdhir al-sājid min Ittikhāz al-Qubur Masājid; al-Tawassul: Anwa'uhu wa Ahkāmuhu; Hijāb al-Mar'ah al-Muslimah fi al-Kitab wa al-Sunnah; Sahih Sunan Abi Dawud; Dhaeef Sunan Abi Dawud; Sahih Sunan al-Tirmidhi; Dhaeef Sunan al-Tirmidhi; Sahih Sunan al-Nsaai; Dhaeef Sunan al-*

Nasai; Sahih Sunan Ibn Majah; Dhaeef Sunan Ibn Majah; Sahih al-Jam'i al-Sagheer wa Dhiyadatuhu; Dhaeef al-Jam'i al-Sagheer wa Dhiyadatuhu; Sahih al-Targhib wa al-Tarhib; Dhaeef al-Targhib wa al-Tarhib; Sahih al-Adab al-Mufrad; Dhaeef al-Adab al-Mufrad; Mukhtasar Sahih al-Bukhari. The magnum opus of his works however, is his series of authentic and forged or fabricated *ahadith* as estimated and evaluated critically by him known as, *Silsilah al-Ahadith al-Sahihah* and *Silsilah al-Ahadith al-Dhaeefah wa al-Maudhu'ah*.

al-Booti, Syeed Ramadhan(Dr.)

Professor in Shariah College, Damascus University, a distinguished scholar and jurist who emphasized on the need of ijtihād to be observed by Ulama while legislating on a new issue keeping in view the main objectives of Shariah and the public interests. His books include: *Dhawābit al-Maslaha fi al-Shariah al-Islamiah; Kubra al-Yaqiniyāt al-Kawniyah; Tajribat al-Tarbiyat al-Islamiah fi Mizān al-Bahth; Manjah Tarbawi Freed fi al-Qur'ān; al-Islam wa Mushkilāt al-Shabāb* and the most important *Fiqh al-Sirah* which is also translated into Urdu by Dr. Muhammad Raziul Islam Nadvi and published in 2003 by Markazi Maktaba Islamic Publishers, New Delhi.

al-Qaradhawi, Yusuf (b. 1926)

The most respectable religious scholar and reformist recognised equally in both the circles of Arab politicians and Ulama and entitled as *mufti al-Jihād*, was born in Egypt. He was graduated from the Faculty of Usul al-Din, of Azhar University in 1953; in 1958, he received the Diploma in Arabic Language and Literature and in 1973 he was awarded Ph.D. degree on the topic of *Role of Zakah in the Solution of Social Problems* from the same faculty. He was the principal of Shariah College in Qatar University for a long time, and occupies now the prestigious post of Director, Centre of Research in Sunnah and Sirah studies in the same University. Being a sincere preacher, moderate and well-balanced Mufti and orator, he visit all the Islamic centres across the Muslim world and attend the seminars, public meetings, conferences in both the Muslim and non-Muslim circles throughout the world. He has always been very sympathetic to the Islamic revivalist movements across the globe and at the same time very realistic taking into active consideration the grossroot causes of the decline of Muslims. He has not been in favour to oppose and condemn onesidedly the misguided Muslim youth—frustrated depressed and sometime turned into terrorists – he is rather supportive to Islamic cause, sympathetic to new generation and its issues and problems and tries his best to guide it in the true, balanced and moderate direction. Due to his sincere efforts, dedication and commitment to Islam he is the most acceptable figure among the Ulama of the present day Muslim world. His *Fatāwa Mu'āsirah* (2 volumes) were translated by Zahid Aghar Falahi and were published from New Delhi. His other works include: *Fiqh al-Zakah; al-Halal wa al-harām fi al-Islam; Mushkilat al-Faqr wa Kaifa 'Aalajaha al-Islam; al-Sabr fi al-Qur'ān al-Karim; al-Imān wa al-Hayat; al-Tarbiyat al-Islamiyah wa Madrasat Hassan al-Banna; Kaifa Nata'āmal m'a al-Sunnah.* All of these works are translated into various languages including Urdu and English.

Umari, Jalaluddin Sayyid (b . 1935)

One of the authoritative Islamic scholars and activists in India, was born in Trupati, Tamil Nadu. He obtained his oriental degrees of Alimiyat and Fadhilat from Jamia Darus Salam, Omarabad, Tamil Nadu; Munshi Fādhil privately from Madras University and then B.A. (English only) from A.M.U., Aligarh. Being a most respectable scholar representing the moderate approach and modern vision of Islam he occupies various key-posts fully involved in all the academic and administrative issues: vice-amir of Jamaat Islami of India; member of both the *Majlis Shura* and *Majlis Numāindagān* of the Jamaat; *Shaykh al-Jamia* of Jamiatul Falah, Azamgarh; the patron of Sirajul Uloom Niswān College, Aligarh; Chairman, Idarah Tahqiq wa Tasneef Islami Aligarh; editor *Tahqiqāt Islami* quarterly, Aligarh and also Chairman, Tasneefi Academy, Jamaat Islami of India, New Delhi. His books included: *'Awrat Islami Muashare Mein; Khuda wa Rasul Ka Tasawwur Islami Taleemāt Mein Musalman Awrat ke Huquq aur Un Par Ietirazāt Ka Jaizah; Maroof wa Munkar* also translated in Arabic by Dr. Mohammad Ajmal Islahi and in English by Ameen Ashraf; *Ghayr Muslimon se*

Talluqāt Aur Unke Huquq; Islam-Insani Huquq Ka Pasbān; Sihhat wa Marz Aur Islami Taleemāt; Islam Mein Khidmat Khalq Ka Tasawwur and *Islam Ki Dawat*. The author portrays a humane, rational Islam that may have coped with the modern challenges of the society. His approach is traditional but not sectarian or rigid. Basically a hanafid scholar but tries to accommodate other schools of jurisprudence in a broader spectrum. His several books are translated into English and some local languages. His specialisation and keen interest in the family system of Islam and faminists' issues places him almost in an unequated position among the Ulama of Indo-Pak subcontinent.

*****

LIST OF QUR'ANIC VERSES

Those who hearken to their Lord, and establish regular prayer; who (conduct) their affairs by mutual consultation; who spend out of what we bestow on them for sustenance. [42: 38] 16, 120

O ye who believe! If you obey the Unbelievers, they will drive you back on your heals, and ye will turn back (from Faith) to your own loss. [3: 149] 1

She said: Ye chiefs! Advise me in (this) my affair: no affair have I decided except in your presence. [27: 32] 18

It is not fitting for an Apostle that he should have prisoners of war until he hath thoroughly subdued the land. Ye look for the temporal goods of this world; but God looketh to the Hereafter: and God is Exalted in might, Wise. [8: 67] 27, 101

Whatever ye cut down (O ye Muslims!) the tender palm trees, or ye left them standing on their roots, it was by leave of God, and in order that He might cover with shame the rebellious transgressors. [59:5] 31

Those who brought forward the lie are a body among yourselves; think it not to be an evil to you; on the contrary it is good for you: to every man among them (will come the punishment) of the sin that he earned, and to him who took on himself the lead among them, will be a penalty grievous. Why did not the Believers – men and women – when ye heard of the affair, - put the best construction on it in their own minds and say, "This charge is an obvious lie"? [24: 11-12] 36

It is part of the Mercy of God that thou dost deal gently with them. Wert thou severe or harsh-hearted, they would have broken away from about thee: so pass over (their faults), and ask for (God's) forgiveness for them; and consult them in affairs (of moment). Then, when thou hast taken a decision, put thy trust in God. For God loves those who put their trust (in Him). [3: 159] 15, 120, 124, 128, 156, 212, 316

The answer of the Believers, when summoned to God and His Apostle, in order that he may judge between them, is no other than this: they say "we hear and we obey": it is such as those that will attain felicity. [24: 51] 1

Nor does he say (aught) of (his own) desire. It is no less than inspiration sent down to him. [53: 3-4] 1

Muhammad is no more than an Apostle: many were the Apostles that passed away before him. If he died or were slain, will ye then turn back on your heels? If any did turn back on his heels, not the least harm will he do to God; but God (on the other hand) will swiftly reward those who (serve him) with gratitude. [3: 144] 1

And God hath full power and control over His affairs; but most among mankind know it not. [12: 21] 112

That (comes) of the Grace of God to us and to mankind: yet most men are not grateful. [12: 38] 112

That is the right religion, but most men understand not. [12: 40] 112

The Hour will certainly come: there is no doubt,

yet most men believe not. [40: 59] 112

But most of them follow nothing but fancy: truly fancy can be of no avail against truth. [10: 36] 112

They are not the ones to believe unless it is in God's plan. But most of them ignore (the truth). [6: 111] 112

They follow nothing but conjecture: they do nothing but lie. [6: 116] 112

It is blasphemers who invent a lie against God; but most of them lack wisdom. [5: 106] 112

(David) said: "He was undoubtedly wronged thee in demanding thy (single) ewe to be added to his (flock of) ewes: truly many are the partners in (business) who wrong each other. [38: 24] 112

It is not fitting for a believer, man or woman, when a matter has been decided by God and His Apostle, to have any option about their decision: if anyone disobeys God and His Apostle, he is indeed on a clearly wrong path. [33: 36] 1

When there comes to them some matter touching (public) safety or fear, they divulge it. If they had only referred it to the Apostle, or to those charged with authority among them, the proper investigators would have tested it from them (direct). Were it not for the Grace and Mercy of God unto you, all but a few of you would have fallen into the clutches of Satan. [4: 83] 177

God doth command you to render back your trusts to those to whom they are due; and when ye judge between man and man, that ye judge with justice: verily how excellent is the teaching which He giveth you! For God is He Who heareth and seeth all things. [4: 58] 190

O mankind! We created you from a single (pair) of a male and female, and made you into nations and tribes, that ye may know each other (not that ye may despise each other. Verily the most honoured of you in the sight of God is (he who is) the most righteous of you. And God has full knowledge and is well acquainted (with all things) [49: 13] 190, 196, 259

Their Prophet said to them: "God hath appointed Talut as King over you". They said: "How can he exercise authority over us when we are better fitted than he to exercise authority, and he is not even gifted with wealth in abundance". He said: "God has chosen him above you, and hath gifted him abundantly with knowledge and bodily prowess: God granteth his authority to whom He pleaseth. God careth for all, and He knoweth all things." [2: 247] 190

And keep thy soul content with those who call on their Lord morning and evening, seeking His Face; and lét not thine eyes pass beyond them, seeking the pomp and glitter of this life; nor obey any whose heart We have permitted to neglect the remembrance of us, one who follows his own desires, whose case has gone beyond all bounds. [18: 28] 190

O ye who believe! When ye are told to make room in the assemblies, (spread out and) make room: (ample) room will God provide for you. And when you are told to rise up, rise up: God will rise up to (suitable) ranks (and degrees), Those of you who believe and who have been granted knowledge. And God is well-acquainted with all ye do. [58: 11] 197

Men are the protectors and maintainers of women, because God has given the one more (strength) than the other, and because they support them from their means. Therefore the righteous women are devoutly obedient, and guard in (the husband's) absence what God would have them guard. [4: 34] 221, 226-227

And women shall have rights similar to the rights against them, according to what is equitable; but men have a degree (of advantage) over them. And God is Exalted in power, Wise. [2: 228] 223, 257-258

And in no wise covet those things in which God hath bestowed His gifts more freely on some of you than on others: to men is allotted what they earn, and to women what they earn: but ask God of his bounty. For God hath full knowledge of all things. To (benefit) everyone appointed sharers and heirs to property left by parents and relatives. To those, also, to whom your right hand was pledged, give their due portion. For truly God is witness to all things. [4: 32-33] 224

O consorts of the Prophet! You are not like any of the (other) women: if ye do fear (God), be not to complaisant of speech, lest one in whose heart is a disease should be moved with desire: but speak ye a speech (that is) just. And stay quietly in your houses, and make not a dazzling display, like that of the former Times of Ignorance; and establish regular prayer, and give regular charity; and obey God and His Apostle. And God only wishes to remove all abomination from you, ye

Members of the Family, and to make you pure 225, 226
and spotless. [33: 32-33]

O ye who believe! Enter not the Prophet's houses, - until leave is given you, - for a meal, (and then) not (so early as) to wait for its preparation: but when ye are invited, enter; and when ye have taken your meal, disperse, without seeking familiar talk. Such (behaviour) annoys the Prophet: he is ashamed to dismiss you, but God is not ashamed (to tell you) the truth. And when ye ask (his ladies) for anything ye want, ask them from before a screen: that makes for greater purity for your hearts and for theirs. Nor is it right for you that ye should annoy God's Apostle, or that ye should marry his widows after him at anytime. Truly such a thing is in God's
sight an enormity. [33: 53] 225, 226-
227, 288

And say to the believing women that they should lower their gaze and guard their modesty: that they should not display their beauty and ornaments except what (must ordinarily) appear these of; that they should draw their veils over
their bosoms. [24: 31] 228

O ye who believe! When ye deal with each other in transactions involving future obligations in a fixed period of time, reduce them to writing. Let a scribe write down faithfully as between the parties: Let not the scribe refuse to write: as God has taught him, so let him write. Let him who incurs liability dictate, but let him fear his Lord God, and not diminish aught of what he owes. If the part liable is mentally deficient, or weak or unable himself to dictate, let his guardian dictate faithfully. And get two witnesses out of your men, and if there are not two men then a man and two women, such as ye choose for witnesses so that if one of them errs, the other can remind her. The witnesses should not refuse when they are called on (for evidence). Disdain not to reduce to writing (your contract) for a future period, whether it be small or big. [2: 282] 231

We have honoured the sons of Adam; provided them with transport on land and sea; given them for sustenance things good and pure; and conferred on them special favours above a great part of our creation. [17: 70] 258

The believers, men and women, are protectors one of another; they enjoin what is just, and forbid what is evil: they observe regular prayers, practice regular charity and obey God and His Apostle. Of them God will pour His Mercy: for God is Exalted in power, Wise. [9: 71] 258

O mankind! Reverence you Guardian-Lord, who created you from a single person, created, of like nature, his mate, and from them his twain scattered (like seeds) countless men and women; - reverence God, through whom ye demand your (mutual) rights, and (reverence) the wombs (that bore you): for God ever watches over you. [4: 1] 259-260

By (the mystery of) the creation of male and female; verily (the ends) ye strive for are diverse. So he who gives (in charity) and fears (God), and (in all sincerity) testifies to the best, we will indeed make smooth for him the path to bliss. [92: 3-7] 260

She said: "ye chief! Advise me in (this) my affair: no affair have I decided except in your presence, "They said: "We are enduced with strength, and given to vehement war: but the command is with thee; so consider what thou wilt command." She said: "Kings when they enter a country, despoil it, and make the noblest of its people its meanest. Thus do they behave. [27: 32-34] 261

O Prophet! When believing women come to thee to take the oath of fealty to thee, that they will not associate in worship any other thing whatever with God, that they will not steal, that they will not commit adultery (or fornication), that they will not kill their children, that they will not utter slander, intentionally forging falsehood, and that they will not disobey thee in any just matter, then do thou receive their fealty and pray to God for the forgiveness (of their sins): for God is Oft-Forgiving, Most Merciful. [60: 12] 263

O ye who believe! Take not into your intimacy those outside your ranks: they will not fail to corrupt you. They only desire your ruin: rank hatred has already appeared from their mouths: what their hearts conceal is far worse. We have made plain to you the Signs, if ye have wisdom. [3: 118] 274

O ye who believe! Take not the Jews and the Christians for your friends and protectors: they are but friends and protectors to each other. And he amongst you that turns to them (for friendship) is of them. Verily God guideth not a people unjust. Those in whose hearts is a disease – thou seest how eagerly they run about amongst them, saying: "We do fear lest a change of fortune bring us disaster." Ah! Perhaps God will (thee) victory, or a decision according His Will. Then will they repent of the thoughts which they secretly harboured in their hearts. [5: 54-55] 274

And he (Sulayman) took a muster of the birds; and he said: "Why is it I see not the Hoopoe? Or is he among the absentees: I will certainly punish him with a severe penalty, or execute him, unless he bring me a clear reason (for absence)".

But the Hoopoe tarried not far: he (came up and) said: "I have compassed (territory) which thou hast not compassed, and I have come to thee from Saba with tidings true.

"I found (there) a woman ruling over them and provided with every requisite; and she has a magnificient throne. I found her and her people worshipping the sun besides God: Satan had made their deeds seem pleasing in their eyes, and has Kept them away from the Path – so they receive no guidance, (Kept them away from the Path) that they should not worship God, who brings to light what is hidden in the heavens and the earth, and knows what ye hide and what ye reveal. God! – there is no god but He! – Lord of the Thorne, Supreme!"

(Sulayman) said: "Soon shall we see whether thou hast told the truth or lied! Go thou, with this letter of mine, and deliver it to them: then draw back from them, and (wait to) see what answer they return."

(The Queen Bilqis) said: "Ye chief! There is – delivered to me – a letter worthy of respect. It is from Sulayman, and is (as follows): "In the name of God, Most Gracious, Most Merciful: "Be ye not arrogant against me, but come to me in submission (to the true religion)."

She said: "Ye chiefs! Advise me in (this) my affair: no affair have I decided except in your presence."

They said: "We are enduced with strength, and given to vehement war: but the command is with thee; so consider what thou wilt command."

She said: "Kings, when they enter a country, despoit it, and make the noblest of its people its meanest, thus do they behave. But I am going to send him a present and (wait) to se with what (answer) return (my) ambassadors."

Now when (the embassy) came to Sulayman, he said: "Will ye give me abundance in wealth? But that which God has given me is better than that He has given you! Nay it is ye who rejoice in your gift! Go back to them and be sure we shall come to them with such hosts as they will never be able to meet: we shall expel them from there in disgrace, and they will feel humbled (indeed)."

He said to his own men: "Ye chiefs! Which of you can bring me her throne before they come to me in submission?"

Said a powerful jinn: "I will bring it to thee before thou rise from thy Council: indeed I have full strength for the purpose, and may be trusted."

Said one who had knowledge of the Books: "I will bring it to thee within the twinkling of an eye!" Then when (Sulayman) saw it placed firmly before him, he said: "This is by the grace of my Lord! – to test me whether I am grateful or ungrateful! And if any is grateful truly his gratitude is (a gain) for his own soul; but if any is ungrateful, truly my Lord is Free of all Needs, Supreme in Honour."

He said: "Transform her thorne out of all recognition by her: let us see whether she is guided (to the truth) or is one of those who receive no guidance."

So when she arrived, she was asked, "Is this thy throne?" She said "It was just like this; and Knowledge was bestowed on us in advance of this, and we have submitted to God".

And he diverted her from the worship of others besides God: for she was (sprung) of a people that had no faith.

She was asked to enter the lofty Palace: but when she saw it, she thought it was a lake of water, and she (tucked up her skirts), uncovering her legs. He said: "This is but a palace paved smooth with slabs of glass." She said: "O my Lord! I have indeed wronged my soul: I do (now) submit (in Islam), with Sulayman, to the Lord of the worlds." [27: 20-44] 289, 291-295

God has indeed heard (and accepted) the statement of the woman who pleads with thee concerning her husband and carries her complaint (in prayer) to God: and God (always) hears the arguments between both sides among you: for God hears and sees (all things). If any men among you divorce their wives by *Zihār* (calling them mothers), they cannot be their mothers except those who gave them birth. And in fact they use words (both) iniquitous and false: but truly God is one that blots out (sins) and forgives (again and again). [58: 1-2] 304

"Those who brought forward the lie are a body among yourselves: think it not to be an evil to you: on the contrary it is good for you: to every man among them (will come the punishment) of the sin that he earned, and to him who took on himself the lead among them, will be a Penalty grievous.

"Why did not the believers – men and women – when ye heard of the affair, - put the best construction on it in their own minds and say "This (charge) is an obvious lie?"

"Why did they not bring four witnesses to prove it? When they had not brought the witnesses, such men, in the sight of God (stand forth) themselves as liars!

"Were it not the grace and mercy of God on you in this world and the Hereafter, a grievous penalty would have seized you in that ye rushed glibly into this affair.

"Behold, ye received it on your tongues and said out of your mouths things of which ye had no knowledge; and ye thought it to be a light matter, while it was most serious in the sight of God."

"And why did ye not, when ye heard it, say? – "It is not right of us to speak of this: Glory to God! This is most serious slander!"

"God doth admonish you, that ye may never repeat such (conduct), if ye are (true) believers. And God makes the Signs plain to you: for God is full of Knowledge and wisdom."

"Those who love (to see) scandal published broadcast among the believers, will have a grievous penalty in this life and in the Hereafter: God knows and ye know not."

"Were it not for the grace and mercy of God on you, and that God is full of Kindness and mercy (ye would be ruined indeed). [24: 11-20] 296-297

LIST OF THE PROPHETIC TRADITIONS

bestows on him a righteous vizier who reminds him of his neglect and once he is reminded of it, helps him and when Allah does not wish for the welfare of *amir*, He gives him a wicked vizier who does not remind him of his neglect and does not help him even when he remembers what he has neglected".

Prophet Muhammad (SAW) once said to K'ab bin 'Ajra "May Allah save you from the mischief of the reign of foolish *amirs*". To the question to K'ab as to what he meant by the expression 'reign of foolish *amirs*', the Prophet (SAW) replied: "After me, the reign of power will come in the hands of people who will not follow my practices and will not read the straight path shown by me. A person who expresses himself in agreement with their wrong practices and participates in perpetrating cruelty will have nothing to do with me, nor would be able to be present by my side at the Cistern on the Day of Judgement. But a person who does not corroborate their wrong pronouncements and does not support them in their tyrannical attitude will be associated with me. He will be able to come to my Cistern on the Day of Judgement." 188-189

"A person who respects innovators (in religious affairs) is a participant in the dismantling of Islam". 191

"By Allah we do not appoint any person to a post of our government who has applied for it or craves it". 191

"According to us, the most dishonest person amongst you is one who himself desires to have a post." 191

Once the Prophet (SAW) said that he had not seen anyone who was more deficient in mind and religiosity than women who can impair the wisdom 230 of even a sane person.

Some Ladies asked the Prophet (SAW) what he meant by saying that they were inferior in matters of wisdom and religion. He asked them whether or not it was true that the evidence of a woman is deemed to be less than half that of a man. When they replied in the affirmative, he said that this was the proof of the inferiority of their minds. He then asked them whether or not it is true that they did not perform *salah* nor did they observe fasts when they were menstruating. When the ladies again replied in the affirmative, the Prophet (SAW) said that this showed that they were inferior in matters of religion". 230-231

"Consult women but not heed their advice". 235

"Obedience to women has to be regretted." 235

"Men have become victims of destruction whenever they have heeded women." 235

"Oppose women since opposing them brings blessing". 235

"None of you ought to do any thing before consulting some one. If one does not find a man to consult he should consult a woman. But he should not heed her advice, since not heeding would bring him the blessing." 235

"When the worst amongst you become *amirs*, when the wealthy in your midst become miserly and when your affairs are put in the charge of women, the bell of the earth would be better than its back." 236

"A nation would never be prosper which has 237-238

handed over its affairs to a woman."

"A person brings a dead piece of land to life will be its owner". 249

"He who obeys me obeys Allah (SWT) and he who disobeys me disobeys Allah (SWT); and he who obeys the *amir* obeys me, and he who disobeys the *amir* disobeys me. Behold, the leader (*imam*) is but a shield from behind which the people fight and by which they protect themselves." 317

"Verily each of you is a shepherd, and each of you is responsible for his flock. The leader who is placed over the people is a shepherd responsible for his flock". 318

"He who has pledged allegiance to an *imam* giving him his hand and the fruit of his heart, shall obey him if he can (as long as he is no ordered to commit a sin), and if another person tries to usurp the *imam*'s rights, smite that other person's neck." 318

"If Allah means well with the *amir*, He provides for him a trustworthy assistant (*wazir*) to remind him whenever he forgets, and to help in whenever he remembers. And if Allah does not mean it well with him, He provides for him a bad assistant, who does not remind him whenever he forgets and does not help him whenever he remembers." 320

Abu Hurairah said to Abu Bakr: How can you start a jihad against these people since the Prophet of Allah has said that he has been asked by Allah to fight against people till they affirmed their faith in His unity. Once they have done so, the security of their life and property is guaranteed, unless it becomes necessary to do so in the cause of Islam and they are accountable only to Allah". Abu Bakr replied: By Allah, if they would refuse to pay a rope already being payed to the Prophet, I will certainly fight against them on the refusal of that. The Zakah is a due in the wealth. By Allah I will fight against those who would distinguish *salah* from Zakah (as both are obligatory)". Umar said spontaneously that he was convinced that Abu Bakr was right. 57-59

Narrates Aisha, the mother of the faithful believers: the Commandment of the Divine Revelation to Allah's Prophet was in the form of good dreams which came true like day light, and then the love of seclusion was bestowed upon him. He used to go in seclusion in the cave of Hira where he used to worship (Allah alone) continuously for many days before his desire to see his family. He used to take with him the journey food for the stay and then come back to (his wife) Khadija to take his food likewise again till suddenly the Truth descended upon him while he was in the cave of Hira. The angel came to him and asked him to read. The Prophet (SAW) replied, "I do not know how to read". The Prophet (SAW) added, "The angel caught me (forcefully) and pressed me so hard that I could not bear it any more. He then released me and again asked me to read and I replied, "I do not know how to read. Thereupon he caught me again and pressed me a second time till I could not bear it any more. He then released me and again asked me to read but again I replied, "I do not know how to read (or what shall I read?)' Thereupon he caught me for the third time and pressed me and then released me and said, "Read in the name of your Lord, who has created (all the exists); has created man from a clot. Read and your Lord is the Most Generous" (96: 1-3). Then Allah's Apostle returned with the Revelation and with his heart beating severely. Then he went to Khadija bint Khuwaylid and said, "Cover me!" They covered him till his fear was over and after that he told her everything that had happened and said, "I fear that something may happen to me", Khadija replied:

> "Never! By Allah, Allah will never disgrace you. You keep good relations with your Kith and Kin, help the poor and the destitute, serve your gests generously and assist the deserving calamity – afflicted one."

Khadija then accompanied him to her cousin Warqua bin Nawfal bin Asad bin Abdul 'Uzza, who during the pre-Islamic period became a Christian and used to write. 300-302

According to Ibn Abbas, the Prophet (SAW) once said that the *Ummah* was blessed by the Hand of Allah (SWT). 135

BIBLIOGRAPHY

References (Arabic)

Al-Aalusi al-Baghdadi, Abul Fazl shahabuddin Syed Mahmood, Rooh al-Maani fi Tafsir al-Qur'ān al-Azeem wa al-Sabe al-Mathani, Dar Ihya al-Turath al-Arabi, Beirut (n.d.).

Abdul Hameed, Ibrahim, Dr., Nizam al-Qaza fi al-Islam (Muhazaraat), Qism al-Siyasah al-Sharyiah, Al-Diraasaat al-Ulya, Kulliyah al-Shariah wa al-Qanoon, Jamea al-Azhar, Egypt. (n.d.)

Abdul Khaliq, Abdul Rahman, Al-Shura fi Zill Nizam al-Hukm al-Islami, Al-Dar al-Salafiyah, Kuwait, 1975.

Abdus Salam, Farooque, Al-Islam wa al-Ahzab al-Siyasiyah, Maktab Qalyub li al-Tibā'ah wa al-Nashr, Egypt, 1978.

Abduh, Mohammad, Al-Islam wa al-Nasraniyah ma al-Ilm wa al-Madniyah, Maktabah Mohd. Ali Sabih, Egypt, 1954.

Abu Daud, Sulayman b. al-Ashas, Sunan, Cairo, 1952.

Abu Ubaid Qasim b. Sallam, Kitab al-Amwal, Cairo, 1353 A.H.

Abu Yusuf, Yaqub bin Ibrahim, Kitab al-Kharaj, Fourth Edition, Egypt, 1392 A.H.

Abu Zahrah, Mohammad, Al-Mujtama al-Insani fi Zill al-Islam, Dar al-Fikr, Beirut, 1970.

____________________, Tarikh al-Mazahib al-Islamiyah fi al-Siyasah wa al-Aqaid, Dar al-Fikr al-Arabi, Cairo, (n.d.)

Al-Adwi, Ibrahim Ahmad, Dr., Al-Nuzum al-Islamiyah: Muqawwamatuha al-Fikriyyah wa Muassasatuha al-Tanfeeziyah fi Sadr al-Islam wa al-Asr al-Umavi, Maktaba Anglo al-Misriyah, Egypt, 1972.

Ahmad, Fazil Zaki, Dr., Al-Fikr al-Siyasi al-Arabi bain Maazeeh wa Hazirih, Dar al-Tabe wa al-Nashr al-Ahliyah, Baghdad, 1971.

Ahmad, Fuad Abdul Munim, Dr., Mabda al-Musawat fi al-Islam ma Muqaranah bi al-Dimiqratiyāh al-Hadithah, Muassash al-Thaqafah al-Jameiyah, Egypt, 1972.

Al-Ajlooni, Ismail Mohammad, Kashf al-Khifa wa Muzeel al-Albas amma Ishtahara min al-Ahadith ala Alsinah al-Nass, Dar Ihya al-Turath al-Arabi, Beirut, 1351 A.H.

Al-Albani, Mohammad Naseruddin, Silsilah al-Ahadith al-Dhaeefah wa al-Mauzuah wa Athruha al-Sayye fi al-Ummah, Al-Maktab al-Islami, Damascus.

Al-Aqqad, Abbas, Al-Dimiqratiyah fi al-Islam, Dar al-Maarif, Egypt, Fourth Edition, 1971.

Al-Arabi, Mohammad Abdullah, Dr., Al-Tanzeem al-Hadith li al-Duwal al-Islamiyah bain al-Shariah wa al-Qanun, Dar al-Maarif, Egypt, 1974.

____________________, Nizam al-Hukm fi al-Islam, Dar al-Fikr, Beirut, 1968.

Audah, Abdul Qadir, Al-Islam wa Awdhauna al-Siyasiyah, second edition, Beirut, 1967.

Bablali, Mahmood, Al-Shura fi al-Islam, Dar al-Irshad, Beirut, 1968.

Badawi, M. Taha, Haqq Muqawamah al-Hukumaat al-Jaairah, Dar al-Kitab al-Arabi, Cairo.

Al-Baghawi, Abu Mohammad al-Husain bin Maswood al-Farra, Maalim al-Tanzeel fi al-Tafsir, Tabaah al-Maktab al-Tijariyah, Egypt.

Al-Bahi, Ahmad Abdul Munim, Dr., Nizam al-Hukm fi al-Islam (Lectures) Al-Diraasaat al-Ulya, Kulliyah al-Shariah wa al-Qanoon, Jamea al-Azhar, Egypt. (n.d.)

Al-Baihaqi, Ahmad bin Husain b. Ali, Al-Sunan al-Kubra, Matabaah Dairah al-Maarif al-Uthmaniyah, Hyderabad, 1354 A.H.

Al-Baladhuri, Ahmad b. Yahya, Futuh al-Buldan, Dar al-Nashr le al-Jamein, Cairo, 1957.

Al-Bukhari, Mohammad bin Ismail, Al-Jame al-Sahih, Cairo, 1938.

Dabboos, Salahuddin, Dr., Al-Khalifah Tauliyatuh wa Azluh: Dirasah Muqaranah, Muassasah al-Thaqafah al-Jameiyah, Alexandria. (n.d.)

Al-Dardiri, Hani Ahmad, al-Tashree Bain al-Fikrain al-Islami wa al-Dusturi, Al-Haiah al-Misriyah al-Aammah, Egypt, 1976.

Al-Darmi, Abu Mohammad Abdullah, Al-Sunan, al-Matba al-Nizami, Kanpur, 1293 A.H.

Darwazah, Mohammad Izzah, Al-Dusṭur al-Qur'āni wa al-Sunnah al-Nabaviyah fi Shuwoon al-Hayat, Isa al-Babi al-Halbī, Egypt, 1966.

__________________________, Al-Marah bain al-Qur'ān wa al-Sunnah, Al-Maktabah al-Asariyah, Beirut, 1967.

Al-Dauri, Qahtan Abdur Rahman, Al-Shura bain al-Nazriah wa al-Tatbeeq, Matbaah al-Ummah, Baghdad, 1974.

Al-Eili, Abdul Hakim Hasan Dr., Al-Hurriyāt al-Aammah fi al-Fikr wa al-Nizam al-Siyasi fi al-Islam Dirasah Muqaranah. Dar al-Fikr al-Arabi, Egypt, 1974.

Al-Fanjari, Ahmad Shauqi, Al-Hurriyah al-Siyasiyah fi al-Islam, Dar al-Qalam, Kuwait, 1973.

________________________, Al-Hurriyah al-Siyasiyah fi al-Islam, Dar al-Qalam, Kuwait, 1973.

Fayyaz, Mahmood, Dr., Al-Fiqh al-Siyasi Ind al-Muslimeen, Silsilah al-Thaqafah al-Islamiyah, Maktaba al-Khanji, Egypt, December, 1959.

Al-Fazili, Ahmad, Nizam al-Hukm fi al-Islam, (Muhazaraat), al-Dirasaat al-Ulya, Qism al-Siyasah al-Sharyiah, Kulliyah al-Shariah wa al-Qanoon, Jamea al-Azhar, Egypt. (n.d.)

Al-Ghazali, Abu Hamid, al-Mustasfa min Ilm al-Usool, Maktaba al-Jundi, Cairo, (n.d.)

Al-Ghazali, Mohammad, al-Islam wa al-Istibdad al-Siyasi, Dar al-Kutub al-Hadithah, Egypt, 1961.

Haykal, Mohammad Husain, al-Farooq Umar, Cairo, 1364 A.H.

Al-Haithami, Nooruddin Ali b. Abu Bakr, Majma al-Zawaid wa Manba al-Fawaid, Dar al-Kitab al-Arabi, Beirut, 1967.

Hakim, Al-Mustadrak ma al-Talkhees li al-Zahabi, Maktabah al-Matbooat al-Islamiyah, Halb.

Hasan Ibrahim Hasan, Tarikh al-Islam al-Siyasi, Cairo, 1935.

Hasan, Ali Ibrami Dr., Al-Tarikh al-Islami al-'Aamin, Al-Nahdhah al-Misriyah, Egypt, 1972.

Hilmi, Mahmood, Dr., Nizam al-Hukm al-Islami Muqaranan bi al-Nuzum al-Muasirah, Dar al-fikr al-Arabi, Cairo, 1970.

Al-Hulv, Majid Ragheb, Al-Isti'fa al-Shabi bain al-Anzemah al-Wadhyiah wa al-Shariah al-Islamiyah, Maktaba al-Manar al-Islamiyah, Kuwait, 1980.

Huwaidi, Hasan, Dr., Al-Shura fi al-Islam, al-Manar al-Islamiyah, Kuwait, 1957.

Ibn Abdul Barr, Yusuf b. Abdullah b. Mohammad, Al-Isteeaab fi Marefah al-Ashaab, ed. Ali Mohammad al-Bajavi, Maktabah Nahdhah, Egypt, (n.d.)

Ibn Abi Sheebah, Abu Bakr Abdullah b. Mohammad b. Ibrahim b. Uthman, Al-Kitab al-Musannaf fi al-Ahadith wa al-Athaar, ed. Abdul Khaliq al-Afghani, Hyderbad, 1867.

Ibn al-Arabi, Abu Bakr Mohammad bin Abdullah, Al-Awasim min al-Qawasim, ed. Muhibbuddin al-Khatib, Al-Matbah al-Salafiyah, Egypt 1387 A.H.

Ibn Hajar Asqalani, Shahabuddin Abul Fazl, Fath al-Bari li Sharh al-Bukhari, Mustafa al-Babi al Halbi wa Auladuhu, Egypt, 1959.

____________________, Al-Kafi al-Shafi fi Takhreej Ahadith al-Kashshaf (with the text of Kashshaf), Dar al-Kitab al-Arabi, Beirut.

____________________, Al-Isabah fi Tamyiz al-Sahabah, Maktaba al-Tijariyah al-Kubra, Egypt, 1939.

Ibn Hanbal, Ahmad b. Muhammad, Al-Musnad, ed. Ahmad Muhammad Shakir, Egypt, 1948.

Ibn Hazm, Mohammad bin Ahmad bin Sayeed, Al-Muhalla, Maktaba al-Jumhuriyah bi al-Azhar, Egypt, 1970.

__________________________, Al-Fisal fi al-Milal wa al-Nihal, Cairo, 1899-1902.

__________________________, al-Ihkam fi Usool al-Ahkam, Maktabah al-Jumhuriyah al-Arabiyah, Al-Azhar, Egypt, 1970.

Ibn Hisham, Abu Muhammad Abdul Malik, Al-Seerah al-Nabaviyah, Mustafa al-Babi al-Halbi, Egypt, 1936.

Ibn Kathir, Abul Fida Ismail, Tafsir al-Qur'ān al-Azeem, Dar Ihya al-Turath al-Arabi, Beirut, 1969.

__________________________, Al-Bidayah wa al-Nihayah, Maktabah al-Maarif, Beirut, First Edition, 1966.

Ibn Khaldun, Abdur Rahman, Al-Muqaddimah, Cairo. (n.d.)

Ibn Maja, Al-Sunan, ed. Muhammad Fuad Abul Baqi, Cairo.

Ibn Manzoor, Jamaluddin Mohammad bin Mukarram, Lisan al-Arab, Dar Sader, Beirut, 1968.

Ibn Qayyim al-Jauziyyah, Samsuddin, Zaad al-Maad fi Hadyi Sayyid al-Ibad, Cairo, 1971.

__________________________, Al-Turuq al-Hukmiyah fi al-Siyasah al-Sharyiah, Al-Muassasah al-Arabiah li al-Tabaah wa al-Nashr, Cairo, 1961.

__________________________, Iélam al-Muaqqieen an Rabb al-Aalameen, Cairo, (n.d.).

Ibn Qudamah, Muaffiquddin, Al-Mughni, Dar al-Kitab al-Arabi, Beirut, 1972.

Ibn Qutaibah, Abdullah b. Muslim, Kitab al-Imamah wa al-Siyasah, Cairo, 1925.

Ibn Sad, Mohammad, Al-Tabaqaat al-Kubra, Dar Sader, Beirut, 1957.

Ibn Taimiyah, Taqiuddin Ahmad, Al-Hisbah fi al-Islam, Al-Matbaah al-Salafiyah, Egypt, 1350 A.H.

__________________________, Al-Siyasah al-Sharyiah fi Islah al-Rai wa al-Rayiah, ed. Mohammad Ibrahim al-Banna and Mohammad Ahmad Aashur, Dar al-Shab, Cairo, 1971.

__________________________, Minjah al-Sunnah al-Nabaviyyah fi Naqdh Kalam al-Shiah al-Qadriyah, Cairo, 1378, A.H.

Jareeshah, Ali Mohammad, Dr., Al-Mashrooyiah al-Islamiyah al-Ulya, Maktaba Wahbah, Egypt, 1975.

Jumah, Mohammad Mahmood, Al-Nuzum al-Ijtimayiah wa al-Siyasiah inda Qudama al-Arab wa al-Umam al-Samiyah, Matbaah al-Saadah, Egypt, 1949.

Khalid, Khalid Mohammad, Al-Dimiqratiyah Abadan, Dar al-Kitab al-Labnani, Fourth Edition, 1974.

Khallaf, Abdul Wahab, Ilm Usool al-Fiqh wa Khulasah Tarikh al-Tashri al-Islami, Seventh Edition, Cairo, 1956.

________________, Al-Siyasah al-Sharyiah Dar al-Ansar, Egypt, 1971.

Al-Khateeb, Abdul Karim, Al-Khilafah wa al-Imamah (diyanah wa Siyasah) Dirasah Muqaranah li al-Hukm al-Islami wa al-Hukumah al-Islamiyah, 1963.

Al-Khayyat, Abdul Aziz, Dr., al-Nizam al-Siyasi fi al-Islam, Beirut, 1974.

Al-Khazin, Alauddin Ali bin Mohammad bin Ibrahim al-Baghdadi al-Soofi, Li Bab al-Taweel fi Maani al-Tanzeel, (Tafsir al-Khazin), Mohammad Ameen Damj, Beirut.

Al-Maleeji, Yaqub Mohammad, Dr., Mabda al-Shura fi al-Islam ma al-Muqaranah bi al-Mabadi al-Dimiqratiyāh al-Gharbiyah wa al-Nizam al-Marxi, Muassasah al-Thaqafah al-Jameiyah, Alexandria, (n.d.).

Mansoor, Mustashār Ali Ali, Nuzum al-Hukm wa al-Idarah fi al-Shariah al-Islamiyah wa al-Qawaneen al-Wadhyiah, Dar al-Fath, Beirut, 1971.

Al-Maraghi, Ahmad Mustafa, Tasfir al-Maraghi, Egypt, 1965.

Al-Mawardi, Abul Hasan Ali, Al-Ahkam al-Sultaniyah wa al-Wilayaat al-Diniyah, Matbaah al-Babi al-Halbi, Egypt, 1966.

Al-Mubarak, Mohammad, Nizam al-Islam: al-Hukm wa al-Dawlah, Dar al-Fikr, Beirut, 1974.

Al-Mubarakpuri, Abul Ali Mohammad Abdur Rahman bin Abdur Rahman, Tuhfah al-Ahwazi bi Sharh Jame al-Tirmizi, ed. Abdur Rahman Mohd. Uthman, Al-Maktabah al-Salafiyah, Madinah Munawwarah, 1964.

Al-Munajji, Jalal Mohammad, Al-Islam wa Al-Shura, Al-Majlis al-Aala li al-Shuwoon al-Islamiyah, Egypt, 1970.

Mutawalli, Abdul Hameed, Dr., Azamah al-Fikr al-Siyasi al-Islami fi al-Asr al-Hadith, Al-Maktab al-Misri al-Hadith, Alexandria, 1970.

_____________________________, Mabda al-Shura fi al-Islam, Alam al-Kutub, Second Edition, Egypt, 1972.

_____________________________, Mabadi Nizam al-Hukm fi al-Islam ma al-Muqaranah bi al-Mabadi al-Dusturiyah al-Hadithah, Manshaah al-Maarif, Alexandria, 1966.

Al-Muteeyi, Mohammad Bakheet, Haqiqah al-Islam wa Usul al-Hukm, Al-Matbah al-Salafiyah, Cairo, 1344 A.H.

Al-Muttaqi, Alauddin, Kanzul Ummal fi Sunan al-Aqwal wa al-Afaal, Hyderabad, 1951.

Al-Nawawi, Muhiuddin Abu Zakaria Yahya bin Sharf, Sahih Muslim bi Sharh al-Navavi, Dar al-Fikr, Beirut, 1972.

Al-Nahwi, Adnan Ali Rida, Malameh al-Shura fi al-Dawah al-Islamiah, Matabi al-Farazdaq al-Tijariyah, Reyadh, 1984.

Al-Qarafi al-Maliki Shihabuddin Abul Abbas Ahmad b. Idris, Al-Ihkam fi Tamyiz al-Fatawa min al-Ahkam wa Tasarrufaat al-Qazi wa al-Imam, ed. Mahmood Urnoos, 1938.

Al-Qaradhawi, Yusuf Dr., Al-Hulul al-Mustawradah wa Kaifa Janat ala Ummatena, Muassasah al-Risalah, Beirut, 1971.

Al-Qasmi, Zaafir, Nizam al-Hukm fi al-Shariah wa al-Tarikh, Dar al-Nafais, Beirut, 1974.

Al-Qastalani, Abul Abbas Shahabuddin Ahmad bin Mohammad, Irshad al-Saari li Sharh Sahih al-Bukhari, Dar al-Kitab al-Arabi, Beirut, (n.d.).

Al-Qirshi, Baqar Sharif, Nizam al-Hukm wa al-Idarah fi al-Islam, Matbaah al-Aadab, Najaf, 1966.

Al-Qurtubi, Abu Abdullah Mohammad bin Ahmad al-Ansari, Al-Jame le Ahkam al-Qur'ān, Dar al-Katib al-Arabi, Cairo, 1967.

Qutb, Syed, Fi Zilal al-Qur'ān, Sixth edition, Beirut.

Al-Razi, Fakhruddin, Mafateeh al-Ghaib, (Al-Tafsir al-Kabeer), Dar al-Kutub al-Ilmiyah, Tehran.

Rida Rashid and Mohammad Abduh, Tafsir al-Qur'ān al-Hakeem, (Tafsir al-Manar), Fourth ed. Cairo, 1960.

Al-Rayyis, Mohammad Ziauddin, Al-Nazriyaat al-Siyaasiyah al-Islamiyah, Dar al-Turath, Egypt, 1976.

Rizwan, Fathi, Al-Islam wa Mushkilat al-Fikr, Dar al-Maarif, Egypt.

Al-Sibai, Mustafa, Dr., Al-Marah bain al-Fiqh wa al-Qanoon, Al-Maktabah al-Asriyah, Halb, 1962.

Al-Saghani, Abu Bakr Abdur Razzaq bin Humam, Al-Musannaf fi al-Hadith ed. Habibur Rahman Azmi, Al-Maktab al-Islami, Beirut, 1972.

Al-Saleh, Subhi, Dr., Al-Nuzum al-Islamiyah: Nashatuha wa Tatawwuruha, Dar al-Ilm li al-Malayin, Beirut, (n.d.)

Al-Sayeedi, Abdul Mutaal, Min Aina Nabda, Maktaba al-Khanji, Egypt, (n.d.).

Shakir, Ahmad Mohamad, Umdah al-Tafsir an al-Hafiz Ibn Kathir, Dat al-Maarif, Egypt, 1957.

Shalbi, Ahmad Dr., Al-Islam wa al-Waei al-Siyasi, Dar al-Maarif, Egypt, 1974.

Shaltoot, Mahmood, Al-Islam: Aqidah wa Shariah, Dar al-Sharooq, Egypt, 1968.

Al-Sharqawi, Mahmood, Al-Dimiqratiyah ind al-Arab, al-Dar al-Qaumiyah li al-Tabaah wa al-Nashr, 1961.

Al-Shaukani, Mohammad bin Ali, Nail al-Awtar Sharh Muntaqa al-Akhbar min Hadith Sayyid al-Akhyar, Mustafa al-Babi al-Halbi wa Auladuhu, Egypt, 1961.

________________________, Fath al-Qadeer al-Jame bain Fannai al-Riwayah wa al-Dirayah fi al-Tafsir, Matbaah al-Babi al-Halbi, Egypt, 1349 A.H.

Al-Suyuti, Jalaluddin bin Abdur Rahman bin Abu Bakr, Al-Durr al-Manthur fi al-Tafsir bi al-Mathur, Dar al-Thaqafah, Beirut (n.d.)

________________________________, Tarikh al-Khulafa, Matba Mujtaba, Delhi, (n.d.)

Al-Tabari, Abu Jafar Muhammad bin Jarir, Tarikh al-Rusul wa al-Muluk, Dar al-Maarif, Egypt, 1962.

________________________, Jame al-Bayan an Taweel Aay al-Qur'ān, ed. Mahmood Mohammad Shakir, Dar al-Maarif, Egypt (n.d.).

Al-Tabatabai, Syed Muhammad Husain, Al-Mizan fi Tafsir al-Qur'ān, Tehran, 1376 A.H.

Tabeelah, Al-Qutb Mohammad Al-Qutb, Al-Islam wa Huquq al-Insan, Dar al-Fikr al-Arabi, Cairo, 1976.

Al-Tabrezi, Waliuddin Mohammad bin Abdullah al-Khatib, Mishkah al-Masabih, ed. Mohd. Naseruddin al-Albani, Al-Maktab al-Islami, Damascus, 1961 A.D.

Tabrisi, Abu Ali bin Hasan, Majma al-Bayan fi Tafsir al-Qur'ān, Dar al-Kitab al-Labnani, Beriut, 1955.

Al-Tamavi, Sulaiman Mohammad Dr., Umar bin al-Khattab wa Usool al-Siyasah wa al-Idarah al-Hadithah, Dar al-Fikr al-Arabi, Cairo, 1969.

________________________, Al-Sultat al-Thalath fi al-Dasatir al-Arabiyah wa fi al-Fikr al-Siyasi al-Islami: Muqaranah, Dar al-Fikr al-Arabi, Cairo, 1973.

Tirmizi, Muhammad b. Isa, Al-Jame al-Sahih, Hims, 1969-71.

Tuaimah, Sabir, al-Islam wa Mushkilaat al-Siyasah, Dar al-Jeel, Beirut, 1974.

Urjoon, Sadeq Ibrahim, Uthman b. Affān, Cairo, 1947.

Uthman, Fathi, Al-Fikr al-Islami wa al-Tatawwur, Dar al-Qalam, Egypt. (n.d.).

Utwah, Abdul Aal, Nizam al-Qaza fi al-Islam (Muhazarat), Qism al-Siyasah al-Sharyiah, al-Dirasaat al-Ulya, Kulliyah al-Shariah wa al-Qanoon, Jamea al-Azhar, Egypt, 1972-73.

Waqidi, Mohammad b. Umar, Kitab al-Maghazi, Oxford University Press, 1966.

Wasfi, Mustafa Kamal Dr., Al-Nizam al-Dusturi fi al-Islam Muqaranan bi al-Nuzum al-Muasirah, Maktabah Wahbah, Egypt, 1974.

Al-Zamkhshari, Mahmood bin Umar, Al-Kashshaaf an Haqaaiq Ghawamiz al-Tanzeel wa Wuyun al-Aqaaweel fi Wajh al-taaweel, Dar al-Kitab al-Arabi, Beirut.

Zuhair, Mohammad Abun Noor, Usool al-Fiqh, Dar al-Taleef al-Maliyah, Egypt. (n.d.)

Al-Zurqani, Mohammad b. Abdul Baqi, Sharh al-Mawahib al-Ladunniyah, Cairo, 1325 A.H. (Ist edition).

References (English)

Ahmad, Ilyas, Sovereignty: Islamic and Modern, Allied Book Corporation, Karachi, 1965.

____________, The Social Contract and the Islamic State, Kitab Bhavan, New Delhi, 1981.

Ahmad, K.. & Ansari, Z., Islamic Perspective: Studies in Honour of Mawlana Sayyid Abul Ala Maududi, The Islamic Foundation, U.K. 1979.

Ahmad, Khurshid, "Islam and the Challenge of the Economic Development", in the Challenge of Islam ed. Altaf Gauhar, Islamic Council of Europe, London, 1978.

Ahmad, Manzooruddin, Islamic Political System in the Modern Age, Saad Publications, Karachi, 1983.

Ahmad, Muhammad Aziz, The Nature of Islamic Political Theory, Maaref, Karachi, 1975.

Allana, G., Muslim Political Thought Through the Ages: 1562-1947, Indian Institute of Applied Political Research, Publication Division, New Delhi, 1987.

Ameer Ali, The Spirit of Islam, Idarah Adabiat, Delhi, 1978.

________, A Short History of Saracens, N. Delhi, 1977.

Apter, E. David & Eckstein, Harry, Comparative Politics, Princeton, N. Jersey, 1963.

Aron, Raymond, France Steadfast and Changing: from the Fourth to the Fifth Republic, Cambridge, 1960.

Asad, Muhammad, The Principles of State and Government in Islam, Dar al-Andalus, Gibraltar, 1980.

El-Awa, Muhammad s., On the Political System of the Islamic State, American Trust Publications, Indiana, 1978.

Banisadr, Abolhassan, The Fundamental Principles and Precepts of Islamic Government, translated by M.R. Ghanoonpravar, Mazda Publications, Lexington, 1981.

Carre, Olivier, Islam and the State in the World Today, Introduction, Imtiaz Ahmad, Manohar, N. Delhi, 1986.

Dunning, W.A., A History of Political Theories: Recent Times, Allahabad, 1969.

Elie, Abid Salem, Political Theory and Institution of the Khawarij, Baltimore, U.S.A., 1956.

Enayat, Hamid, Modern Islamic Political Thought, Macmillan, London, 1977.

Fahad, Obaidullah, Principles of Diplomacy in Islam, Islamic Publications, Lahore, 1996.

________________, Islamic Polity and Orientalists, Institute of Islamic Studies, A.M.U., Aligarh, 2001.

________________, Islamic Revivalism: An Approach Study, Institute of Islamic Studies, A.M.U., Aligarh, 2001.

________________, Redefining Islamic Political Thought, A Critique in Methodological Perspective, Serials Publications, New Delhi.

The Government of France, The Constitution of Fifth Republic of France.

The Government of U.S.A., The Constitution of U.S.A.

Hasan Ahmad, The Doctrine of Ijma in Islam, Islamic Research Institute, Islamabad, 1978.

Hassan, Farooq, The Concept of State and Law in Islam, University Press of America, Lanham, 1981.

Iqbal, Afzal, The Prophet's Diplomacy: The Art of Negotiations as Conceived and Developed by the Prophet of Islam, Claude Stark and Co., Cape Cod, Mass, 1975.

Jaffery, Syeda Razia, An Approach to Politics in Islam, P. Ebrahim Trust, Karachi, 1973.

Khan, Qamaruddin, The Political Thought of Ibn Taimiyah, Islamic Book Foundation, Lahore, 1983.

________________, Political Concepts in the Qur'ān, Institute of Islamic Studies, Karachi, 1973.

Lambton, A.K.S., State and Government in Medieval Islam, Oxford University Press, Oxford, 1981.

Litterdate, D.W.S., The Parliament of France, London, 1951.

Palmer & Perkins, International Relations: The World Community in Transition, Scientific Book Agency, Calcutta, 1973.

Pickles, Dorothly, The Fifth Republic, New York, 1960.

Piscatori, James, Islam in a World of Nation-States, Cambridge University Press, 1986.

Quddus, Syed Abdul, Islamic Polity in Modern Times, Feroz Sons, Lahore, 1987.

Rosenthal, E.I.J., Political Thought in Medieval Islam, Cambridge University Press, 1958.

Sabine, George H., A History of Political Theory, Oxford and IBH Publishing Co., N. Delhi, 1973.

Al-Sadr, Baqir, Introduction to Islamic Political System, Islamic Seminary, 1982.

Al-Sayed, Abdul Malik A., Social Ethics of Islam: Classical Islamic Arabic Political Theory and Practices, Vantage Press, New York, 1982.

Shafique, Mohammad, Islamic Concept of a Modern State, The centre for Islamic Research, Zamindar Educational Association, Gujrat, 1987.

Sherwanj, H.K., Studies in Muslim Political Thought and Administration, Ashraf Publications, Lahore, 1985.

Siddiqui, Abdul Hameed, Theocracy and the Islamic State, Islamic Book Centre, Lahore, 1976.

Siddiqui, M.Y.M., Organization of Government under the Prophet, Idarah Adabiyat, Delhi, 1987.

Vatikiotis, P.J., Islam and State, Croom Helm, London, 1987.

Verney, Douglas V., Analysis of Political System, Routledge and Kegan Paul Ltd., London, 1959.

Watt, W.M., Islamic Political Thought: The Basic Concepts, Edinburgh, 1968.

Williams, Philip, Politics in Post-War France, London, 1958.

Yousuf Ali, M. The Holy Qur'ān, Text, Translation and Commentary, Amanah Corp. Maryland, U.S.A., 1989.

Zaydan, Abdul Karim, The Role of State and Individual in Islam, Hindustan Publications, Delhi, 1983.

Zaidi, A.H., Evolution of Muslim Political Thought in India, Vol. 1 to 6, S. Chand & Co., New Delhi, 1978.

Zaman, Hasan, Nature of Politics in Islam, Society for Pakistan Studies, Dhaka, 1969.

Articles (Arabic)

Al-Abasiri, Mohammad, Al-Shura fi al-Islam, Al-Waye al-Islami, No. 131, Kuwait.

Abu Izzah, Abdullah, Al-Shura am al-Istibdaad, al-Mujtama, Kuwait, No. 38, 41, 43, Dec. 1970 – Jan. 1971.

Abul Majd, Ahmad Kamal, Al-Shura wa al-Dimiqratiyah wa Ruyah al-Islam al-Siyasiyah, Al-Arabi, Kuwait, No. 80.

______________________, Qaziyyah al-Shura bi hajatin Kulliha ila Ruyah Jadeedah. Al-Arabi, Kuwait, 262, September, 80, 18.

______________________, Al-Islam Dusturan, Al-Hilal, Egypt, No. 250, Nov. 1971.

______________________, Muajahah Ma Anaasir al-Jamud fi al-Fikr al-Islami al-Muasir, Al-Arabi, Kuwait, No. 222, May, 1977.

Abu Zahrah, Mohammad, Al-Shura fi al-Islam, Majallah Hadharah al-Islam, Damascus, No. 3, 1960.

Abu Zayd, Al-Shura: Aa Hiya Asasun li Tanzim al-Mujtama al-Islami am Hilyah Umkin al-Istighnau anha? Al-Shahab, Beirut, Vol. 2, No. 15, 17 Sep. – Oct., 1968.

Ayyub, Midhat, Shura al-Aadaab wa al-Funun, Majallah al-Shura Vol. V, No. 7, Al-Jamahiriyah al-arabiyah al-Libiyah, July, 1978.

Al-Booti, Mohammad Sayeed Ramadhan, Al-Shura fi al-Islam Laisat Mulzamah Dayman, Al-Arabi, Kuwait, No. 262, 1980.

Al-Faasi, Mohammad bin Salim al-Fahri, Al-Fiqh al-Islami wa Hurriyah al-Tafkeer, Al-Isalah, No. 51, Nov. 77-119.

Al-Fanjari, Ahmad Shauqi, Dr., Al-Marah al-Muslimah fi Mayadin al-Qital, Al-Arabi, Kuwait, No 198. May 1975.

Al-Hawfi, Ahmad, Dr., Wa Shaawir Hum fi al-Amr, Al-Waye al-Islami, No. 118, October, 1974.

Ibadah, Abdul Latif, al-Dawlah wa Tanzeem al-Sultah fi al-Islam, Al-Isālah, No. 85, 86.

Ibrahim, Mohammad, Al-Shura fi al-Islam: Tatbeeq li Hurriah al-Rae wa Ilzam al-Hakim wa al-Mahkum, Al-Ahram 3rd June, 1977.

Islahi, Amin Ahsan, Makianah al-Jamaheer fi al-Dawlah al-Islamiyah, Al-Bath al-Islami, Lucknow, June – August 1969, Vol. 13, No. 9-10, Vol. 14, No. 1.

Khalfullah, Ahmad, Dr., Al-Qur'ān wa al-Dawlah, Majallah al-Katib, Egypt, Vol. 13, No. 148, July, 1973.

Al-Khateeb, Abdul Karim, Al-Shura fi al-Islam, Al-Waye, Kuwait, 79, 10, 70, 40.

Madkoor, Mohammad Salam, Dr., Al-Ijma fi al-Tashrei al-Islami, Al-Waye al-Islami, Kuwait, No. 127, July, 1975.

Mansoor, Abdul Azim, Ietibaaraat al-Zamaan wa al-Makaan fi Shariah al-Islam, Majallah Minbar al-Islam, No. 32, Nov. 1974.

Najeeb, Ibrahim, Dr., Al-Shura fi al-Islam, Daily Al-Ahram, Ist October 1976.

Al-Namer, Abdul Munim, Dr., Ala Abwaab Taqneen al-Shariah, Al-Ahram, Ist April, 1978.

al-Qaradhawi, Yusuf, Dr., Nazraat, Al-Muslim al-Muasir, Beirut, No. 1-2, April, 1975.

Al-Saih, Abdul Hameed, Hal lil Akhz bi Rae al-Akthariyah Asasun fi al-Islam? Al-Waye al-Islam, Kuwait, No. 25, April, 1967.

Shaltoot, Mahmood, Al-Shura fi al-Islam, Majallah al-Azhar, First part of Vol. 32, 1960.

Sharf, Moosa, Al-Wahy wa al-Shura, Manar al-Islam, No. 8, 1976.

Tamawi, Sulaiman Mohammad, Dr., Muqaranah bain al-Shura fi al-Islam wa al-Nuzum al-Niyabiyah al-Muasirah, Majallah al-Arabi, Kuwait, No. 198, 1975.

Al-Taweel, Mohammad, Dr., Al-Shura Mulzamah fi al-Amr al-Aamm, Al-Arabi, Kuwait, No. 269, 1981.

Uthman, Mohd. Fathi, Al-Shariah al-Islamiyah fi Seghah Muasihar Kilaf al-Rae wa al-Aqeedah Laisa Harban ala Allah wa Rasulih, Al-Arabi, Kuwait, Vol. 18, Nov. 1978.

_________________, Ahl al-Hall wa al-Aqd Man Hum? Al-Arabi, Kuwait, July, 1980.

_________________, Haula Maqalaat al-Shura, Al-Mujtama, Kuwait, No. 46, Feb. 1971.

Zaydan, Abdul Karim, Dr., Al-Shura: Al-Khilaf bain Rayees al-Dawlah wa Ahl al-Shura, Al-Mujtama, Kuwait, No. 47, 1971.

Articles (English)

Abu-Sulayman, A. Abdul Hamid, Islamization of Knowledge with special Reference to Political Science, The American Journal of Islamic Social Sciences, U.S.A., 2.2 (December 1985).

Ahmad, Muhammad Aziz, Islam and Democracy, University Studies, Karachi, 2, 1 (1965).

______________________, The Concept of Mulk in Political Theory of Islam, University Studies, Karachi, 5, 1 (1968).

Anwarul, M., Influence of Muslim Political theorists on Medieval European Political Thought, Islamic Culture, Hyderabad, 32, 1958.

Daabla, Basheer A., Muslim Political Thought in colonial India: A comparative study of Sir Sayyid Ahmad Khan and Mawlana Abul Kalam Azad, Islamic Culture, Hyderabad, 61, 1 (1988).

Ghazi Mahmood A., The Institution of Shura in Islamic Polity, Islamic Order, 3, 2 (1981).

Husaini, S.A. Qadir, The Shura, Journal of Pakistan Historical Society, 3 (1955).

Kakakhel, M. Nazeer, The Conceptual and Institutional Development of Shura in Early Islam, Islamic Studies, Islamabad, 17 (1978).

Shafiq, Muhammad, The Role of Shura in Islamic Polity, Journal of the World Muslim League, 12, 6 March, 1985.

References (Urdu)

Chowdhry, M.A., Musalmanon Ka Baladiyati Nizam, Lahore, 1983.

Al-Ghamidi, J.A., Islam Ka Siyasi Nizam, Dar al-Ishraq, Lahore, 1986.

Ghazi, Hamid al-Ansari, Islam Ka Nizam e Hukumat, Lahore, (n.d.)

Hamidullah, Mohammad, Islami Reyasat, Dar al-Qur'ān, Delhi, 1988.

________________________, Ahd Nabavi Main Nizam Hukmrani, Urdu Academy, Karachi, 1987.

Islahi, Amin Ahsan, Tadabbur i Qur'ān, Faran Foundation, Lahore, Ist edition.

Keelani, Abdur Rahman, Khilafat wa Jumhuriyat, Lahore, 1985.

Maududi, Abul Ala, Tafhimul Qur'ān, Markazi Maktaba Islami, Delhi.

Nadwi, Rasheed Akhtar, Islam main Markazi Hukumat ka Tasawwur, Lahore, 1986.

Naushahrwi, Abu Yahya Imam Khan, Hazrat Umar ke Siyasi Nazriye, Maktaba Nazeeriyah, Lahore, 1979.

Qadiri, Syed Shamim Husain, Islami Reyasat Qur'ān O Sunnat Ki Roshni main, Ulama Academy, Mahkama Awqaf Punjab, Lahore, 1984.

Rahman, Gauhar, Islami Siyasat, Maktaba Zikra, Rampur, 1982.

Shibli Nomani, Al-Farooque, Azamgarh, 1956.

Umari, Jalaluddin Sayyid, Islam ka Shuraai Nizam, Lahore 1983.

*****

INDEX

J

V

W